X-MEN

THE MOVIE ADAPTATION

RALPH MACCHIO
writer
adapted from a screenplay

ANTHONY WILLIAMS
penciler

ANDY LANNING
inker

CHRIS ELIOPOULOS
letterer

ATOMIC PAINTBRUSH
color art

MIKE RAICH
assistant editor

MIKE MART...
editor

BOB HARRAS
editor in chief

X-MEN® MOVIE ADAPTION, September, 2000. Published by MARVEL COMICS, Bill Jemas, President; Bob Harras, Editor-in-Chief; Stan Lee, Chairman Emeritus. OFFICE OF PUBLICATION: 387 PARK AVENUE SOUTH, NEW YORK, N.Y. 10016. Copyright © 2000 Marvel Characters, Inc. All rights reserved. Price $5.95 per copy in the U.S. and $8.95 in Canada. GST #R127032852. No similarity between any of the names, characters, persons, and/or institutions in this magazine with those of any living or dead person or institution is intended, and any such similarity which may exist is purely coincidental. This periodical may not be sold except by authorized dealers and is sold subject to the condition that it shall not be sold or distributed with any part of its cover or markings removed, nor in a mutilated condition. X-MEN (including all prominent characters featured in this issue and the distinctive likenesses thereof) is a trademark of MARVEL CHARACTERS, INC. Printed in the U.S.A. MARVEL COMICS is a division of MARVEL ENTERPRISES, INC. Peter Cuneo, Chief Executive Officer; Avi Arad, Chief Creative Officer.

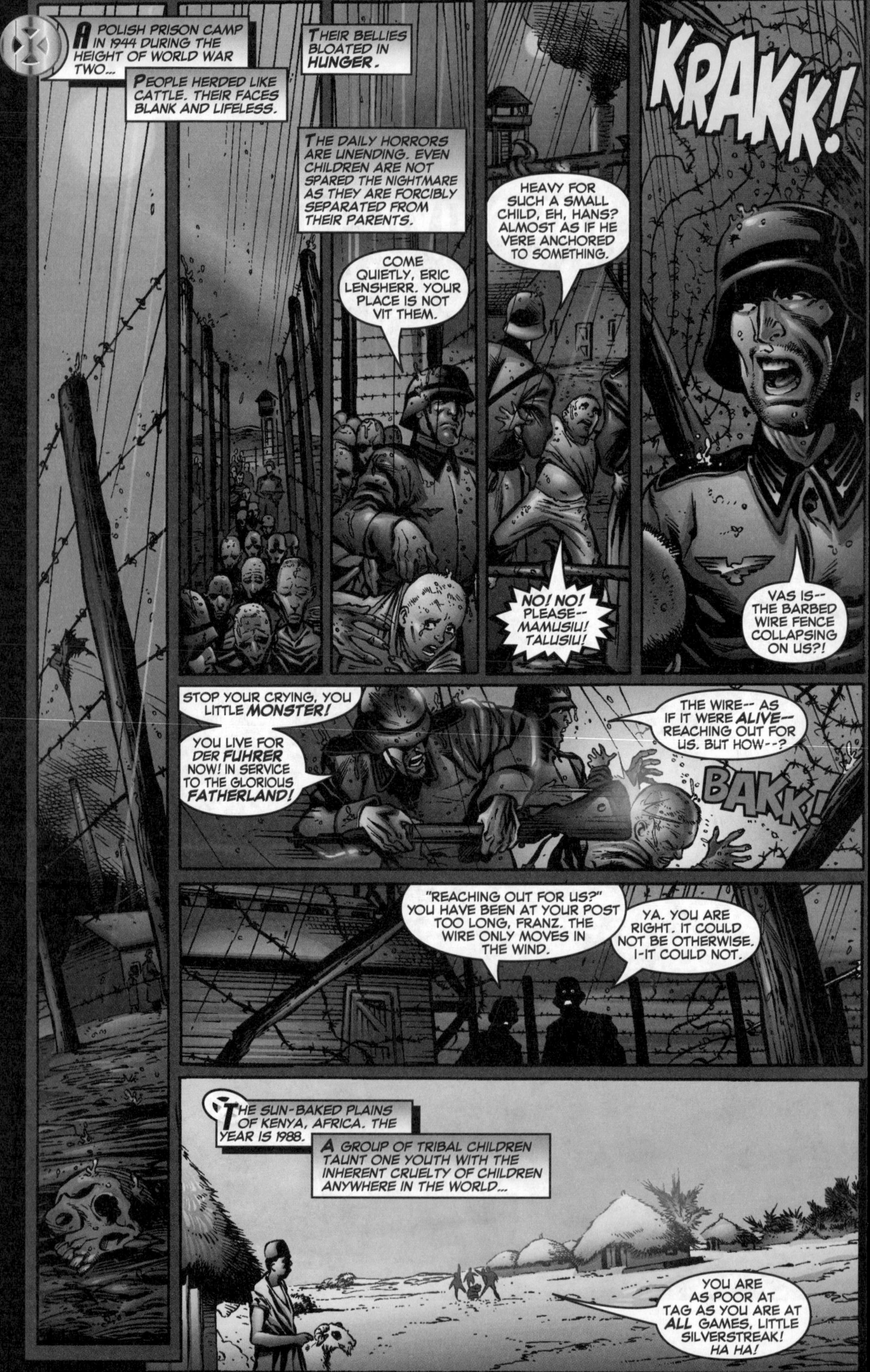
A POLISH PRISON CAMP IN 1944 DURING THE HEIGHT OF WORLD WAR TWO...
PEOPLE HERDED LIKE CATTLE. THEIR FACES BLANK AND LIFELESS.
THEIR BELLIES BLOATED IN HUNGER.
THE DAILY HORRORS ARE UNENDING. EVEN CHILDREN ARE NOT SPARED THE NIGHTMARE AS THEY ARE FORCIBLY SEPARATED FROM THEIR PARENTS.
COME QUIETLY, ERIC LENSHERR. YOUR PLACE IS NOT VIT THEM.
HEAVY FOR SUCH A SMALL CHILD, EH, HANS? ALMOST AS IF HE VERE ANCHORED TO SOMETHING.
NO! NO! PLEASE-- MAMUSIU! TALUSIU!
KRAKK!
VAS IS-- THE BARBED WIRE FENCE COLLAPSING ON US?!
STOP YOUR CRYING, YOU LITTLE MONSTER!
YOU LIVE FOR DER FUHRER NOW! IN SERVICE TO THE GLORIOUS FATHERLAND!
THE WIRE-- AS IF IT WERE ALIVE-- REACHING OUT FOR US. BUT HOW--?
BAKK!
"REACHING OUT FOR US?" YOU HAVE BEEN AT YOUR POST TOO LONG, FRANZ. THE WIRE ONLY MOVES IN THE WIND.
YA. YOU ARE RIGHT. IT COULD NOT BE OTHERWISE. I-IT COULD NOT.
THE SUN-BAKED PLAINS OF KENYA, AFRICA. THE YEAR IS 1988.
A GROUP OF TRIBAL CHILDREN TAUNT ONE YOUTH WITH THE INHERENT CRUELTY OF CHILDREN ANYWHERE IN THE WORLD...
YOU ARE AS POOR AT TAG AS YOU ARE AT ALL GAMES, LITTLE SILVERSTREAK! HA HA!

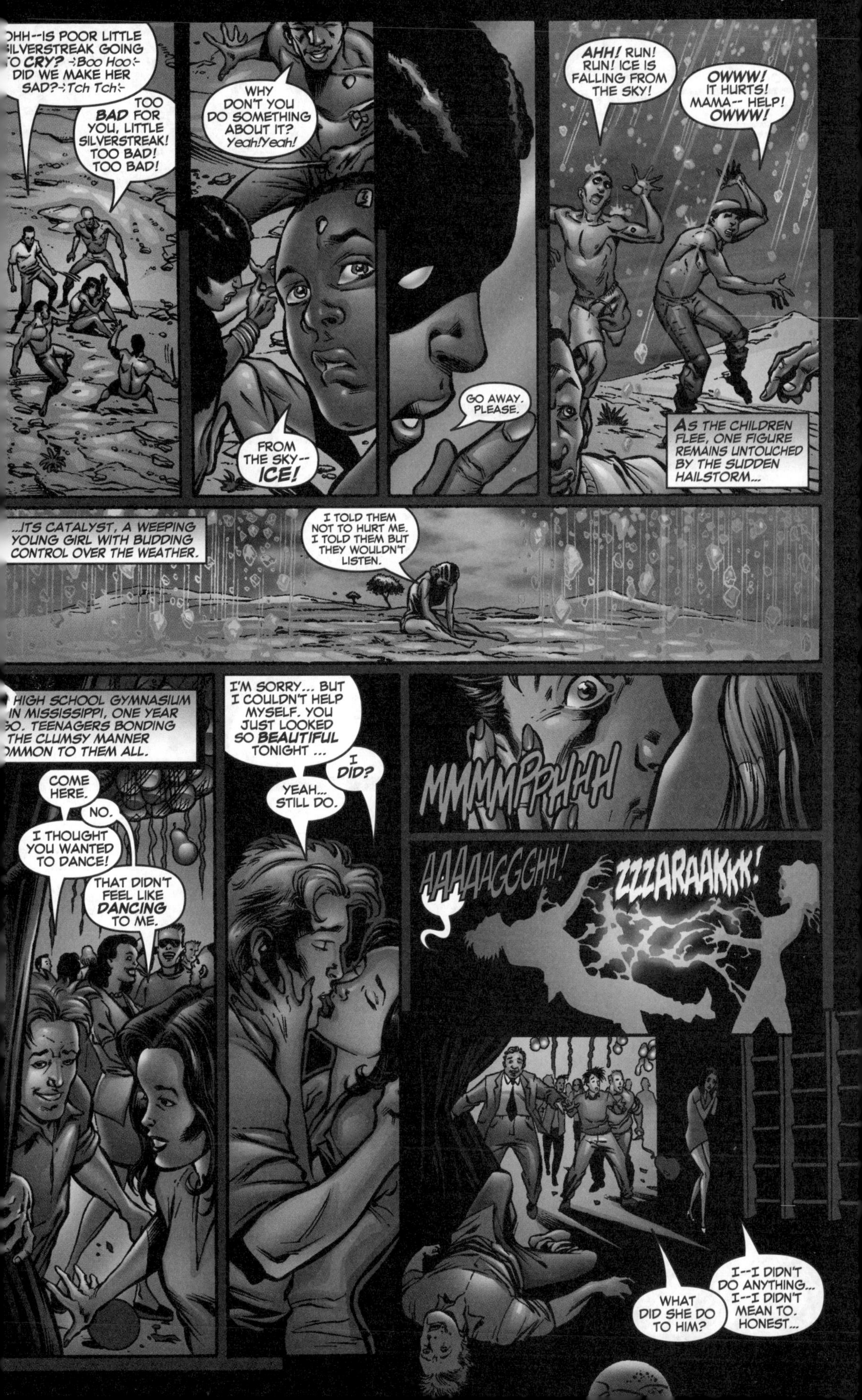
OHH--IS POOR LITTLE SILVERSTREAK GOING TO CRY? -:-Boo Hoo-:- DID WE MAKE HER SAD?-:-Tch Tch-:-
TOO BAD FOR YOU, LITTLE SILVERSTREAK! TOO BAD! TOO BAD!
WHY DON'T YOU DO SOMETHING ABOUT IT? Yeah!Yeah!
FROM THE SKY-- ICE!
GO AWAY. PLEASE.
AHH! RUN! RUN! ICE IS FALLING FROM THE SKY!
OWWW! IT HURTS! MAMA-- HELP! OWWW!
AS THE CHILDREN FLEE, ONE FIGURE REMAINS UNTOUCHED BY THE SUDDEN HAILSTORM...
...ITS CATALYST, A WEEPING YOUNG GIRL WITH BUDDING CONTROL OVER THE WEATHER.
I TOLD THEM NOT TO HURT ME. I TOLD THEM BUT THEY WOULDN'T LISTEN.
HIGH SCHOOL GYMNASIUM IN MISSISSIPPI, ONE YEAR GO. TEENAGERS BONDING THE CLUMSY MANNER OMMON TO THEM ALL.
COME HERE.
NO.
I THOUGHT YOU WANTED TO DANCE!
THAT DIDN'T FEEL LIKE DANCING TO ME.
I'M SORRY... BUT I COULDN'T HELP MYSELF. YOU JUST LOOKED SO BEAUTIFUL TONIGHT ...
I DID?
YEAH... STILL DO.
MMMMPPHHH
AAAAAGGGHH!
ZZZARAAKKK!
WHAT DID SHE DO TO HIM?
I--I DIDN'T DO ANYTHING... I--I DIDN'T MEAN TO. HONEST...

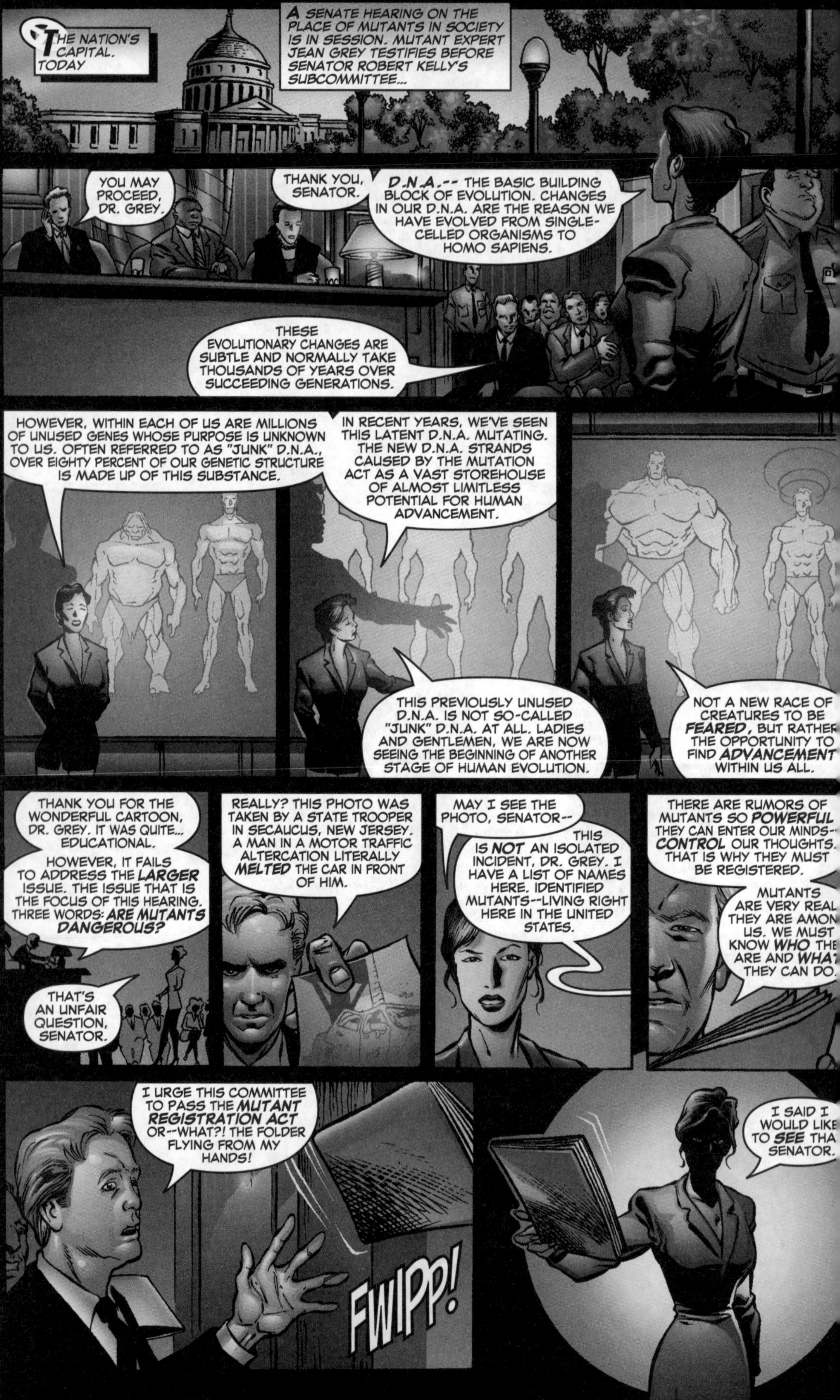
THE NATION'S CAPITAL. TODAY
A SENATE HEARING ON THE PLACE OF MUTANTS IN SOCIETY IS IN SESSION. MUTANT EXPERT JEAN GREY TESTIFIES BEFORE SENATOR ROBERT KELLY'S SUBCOMMITTEE...
YOU MAY PROCEED, DR. GREY.
THANK YOU, SENATOR.
D.N.A.-- THE BASIC BUILDING BLOCK OF EVOLUTION. CHANGES IN OUR D.N.A. ARE THE REASON WE HAVE EVOLVED FROM SINGLE-CELLED ORGANISMS TO HOMO SAPIENS.
THESE EVOLUTIONARY CHANGES ARE SUBTLE AND NORMALLY TAKE THOUSANDS OF YEARS OVER SUCCEEDING GENERATIONS.
HOWEVER, WITHIN EACH OF US ARE MILLIONS OF UNUSED GENES WHOSE PURPOSE IS UNKNOWN TO US. OFTEN REFERRED TO AS "JUNK" D.N.A., OVER EIGHTY PERCENT OF OUR GENETIC STRUCTURE IS MADE UP OF THIS SUBSTANCE.
IN RECENT YEARS, WE'VE SEEN THIS LATENT D.N.A. MUTATING. THE NEW D.N.A. STRANDS CAUSED BY THE MUTATION ACT AS A VAST STOREHOUSE OF ALMOST LIMITLESS POTENTIAL FOR HUMAN ADVANCEMENT.
THIS PREVIOUSLY UNUSED D.N.A. IS NOT SO-CALLED "JUNK" D.N.A. AT ALL. LADIES AND GENTLEMEN, WE ARE NOW SEEING THE BEGINNING OF ANOTHER STAGE OF HUMAN EVOLUTION.
NOT A NEW RACE OF CREATURES TO BE FEARED, BUT RATHER THE OPPORTUNITY TO FIND ADVANCEMENT WITHIN US ALL.
THANK YOU FOR THE WONDERFUL CARTOON, DR. GREY. IT WAS QUITE... EDUCATIONAL.
HOWEVER, IT FAILS TO ADDRESS THE LARGER ISSUE. THE ISSUE THAT IS THE FOCUS OF THIS HEARING. THREE WORDS: ARE MUTANTS DANGEROUS?
THAT'S AN UNFAIR QUESTION, SENATOR.
REALLY? THIS PHOTO WAS TAKEN BY A STATE TROOPER IN SECAUCUS, NEW JERSEY. A MAN IN A MOTOR TRAFFIC ALTERCATION LITERALLY MELTED THE CAR IN FRONT OF HIM.
MAY I SEE THE PHOTO, SENATOR--
THIS IS NOT AN ISOLATED INCIDENT, DR. GREY. I HAVE A LIST OF NAMES HERE. IDENTIFIED MUTANTS--LIVING RIGHT HERE IN THE UNITED STATES.
THERE ARE RUMORS OF MUTANTS SO POWERFUL THEY CAN ENTER OUR MINDS-- CONTROL OUR THOUGHTS. THAT IS WHY THEY MUST BE REGISTERED.
MUTANTS ARE VERY REAL THEY ARE AMON US. WE MUST KNOW WHO THE ARE AND WHA THEY CAN DO.
I URGE THIS COMMITTEE TO PASS THE MUTANT REGISTRATION ACT OR--WHAT?! THE FOLDER FLYING FROM MY HANDS!
FWIPP!
I SAID I WOULD LIKE TO SEE THA SENATOR.

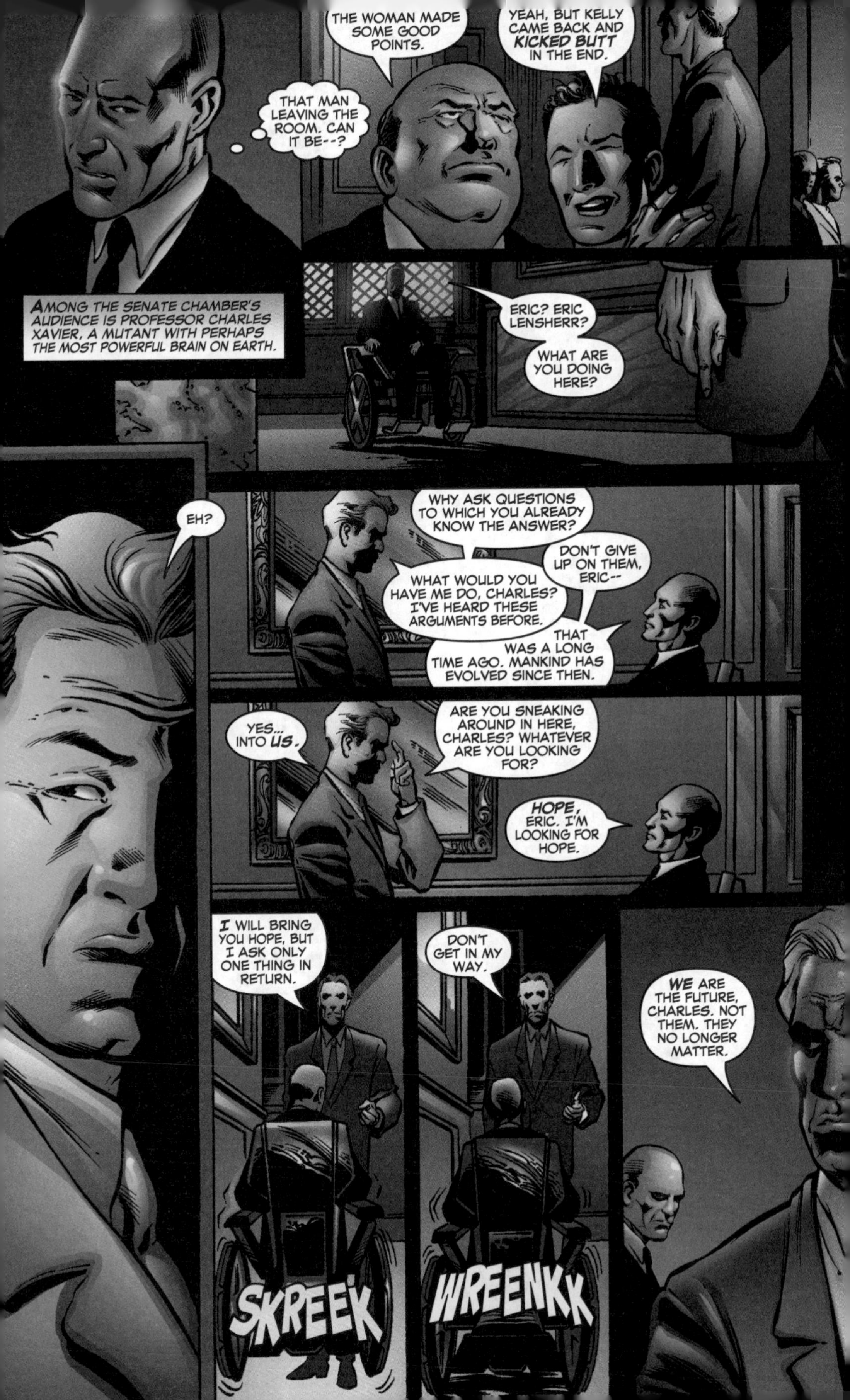

THE WOMAN MADE SOME GOOD POINTS.
YEAH, BUT KELLY CAME BACK AND KICKED BUTT IN THE END.
THAT MAN LEAVING THE ROOM. CAN IT BE--?
AMONG THE SENATE CHAMBER'S AUDIENCE IS PROFESSOR CHARLES XAVIER, A MUTANT WITH PERHAPS THE MOST POWERFUL BRAIN ON EARTH.
ERIC? ERIC LENSHERR?
WHAT ARE YOU DOING HERE?
EH?
WHY ASK QUESTIONS TO WHICH YOU ALREADY KNOW THE ANSWER?
DON'T GIVE UP ON THEM, ERIC--
WHAT WOULD YOU HAVE ME DO, CHARLES? I'VE HEARD THESE ARGUMENTS BEFORE.
THAT WAS A LONG TIME AGO. MANKIND HAS EVOLVED SINCE THEN.
YES... INTO US.
ARE YOU SNEAKING AROUND IN HERE, CHARLES? WHATEVER ARE YOU LOOKING FOR?
HOPE, ERIC. I'M LOOKING FOR HOPE.
I WILL BRING YOU HOPE, BUT I ASK ONLY ONE THING IN RETURN.
SKREEK
DON'T GET IN MY WAY.
WREENKK
WE ARE THE FUTURE, CHARLES. NOT THEM. THEY NO LONGER MATTER.

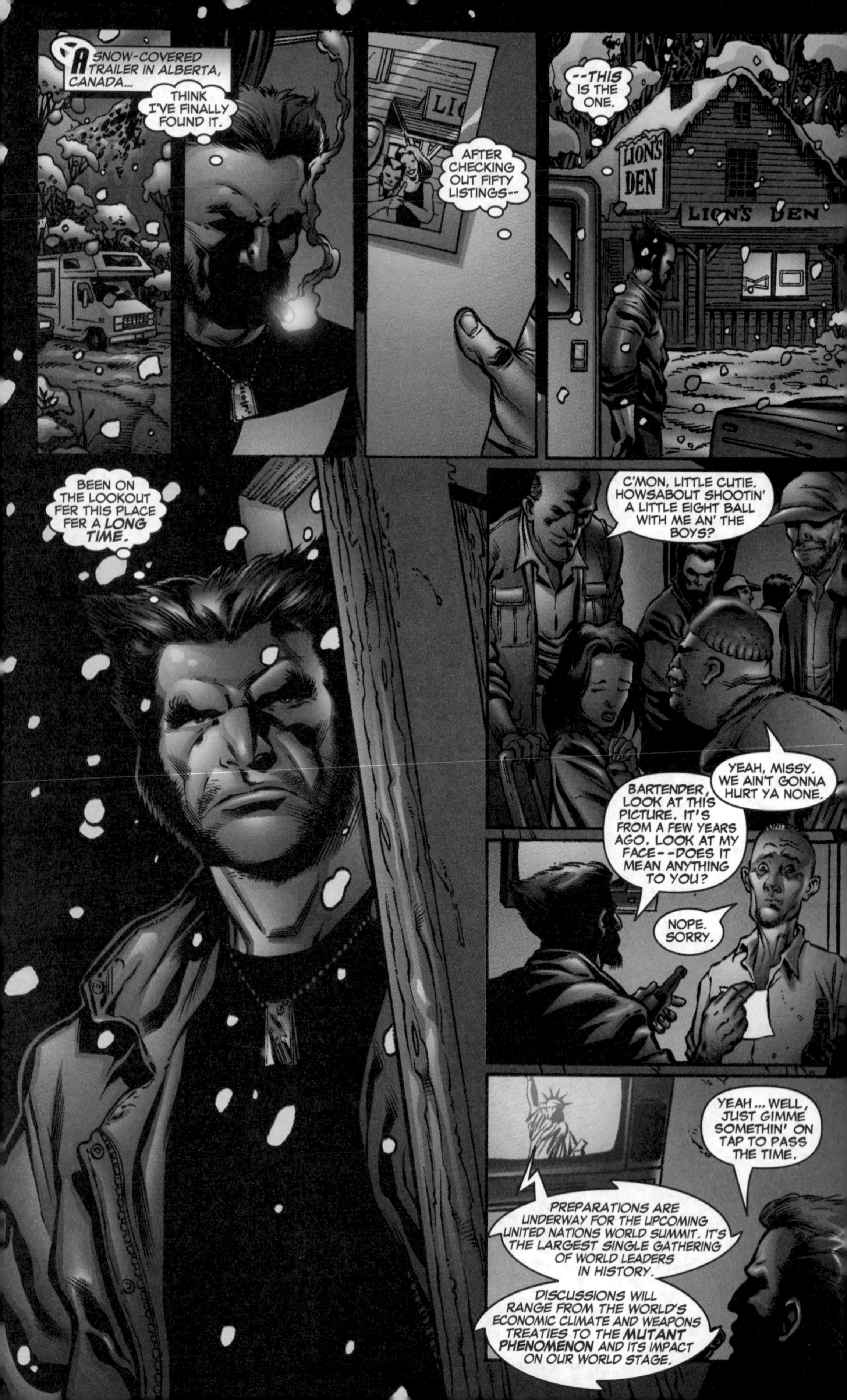

A SNOW-COVERED TRAILER IN ALBERTA, CANADA...
THINK I'VE FINALLY FOUND IT.
AFTER CHECKING OUT FIFTY LISTINGS--
--THIS IS THE ONE.
LION'S DEN
LION'S DEN
BEEN ON THE LOOKOUT FER THIS PLACE FER A LONG TIME.
C'MON, LITTLE CUTIE. HOWSABOUT SHOOTIN' A LITTLE EIGHT BALL WITH ME AN' THE BOYS?
YEAH, MISSY. WE AIN'T GONNA HURT YA NONE.
BARTENDER, LOOK AT THIS PICTURE. IT'S FROM A FEW YEARS AGO. LOOK AT MY FACE--DOES IT MEAN ANYTHING TO YOU?
NOPE. SORRY.
YEAH... WELL, JUST GIMME SOMETHIN' ON TAP TO PASS THE TIME.
PREPARATIONS ARE UNDERWAY FOR THE UPCOMING UNITED NATIONS WORLD SUMMIT. IT'S THE LARGEST SINGLE GATHERING OF WORLD LEADERS IN HISTORY.
DISCUSSIONS WILL RANGE FROM THE WORLD'S ECONOMIC CLIMATE AND WEAPONS TREATIES TO THE MUTANT PHENOMENON AND ITS IMPACT ON OUR WORLD STAGE.

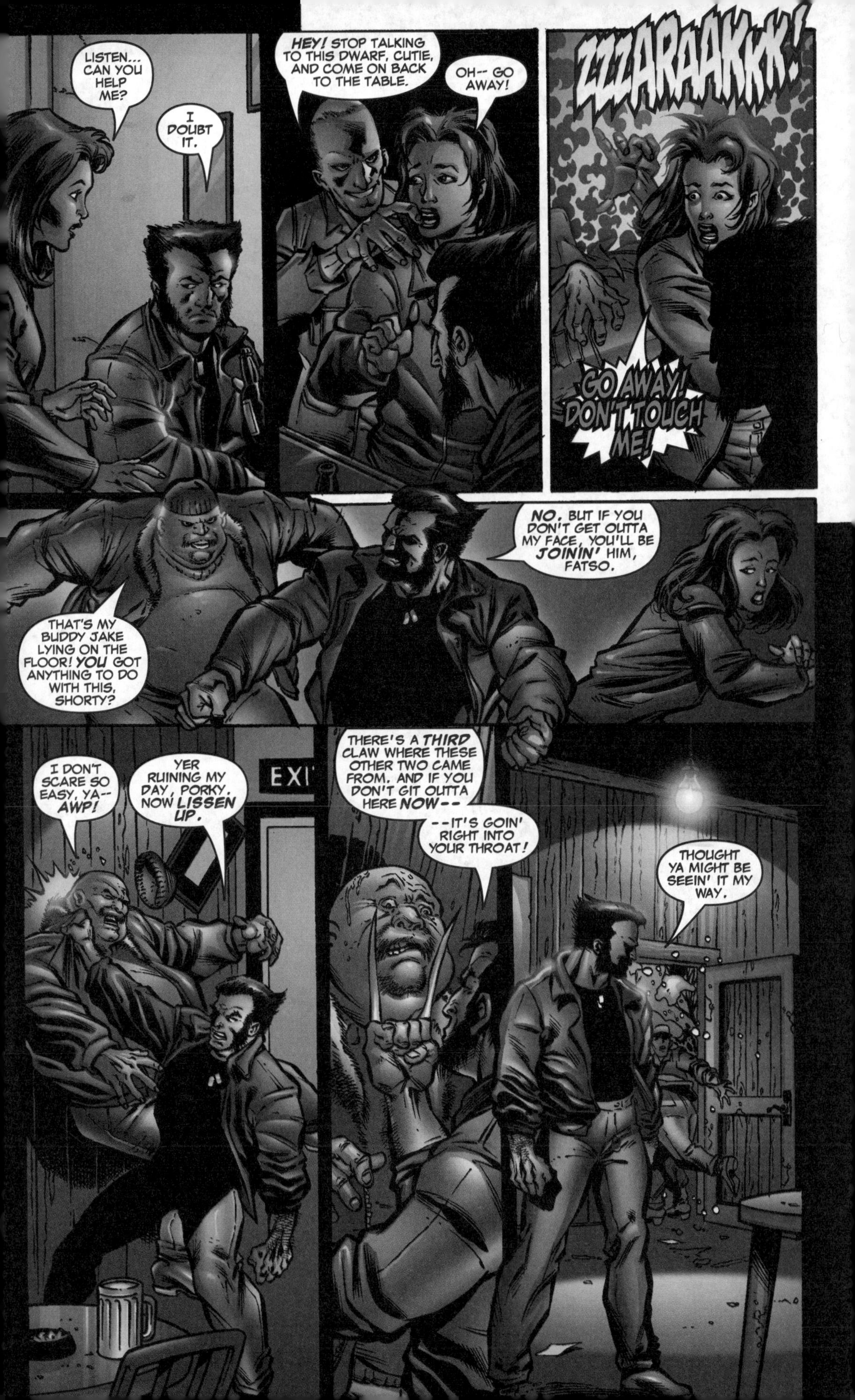
LISTEN... CAN YOU HELP ME?
I DOUBT IT.
HEY! STOP TALKING TO THIS DWARF, CUTIE, AND COME ON BACK TO THE TABLE.
OH-- GO AWAY!
ZZZARAAKKK!
GO AWAY! DON'T TOUCH ME!
THAT'S MY BUDDY JAKE LYING ON THE FLOOR! YOU GOT ANYTHING TO DO WITH THIS, SHORTY?
NO. BUT IF YOU DON'T GET OUTTA MY FACE, YOU'LL BE JOININ' HIM, FATSO.
I DON'T SCARE SO EASY, YA-- AWP!
YER RUINING MY DAY, PORKY. NOW LISSEN UP.
EXIT
THERE'S A THIRD CLAW WHERE THESE OTHER TWO CAME FROM. AND IF YOU DON'T GIT OUTTA HERE NOW--
--IT'S GOIN' RIGHT INTO YOUR THROAT!
THOUGHT YA MIGHT BE SEEIN' IT MY WAY.

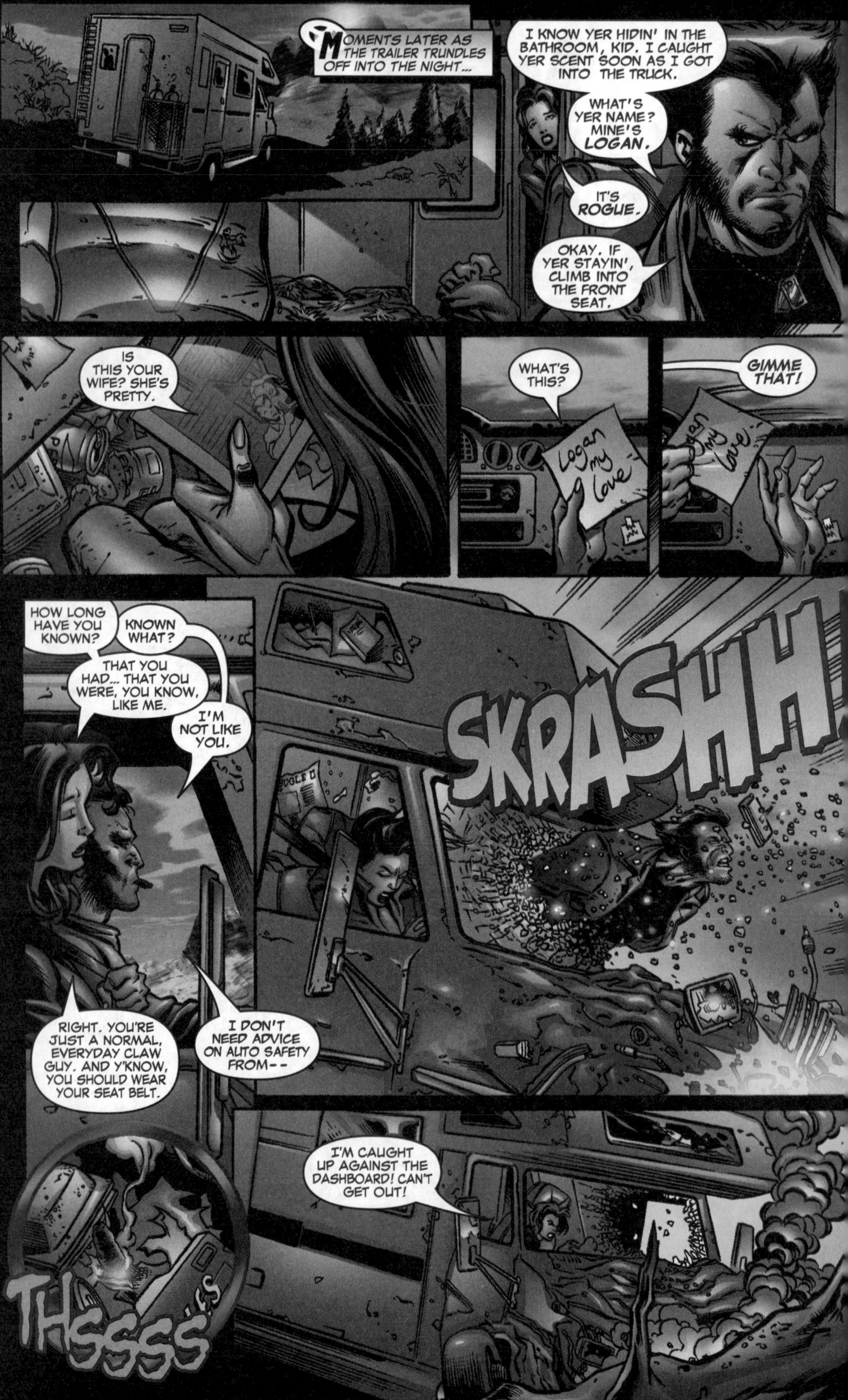
MOMENTS LATER AS THE TRAILER TRUNDLES OFF INTO THE NIGHT...
I KNOW YER HIDIN' IN THE BATHROOM, KID. I CAUGHT YER SCENT SOON AS I GOT INTO THE TRUCK.
WHAT'S YER NAME? MINE'S LOGAN.
IT'S ROGUE.
OKAY. IF YER STAYIN', CLIMB INTO THE FRONT SEAT.
IS THIS YOUR WIFE? SHE'S PRETTY.
WHAT'S THIS?
Logan my love
GIMME THAT!
Logan my love
HOW LONG HAVE YOU KNOWN?
KNOWN WHAT?
THAT YOU HAD... THAT YOU WERE, YOU KNOW, LIKE ME.
I'M NOT LIKE YOU.
RIGHT. YOU'RE JUST A NORMAL, EVERYDAY CLAW GUY. AND Y'KNOW, YOU SHOULD WEAR YOUR SEAT BELT.
I DON'T NEED ADVICE ON AUTO SAFETY FROM--
SKRASHH!
I'M CAUGHT UP AGAINST THE DASHBOARD! CAN'T GET OUT!
THSSSS

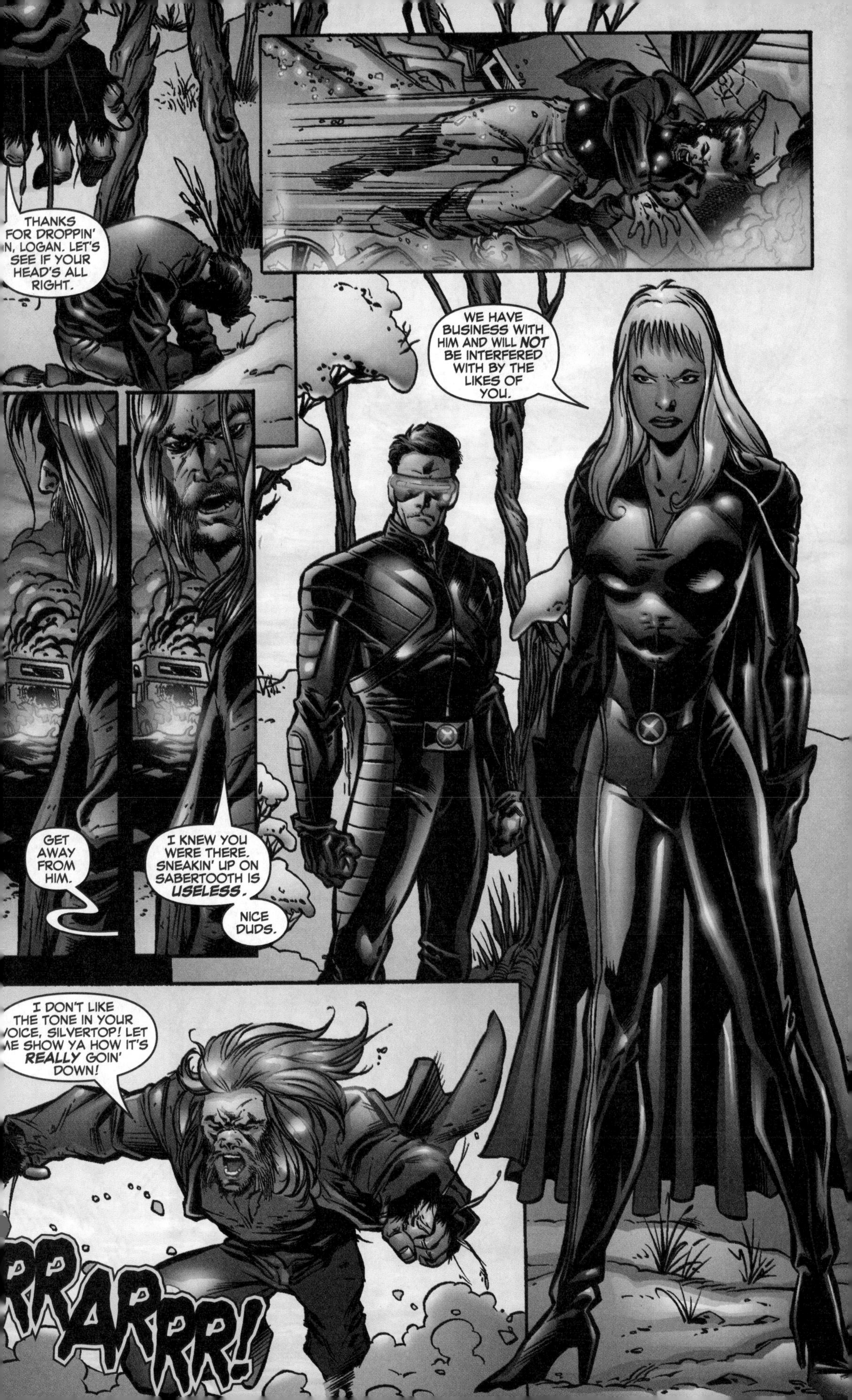
THANKS FOR DROPPIN' IN, LOGAN. LET'S SEE IF YOUR HEAD'S ALL RIGHT.
WE HAVE BUSINESS WITH HIM AND WILL NOT BE INTERFERED WITH BY THE LIKES OF YOU.
GET AWAY FROM HIM.
I KNEW YOU WERE THERE. SNEAKIN' UP ON SABERTOOTH IS USELESS.
NICE DUDS.
I DON'T LIKE THE TONE IN YOUR VOICE, SILVERTOP! LET ME SHOW YA HOW IT'S REALLY GOIN' DOWN!
RRARRRR!

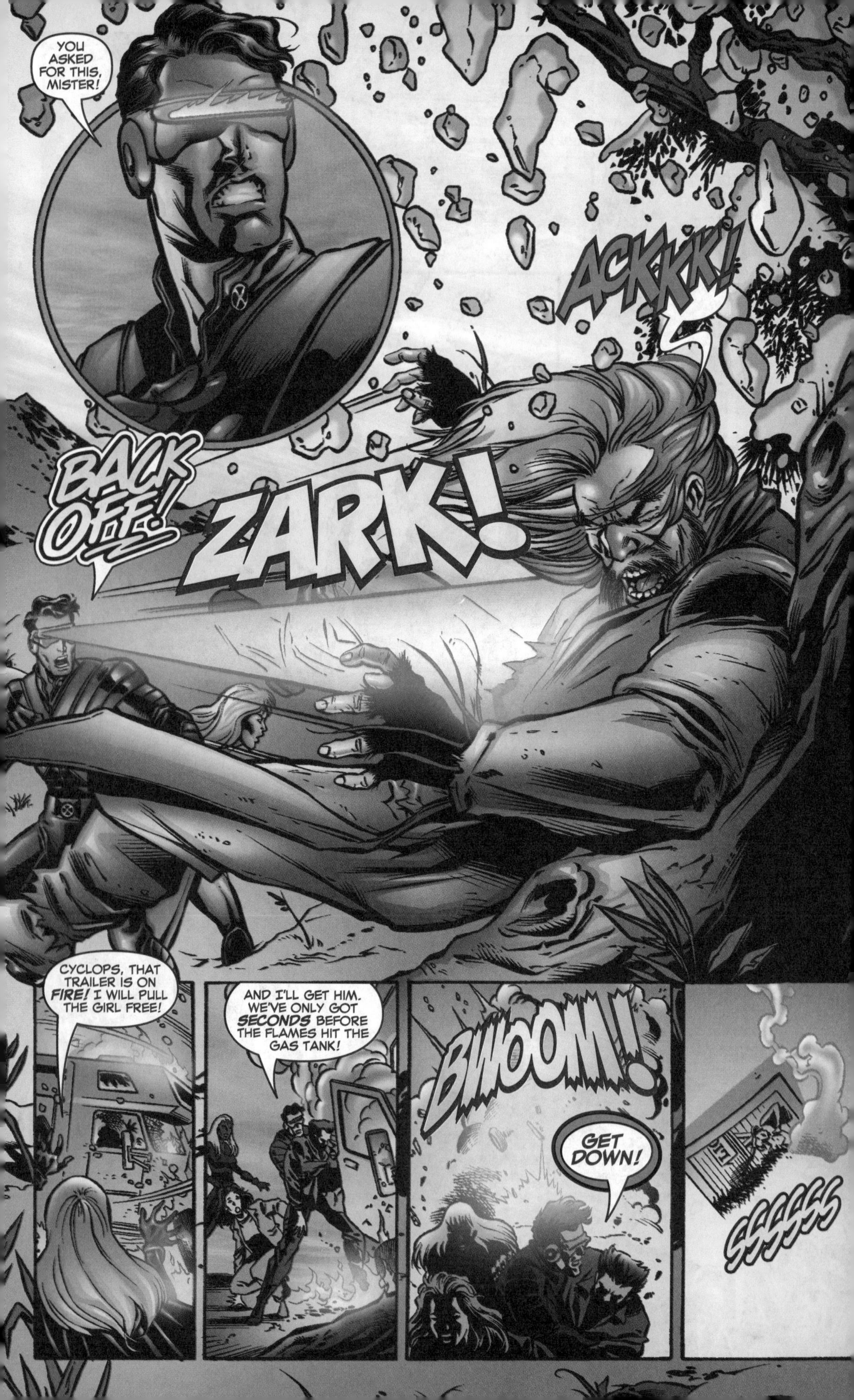
YOU ASKED FOR THIS, MISTER!
ACKKK!
BACK OFF!
ZARK!
CYCLOPS, THAT TRAILER IS ON FIRE! I WILL PULL THE GIRL FREE!
AND I'LL GET HIM. WE'VE ONLY GOT SECONDS BEFORE THE FLAMES HIT THE GAS TANK!
BWOOOM!!
GET DOWN!
SSSSSS

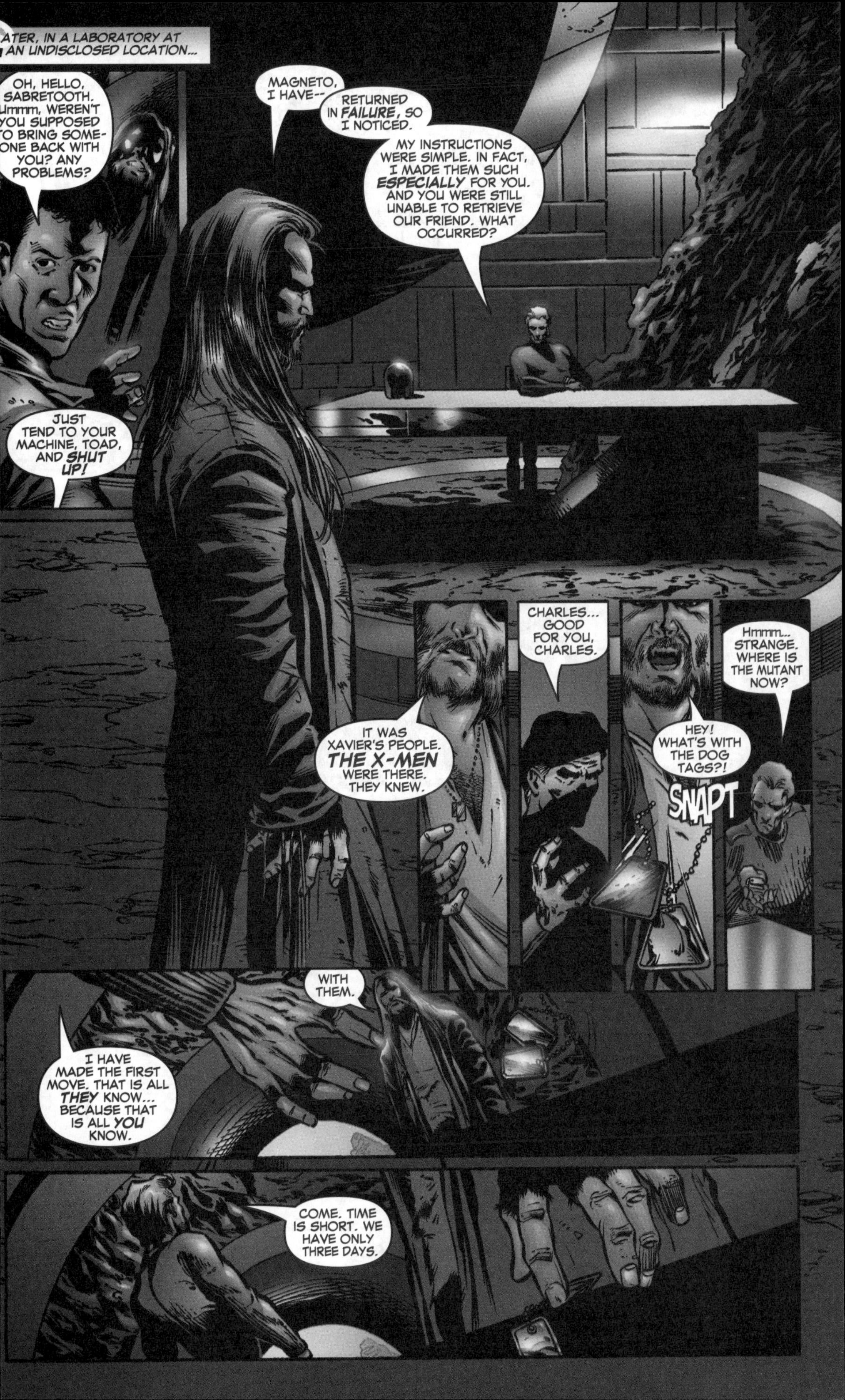

ATER, IN A LABORATORY AT AN UNDISCLOSED LOCATION...
OH, HELLO, SABRETOOTH. Ummm, WEREN'T YOU SUPPOSED TO BRING SOME-ONE BACK WITH YOU? ANY PROBLEMS?
MAGNETO, I HAVE--
RETURNED IN FAILURE, SO I NOTICED.
MY INSTRUCTIONS WERE SIMPLE. IN FACT, I MADE THEM SUCH ESPECIALLY FOR YOU. AND YOU WERE STILL UNABLE TO RETRIEVE OUR FRIEND. WHAT OCCURRED?
JUST TEND TO YOUR MACHINE, TOAD, AND SHUT UP!
IT WAS XAVIER'S PEOPLE. THE X-MEN WERE THERE. THEY KNEW.
CHARLES... GOOD FOR YOU, CHARLES.
HEY! WHAT'S WITH THE DOG TAGS?!
SNAPT
Hmmm... STRANGE. WHERE IS THE MUTANT NOW?
WITH THEM.
I HAVE MADE THE FIRST MOVE. THAT IS ALL THEY KNOW... BECAUSE THAT IS ALL YOU KNOW.
COME. TIME IS SHORT. WE HAVE ONLY THREE DAYS.

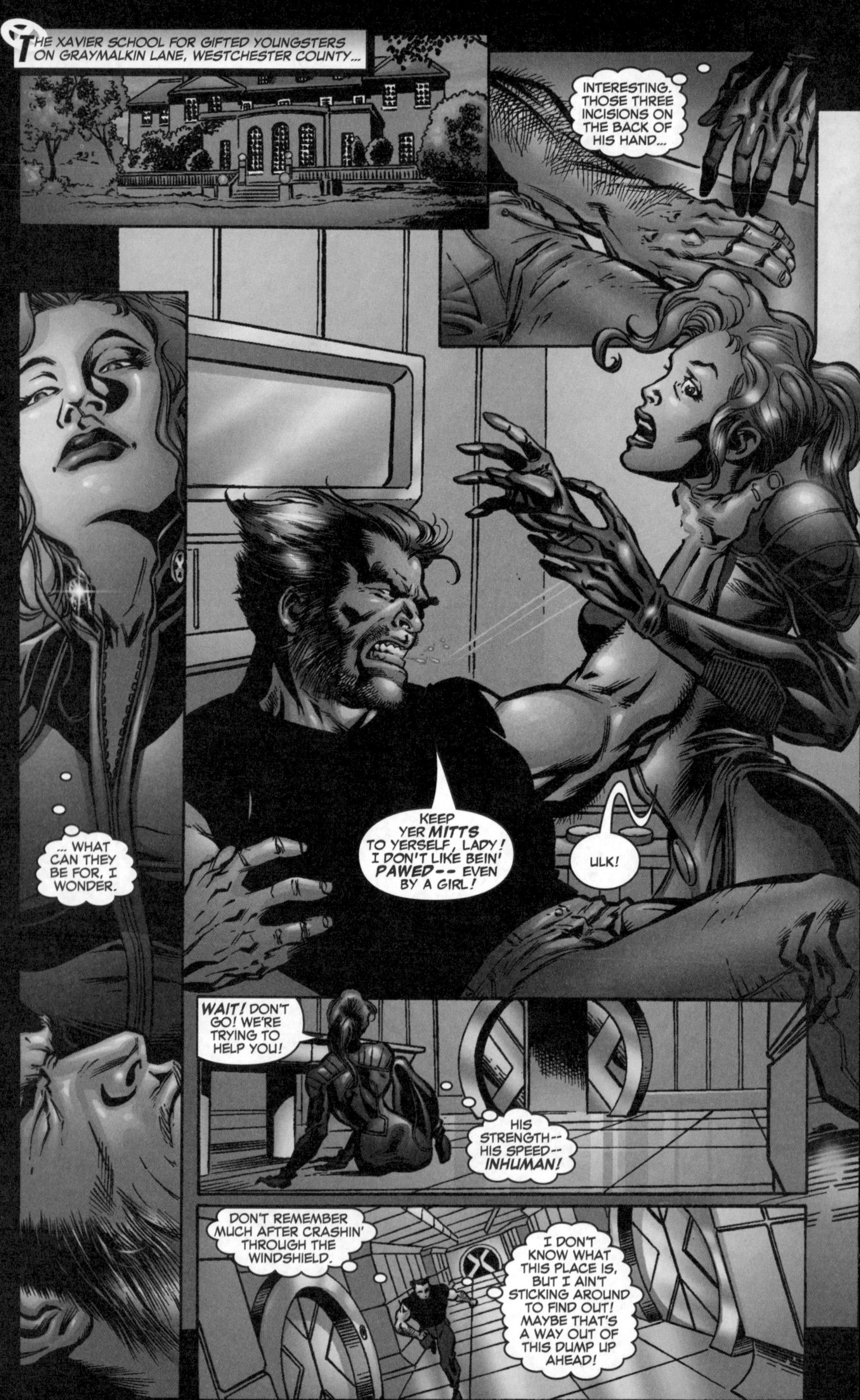
THE XAVIER SCHOOL FOR GIFTED YOUNGSTERS ON GRAYMALKIN LANE, WESTCHESTER COUNTY...
INTERESTING. THOSE THREE INCISIONS ON THE BACK OF HIS HAND...
... WHAT CAN THEY BE FOR, I WONDER.
KEEP YER MITTS TO YERSELF, LADY! I DON'T LIKE BEIN' PAWED-- EVEN BY A GIRL!
ULK!
WAIT! DON'T GO! WE'RE TRYING TO HELP YOU!
HIS STRENGTH-- HIS SPEED-- INHUMAN!
DON'T REMEMBER MUCH AFTER CRASHIN' THROUGH THE WINDSHIELD.
I DON'T KNOW WHAT THIS PLACE IS, BUT I AIN'T STICKING AROUND TO FIND OUT! MAYBE THAT'S A WAY OUT OF THIS DUMP UP AHEAD!

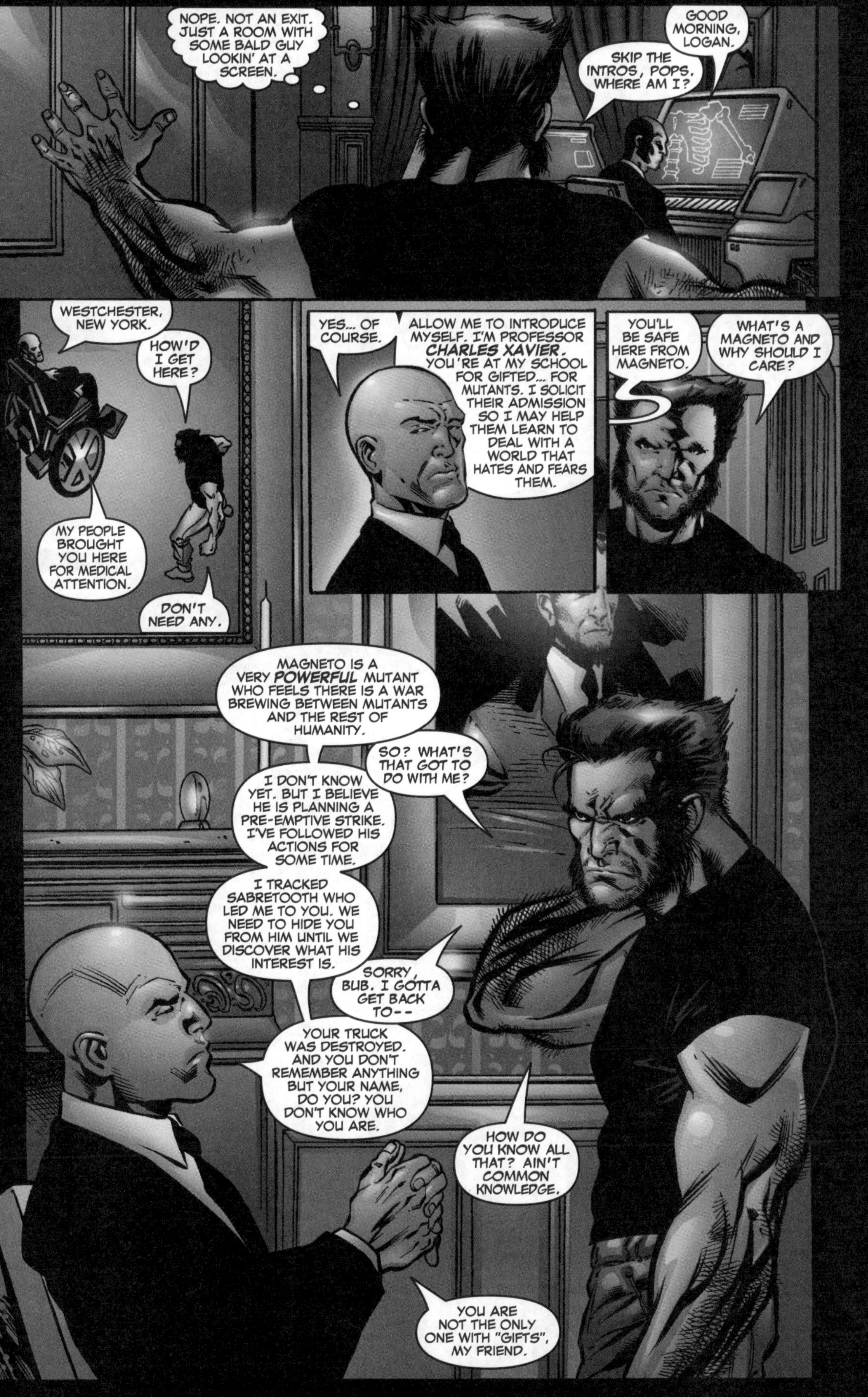
NOPE. NOT AN EXIT. JUST A ROOM WITH SOME BALD GUY LOOKIN' AT A SCREEN.
GOOD MORNING, LOGAN.
SKIP THE INTROS, POPS. WHERE AM I?
WESTCHESTER, NEW YORK.
HOW'D I GET HERE?
MY PEOPLE BROUGHT YOU HERE FOR MEDICAL ATTENTION.
DON'T NEED ANY.
YES... OF COURSE.
ALLOW ME TO INTRODUCE MYSELF. I'M PROFESSOR **CHARLES XAVIER.** YOU'RE AT MY SCHOOL FOR GIFTED... FOR MUTANTS. I SOLICIT THEIR ADMISSION SO I MAY HELP THEM LEARN TO DEAL WITH A WORLD THAT HATES AND FEARS THEM.
YOU'LL BE SAFE HERE FROM MAGNETO.
WHAT'S A MAGNETO AND WHY SHOULD I CARE?
MAGNETO IS A VERY ***POWERFUL*** MUTANT WHO FEELS THERE IS A WAR BREWING BETWEEN MUTANTS AND THE REST OF HUMANITY.
SO? WHAT'S THAT GOT TO DO WITH ME?
I DON'T KNOW YET. BUT I BELIEVE HE IS PLANNING A PRE-EMPTIVE STRIKE. I'VE FOLLOWED HIS ACTIONS FOR SOME TIME.
I TRACKED SABRETOOTH WHO LED ME TO YOU. WE NEED TO HIDE YOU FROM HIM UNTIL WE DISCOVER WHAT HIS INTEREST IS.
SORRY, BUB. I GOTTA GET BACK TO--
YOUR TRUCK WAS DESTROYED. AND YOU DON'T REMEMBER ANYTHING BUT YOUR NAME, DO YOU? YOU DON'T KNOW WHO YOU ARE.
HOW DO YOU KNOW ALL THAT? AIN'T COMMON KNOWLEDGE.
YOU ARE NOT THE ONLY ONE WITH "GIFTS", MY FRIEND.

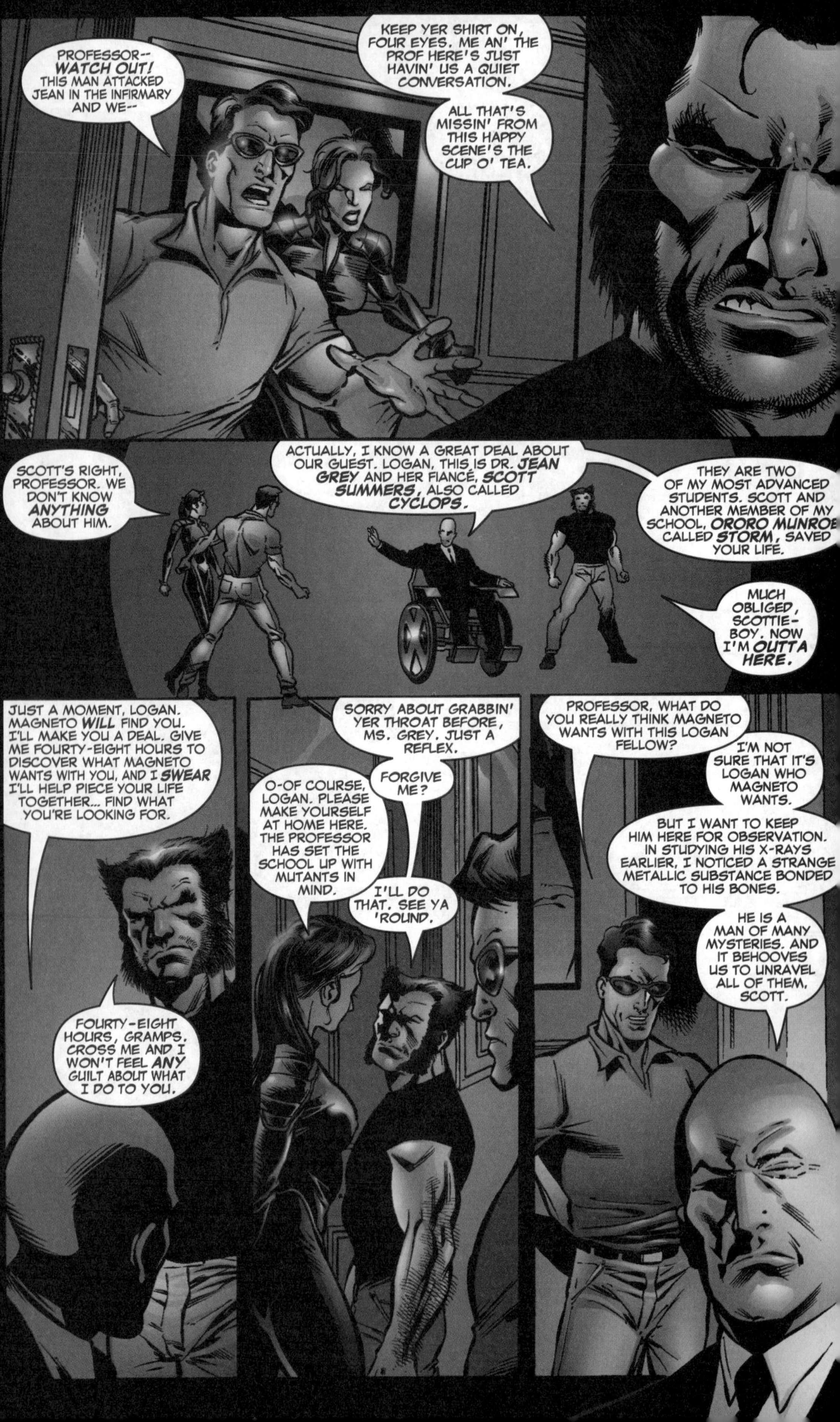
PROFESSOR-- WATCH OUT! THIS MAN ATTACKED JEAN IN THE INFIRMARY AND WE--
KEEP YER SHIRT ON, FOUR EYES. ME AN' THE PROF HERE'S JUST HAVIN' US A QUIET CONVERSATION.
ALL THAT'S MISSIN' FROM THIS HAPPY SCENE'S THE CUP O' TEA.
SCOTT'S RIGHT, PROFESSOR. WE DON'T KNOW ANYTHING ABOUT HIM.
ACTUALLY, I KNOW A GREAT DEAL ABOUT OUR GUEST. LOGAN, THIS IS DR. JEAN GREY AND HER FIANCÉ, SCOTT SUMMERS, ALSO CALLED CYCLOPS.
THEY ARE TWO OF MY MOST ADVANCED STUDENTS. SCOTT AND ANOTHER MEMBER OF MY SCHOOL, ORORO MUNROE, CALLED STORM, SAVED YOUR LIFE.
MUCH OBLIGED, SCOTTIE-BOY. NOW I'M OUTTA HERE.
JUST A MOMENT, LOGAN. MAGNETO WILL FIND YOU. I'LL MAKE YOU A DEAL. GIVE ME FOURTY-EIGHT HOURS TO DISCOVER WHAT MAGNETO WANTS WITH YOU, AND I SWEAR I'LL HELP PIECE YOUR LIFE TOGETHER... FIND WHAT YOU'RE LOOKING FOR.
FOURTY-EIGHT HOURS, GRAMPS. CROSS ME AND I WON'T FEEL ANY GUILT ABOUT WHAT I DO TO YOU.
SORRY ABOUT GRABBIN' YER THROAT BEFORE, MS. GREY. JUST A REFLEX.
FORGIVE ME?
O-OF COURSE, LOGAN. PLEASE MAKE YOURSELF AT HOME HERE. THE PROFESSOR HAS SET THE SCHOOL UP WITH MUTANTS IN MIND.
I'LL DO THAT. SEE YA 'ROUND.
PROFESSOR, WHAT DO YOU REALLY THINK MAGNETO WANTS WITH THIS LOGAN FELLOW?
I'M NOT SURE THAT IT'S LOGAN WHO MAGNETO WANTS.
BUT I WANT TO KEEP HIM HERE FOR OBSERVATION. IN STUDYING HIS X-RAYS EARLIER, I NOTICED A STRANGE METALLIC SUBSTANCE BONDED TO HIS BONES.
HE IS A MAN OF MANY MYSTERIES. AND IT BEHOOVES US TO UNRAVEL ALL OF THEM, SCOTT.

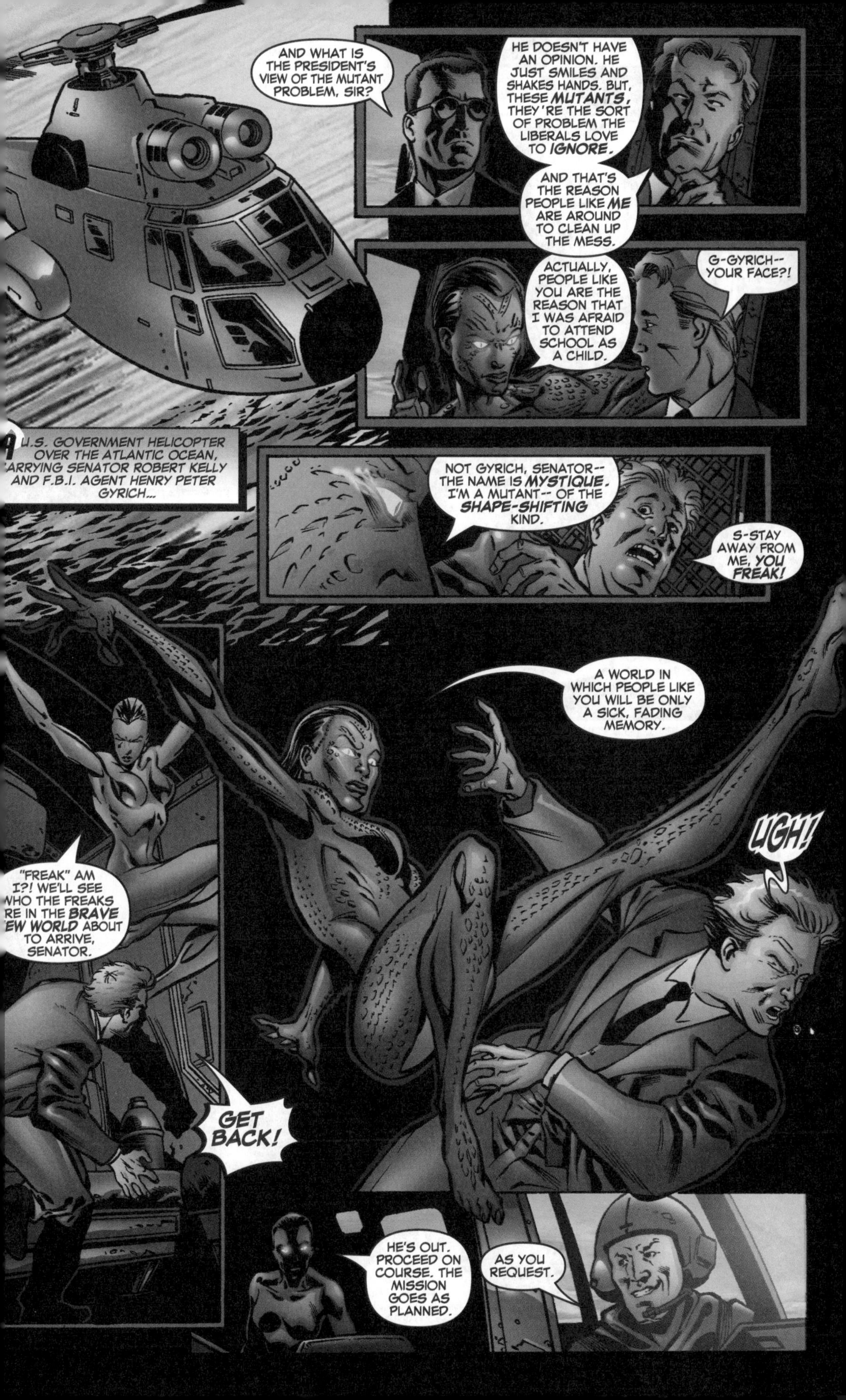
U.S. GOVERNMENT HELICOPTER OVER THE ATLANTIC OCEAN, CARRYING SENATOR ROBERT KELLY AND F.B.I. AGENT HENRY PETER GYRICH...
AND WHAT IS THE PRESIDENT'S VIEW OF THE MUTANT PROBLEM, SIR?
HE DOESN'T HAVE AN OPINION. HE JUST SMILES AND SHAKES HANDS. BUT, THESE MUTANTS, THEY'RE THE SORT OF PROBLEM THE LIBERALS LOVE TO IGNORE.
AND THAT'S THE REASON PEOPLE LIKE ME ARE AROUND TO CLEAN UP THE MESS.
ACTUALLY, PEOPLE LIKE YOU ARE THE REASON THAT I WAS AFRAID TO ATTEND SCHOOL AS A CHILD.
G-GYRICH-- YOUR FACE?!
NOT GYRICH, SENATOR-- THE NAME IS MYSTIQUE. I'M A MUTANT-- OF THE SHAPE-SHIFTING KIND.
S-STAY AWAY FROM ME, YOU FREAK!
"FREAK" AM I?! WE'LL SEE WHO THE FREAKS ARE IN THE BRAVE NEW WORLD ABOUT TO ARRIVE, SENATOR.
A WORLD IN WHICH PEOPLE LIKE YOU WILL BE ONLY A SICK, FADING MEMORY.
UGH!
GET BACK!
HE'S OUT. PROCEED ON COURSE. THE MISSION GOES AS PLANNED.
AS YOU REQUEST.

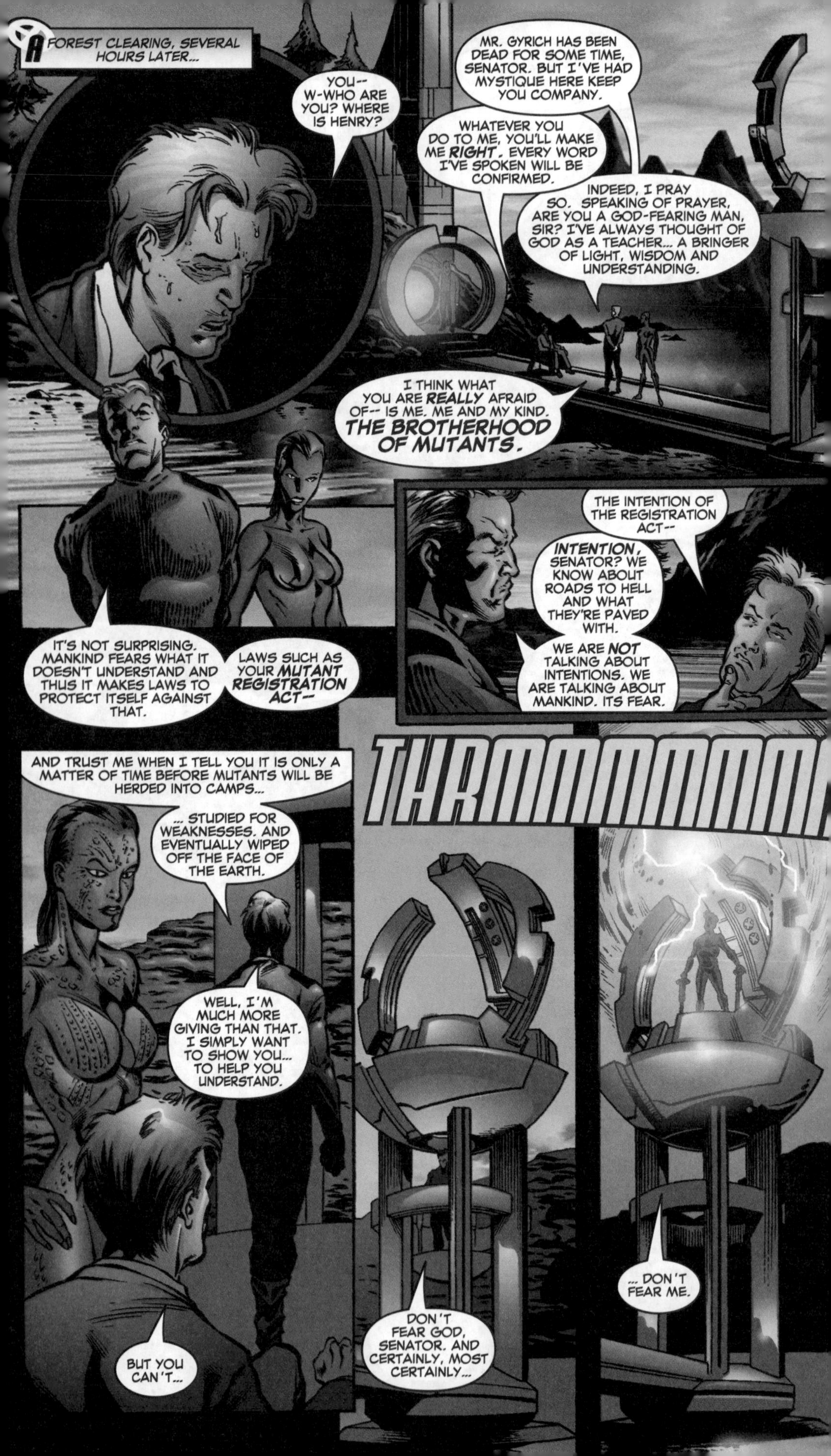
A FOREST CLEARING, SEVERAL HOURS LATER...
YOU-- W-WHO ARE YOU? WHERE IS HENRY?
MR. GYRICH HAS BEEN DEAD FOR SOME TIME, SENATOR. BUT I'VE HAD MYSTIQUE HERE KEEP YOU COMPANY.
WHATEVER YOU DO TO ME, YOU'LL MAKE ME RIGHT. EVERY WORD I'VE SPOKEN WILL BE CONFIRMED.
INDEED, I PRAY SO. SPEAKING OF PRAYER, ARE YOU A GOD-FEARING MAN, SIR? I'VE ALWAYS THOUGHT OF GOD AS A TEACHER... A BRINGER OF LIGHT, WISDOM AND UNDERSTANDING.
I THINK WHAT YOU ARE REALLY AFRAID OF-- IS ME. ME AND MY KIND. THE BROTHERHOOD OF MUTANTS.
IT'S NOT SURPRISING. MANKIND FEARS WHAT IT DOESN'T UNDERSTAND AND THUS IT MAKES LAWS TO PROTECT ITSELF AGAINST THAT.
LAWS SUCH AS YOUR MUTANT REGISTRATION ACT--
THE INTENTION OF THE REGISTRATION ACT--
INTENTION, SENATOR? WE KNOW ABOUT ROADS TO HELL AND WHAT THEY'RE PAVED WITH.
WE ARE NOT TALKING ABOUT INTENTIONS. WE ARE TALKING ABOUT MANKIND. ITS FEAR.
AND TRUST ME WHEN I TELL YOU IT IS ONLY A MATTER OF TIME BEFORE MUTANTS WILL BE HERDED INTO CAMPS...
... STUDIED FOR WEAKNESSES. AND EVENTUALLY WIPED OFF THE FACE OF THE EARTH.
WELL, I'M MUCH MORE GIVING THAN THAT. I SIMPLY WANT TO SHOW YOU... TO HELP YOU UNDERSTAND.
BUT YOU CAN'T...
THRMMMMMMM
DON'T FEAR GOD, SENATOR. AND CERTAINLY, MOST CERTAINLY...
... DON'T FEAR ME.

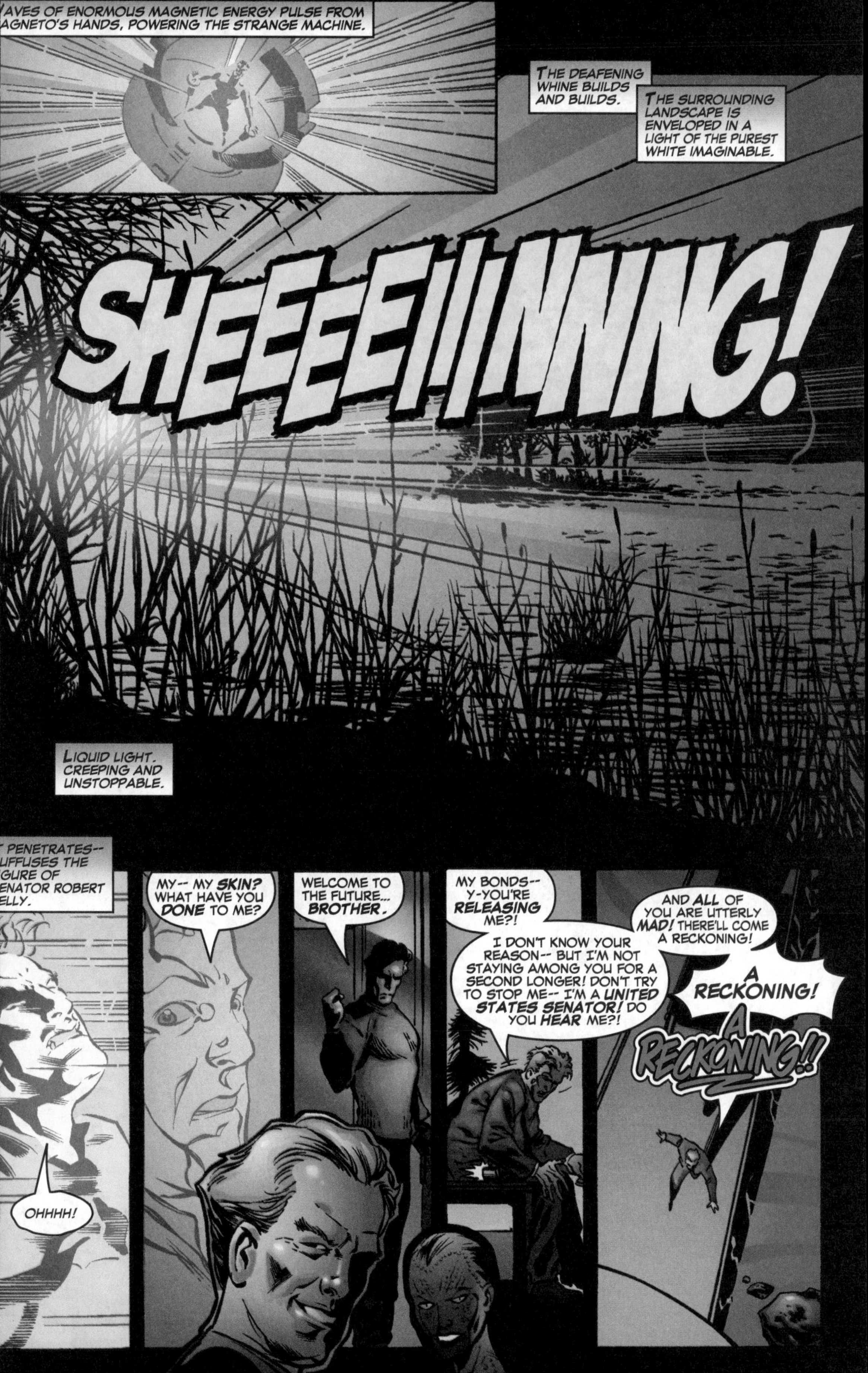
AVES OF ENORMOUS MAGNETIC ENERGY PULSE FROM
AGNETO'S HANDS, POWERING THE STRANGE MACHINE.
THE DEAFENING WHINE BUILDS AND BUILDS.
THE SURROUNDING LANDSCAPE IS ENVELOPED IN A LIGHT OF THE PUREST WHITE IMAGINABLE.
SHEEEEIIIINNNNG!
LIQUID LIGHT. CREEPING AND UNSTOPPABLE.
T PENETRATES-- UFFUSES THE IGURE OF ENATOR ROBERT ELLY.
OHHHH!
MY-- MY SKIN? WHAT HAVE YOU DONE TO ME?
WELCOME TO THE FUTURE... BROTHER.
MY BONDS-- Y-YOU'RE RELEASING ME?!
I DON'T KNOW YOUR REASON-- BUT I'M NOT STAYING AMONG YOU FOR A SECOND LONGER! DON'T TRY TO STOP ME-- I'M A UNITED STATES SENATOR! DO YOU HEAR ME?!
AND ALL OF YOU ARE UTTERLY MAD! THERE'LL COME A RECKONING!
A RECKONING!
A RECKONING!!

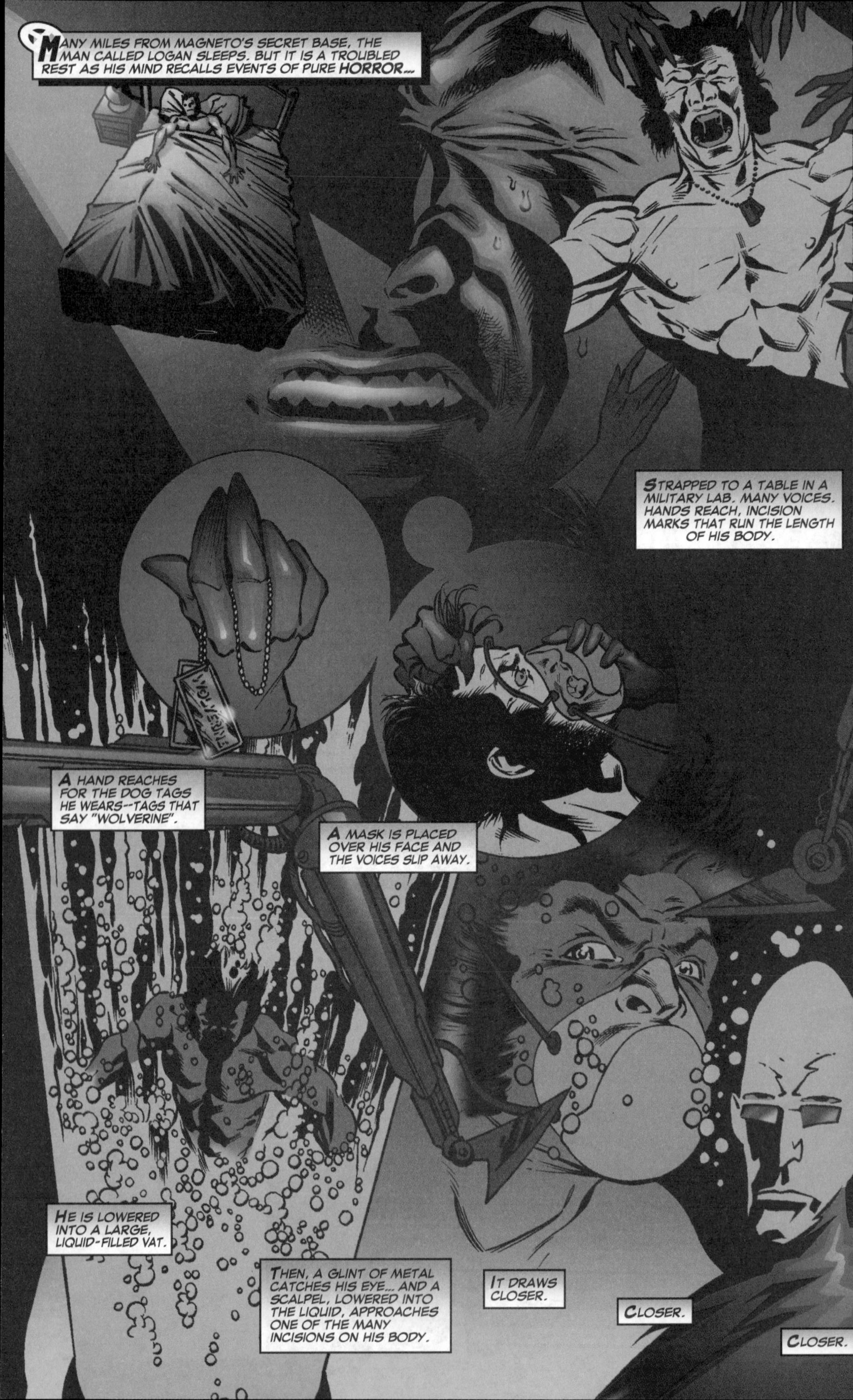
MANY MILES FROM MAGNETO'S SECRET BASE, THE MAN CALLED LOGAN SLEEPS. BUT IT IS A TROUBLED REST AS HIS MIND RECALLS EVENTS OF PURE HORROR...
STRAPPED TO A TABLE IN A MILITARY LAB. MANY VOICES. HANDS REACH. INCISION MARKS THAT RUN THE LENGTH OF HIS BODY.
A HAND REACHES FOR THE DOG TAGS HE WEARS--TAGS THAT SAY "WOLVERINE".
A MASK IS PLACED OVER HIS FACE AND THE VOICES SLIP AWAY.
HE IS LOWERED INTO A LARGE, LIQUID-FILLED VAT.
THEN, A GLINT OF METAL CATCHES HIS EYE... AND A SCALPEL, LOWERED INTO THE LIQUID, APPROACHES ONE OF THE MANY INCISIONS ON HIS BODY.
IT DRAWS CLOSER.
CLOSER.
CLOSER.

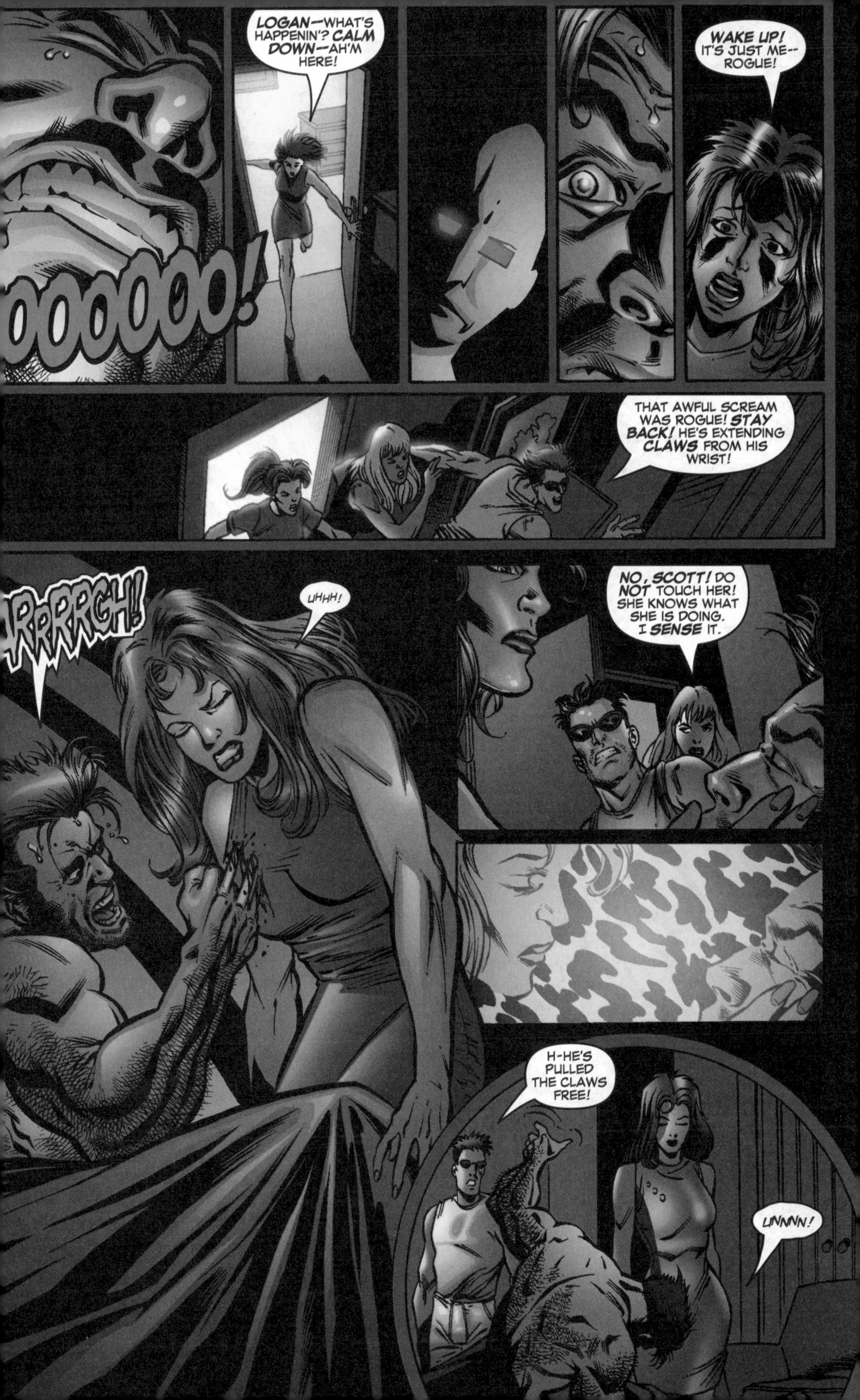

OOOOOO!
LOGAN--WHAT'S HAPPENIN'? CALM DOWN--AH'M HERE!
WAKE UP! IT'S JUST ME--ROGUE!
THAT AWFUL SCREAM WAS ROGUE! STAY BACK! HE'S EXTENDING CLAWS FROM HIS WRIST!
RRRRGH!!
UHHH!
NO, SCOTT! DO NOT TOUCH HER! SHE KNOWS WHAT SHE IS DOING. I SENSE IT.
H-HE'S PULLED THE CLAWS FREE!
UNNNN!

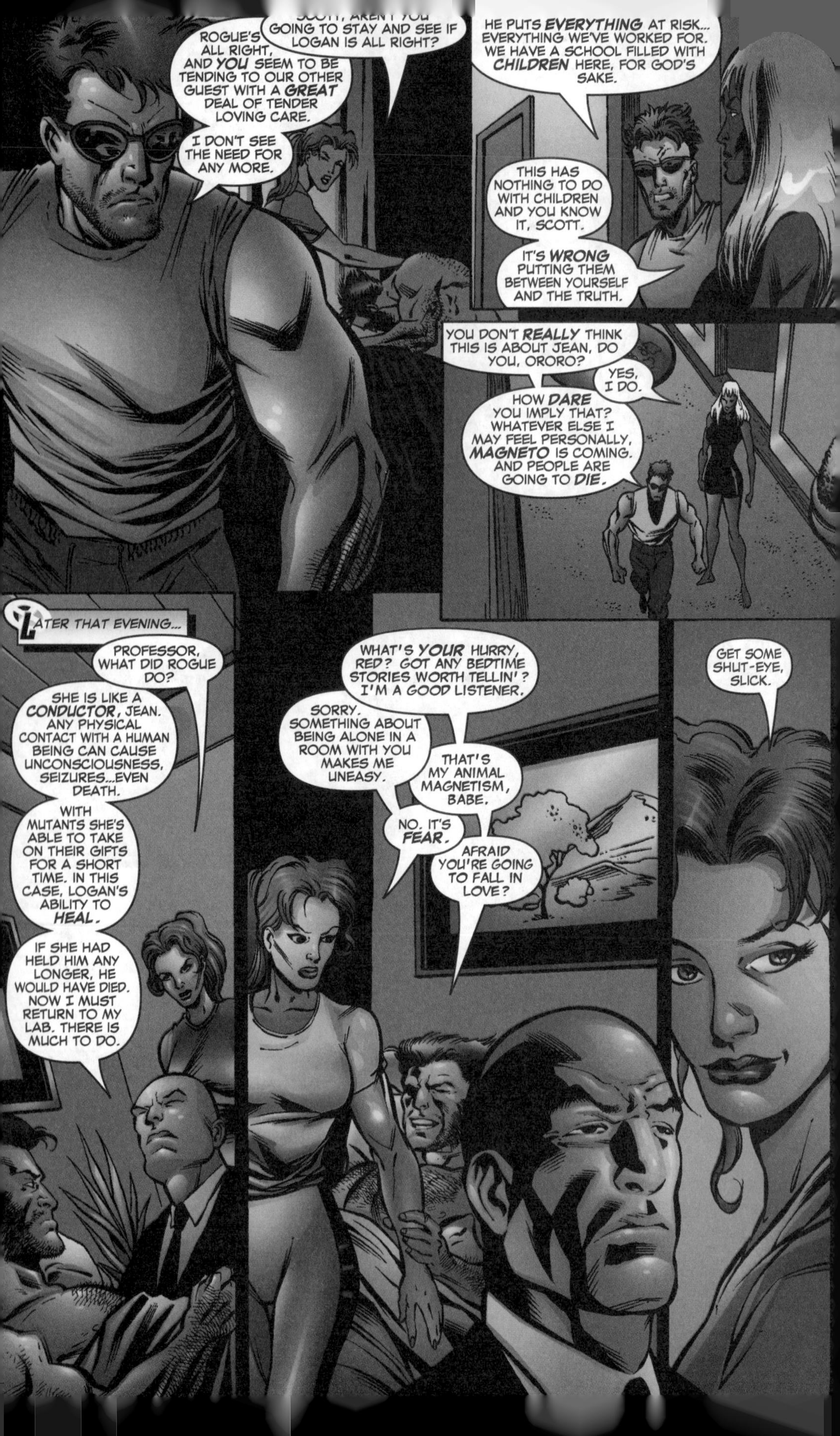
SCOTT, AREN'T YOU GOING TO STAY AND SEE IF LOGAN IS ALL RIGHT?
ROGUE'S ALL RIGHT, AND YOU SEEM TO BE TENDING TO OUR OTHER GUEST WITH A GREAT DEAL OF TENDER LOVING CARE.
I DON'T SEE THE NEED FOR ANY MORE.
HE PUTS EVERYTHING AT RISK... EVERYTHING WE'VE WORKED FOR. WE HAVE A SCHOOL FILLED WITH CHILDREN HERE, FOR GOD'S SAKE.
THIS HAS NOTHING TO DO WITH CHILDREN AND YOU KNOW IT, SCOTT.
IT'S WRONG PUTTING THEM BETWEEN YOURSELF AND THE TRUTH.
YOU DON'T REALLY THINK THIS IS ABOUT JEAN, DO YOU, ORORO?
YES, I DO.
HOW DARE YOU IMPLY THAT? WHATEVER ELSE I MAY FEEL PERSONALLY, MAGNETO IS COMING. AND PEOPLE ARE GOING TO DIE.
LATER THAT EVENING...
PROFESSOR, WHAT DID ROGUE DO?
SHE IS LIKE A CONDUCTOR, JEAN. ANY PHYSICAL CONTACT WITH A HUMAN BEING CAN CAUSE UNCONSCIOUSNESS, SEIZURES...EVEN DEATH.
WITH MUTANTS SHE'S ABLE TO TAKE ON THEIR GIFTS FOR A SHORT TIME. IN THIS CASE, LOGAN'S ABILITY TO HEAL.
IF SHE HAD HELD HIM ANY LONGER, HE WOULD HAVE DIED. NOW I MUST RETURN TO MY LAB. THERE IS MUCH TO DO.
WHAT'S YOUR HURRY, RED? GOT ANY BEDTIME STORIES WORTH TELLIN'? I'M A GOOD LISTENER.
SORRY. SOMETHING ABOUT BEING ALONE IN A ROOM WITH YOU MAKES ME UNEASY.
THAT'S MY ANIMAL MAGNETISM, BABE.
NO. IT'S FEAR.
AFRAID YOU'RE GOING TO FALL IN LOVE?
GET SOME SHUT-EYE, SLICK.

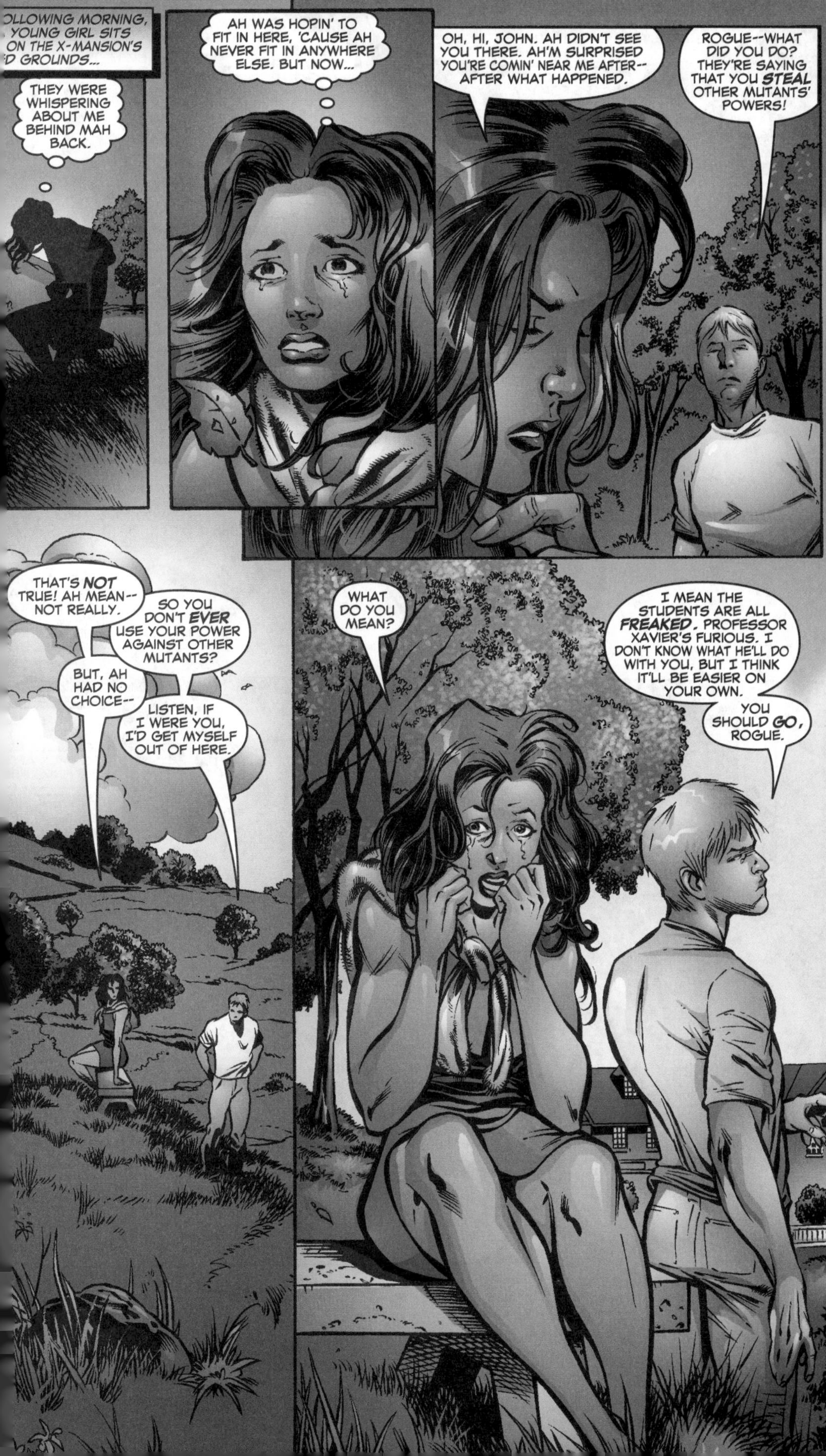
OLLOWING MORNING, YOUNG GIRL SITS ON THE X-MANSION'S ED GROUNDS...
THEY WERE WHISPERING ABOUT ME BEHIND MAH BACK.
AH WAS HOPIN' TO FIT IN HERE, 'CAUSE AH NEVER FIT IN ANYWHERE ELSE. BUT NOW...
OH, HI, JOHN. AH DIDN'T SEE YOU THERE. AH'M SURPRISED YOU'RE COMIN' NEAR ME AFTER--AFTER WHAT HAPPENED.
ROGUE--WHAT DID YOU DO? THEY'RE SAYING THAT YOU STEAL OTHER MUTANTS' POWERS!
THAT'S NOT TRUE! AH MEAN--NOT REALLY.
SO YOU DON'T EVER USE YOUR POWER AGAINST OTHER MUTANTS?
BUT, AH HAD NO CHOICE--
LISTEN, IF I WERE YOU, I'D GET MYSELF OUT OF HERE.
WHAT DO YOU MEAN?
I MEAN THE STUDENTS ARE ALL FREAKED. PROFESSOR XAVIER'S FURIOUS. I DON'T KNOW WHAT HE'LL DO WITH YOU, BUT I THINK IT'LL BE EASIER ON YOUR OWN.
YOU SHOULD GO, ROGUE.

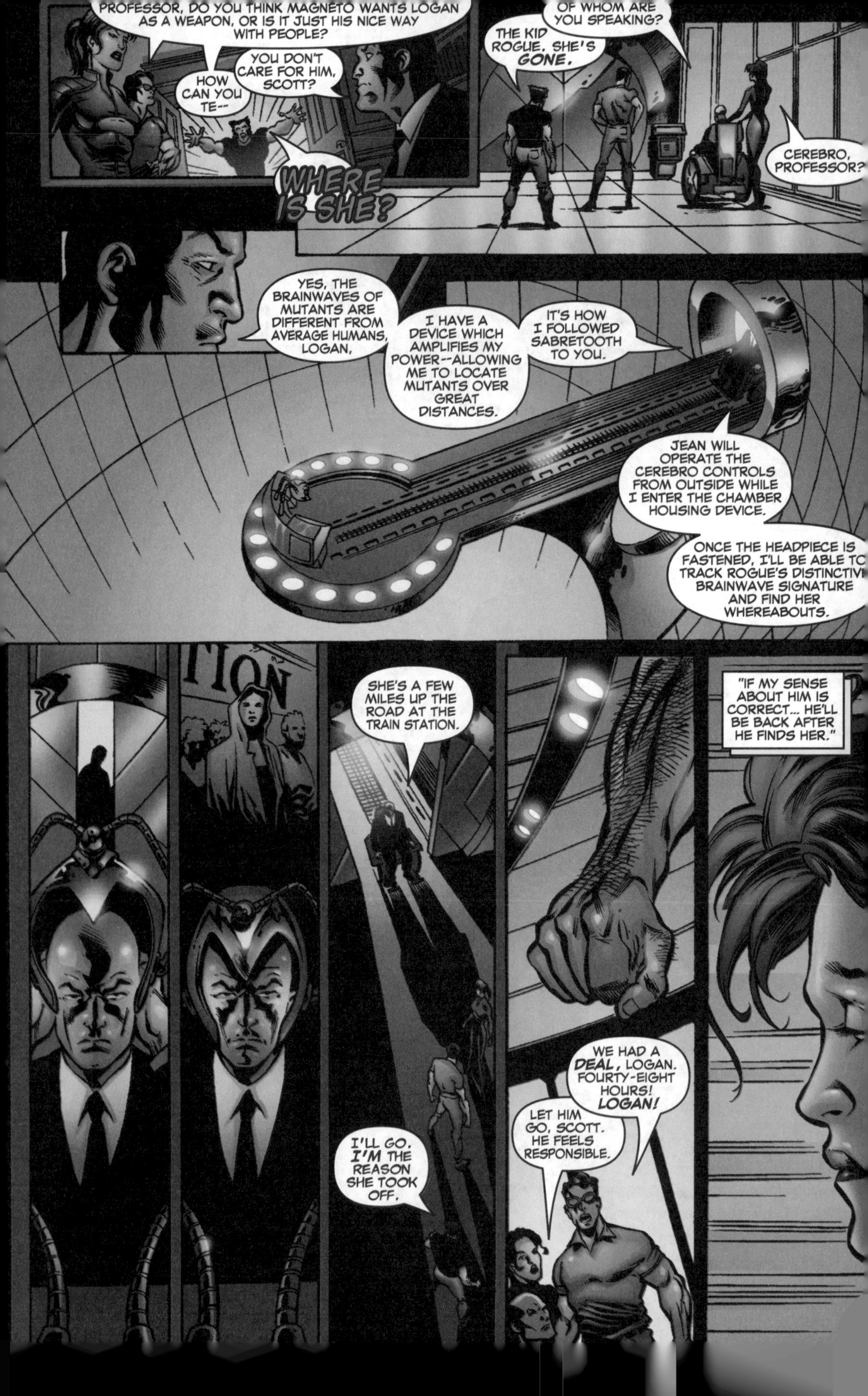
PROFESSOR, DO YOU THINK MAGNETO WANTS LOGAN AS A WEAPON, OR IS IT JUST HIS NICE WAY WITH PEOPLE?
HOW CAN YOU TE--
YOU DON'T CARE FOR HIM, SCOTT?
WHERE IS SHE?
OF WHOM ARE YOU SPEAKING?
THE KID ROGUE. SHE'S GONE.
CEREBRO, PROFESSOR?
YES, THE BRAINWAVES OF MUTANTS ARE DIFFERENT FROM AVERAGE HUMANS, LOGAN,
I HAVE A DEVICE WHICH AMPLIFIES MY POWER--ALLOWING ME TO LOCATE MUTANTS OVER GREAT DISTANCES.
IT'S HOW I FOLLOWED SABRETOOTH TO YOU.
JEAN WILL OPERATE THE CEREBRO CONTROLS FROM OUTSIDE WHILE I ENTER THE CHAMBER HOUSING DEVICE.
ONCE THE HEADPIECE IS FASTENED, I'LL BE ABLE TO TRACK ROGUE'S DISTINCTIVE BRAINWAVE SIGNATURE AND FIND HER WHEREABOUTS.
TION
SHE'S A FEW MILES UP THE ROAD AT THE TRAIN STATION.
I'LL GO. I'M THE REASON SHE TOOK OFF.
WE HAD A DEAL, LOGAN. FOURTY-EIGHT HOURS! LOGAN!
LET HIM GO, SCOTT. HE FEELS RESPONSIBLE.
"IF MY SENSE ABOUT HIM IS CORRECT... HE'LL BE BACK AFTER HE FINDS HER."

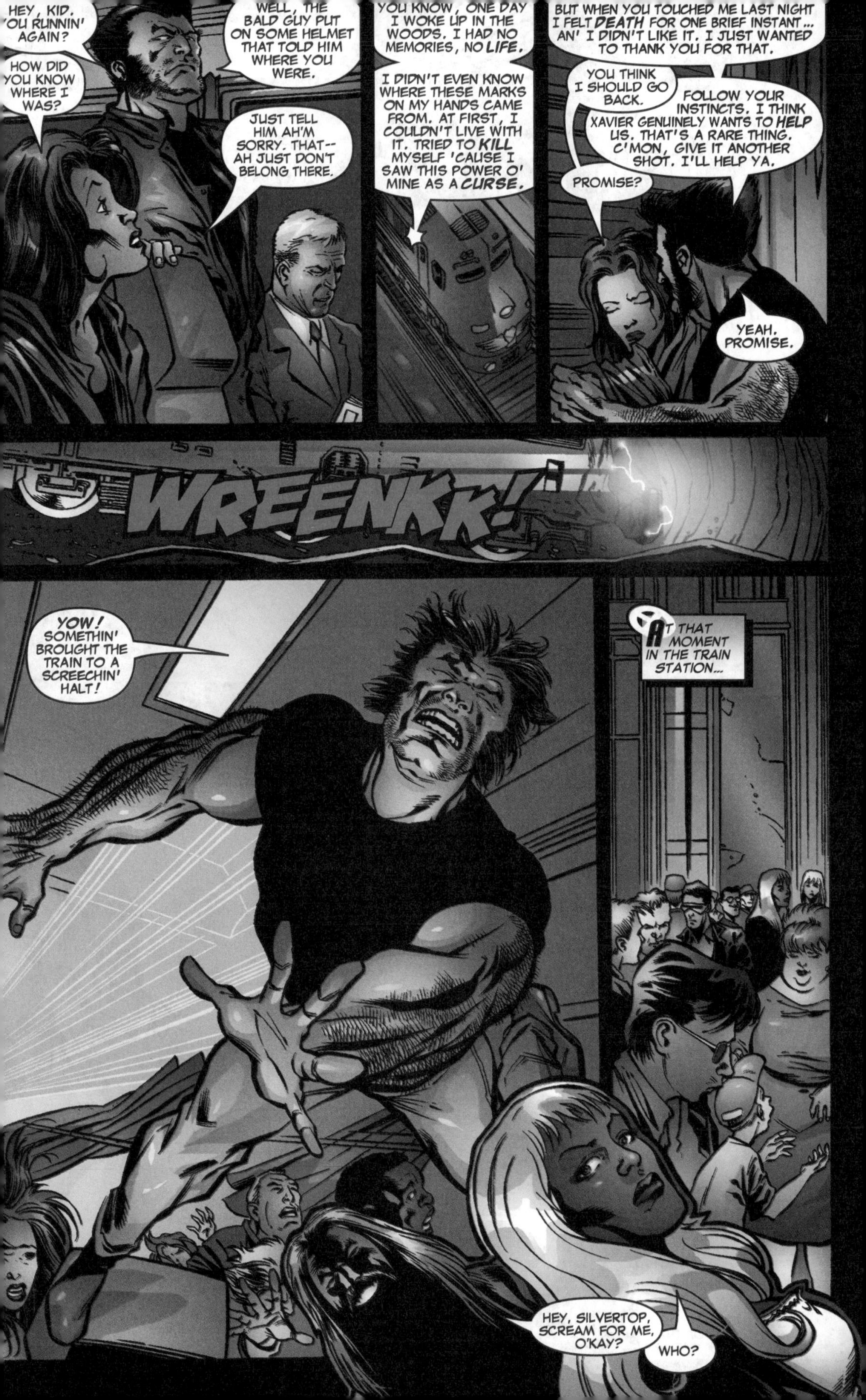
HEY, KID. 'OU RUNNIN' AGAIN?
HOW DID YOU KNOW WHERE I WAS?
WELL, THE BALD GUY PUT ON SOME HELMET THAT TOLD HIM WHERE YOU WERE.
JUST TELL HIM AH'M SORRY. THAT-- AH JUST DON'T BELONG THERE.
YOU KNOW, ONE DAY I WOKE UP IN THE WOODS. I HAD NO MEMORIES, NO LIFE.
I DIDN'T EVEN KNOW WHERE THESE MARKS ON MY HANDS CAME FROM. AT FIRST, I COULDN'T LIVE WITH IT. TRIED TO KILL MYSELF 'CAUSE I SAW THIS POWER O' MINE AS A CURSE.
BUT WHEN YOU TOUCHED ME LAST NIGHT I FELT DEATH FOR ONE BRIEF INSTANT... AN' I DIDN'T LIKE IT. I JUST WANTED TO THANK YOU FOR THAT.
YOU THINK I SHOULD GO BACK.
FOLLOW YOUR INSTINCTS. I THINK XAVIER GENUINELY WANTS TO HELP US. THAT'S A RARE THING. C'MON, GIVE IT ANOTHER SHOT. I'LL HELP YA.
PROMISE?
YEAH. PROMISE.
WREENKK!
YOW! SOMETHIN' BROUGHT THE TRAIN TO A SCREECHIN' HALT!
AT THAT MOMENT IN THE TRAIN STATION...
HEY, SILVERTOP, SCREAM FOR ME, O'KAY?
WHO?

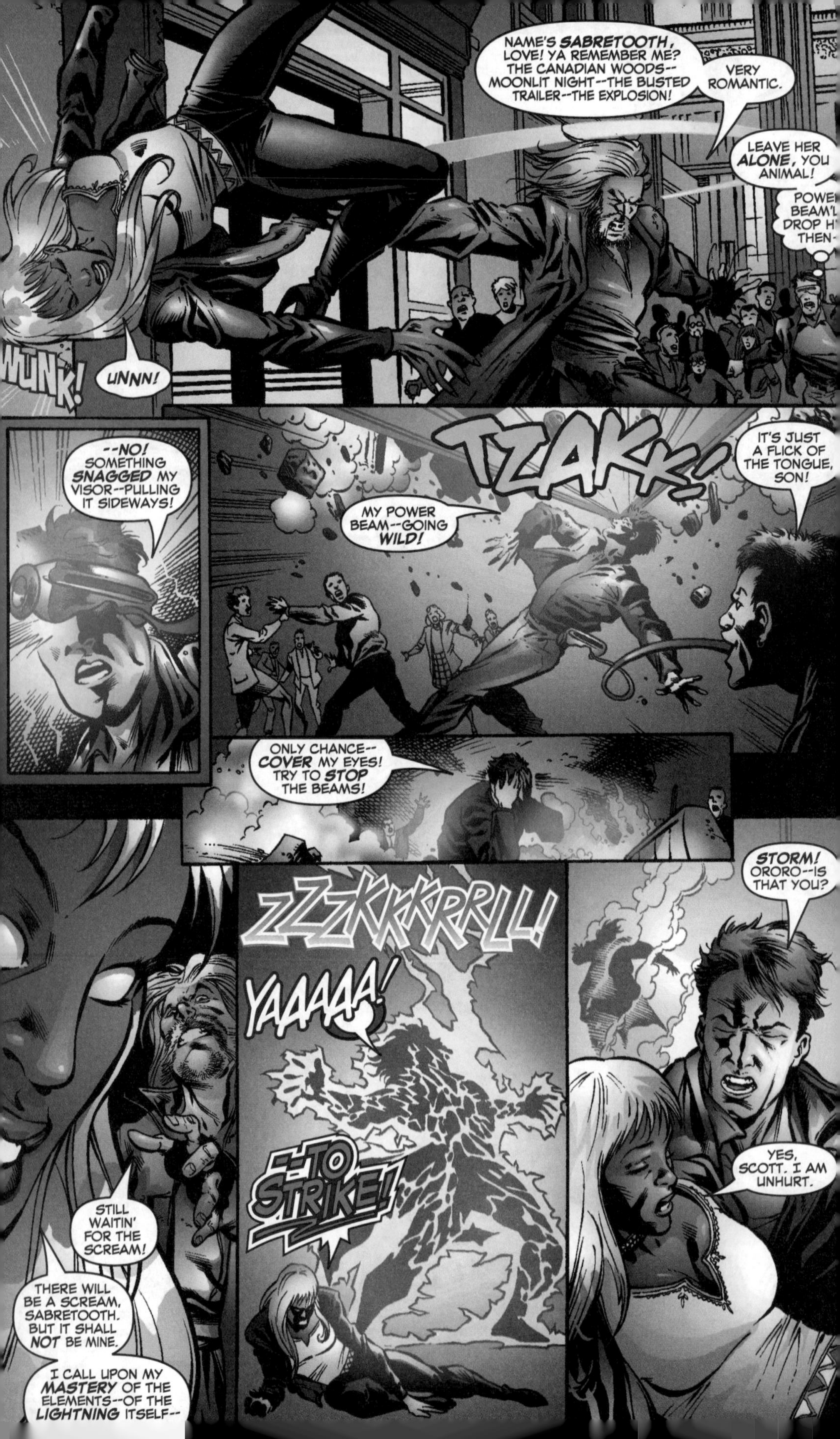

NAME'S SABRETOOTH, LOVE! YA REMEMBER ME? THE CANADIAN WOODS-- MOONLIT NIGHT--THE BUSTED TRAILER--THE EXPLOSION!
VERY ROMANTIC.
LEAVE HER ALONE, YOU ANIMAL!
POWE BEAM'L DROP H THEN-
WUNK!
UNNN!
--NO! SOMETHING SNAGGED MY VISOR--PULLING IT SIDEWAYS!
TZAKK!
MY POWER BEAM--GOING WILD!
IT'S JUST A FLICK OF THE TONGUE, SON!
ONLY CHANCE-- COVER MY EYES! TRY TO STOP THE BEAMS!
STILL WAITIN' FOR THE SCREAM!
THERE WILL BE A SCREAM, SABRETOOTH. BUT IT SHALL NOT BE MINE.
I CALL UPON MY MASTERY OF THE ELEMENTS--OF THE LIGHTNING ITSELF--
ZZZKKKRRLL!
YAAAAA!
--TO STRIKE!
STORM! ORORO--IS THAT YOU?
YES, SCOTT. I AM UNHURT.

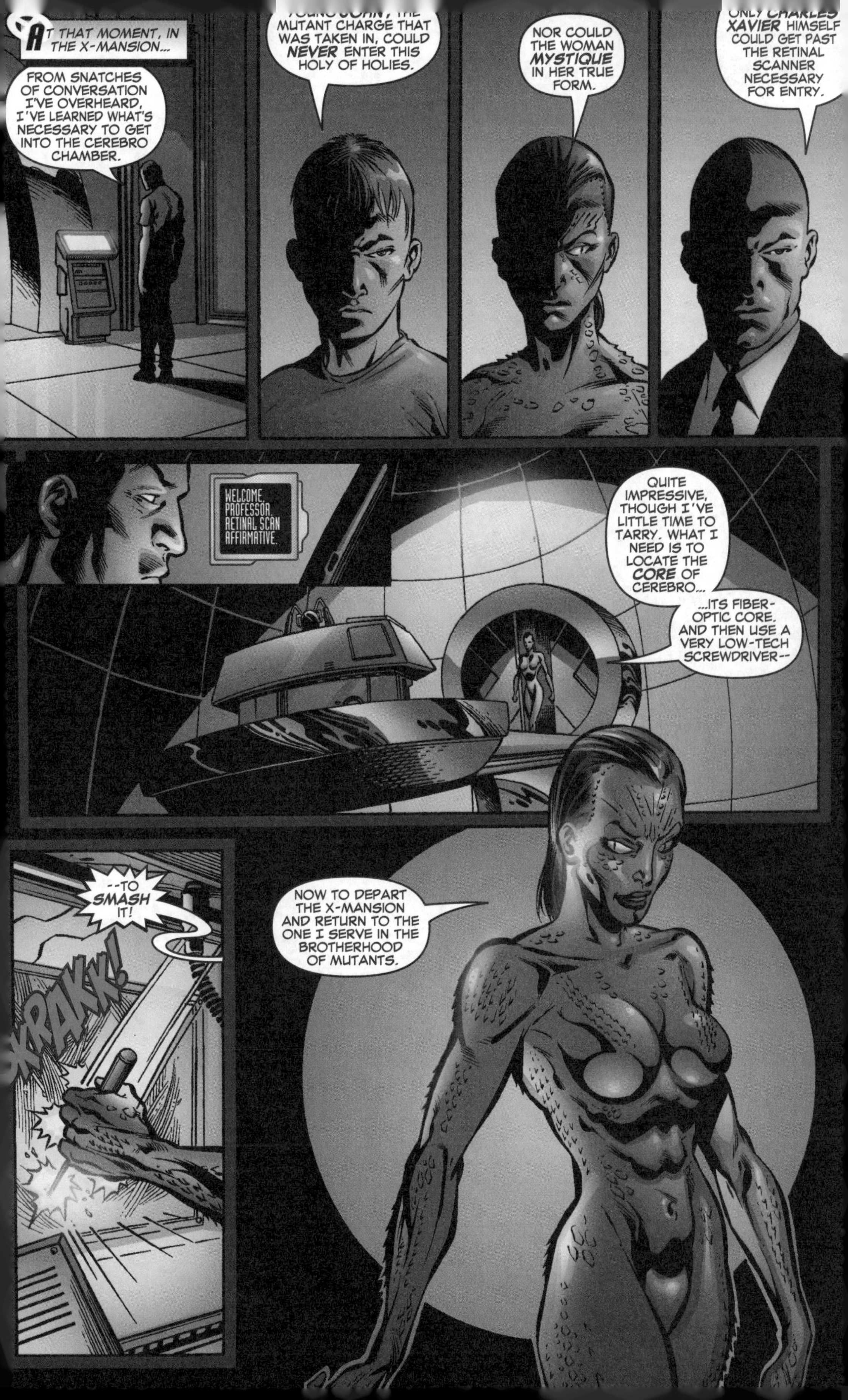
AT THAT MOMENT, IN THE X-MANSION...
FROM SNATCHES OF CONVERSATION I'VE OVERHEARD, I'VE LEARNED WHAT'S NECESSARY TO GET INTO THE CEREBRO CHAMBER.
MUTANT CHARGE THAT WAS TAKEN IN, COULD NEVER ENTER THIS HOLY OF HOLIES.
NOR COULD THE WOMAN MYSTIQUE IN HER TRUE FORM.
XAVIER HIMSELF COULD GET PAST THE RETINAL SCANNER NECESSARY FOR ENTRY.
WELCOME, PROFESSOR. RETINAL SCAN AFFIRMATIVE.
QUITE IMPRESSIVE, THOUGH I'VE LITTLE TIME TO TARRY. WHAT I NEED IS TO LOCATE THE CORE OF CEREBRO...
...ITS FIBER-OPTIC CORE. AND THEN USE A VERY LOW-TECH SCREWDRIVER--
--TO SMASH IT!
KRAKK!
NOW TO DEPART THE X-MANSION AND RETURN TO THE ONE I SERVE IN THE BROTHERHOOD OF MUTANTS.

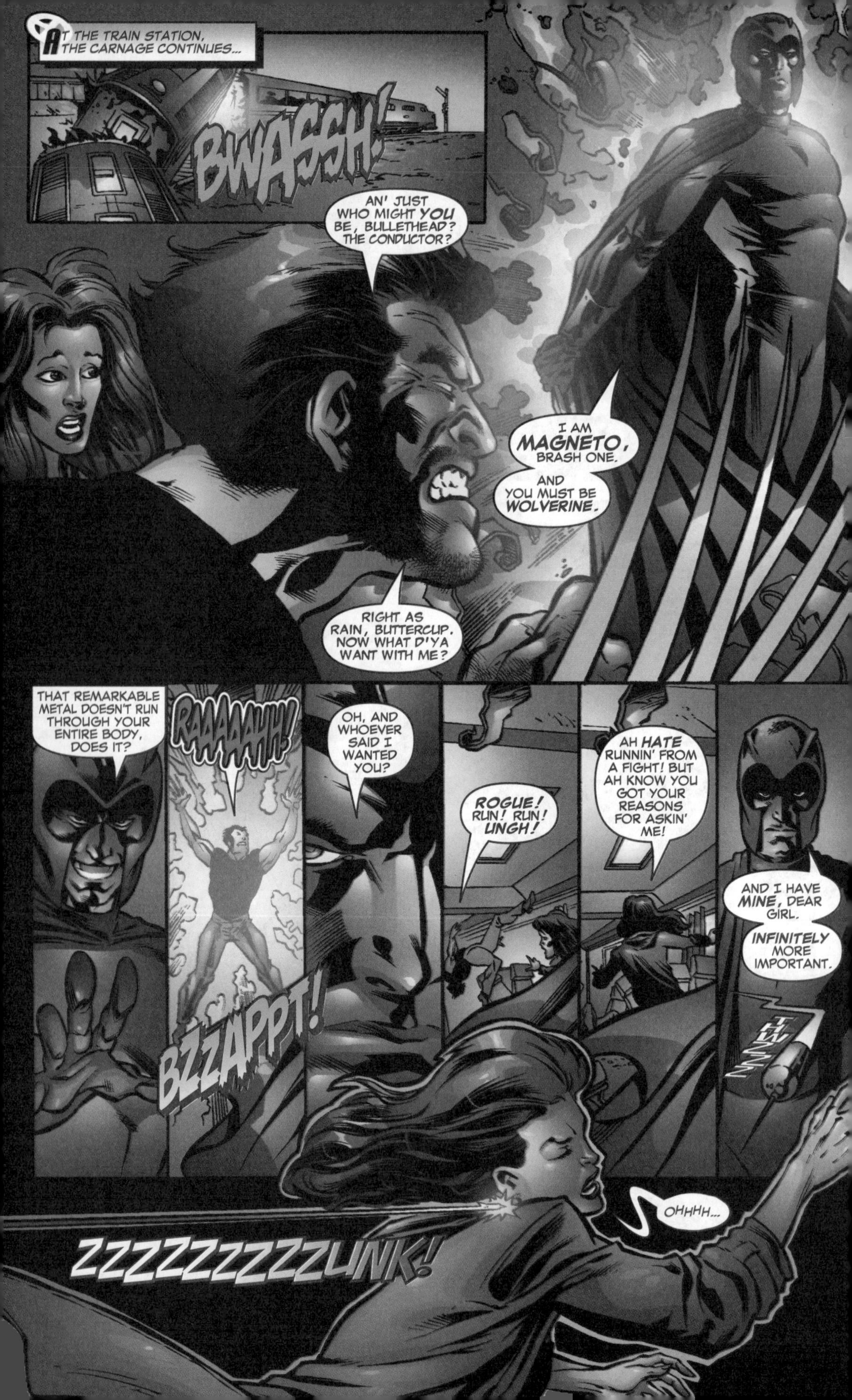
AT THE TRAIN STATION, THE CARNAGE CONTINUES...
BWASSH!
AN' JUST WHO MIGHT YOU BE, BULLETHEAD? THE CONDUCTOR?
I AM MAGNETO, BRASH ONE.
AND YOU MUST BE WOLVERINE.
RIGHT AS RAIN, BUTTERCUP. NOW WHAT D'YA WANT WITH ME?
THAT REMARKABLE METAL DOESN'T RUN THROUGH YOUR ENTIRE BODY, DOES IT?
RAAAAAHH!
BZZAPPT!
OH, AND WHOEVER SAID I WANTED YOU?
ROGUE! RUN! RUN! UNGH!
AH HATE RUNNIN' FROM A FIGHT! BUT AH KNOW YOU GOT YOUR REASONS FOR ASKIN' ME!
AND I HAVE MINE, DEAR GIRL.
INFINITELY MORE IMPORTANT.
THWZZ
OHHHH...
ZZZZZZZZZZUNK!

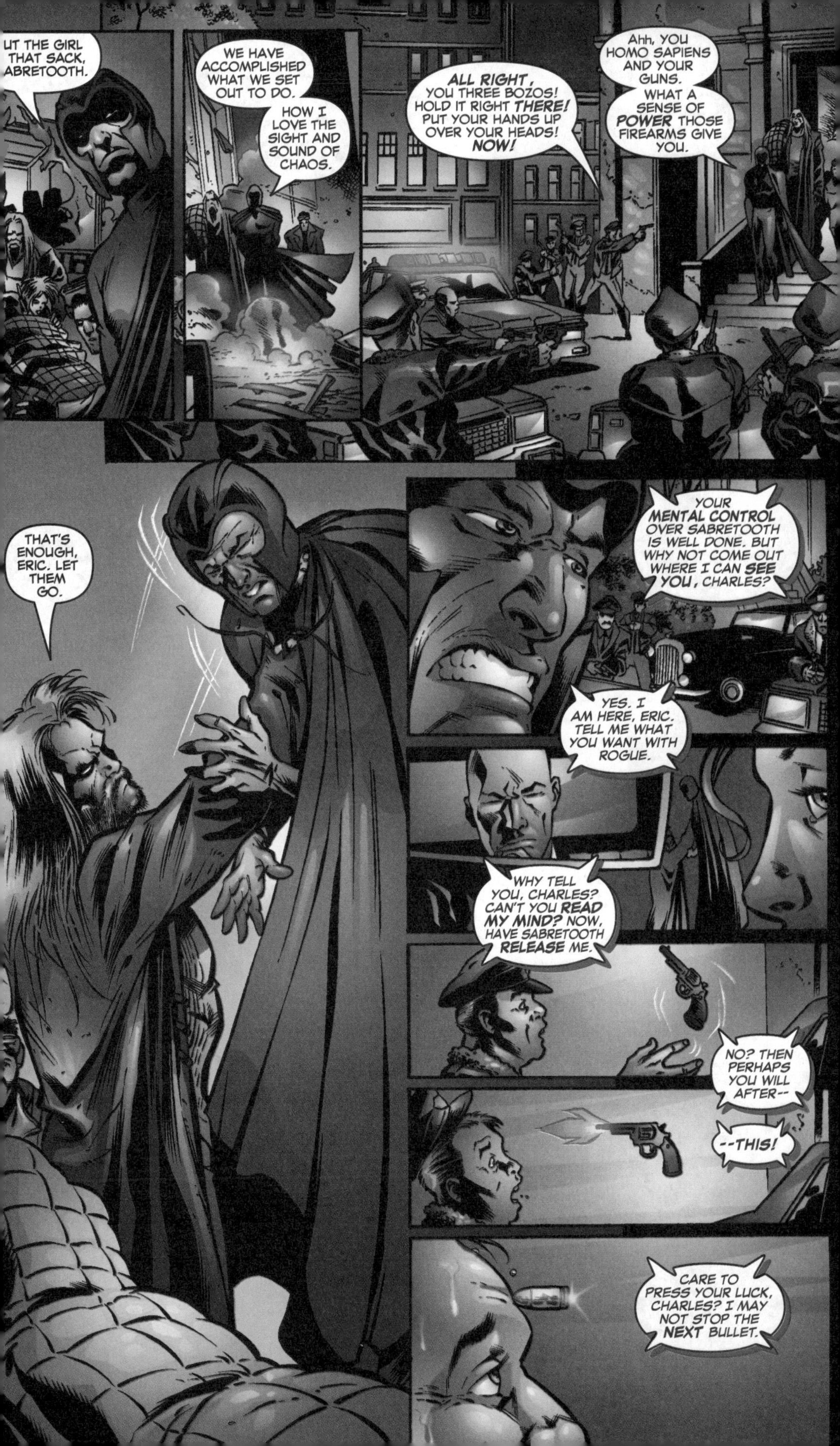

UT THE GIRL THAT SACK, ABRETOOTH.
WE HAVE ACCOMPLISHED WHAT WE SET OUT TO DO.
HOW I LOVE THE SIGHT AND SOUND OF CHAOS.
ALL RIGHT, YOU THREE BOZOS! HOLD IT RIGHT THERE! PUT YOUR HANDS UP OVER YOUR HEADS! NOW!
Ahh, YOU HOMO SAPIENS AND YOUR GUNS.
WHAT A SENSE OF POWER THOSE FIREARMS GIVE YOU.
THAT'S ENOUGH, ERIC. LET THEM GO.
YOUR MENTAL CONTROL OVER SABRETOOTH IS WELL DONE. BUT WHY NOT COME OUT WHERE I CAN SEE YOU, CHARLES?
YES. I AM HERE, ERIC. TELL ME WHAT YOU WANT WITH ROGUE.
WHY TELL YOU, CHARLES? CAN'T YOU READ MY MIND? NOW, HAVE SABRETOOTH RELEASE ME.
NO? THEN PERHAPS YOU WILL AFTER--
--THIS!
CARE TO PRESS YOUR LUCK, CHARLES? I MAY NOT STOP THE NEXT BULLET.

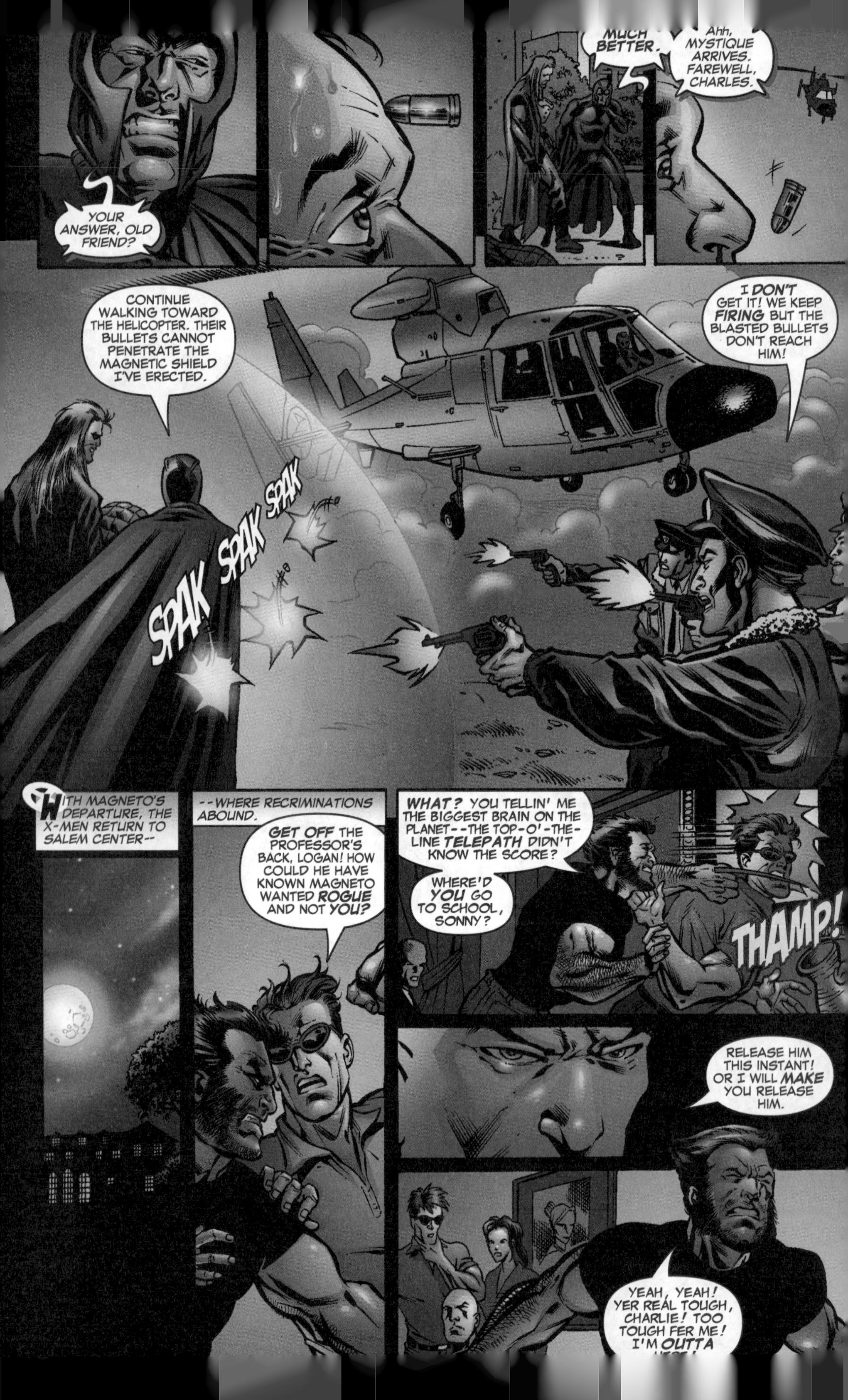

YOUR ANSWER, OLD FRIEND?
MUCH BETTER.
Ahh, MYSTIQUE ARRIVES. FAREWELL, CHARLES.
CONTINUE WALKING TOWARD THE HELICOPTER. THEIR BULLETS CANNOT PENETRATE THE MAGNETIC SHIELD I'VE ERECTED.
I DON'T GET IT! WE KEEP FIRING BUT THE BLASTED BULLETS DON'T REACH HIM!
SPAK SPAK SPAK
WITH MAGNETO'S DEPARTURE, THE X-MEN RETURN TO SALEM CENTER--
--WHERE RECRIMINATIONS ABOUND.
GET OFF THE PROFESSOR'S BACK, LOGAN! HOW COULD HE HAVE KNOWN MAGNETO WANTED ROGUE AND NOT YOU?
WHAT? YOU TELLIN' ME THE BIGGEST BRAIN ON THE PLANET--THE TOP-O'-THE-LINE TELEPATH DIDN'T KNOW THE SCORE?
WHERE'D YOU GO TO SCHOOL, SONNY?
THAMP!
RELEASE HIM THIS INSTANT! OR I WILL MAKE YOU RELEASE HIM.
YEAH, YEAH! YER REAL TOUGH, CHARLIE! TOO TOUGH FER ME! I'M OUTTA

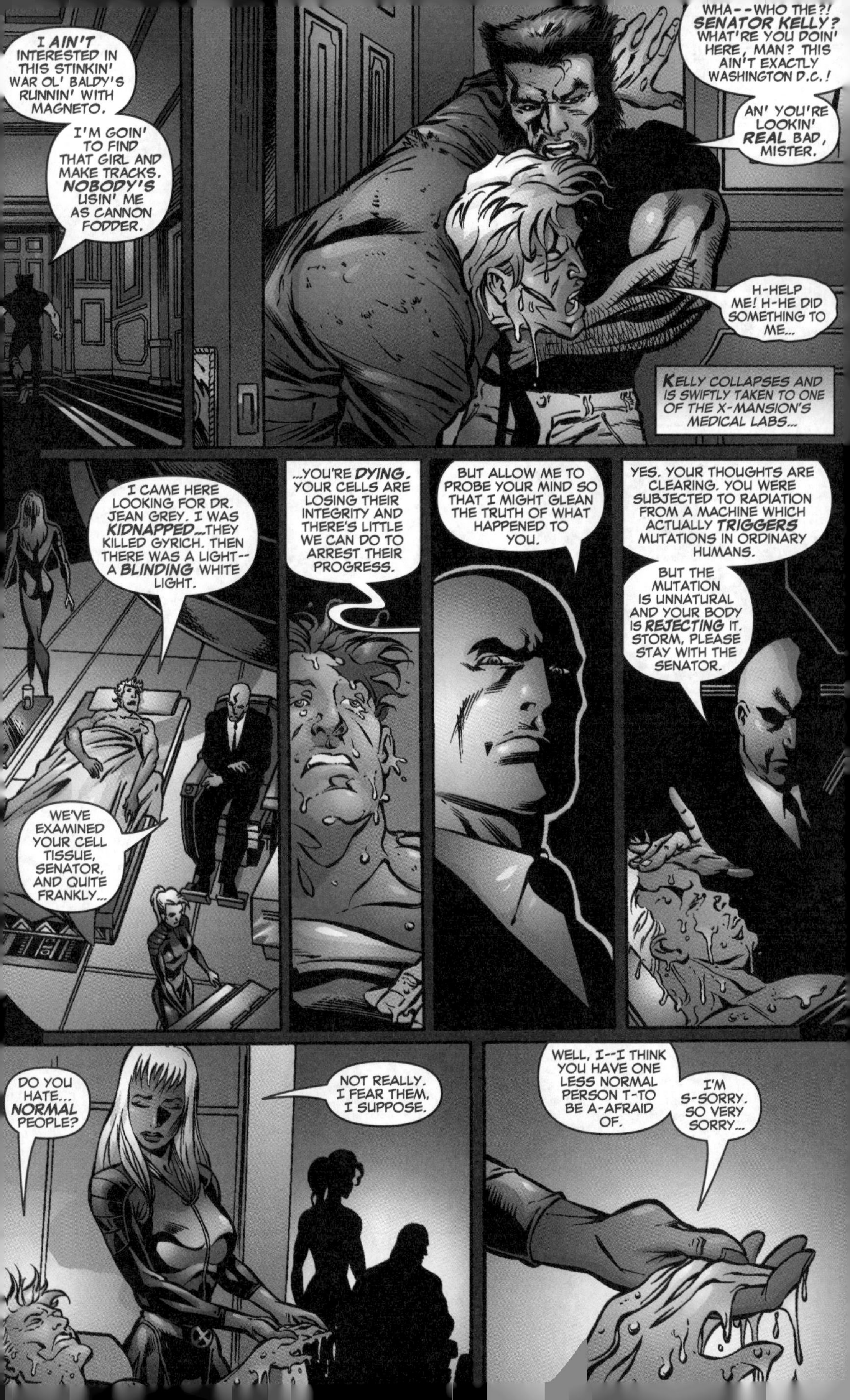
I AIN'T INTERESTED IN THIS STINKIN' WAR OL' BALDY'S RUNNIN' WITH MAGNETO.
I'M GOIN' TO FIND THAT GIRL AND MAKE TRACKS. NOBODY'S USIN' ME AS CANNON FODDER.
WHA--WHO THE?! SENATOR KELLY? WHAT'RE YOU DOIN' HERE, MAN? THIS AIN'T EXACTLY WASHINGTON D.C.!
AN' YOU'RE LOOKIN' REAL BAD, MISTER.
H-HELP ME! H-HE DID SOMETHING TO ME...
KELLY COLLAPSES AND IS SWIFTLY TAKEN TO ONE OF THE X-MANSION'S MEDICAL LABS...
I CAME HERE LOOKING FOR DR. JEAN GREY. I WAS KIDNAPPED...THEY KILLED GYRICH. THEN THERE WAS A LIGHT--A BLINDING WHITE LIGHT.
WE'VE EXAMINED YOUR CELL TISSUE, SENATOR, AND QUITE FRANKLY...
...YOU'RE DYING. YOUR CELLS ARE LOSING THEIR INTEGRITY AND THERE'S LITTLE WE CAN DO TO ARREST THEIR PROGRESS.
BUT ALLOW ME TO PROBE YOUR MIND SO THAT I MIGHT GLEAN THE TRUTH OF WHAT HAPPENED TO YOU.
YES. YOUR THOUGHTS ARE CLEARING. YOU WERE SUBJECTED TO RADIATION FROM A MACHINE WHICH ACTUALLY TRIGGERS MUTATIONS IN ORDINARY HUMANS.
BUT THE MUTATION IS UNNATURAL AND YOUR BODY IS REJECTING IT. STORM, PLEASE STAY WITH THE SENATOR.
DO YOU HATE... NORMAL PEOPLE?
NOT REALLY. I FEAR THEM, I SUPPOSE.
WELL, I--I THINK YOU HAVE ONE LESS NORMAL PERSON T-TO BE A-AFRAID OF.
I'M S-SORRY. SO VERY SORRY...

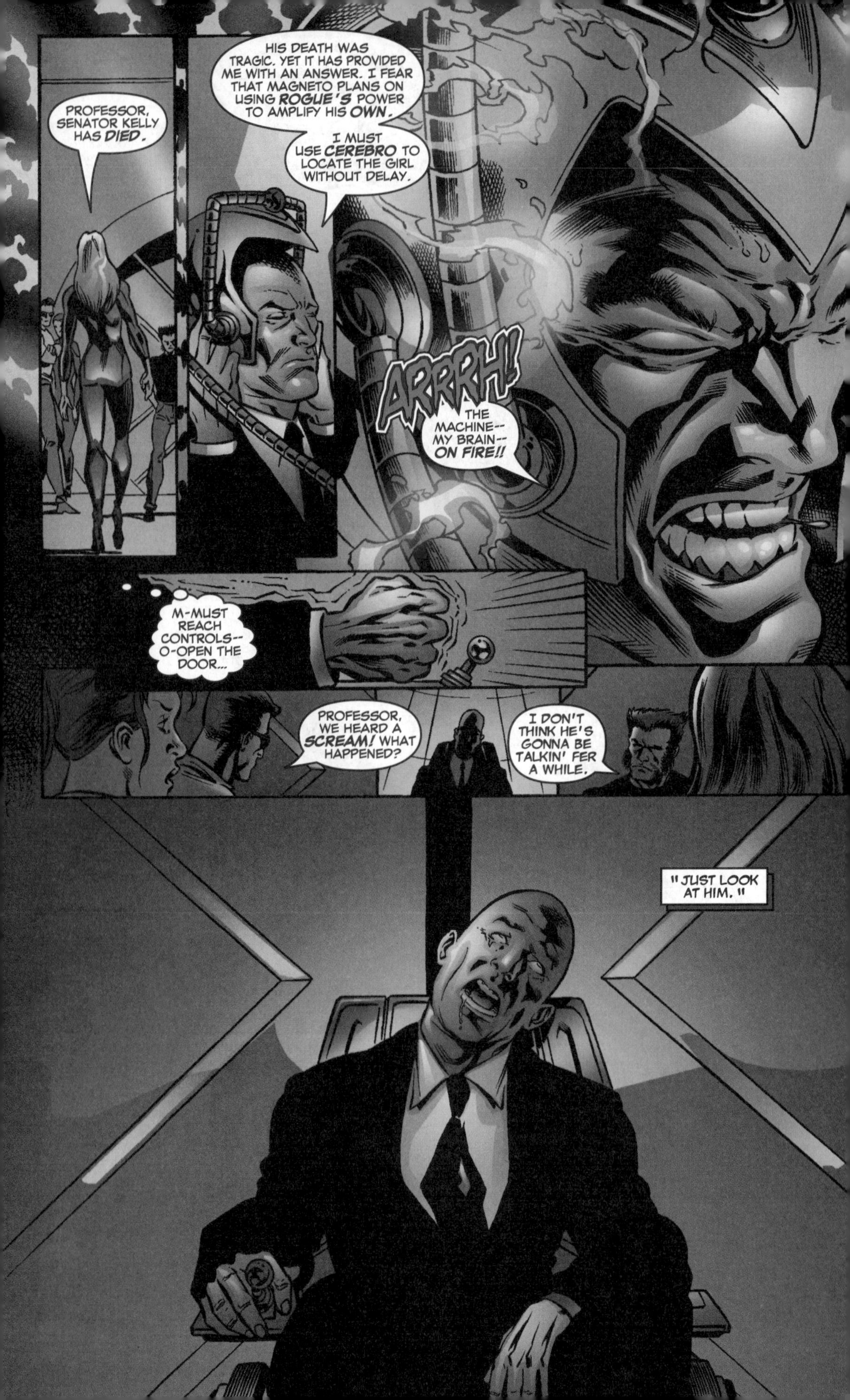
PROFESSOR, SENATOR KELLY HAS DIED.
HIS DEATH WAS TRAGIC. YET IT HAS PROVIDED ME WITH AN ANSWER. I FEAR THAT MAGNETO PLANS ON USING ROGUE'S POWER TO AMPLIFY HIS OWN.
I MUST USE CEREBRO TO LOCATE THE GIRL WITHOUT DELAY.
ARRRH!
THE MACHINE-- MY BRAIN-- ON FIRE!!
M-MUST REACH CONTROLS-- O-OPEN THE DOOR...
PROFESSOR, WE HEARD A SCREAM! WHAT HAPPENED?
I DON'T THINK HE'S GONNA BE TALKIN' FER A WHILE.
"JUST LOOK AT HIM."

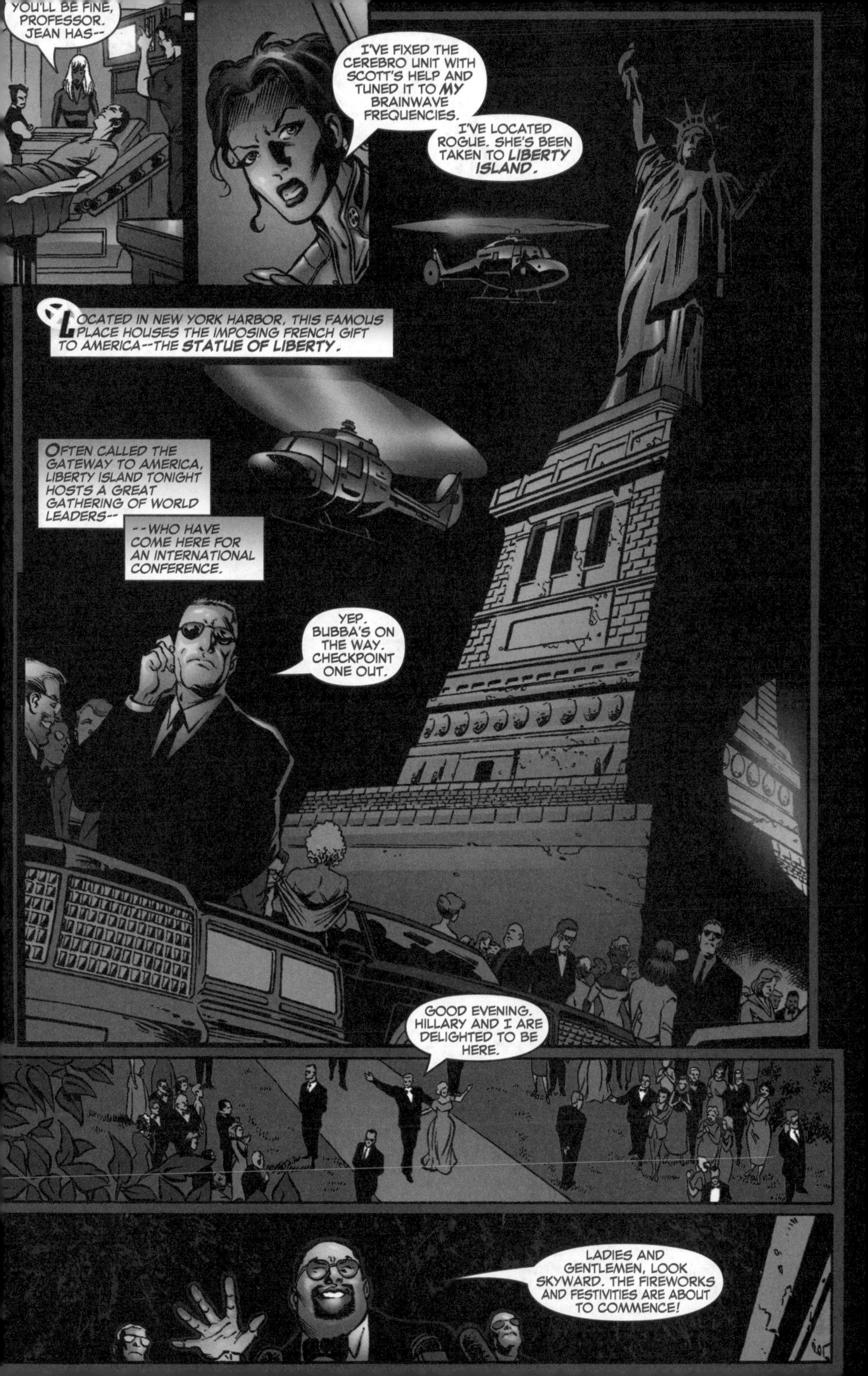

YOU'LL BE FINE, PROFESSOR. JEAN HAS--
I'VE FIXED THE CEREBRO UNIT WITH SCOTT'S HELP AND TUNED IT TO MY BRAINWAVE FREQUENCIES.
I'VE LOCATED ROGUE. SHE'S BEEN TAKEN TO LIBERTY ISLAND.
LOCATED IN NEW YORK HARBOR, THIS FAMOUS PLACE HOUSES THE IMPOSING FRENCH GIFT TO AMERICA--THE STATUE OF LIBERTY.
OFTEN CALLED THE GATEWAY TO AMERICA, LIBERTY ISLAND TONIGHT HOSTS A GREAT GATHERING OF WORLD LEADERS--
--WHO HAVE COME HERE FOR AN INTERNATIONAL CONFERENCE.
YEP. BUBBA'S ON THE WAY. CHECKPOINT ONE OUT.
GOOD EVENING. HILLARY AND I ARE DELIGHTED TO BE HERE.
LADIES AND GENTLEMEN, LOOK SKYWARD. THE FIREWORKS AND FESTIVITIES ARE ABOUT TO COMMENCE!

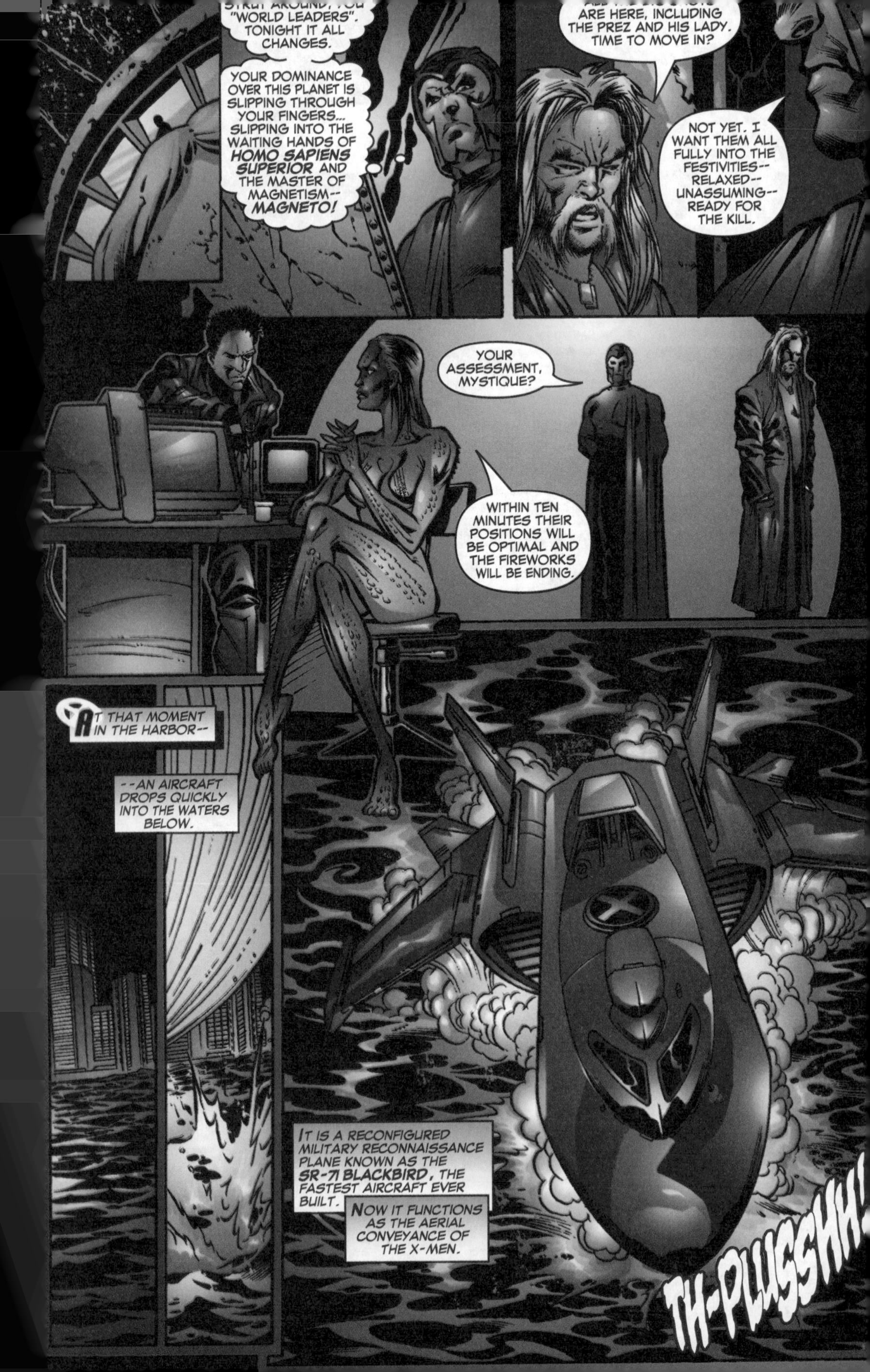
"WORLD LEADERS". TONIGHT IT ALL CHANGES.
YOUR DOMINANCE OVER THIS PLANET IS SLIPPING THROUGH YOUR FINGERS... SLIPPING INTO THE WAITING HANDS OF HOMO SAPIENS SUPERIOR AND THE MASTER OF MAGNETISM-- MAGNETO!
ARE HERE, INCLUDING THE PREZ AND HIS LADY. TIME TO MOVE IN?
NOT YET. I WANT THEM ALL FULLY INTO THE FESTIVITIES-- RELAXED-- UNASSUMING-- READY FOR THE KILL.
YOUR ASSESSMENT, MYSTIQUE?
WITHIN TEN MINUTES THEIR POSITIONS WILL BE OPTIMAL AND THE FIREWORKS WILL BE ENDING.
AT THAT MOMENT IN THE HARBOR--
--AN AIRCRAFT DROPS QUICKLY INTO THE WATERS BELOW.
IT IS A RECONFIGURED MILITARY RECONNAISSANCE PLANE KNOWN AS THE SR-71 BLACKBIRD, THE FASTEST AIRCRAFT EVER BUILT.
NOW IT FUNCTIONS AS THE AERIAL CONVEYANCE OF THE X-MEN.
TH-PLUSSHH!

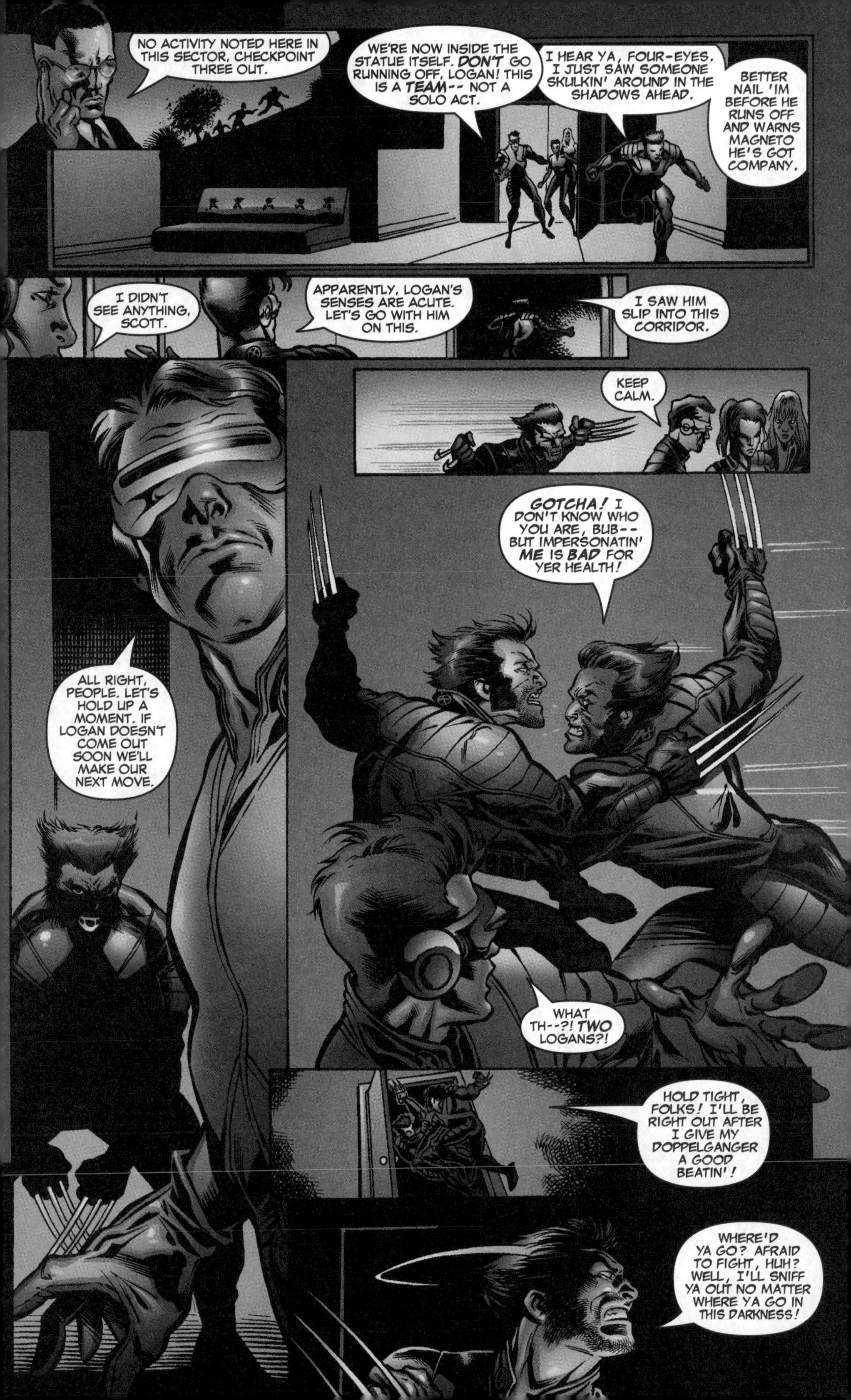

NO ACTIVITY NOTED HERE IN THIS SECTOR, CHECKPOINT THREE OUT.
WE'RE NOW INSIDE THE STATUE ITSELF. DON'T GO RUNNING OFF, LOGAN! THIS IS A TEAM-- NOT A SOLO ACT.
I HEAR YA, FOUR-EYES. I JUST SAW SOMEONE SKULKIN' AROUND IN THE SHADOWS AHEAD.
BETTER NAIL 'IM BEFORE HE RUNS OFF AND WARNS MAGNETO HE'S GOT COMPANY.
I DIDN'T SEE ANYTHING, SCOTT.
APPARENTLY, LOGAN'S SENSES ARE ACUTE. LET'S GO WITH HIM ON THIS.
I SAW HIM SLIP INTO THIS CORRIDOR.
KEEP CALM.
GOTCHA! I DON'T KNOW WHO YOU ARE, BUB-- BUT IMPERSONATIN' ME IS BAD FOR YER HEALTH!
WHAT TH--?! TWO LOGANS?!
ALL RIGHT, PEOPLE. LET'S HOLD UP A MOMENT. IF LOGAN DOESN'T COME OUT SOON WE'LL MAKE OUR NEXT MOVE.
HOLD TIGHT, FOLKS! I'LL BE RIGHT OUT AFTER I GIVE MY DOPPELGANGER A GOOD BEATIN'!
WHERE'D YA GO? AFRAID TO FIGHT, HUH? WELL, I'LL SNIFF YA OUT NO MATTER WHERE YA GO IN THIS DARKNESS!

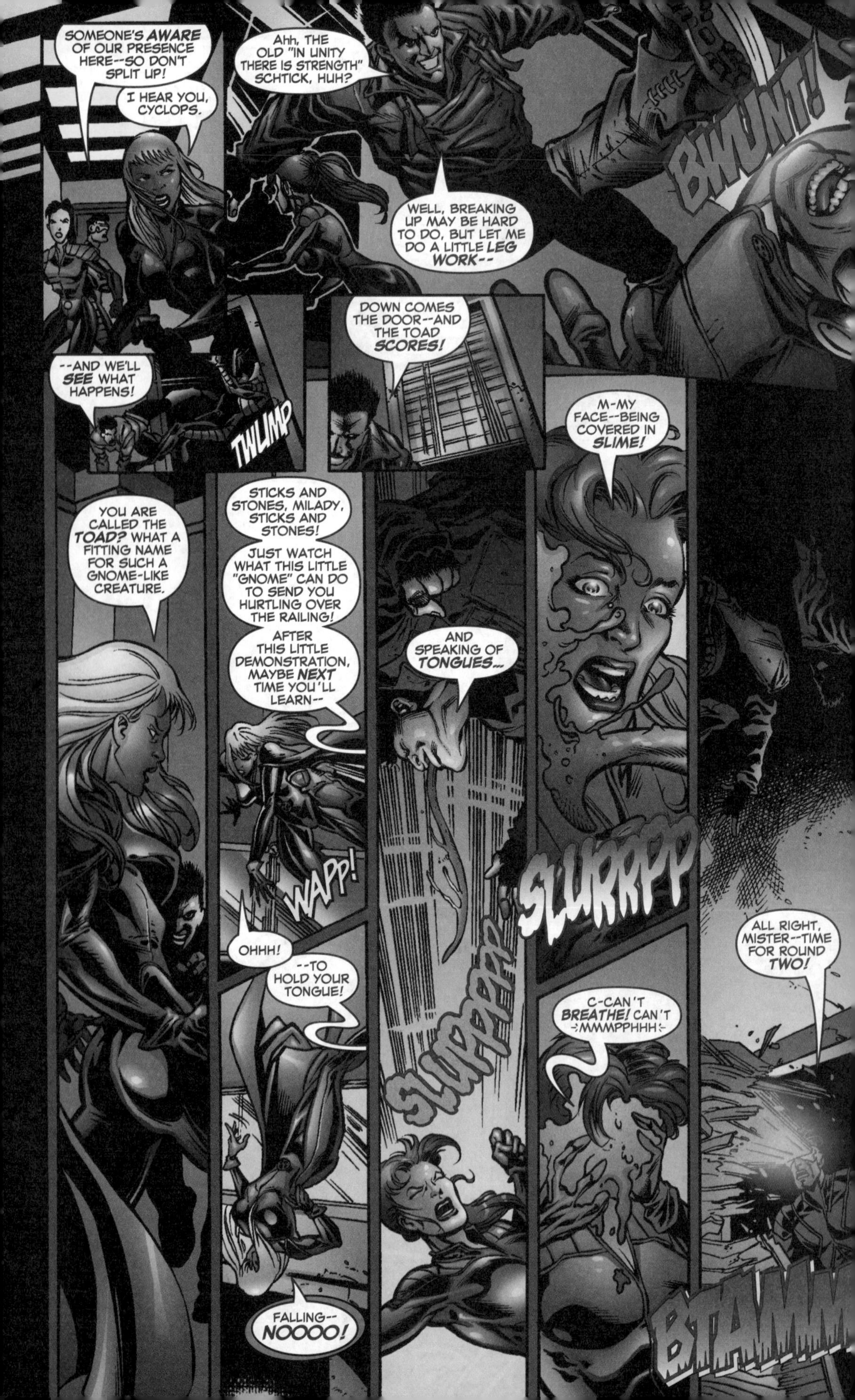
SOMEONE'S AWARE OF OUR PRESENCE HERE--SO DON'T SPLIT UP!
I HEAR YOU, CYCLOPS.
Ahh, THE OLD "IN UNITY THERE IS STRENGTH" SCHTICK, HUH?
WELL, BREAKING UP MAY BE HARD TO DO, BUT LET ME DO A LITTLE LEG WORK--
BWUNT!
--AND WE'LL SEE WHAT HAPPENS!
TWUMP
DOWN COMES THE DOOR--AND THE TOAD SCORES!
YOU ARE CALLED THE TOAD? WHAT A FITTING NAME FOR SUCH A GNOME-LIKE CREATURE.
STICKS AND STONES, MILADY, STICKS AND STONES!
JUST WATCH WHAT THIS LITTLE "GNOME" CAN DO TO SEND YOU HURTLING OVER THE RAILING!
AFTER THIS LITTLE DEMONSTRATION, MAYBE NEXT TIME YOU'LL LEARN--
WAPP!
OHHH!
--TO HOLD YOUR TONGUE!
FALLING-- NOOOO!
AND SPEAKING OF TONGUES...
SLURPPP
M-MY FACE--BEING COVERED IN SLIME!
SLURRPP
C-CAN'T BREATHE! CAN'T MMMPPHHH
ALL RIGHT, MISTER--TIME FOR ROUND TWO!
BTAMM

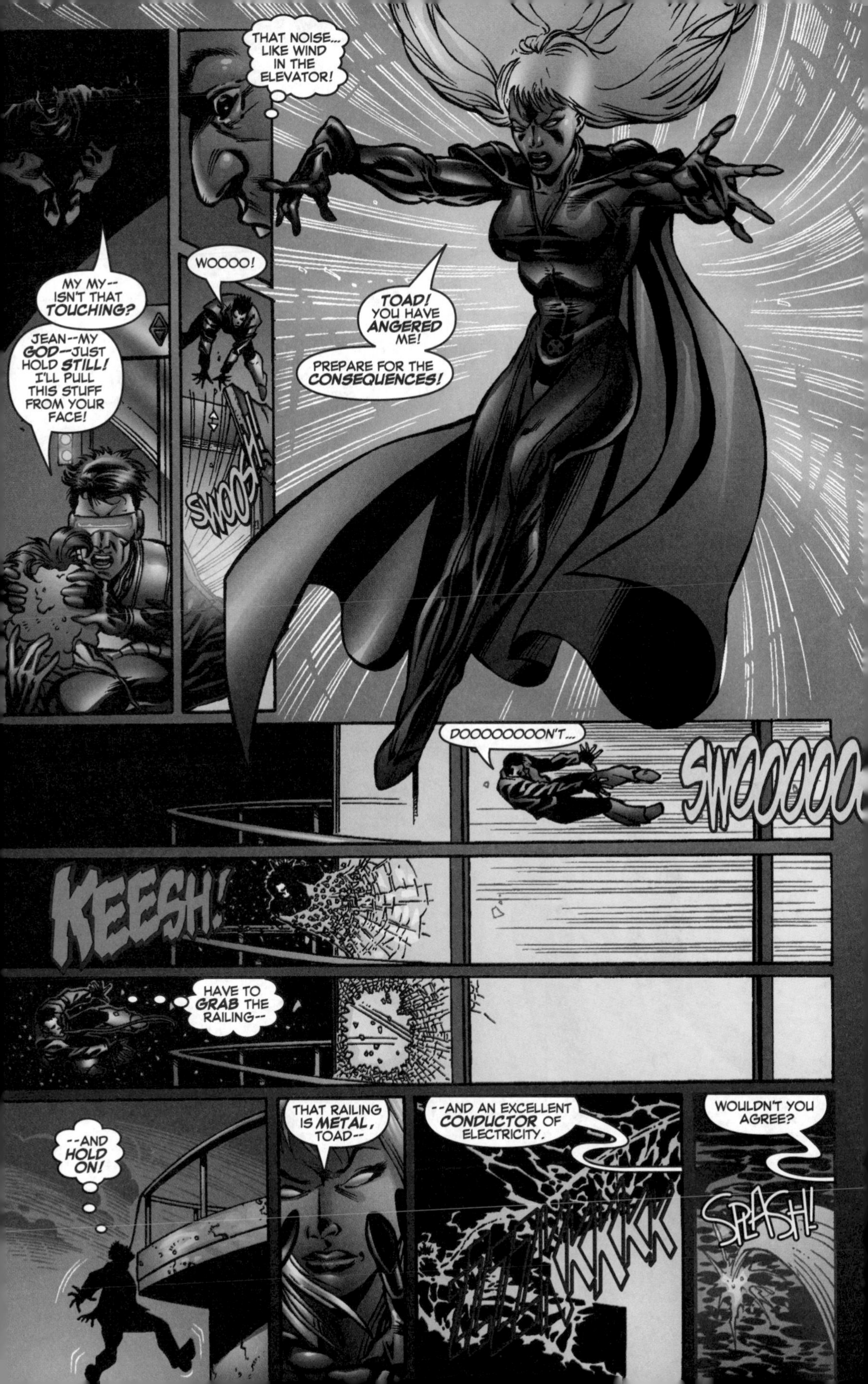
THAT NOISE... LIKE WIND IN THE ELEVATOR!
MY MY-- ISN'T THAT TOUCHING?
JEAN--MY GOD--JUST HOLD STILL! I'LL PULL THIS STUFF FROM YOUR FACE!
WOOOO!
SWOOSH!
TOAD! YOU HAVE ANGERED ME!
PREPARE FOR THE CONSEQUENCES!
DOOOOOOOON'T...
SWOOOOO
KEESH!
HAVE TO GRAB THE RAILING--
--AND HOLD ON!
THAT RAILING IS METAL, TOAD--
--AND AN EXCELLENT CONDUCTOR OF ELECTRICITY.
WOULDN'T YOU AGREE?
SPLASH!

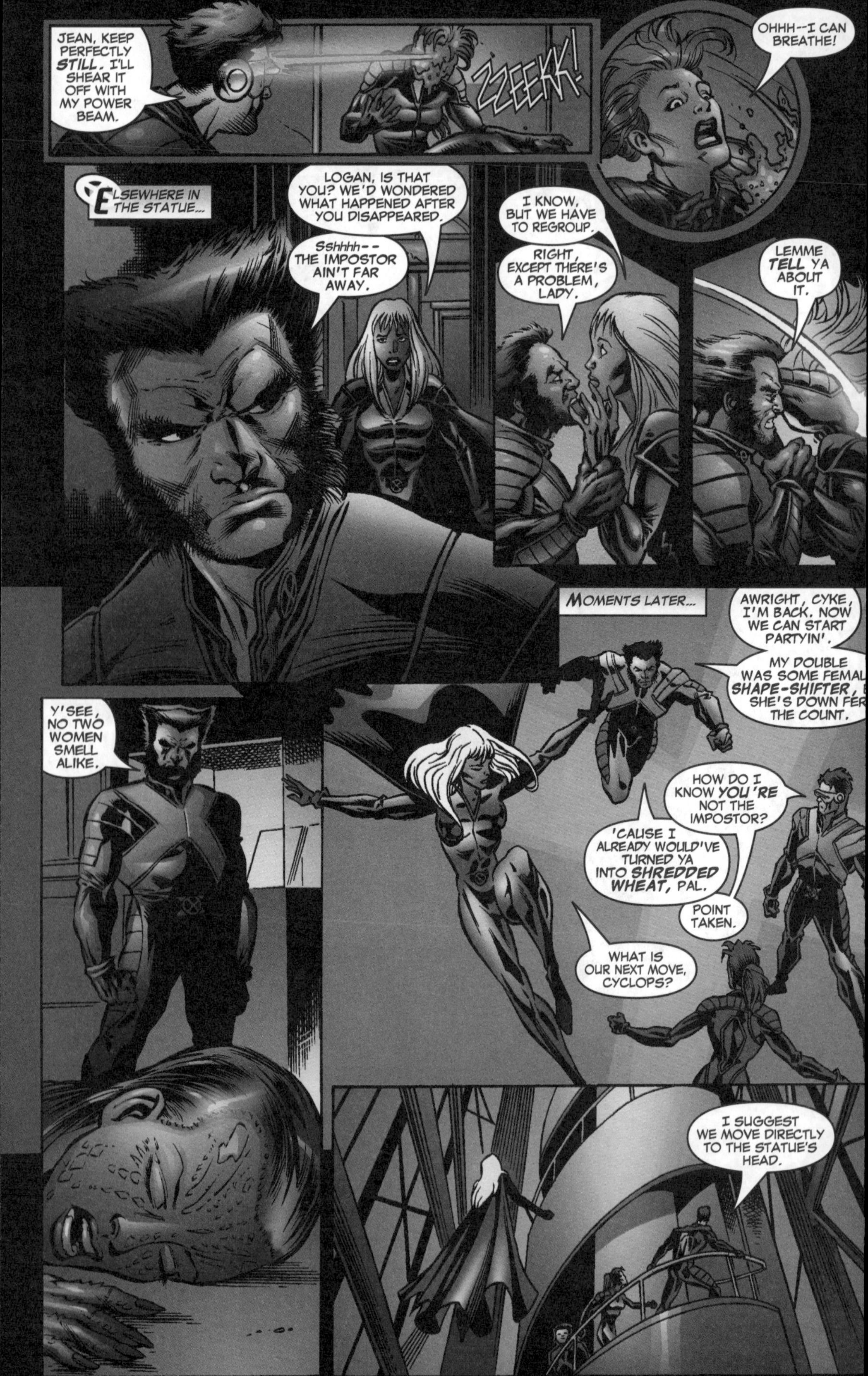

JEAN, KEEP PERFECTLY STILL. I'LL SHEAR IT OFF WITH MY POWER BEAM.
ZZEEKK!
OHHH--I CAN BREATHE!
ELSEWHERE IN THE STATUE...
LOGAN, IS THAT YOU? WE'D WONDERED WHAT HAPPENED AFTER YOU DISAPPEARED.
Sshhhh-- THE IMPOSTOR AIN'T FAR AWAY.
I KNOW, BUT WE HAVE TO REGROUP.
RIGHT, EXCEPT THERE'S A PROBLEM, LADY.
LEMME TELL YA ABOUT IT.
MOMENTS LATER...
AWRIGHT, CYKE, I'M BACK. NOW WE CAN START PARTYIN'.
Y'SEE, NO TWO WOMEN SMELL ALIKE.
HOW DO I KNOW YOU'RE NOT THE IMPOSTOR?
'CAUSE I ALREADY WOULD'VE TURNED YA INTO SHREDDED WHEAT, PAL.
POINT TAKEN.
WHAT IS OUR NEXT MOVE, CYCLOPS?
I SUGGEST WE MOVE DIRECTLY TO THE STATUE'S HEAD.

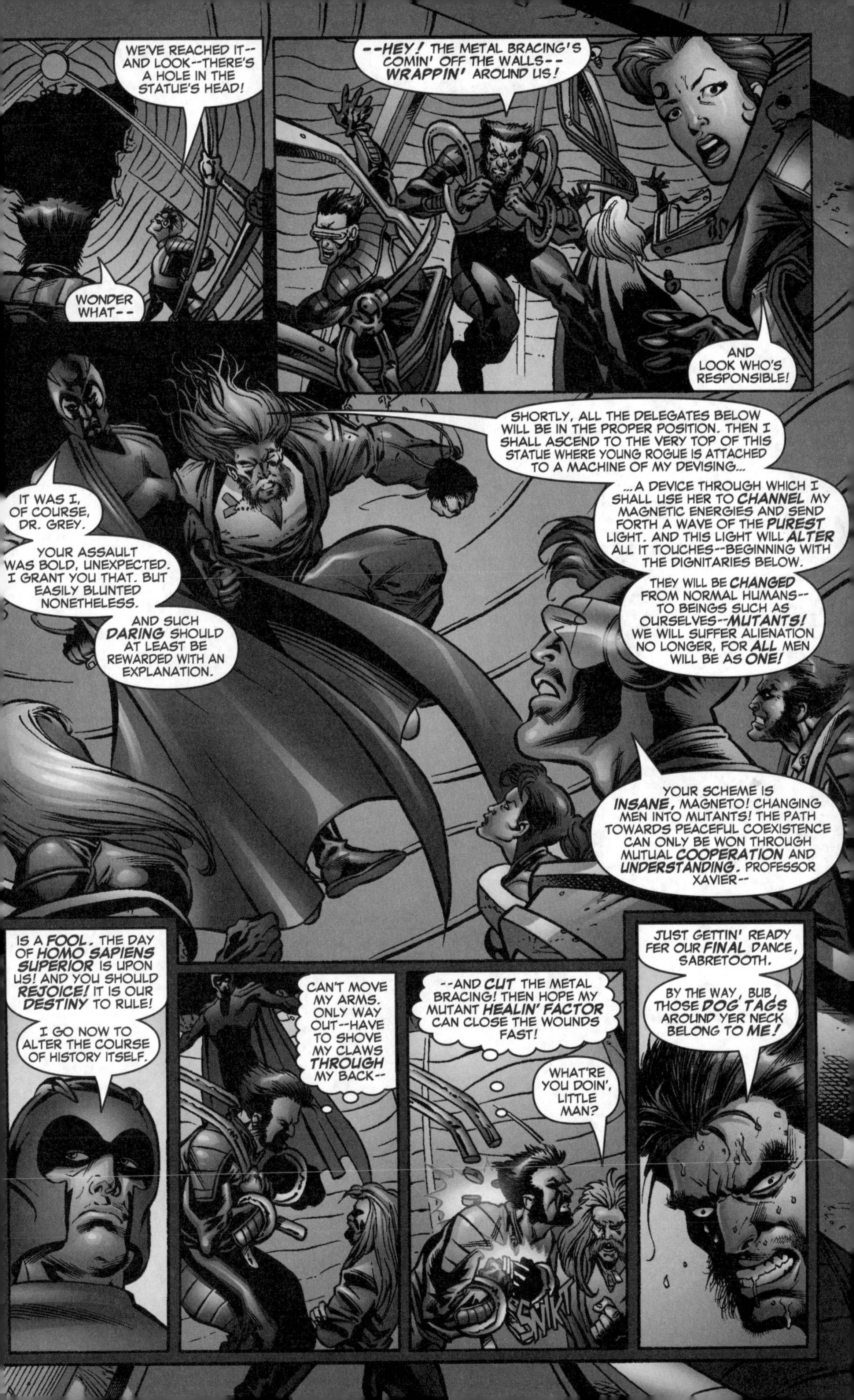
WE'VE REACHED IT--AND LOOK--THERE'S A HOLE IN THE STATUE'S HEAD!
WONDER WHAT--
--HEY! THE METAL BRACING'S COMIN' OFF THE WALLS--WRAPPIN' AROUND US!
AND LOOK WHO'S RESPONSIBLE!
IT WAS I, OF COURSE, DR. GREY.
YOUR ASSAULT WAS BOLD, UNEXPECTED. I GRANT YOU THAT. BUT EASILY BLUNTED NONETHELESS.
AND SUCH DARING SHOULD AT LEAST BE REWARDED WITH AN EXPLANATION.
SHORTLY, ALL THE DELEGATES BELOW WILL BE IN THE PROPER POSITION. THEN I SHALL ASCEND TO THE VERY TOP OF THIS STATUE WHERE YOUNG ROGUE IS ATTACHED TO A MACHINE OF MY DEVISING...
...A DEVICE THROUGH WHICH I SHALL USE HER TO CHANNEL MY MAGNETIC ENERGIES AND SEND FORTH A WAVE OF THE PUREST LIGHT. AND THIS LIGHT WILL ALTER ALL IT TOUCHES--BEGINNING WITH THE DIGNITARIES BELOW.
THEY WILL BE CHANGED FROM NORMAL HUMANS--TO BEINGS SUCH AS OURSELVES--MUTANTS! WE WILL SUFFER ALIENATION NO LONGER, FOR ALL MEN WILL BE AS ONE!
YOUR SCHEME IS INSANE, MAGNETO! CHANGING MEN INTO MUTANTS! THE PATH TOWARDS PEACEFUL COEXISTENCE CAN ONLY BE WON THROUGH MUTUAL COOPERATION AND UNDERSTANDING. PROFESSOR XAVIER--
IS A FOOL. THE DAY OF HOMO SAPIENS SUPERIOR IS UPON US! AND YOU SHOULD REJOICE! IT IS OUR DESTINY TO RULE!
I GO NOW TO ALTER THE COURSE OF HISTORY ITSELF.
CAN'T MOVE MY ARMS. ONLY WAY OUT--HAVE TO SHOVE MY CLAWS THROUGH MY BACK--
--AND CUT THE METAL BRACING! THEN HOPE MY MUTANT HEALIN' FACTOR CAN CLOSE THE WOUNDS FAST!
WHAT'RE YOU DOIN', LITTLE MAN?
SNIKT
JUST GETTIN' READY FER OUR FINAL DANCE, SABRETOOTH.
BY THE WAY, BUB, THOSE DOG TAGS AROUND YER NECK BELONG TO ME!

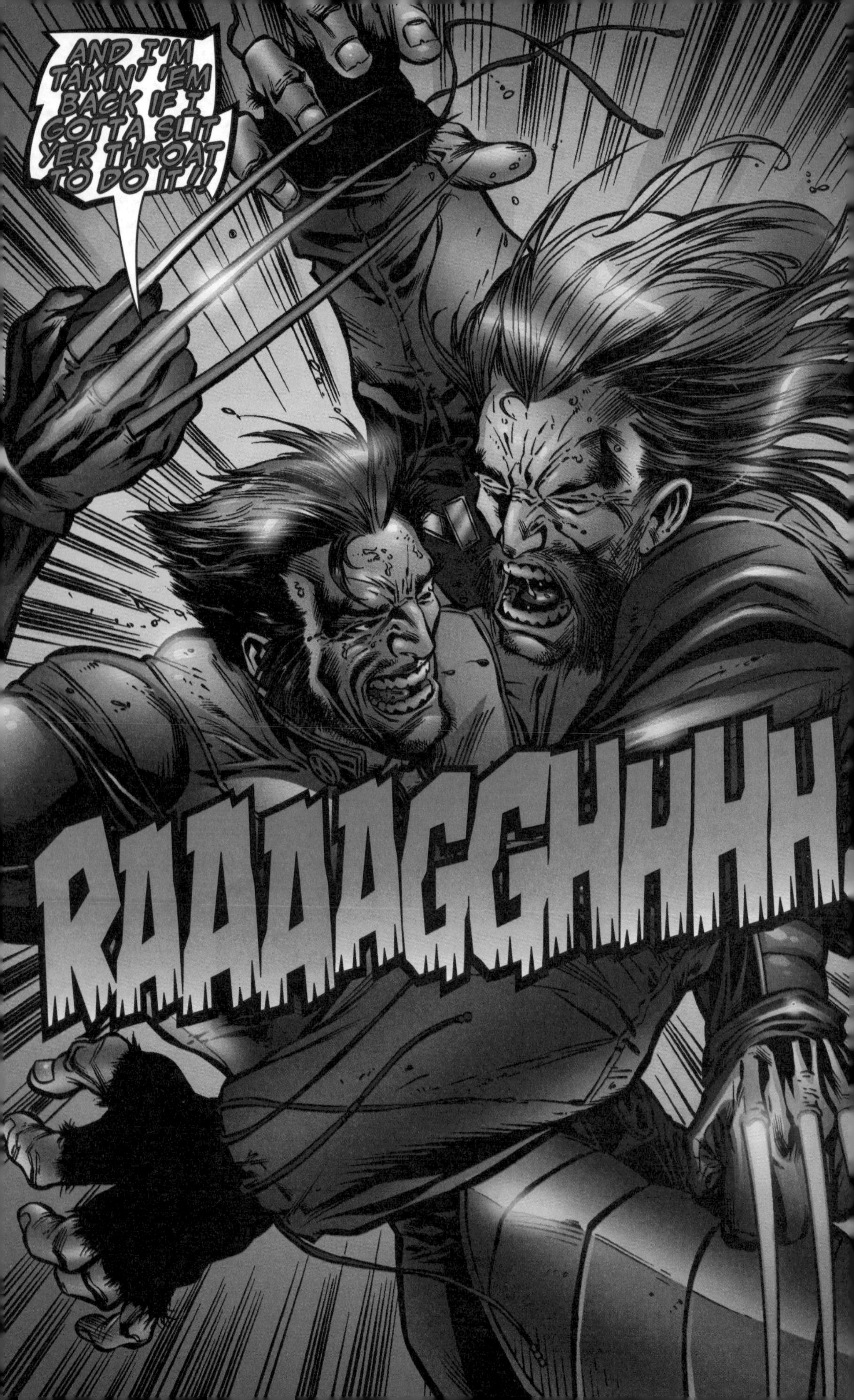
AND I'M TAKIN' 'EM BACK IF I GOTTA SLIT YER THROAT TO DO IT!!
RAAAGHHHH

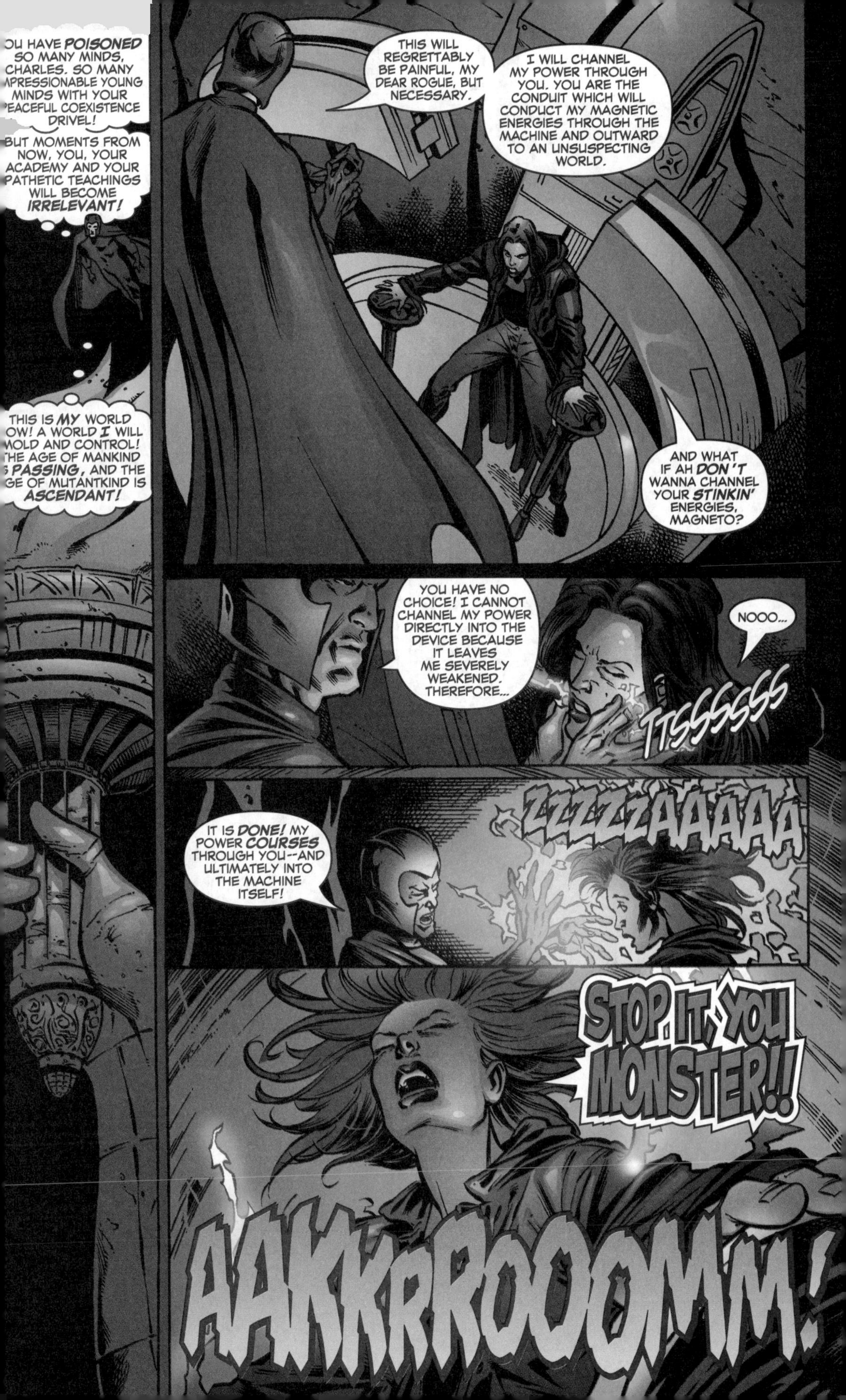

OU HAVE POISONED SO MANY MINDS, CHARLES. SO MANY IMPRESSIONABLE YOUNG MINDS WITH YOUR PEACEFUL COEXISTENCE DRIVEL!
BUT MOMENTS FROM NOW, YOU, YOUR ACADEMY AND YOUR PATHETIC TEACHINGS WILL BECOME IRRELEVANT!
THIS IS MY WORLD OW! A WORLD I WILL MOLD AND CONTROL! THE AGE OF MANKIND S PASSING, AND THE GE OF MUTANTKIND IS ASCENDANT!
THIS WILL REGRETTABLY BE PAINFUL, MY DEAR ROGUE, BUT NECESSARY.
I WILL CHANNEL MY POWER THROUGH YOU. YOU ARE THE CONDUIT WHICH WILL CONDUCT MY MAGNETIC ENERGIES THROUGH THE MACHINE AND OUTWARD TO AN UNSUSPECTING WORLD.
AND WHAT IF AH DON'T WANNA CHANNEL YOUR STINKIN' ENERGIES, MAGNETO?
YOU HAVE NO CHOICE! I CANNOT CHANNEL MY POWER DIRECTLY INTO THE DEVICE BECAUSE IT LEAVES ME SEVERELY WEAKENED. THEREFORE...
NOOO...
TTSSSSSS
ZZZZZAAAAAA
IT IS DONE! MY POWER COURSES THROUGH YOU--AND ULTIMATELY INTO THE MACHINE ITSELF!
STOP IT, YOU MONSTER!!
AAKKRROOOMM!

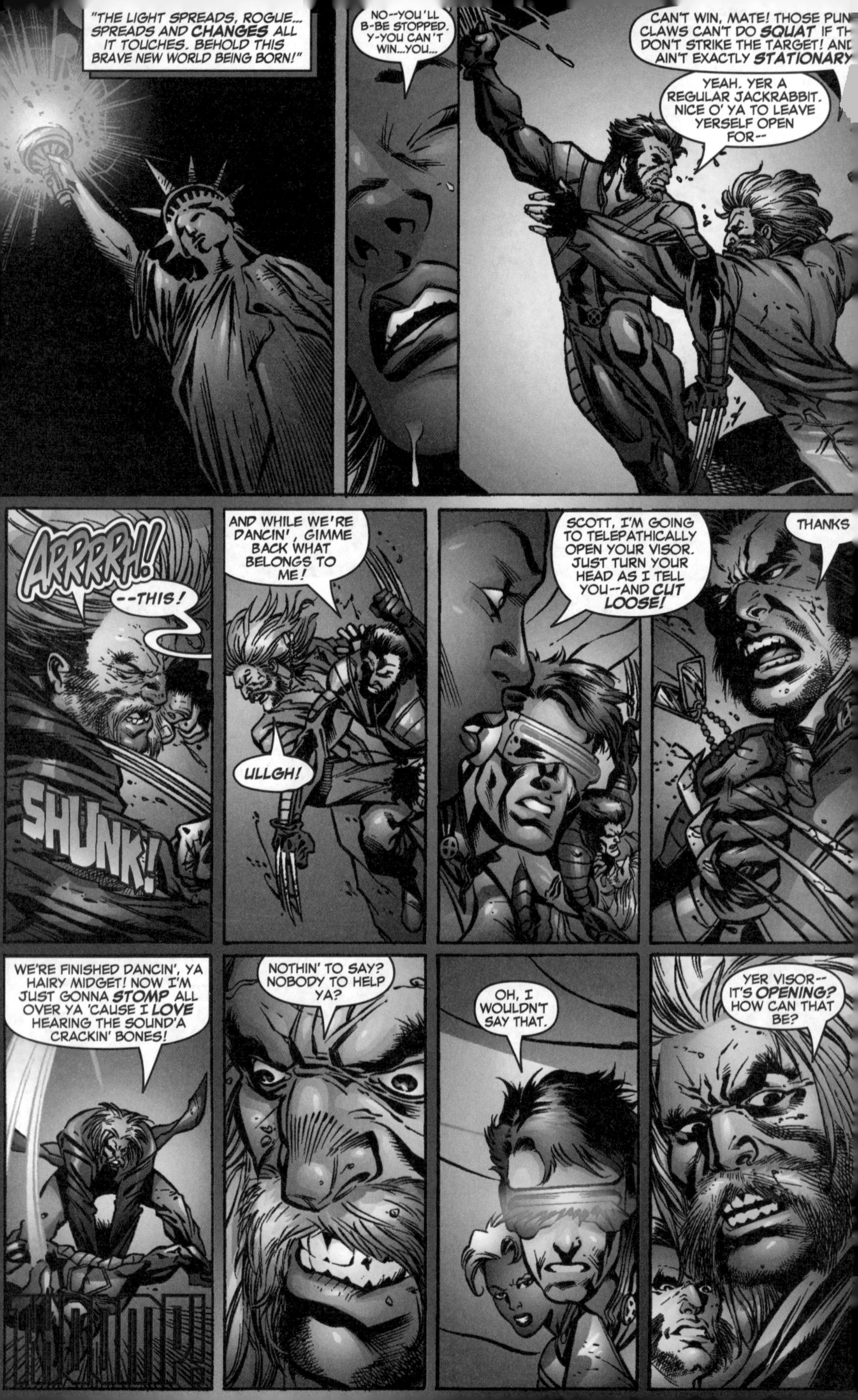
"THE LIGHT SPREADS, ROGUE... SPREADS AND CHANGES ALL IT TOUCHES. BEHOLD THIS BRAVE NEW WORLD BEING BORN!"
NO--YOU'LL B-BE STOPPED. Y-YOU CAN'T WIN...YOU...
YEAH. YER A REGULAR JACKRABBIT. NICE O' YA TO LEAVE YERSELF OPEN FOR--
ARRRRH!
--THIS!
SHUNK!
AND WHILE WE'RE DANCIN', GIMME BACK WHAT BELONGS TO ME!
ULLGH!
SCOTT, I'M GOING TO TELEPATHICALLY OPEN YOUR VISOR. JUST TURN YOUR HEAD AS I TELL YOU--AND CUT LOOSE!
WE'RE FINISHED DANCIN', YA HAIRY MIDGET! NOW I'M JUST GONNA STOMP ALL OVER YA 'CAUSE I LOVE HEARING THE SOUND'A CRACKIN' BONES!
NOTHIN' TO SAY? NOBODY TO HELP YA?
OH, I WOULDN'T SAY THAT.
YER VISOR--IT'S OPENING? HOW CAN THAT BE?

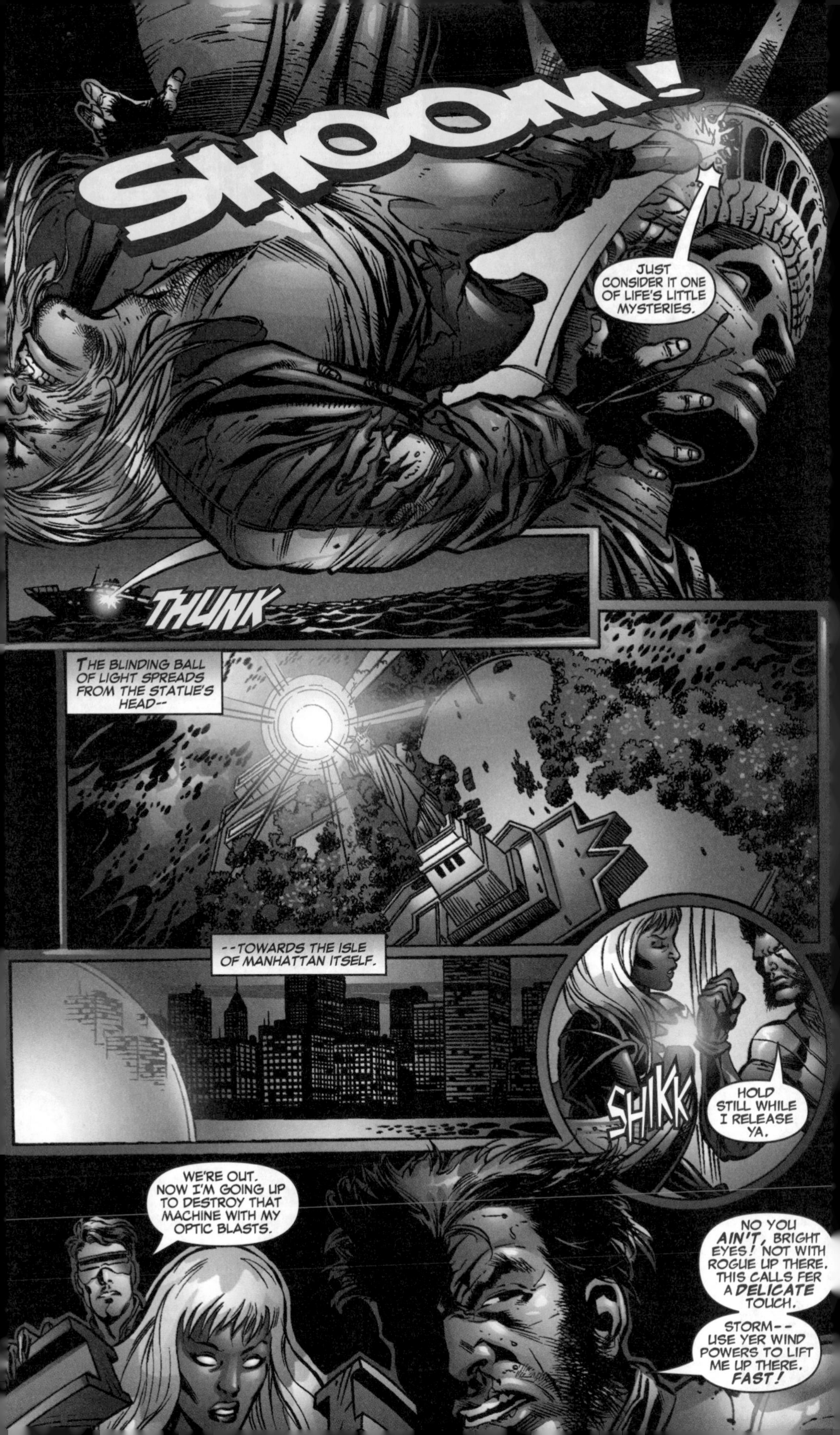
SHOOM!
JUST CONSIDER IT ONE OF LIFE'S LITTLE MYSTERIES.
THUNK
THE BLINDING BALL OF LIGHT SPREADS FROM THE STATUE'S HEAD--
--TOWARDS THE ISLE OF MANHATTAN ITSELF.
SHIKK
HOLD STILL WHILE I RELEASE YA.
WE'RE OUT. NOW I'M GOING UP TO DESTROY THAT MACHINE WITH MY OPTIC BLASTS.
NO YOU AIN'T, BRIGHT EYES! NOT WITH ROGUE UP THERE. THIS CALLS FER A DELICATE TOUCH.
STORM-- USE YER WIND POWERS TO LIFT ME UP THERE. FAST!

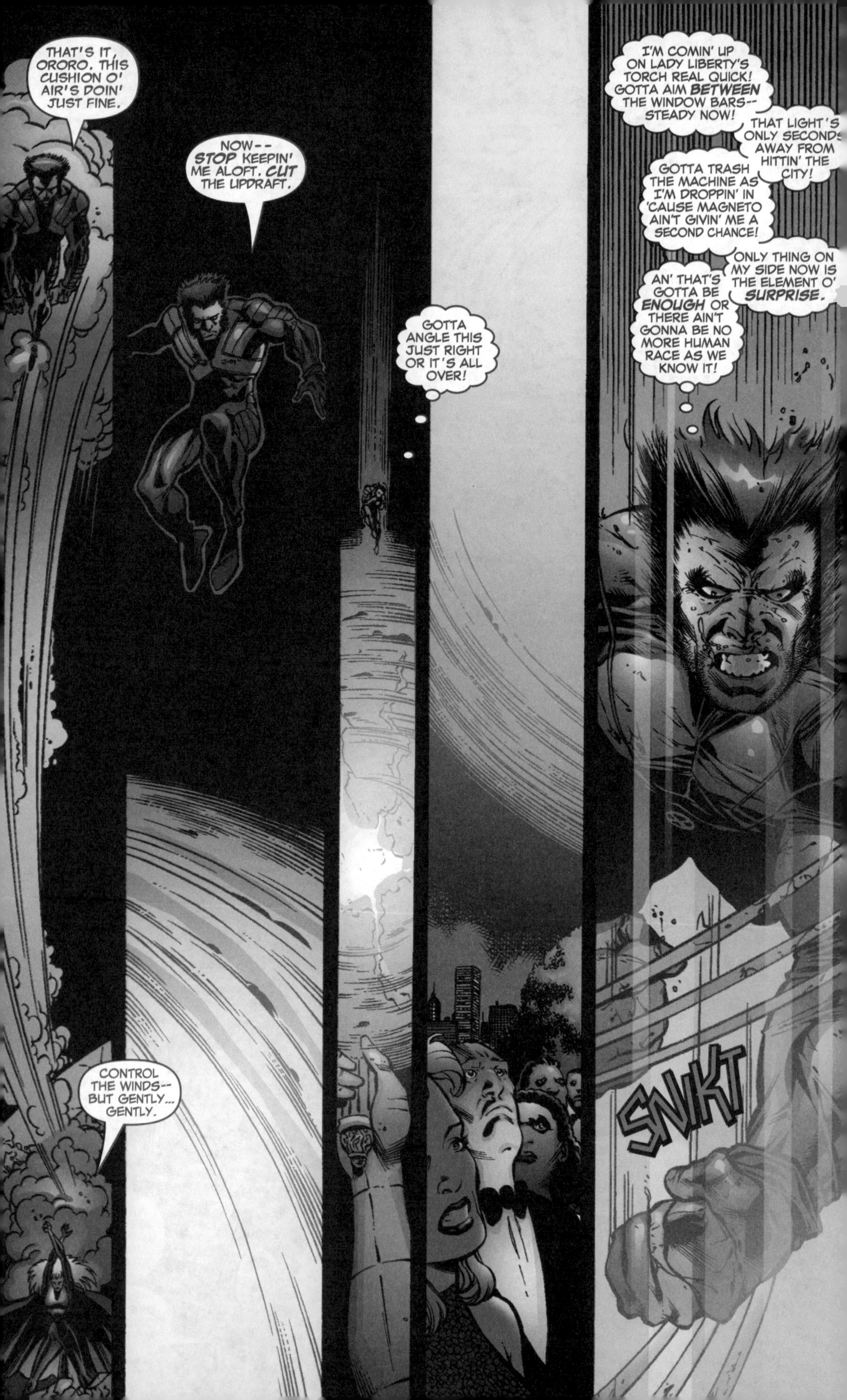
THAT'S IT, ORORO. THIS CUSHION O' AIR'S DOIN' JUST FINE.
CONTROL THE WINDS-- BUT GENTLY... GENTLY.
NOW-- STOP KEEPIN' ME ALOFT. CUT THE UPDRAFT.
GOTTA ANGLE THIS JUST RIGHT OR IT'S ALL OVER!
I'M COMIN' UP ON LADY LIBERTY'S TORCH REAL QUICK! GOTTA AIM BETWEEN THE WINDOW BARS-- STEADY NOW!
THAT LIGHT'S ONLY SECONDS AWAY FROM HITTIN' THE CITY!
GOTTA TRASH THE MACHINE AS I'M DROPPIN' IN 'CAUSE MAGNETO AIN'T GIVIN' ME A SECOND CHANCE!
ONLY THING ON MY SIDE NOW IS THE ELEMENT O' SURPRISE.
AN' THAT'S GOTTA BE ENOUGH OR THERE AIN'T GONNA BE NO MORE HUMAN RACE AS WE KNOW IT!
SNKT

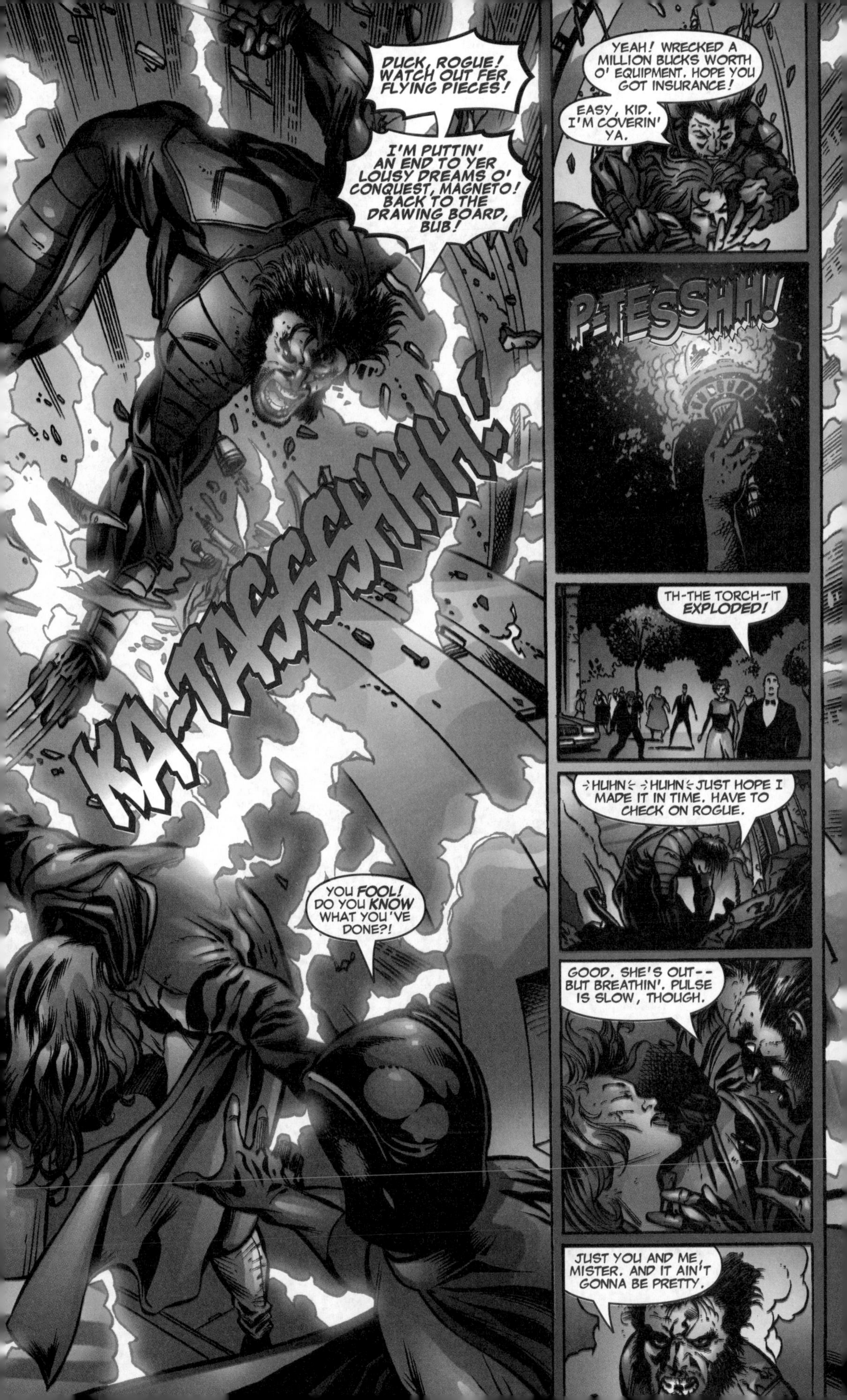
DUCK, ROGUE! WATCH OUT FER FLYING PIECES!
I'M PUTTIN' AN END TO YER LOUSY DREAMS O' CONQUEST, MAGNETO! BACK TO THE DRAWING BOARD, BUB!
KA-TASSSHH!
YOU FOOL! DO YOU KNOW WHAT YOU'VE DONE?!
YEAH! WRECKED A MILLION BUCKS WORTH O' EQUIPMENT. HOPE YOU GOT INSURANCE!
EASY, KID. I'M COVERIN' YA.
P-TESSHH!!
TH-THE TORCH--IT EXPLODED!
HUHN HUHN JUST HOPE I MADE IT IN TIME. HAVE TO CHECK ON ROGUE.
GOOD. SHE'S OUT--BUT BREATHIN'. PULSE IS SLOW, THOUGH.
JUST YOU AND ME, MISTER. AND IT AIN'T GONNA BE PRETTY.

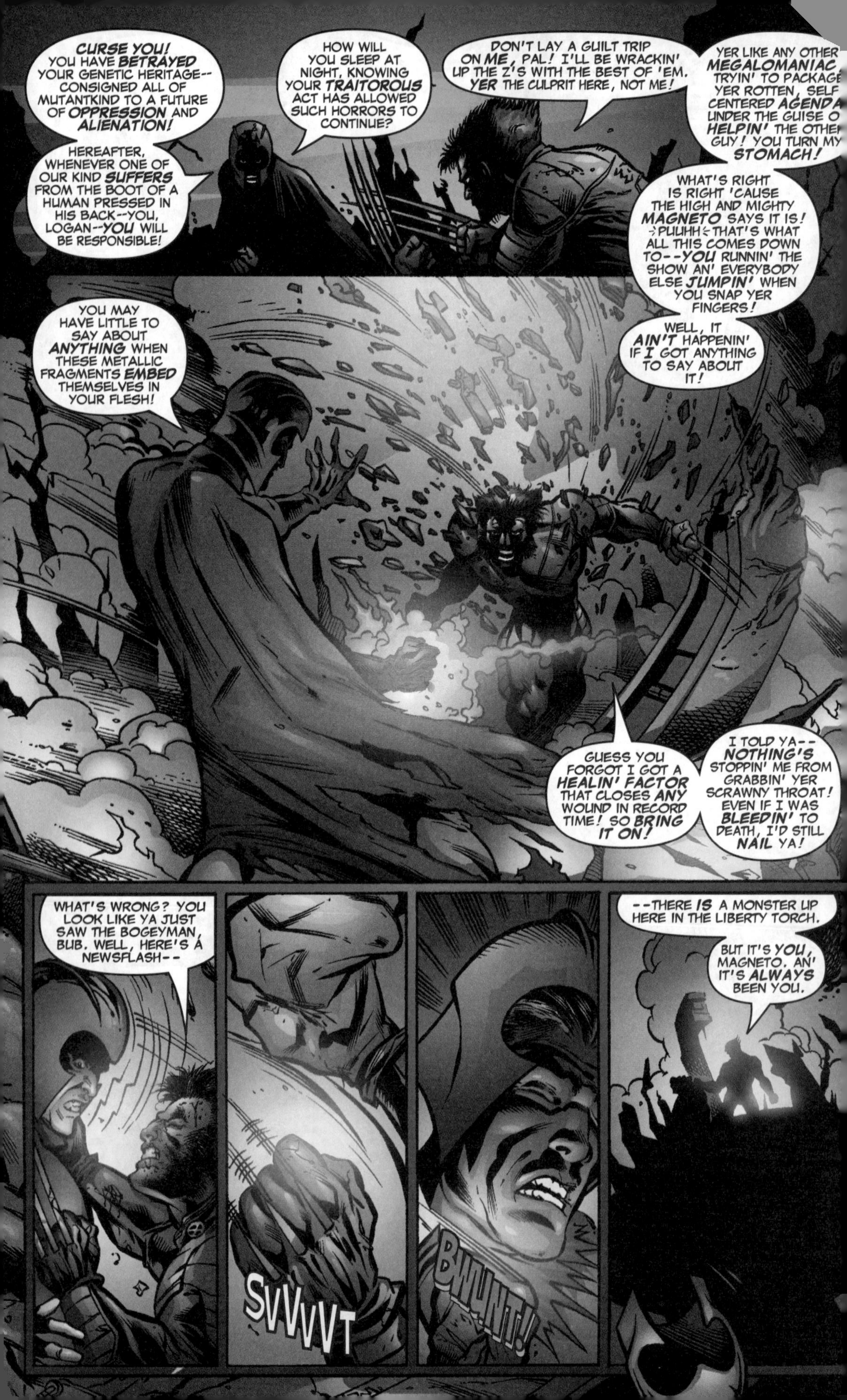

CURSE YOU! YOU HAVE BETRAYED YOUR GENETIC HERITAGE--CONSIGNED ALL OF MUTANTKIND TO A FUTURE OF OPPRESSION AND ALIENATION!
HEREAFTER, WHENEVER ONE OF OUR KIND SUFFERS FROM THE BOOT OF A HUMAN PRESSED IN HIS BACK--YOU, LOGAN--YOU WILL BE RESPONSIBLE!
HOW WILL YOU SLEEP AT NIGHT, KNOWING YOUR TRAITOROUS ACT HAS ALLOWED SUCH HORRORS TO CONTINUE?
DON'T LAY A GUILT TRIP ON ME, PAL! I'LL BE WRACKIN' UP THE Z'S WITH THE BEST OF 'EM. YER THE CULPRIT HERE, NOT ME!
YER LIKE ANY OTHER MEGALOMANIAC, TRYIN' TO PACKAGE YER ROTTEN, SELF CENTERED AGENDA UNDER THE GUISE O HELPIN' THE OTHER GUY! YOU TURN MY STOMACH!
WHAT'S RIGHT IS RIGHT 'CAUSE THE HIGH AND MIGHTY MAGNETO SAYS IT IS! PUUHH THAT'S WHAT ALL THIS COMES DOWN TO--YOU RUNNIN' THE SHOW AN' EVERYBODY ELSE JUMPIN' WHEN YOU SNAP YER FINGERS!
YOU MAY HAVE LITTLE TO SAY ABOUT ANYTHING WHEN THESE METALLIC FRAGMENTS EMBED THEMSELVES IN YOUR FLESH!
WELL, IT AIN'T HAPPENIN' IF I GOT ANYTHING TO SAY ABOUT IT!
GUESS YOU FORGOT I GOT A HEALIN' FACTOR THAT CLOSES ANY WOUND IN RECORD TIME! SO BRING IT ON!
I TOLD YA--NOTHING'S STOPPIN' ME FROM GRABBIN' YER SCRAWNY THROAT! EVEN IF I WAS BLEEDIN' TO DEATH, I'D STILL NAIL YA!
WHAT'S WRONG? YOU LOOK LIKE YA JUST SAW THE BOGEYMAN, BUB. WELL, HERE'S A NEWSFLASH--
SVVVVT
BWUNT!!
--THERE IS A MONSTER UP HERE IN THE LIBERTY TORCH.
BUT IT'S YOU, MAGNETO. AN' IT'S ALWAYS BEEN YOU.

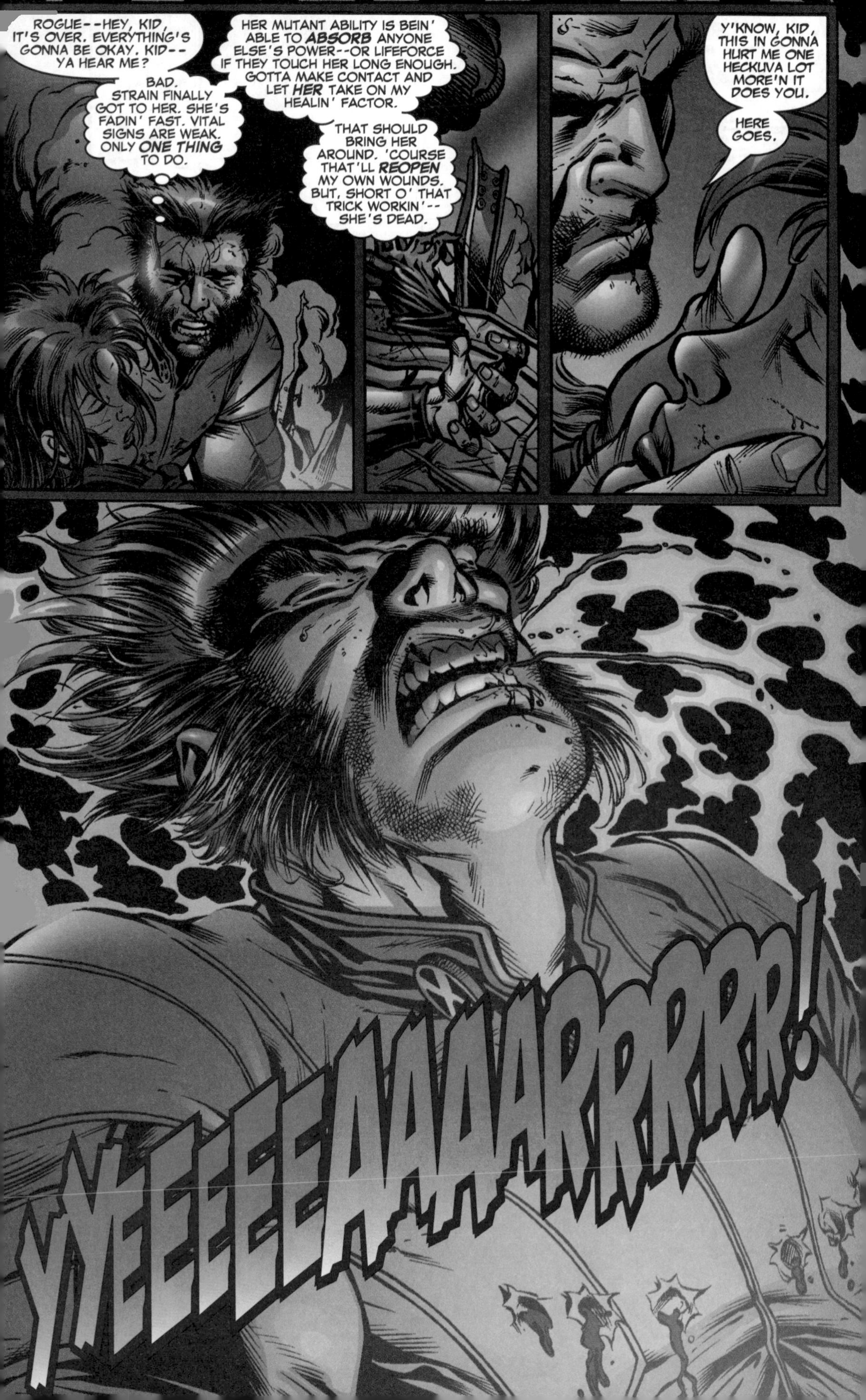
ROGUE--HEY, KID, IT'S OVER. EVERYTHING'S GONNA BE OKAY. KID--YA HEAR ME?
BAD. STRAIN FINALLY GOT TO HER. SHE'S FADIN' FAST. VITAL SIGNS ARE WEAK. ONLY ONE THING TO DO.
HER MUTANT ABILITY IS BEIN' ABLE TO ABSORB ANYONE ELSE'S POWER--OR LIFEFORCE IF THEY TOUCH HER LONG ENOUGH. GOTTA MAKE CONTACT AND LET HER TAKE ON MY HEALIN' FACTOR.
THAT SHOULD BRING HER AROUND. 'COURSE THAT'LL REOPEN MY OWN WOUNDS. BUT, SHORT O' THAT TRICK WORKIN'--SHE'S DEAD.
Y'KNOW, KID, THIS IN GONNA HURT ME ONE HECKUVA LOT MORE'N IT DOES YOU.
HERE GOES.
YYEEEEEAAAARRRRR!

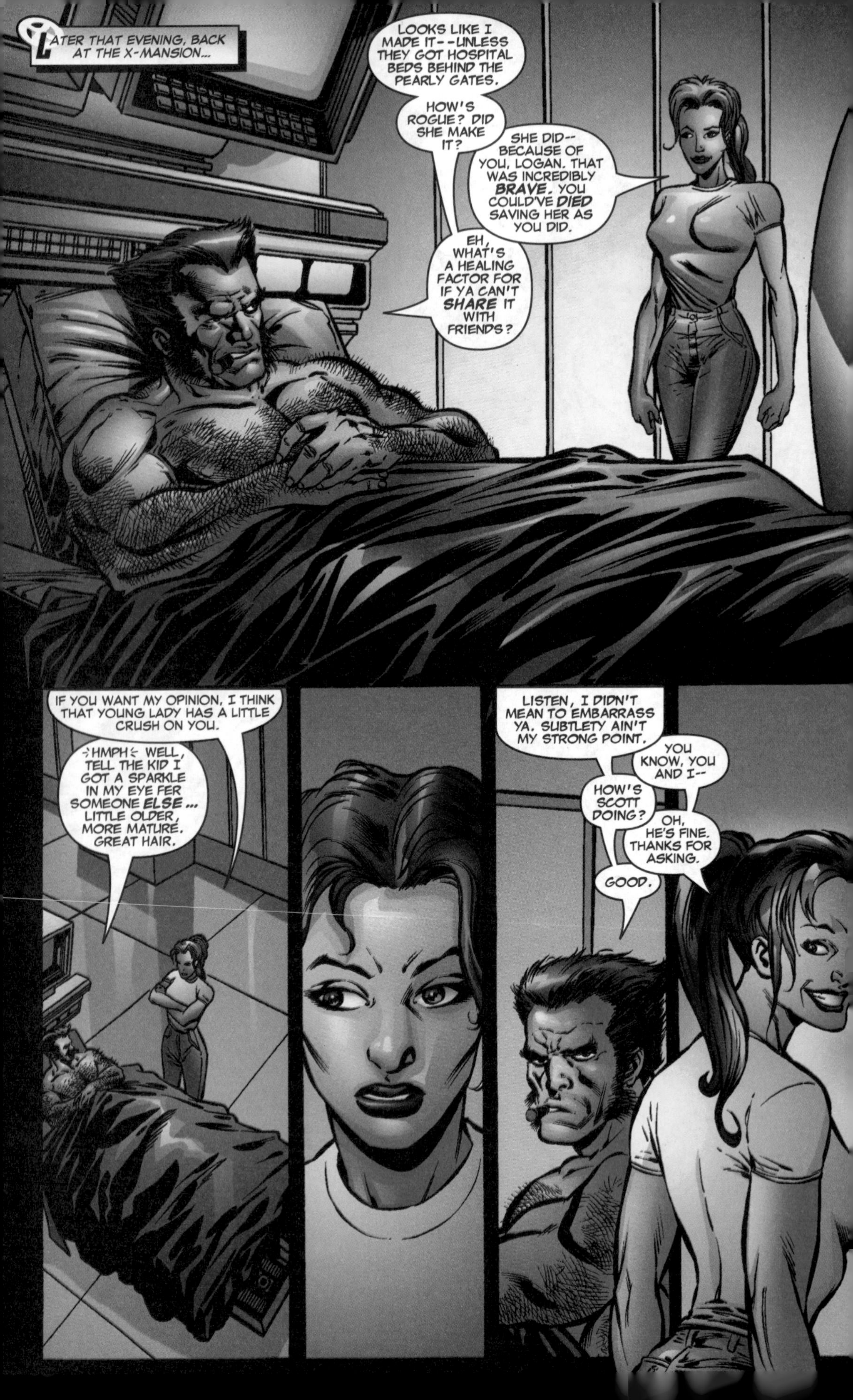
LATER THAT EVENING, BACK AT THE X-MANSION...
LOOKS LIKE I MADE IT--UNLESS THEY GOT HOSPITAL BEDS BEHIND THE PEARLY GATES.
HOW'S ROGUE? DID SHE MAKE IT?
SHE DID-- BECAUSE OF YOU, LOGAN. THAT WAS INCREDIBLY BRAVE. YOU COULD'VE DIED SAVING HER AS YOU DID.
EH, WHAT'S A HEALING FACTOR FOR IF YA CAN'T SHARE IT WITH FRIENDS?
IF YOU WANT MY OPINION, I THINK THAT YOUNG LADY HAS A LITTLE CRUSH ON YOU.
HMPH WELL, TELL THE KID I GOT A SPARKLE IN MY EYE FER SOMEONE ELSE... LITTLE OLDER, MORE MATURE. GREAT HAIR.
LISTEN, I DIDN'T MEAN TO EMBARRASS YA. SUBTLETY AIN'T MY STRONG POINT.
YOU KNOW, YOU AND I--
HOW'S SCOTT DOING?
OH, HE'S FINE. THANKS FOR ASKING.
GOOD.

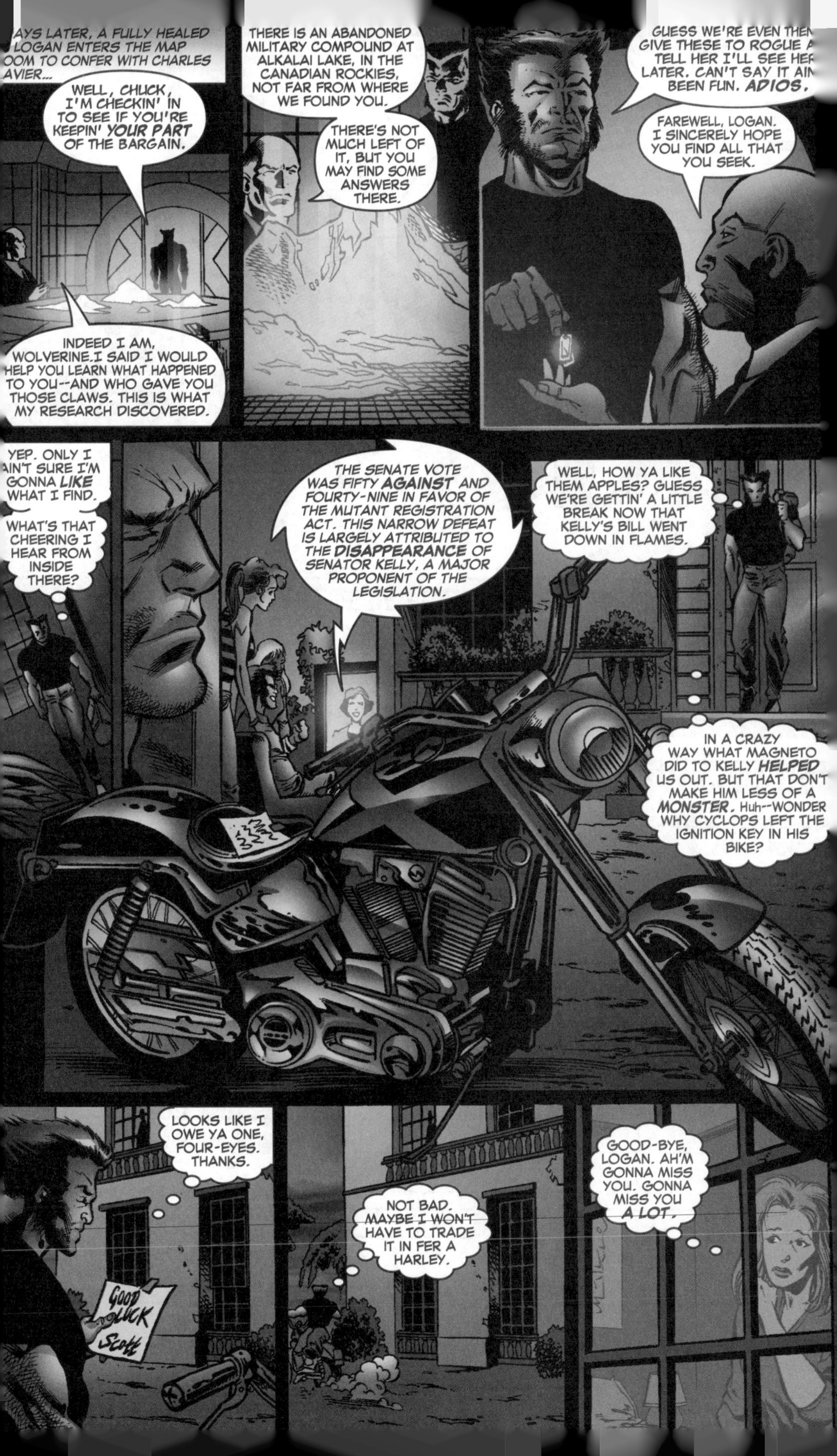
AYS LATER, A FULLY HEALED LOGAN ENTERS THE MAP OOM TO CONFER WITH CHARLES AVIER...
WELL, CHUCK, I'M CHECKIN' IN TO SEE IF YOU'RE KEEPIN' YOUR PART OF THE BARGAIN.
INDEED I AM, WOLVERINE. I SAID I WOULD HELP YOU LEARN WHAT HAPPENED TO YOU--AND WHO GAVE YOU THOSE CLAWS. THIS IS WHAT MY RESEARCH DISCOVERED.
THERE IS AN ABANDONED MILITARY COMPOUND AT ALKALAI LAKE, IN THE CANADIAN ROCKIES, NOT FAR FROM WHERE WE FOUND YOU.
THERE'S NOT MUCH LEFT OF IT, BUT YOU MAY FIND SOME ANSWERS THERE.
GUESS WE'RE EVEN THEN GIVE THESE TO ROGUE A TELL HER I'LL SEE HER LATER. CAN'T SAY IT AIN BEEN FUN. ADIOS.
FAREWELL, LOGAN. I SINCERELY HOPE YOU FIND ALL THAT YOU SEEK.
YEP. ONLY I AIN'T SURE I'M GONNA LIKE WHAT I FIND.
WHAT'S THAT CHEERING I HEAR FROM INSIDE THERE?
THE SENATE VOTE WAS FIFTY AGAINST AND FOURTY-NINE IN FAVOR OF THE MUTANT REGISTRATION ACT. THIS NARROW DEFEAT IS LARGELY ATTRIBUTED TO THE DISAPPEARANCE OF SENATOR KELLY, A MAJOR PROPONENT OF THE LEGISLATION.
WELL, HOW YA LIKE THEM APPLES? GUESS WE'RE GETTIN' A LITTLE BREAK NOW THAT KELLY'S BILL WENT DOWN IN FLAMES.
IN A CRAZY WAY WHAT MAGNETO DID TO KELLY HELPED US OUT. BUT THAT DON'T MAKE HIM LESS OF A MONSTER. Huh--WONDER WHY CYCLOPS LEFT THE IGNITION KEY IN HIS BIKE?
LOOKS LIKE I OWE YA ONE, FOUR-EYES. THANKS.
GOOD LUCK Scott
NOT BAD. MAYBE I WON'T HAVE TO TRADE IT IN FER A HARLEY.
GOOD-BYE, LOGAN. AH'M GONNA MISS YOU. GONNA MISS YOU A LOT.

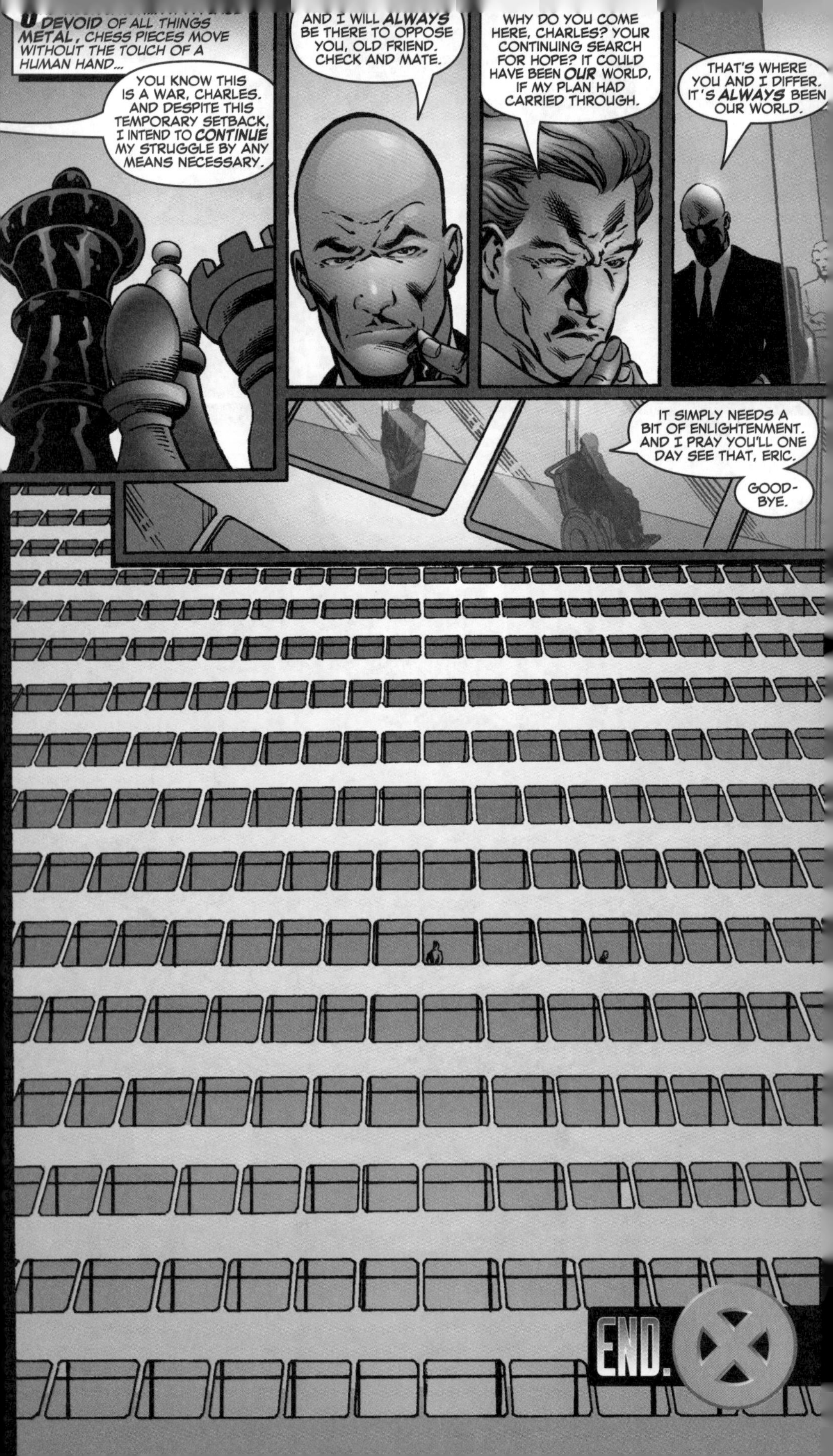
DEVOID OF ALL THINGS METAL, CHESS PIECES MOVE WITHOUT THE TOUCH OF A HUMAN HAND...
YOU KNOW THIS IS A WAR, CHARLES. AND DESPITE THIS TEMPORARY SETBACK, I INTEND TO CONTINUE MY STRUGGLE BY ANY MEANS NECESSARY.
AND I WILL ALWAYS BE THERE TO OPPOSE YOU, OLD FRIEND. CHECK AND MATE.
WHY DO YOU COME HERE, CHARLES? YOUR CONTINUING SEARCH FOR HOPE? IT COULD HAVE BEEN OUR WORLD, IF MY PLAN HAD CARRIED THROUGH.
THAT'S WHERE YOU AND I DIFFER. IT'S ALWAYS BEEN OUR WORLD.
IT SIMPLY NEEDS A BIT OF ENLIGHTENMENT. AND I PRAY YOU'LL ONE DAY SEE THAT, ERIC.
GOOD-BYE.
END.

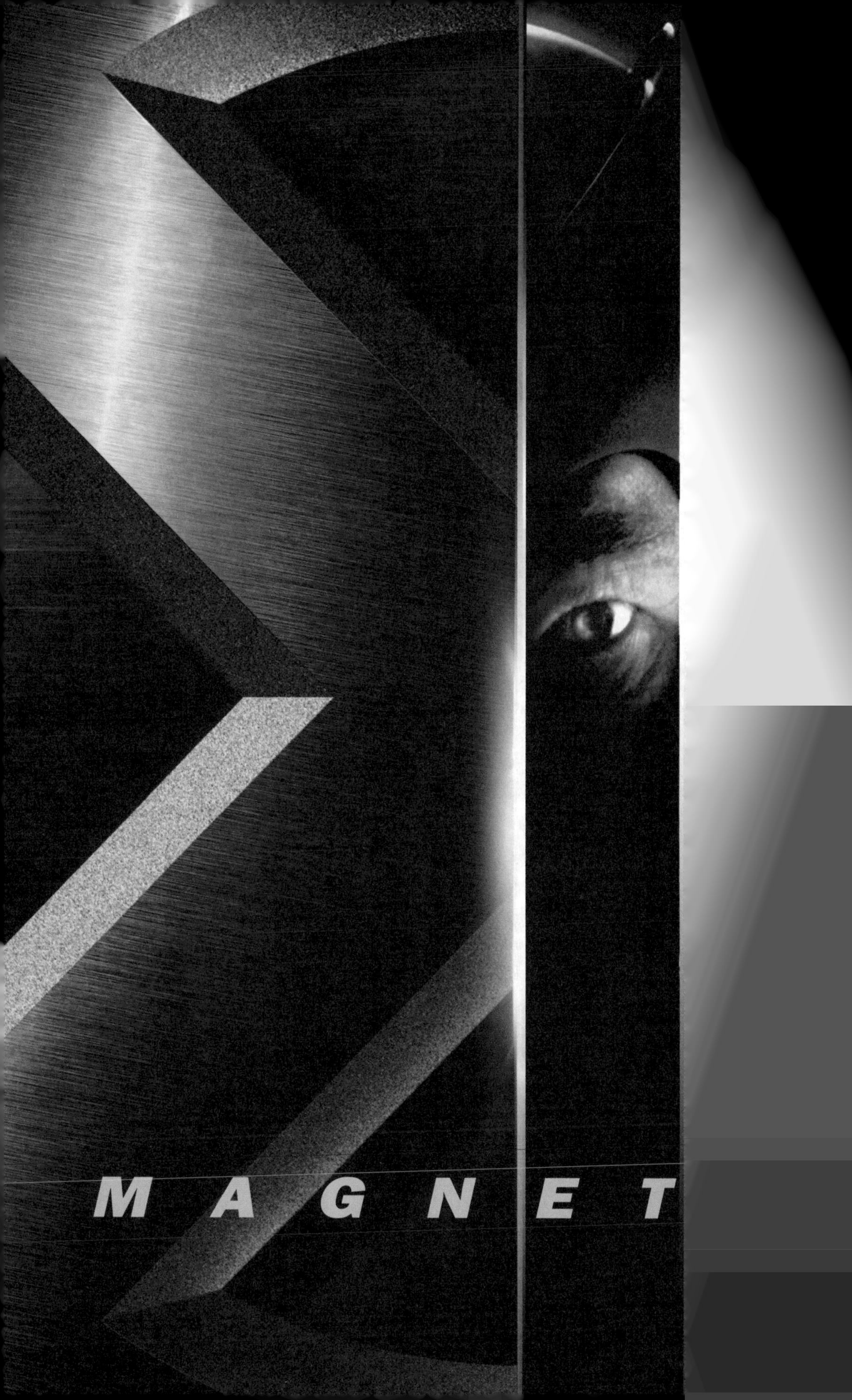
MAGNET

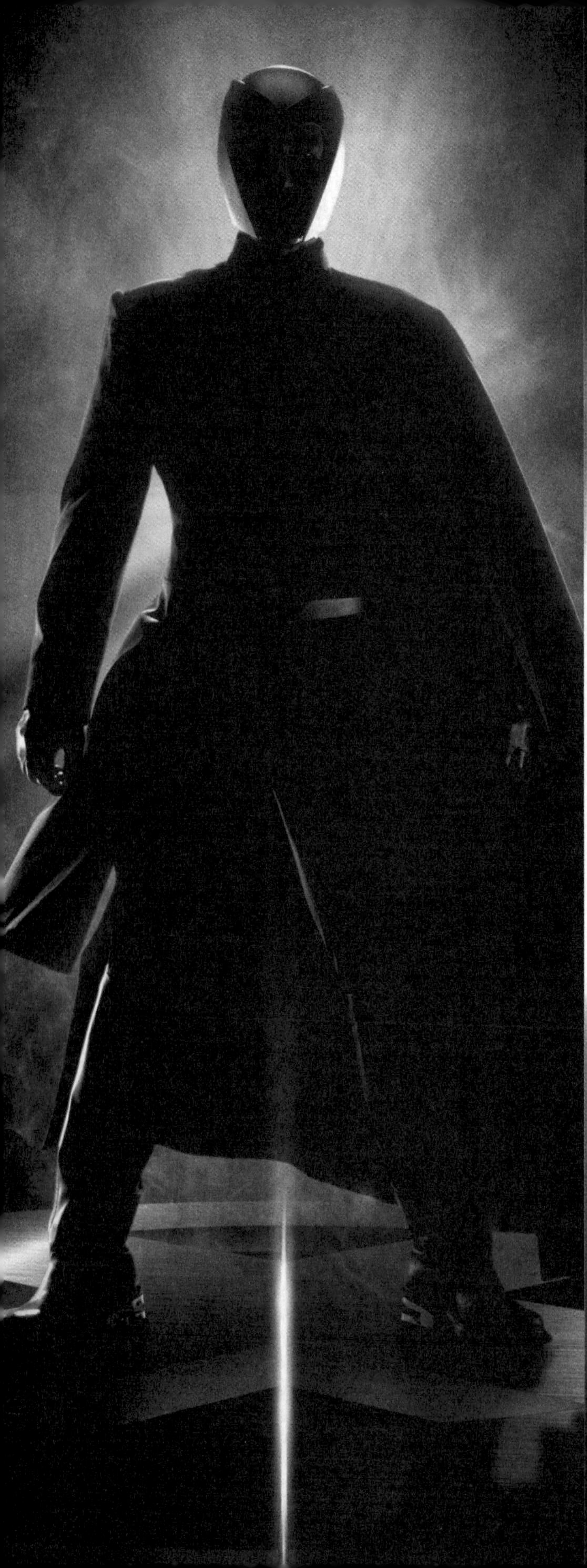

MAGNETO

SCATTERS

THE X-MEN

LIKE TOYS

IN THIS

CLASSIC

TALE!

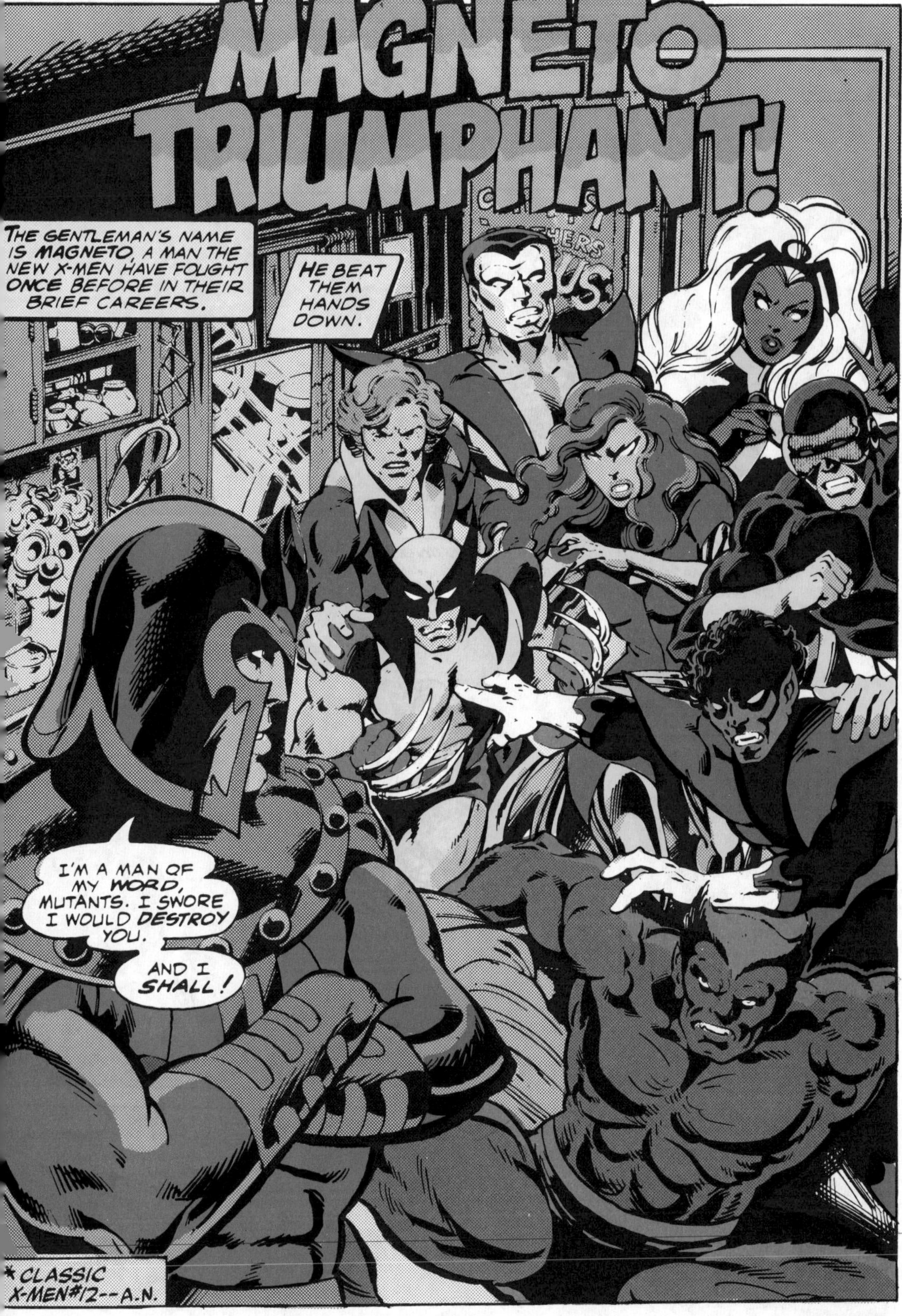
MAGNETO TRIUMPHANT!
THE GENTLEMAN'S NAME IS MAGNETO, A MAN THE NEW X-MEN HAVE FOUGHT ONCE BEFORE IN THEIR BRIEF CAREERS.
HE BEAT THEM HANDS DOWN.
I'M A MAN OF MY WORD, MUTANTS. I SWORE I WOULD DESTROY YOU.
AND I SHALL!
*CLASSIC X-MEN #12--A.N.

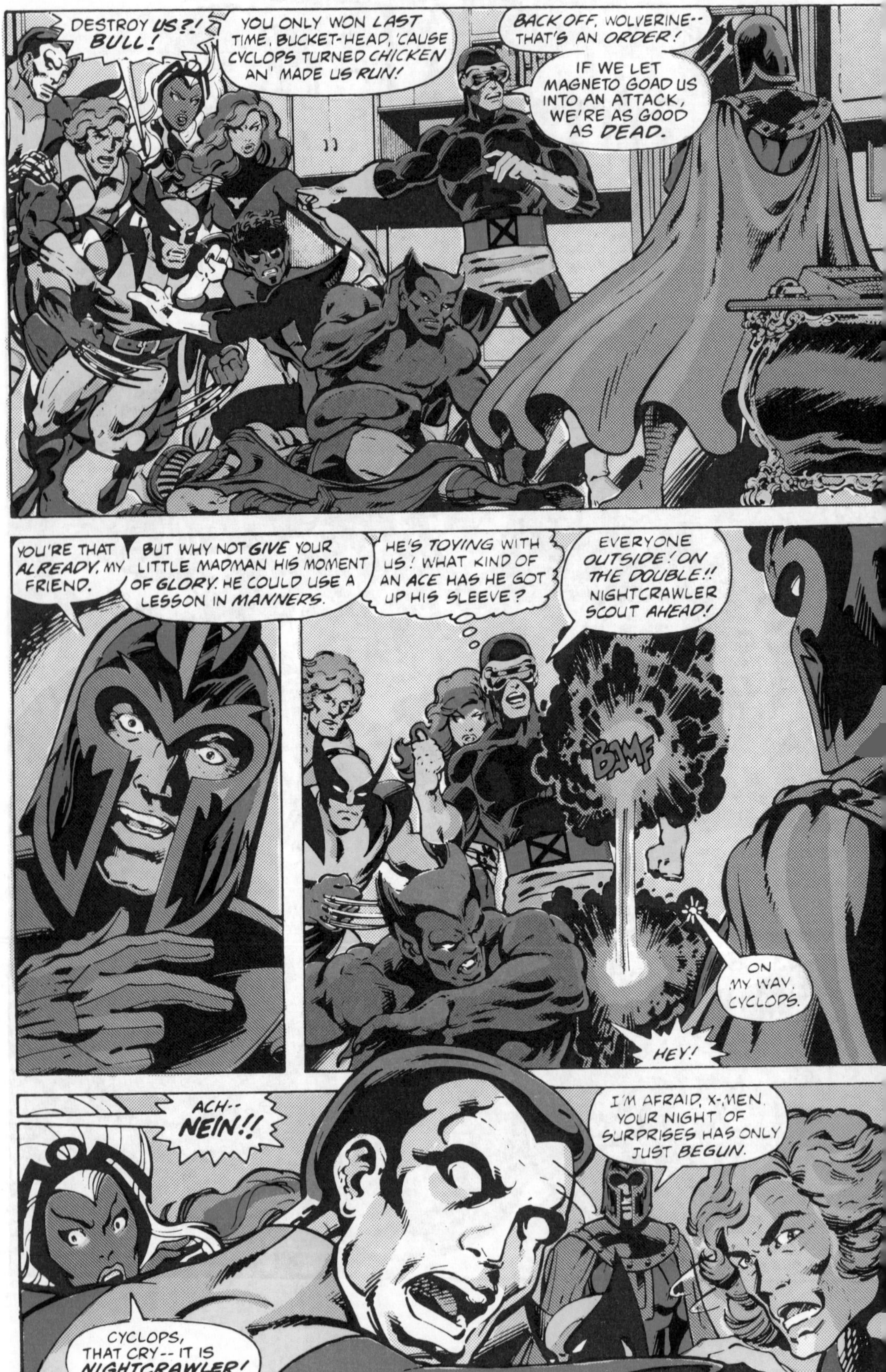
DESTROY US?! BULL!
YOU ONLY WON LAST TIME, BUCKET-HEAD, 'CAUSE CYCLOPS TURNED CHICKEN AN' MADE US RUN!
BACK OFF, WOLVERINE-- THAT'S AN ORDER!
IF WE LET MAGNETO GOAD US INTO AN ATTACK, WE'RE AS GOOD AS DEAD.
YOU'RE THAT ALREADY, MY FRIEND.
BUT WHY NOT GIVE YOUR LITTLE MADMAN HIS MOMENT OF GLORY. HE COULD USE A LESSON IN MANNERS.
HE'S TOYING WITH US! WHAT KIND OF AN ACE HAS HE GOT UP HIS SLEEVE?
EVERYONE OUTSIDE! ON THE DOUBLE!! NIGHTCRAWLER SCOUT AHEAD!
BAMF
ON MY WAY, CYCLOPS.
HEY!
ACH-- NEIN!!
I'M AFRAID, X-MEN, YOUR NIGHT OF SURPRISES HAS ONLY JUST BEGUN.
CYCLOPS, THAT CRY-- IT IS NIGHTCRAWLER!

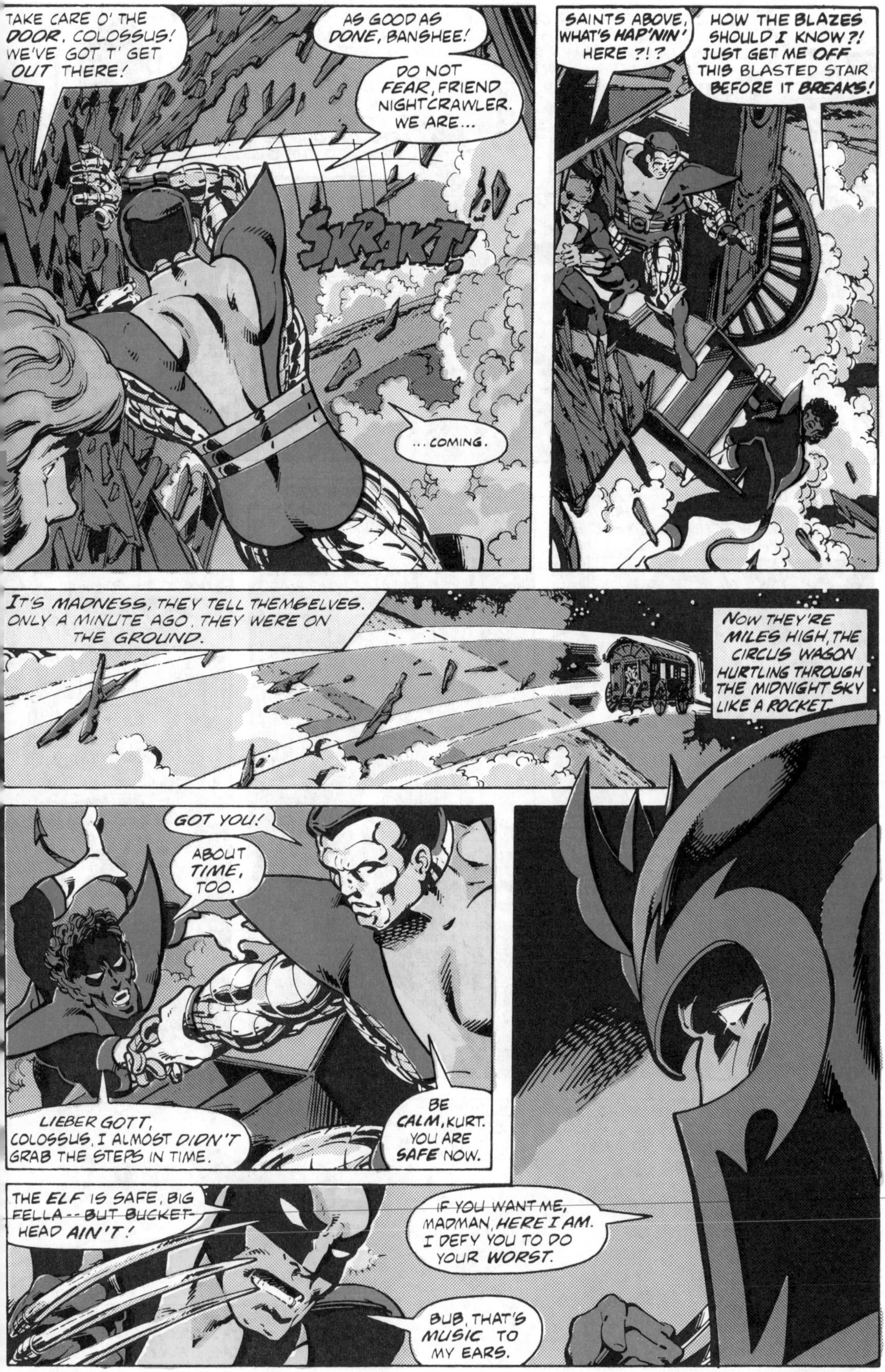
TAKE CARE O' THE DOOR, COLOSSUS! WE'VE GOT T' GET OUT THERE!
AS GOOD AS DONE, BANSHEE!
DO NOT FEAR, FRIEND NIGHTCRAWLER. WE ARE...
SKRAKT!
...COMING.
SAINTS ABOVE, WHAT'S HAP'NIN' HERE ?!?
HOW THE BLAZES SHOULD I KNOW?! JUST GET ME OFF THIS BLASTED STAIR BEFORE IT BREAKS!
IT'S MADNESS, THEY TELL THEMSELVES. ONLY A MINUTE AGO, THEY WERE ON THE GROUND.
NOW THEY'RE MILES HIGH, THE CIRCUS WAGON HURTLING THROUGH THE MIDNIGHT SKY LIKE A ROCKET.
GOT YOU!
ABOUT TIME, TOO.
LIEBER GOTT, COLOSSUS, I ALMOST DIDN'T GRAB THE STEPS IN TIME.
BE CALM, KURT. YOU ARE SAFE NOW.
THE ELF IS SAFE, BIG FELLA--BUT BUCKET-HEAD AIN'T!
IF YOU WANT ME, MADMAN, HERE I AM. I DEFY YOU TO DO YOUR WORST.
BUB, THAT'S MUSIC TO MY EARS.

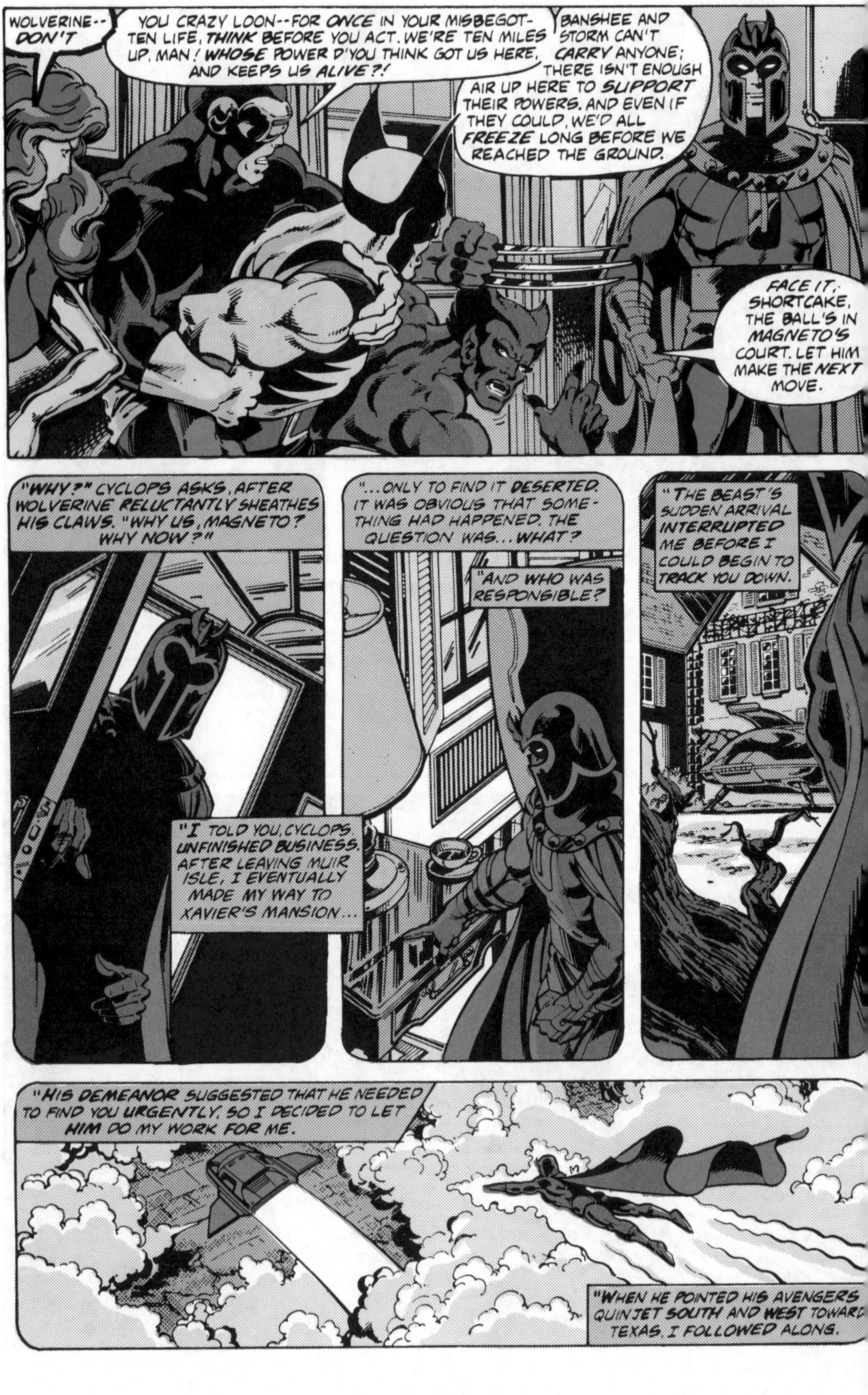
WOLVERINE-- DON'T
YOU CRAZY LOON--FOR ONCE IN YOUR MISBEGOTTEN LIFE, THINK BEFORE YOU ACT. WE'RE TEN MILES UP, MAN! WHOSE POWER D'YOU THINK GOT US HERE, AND KEEPS US ALIVE?!
BANSHEE AND STORM CAN'T CARRY ANYONE; THERE ISN'T ENOUGH AIR UP HERE TO SUPPORT THEIR POWERS. AND EVEN IF THEY COULD, WE'D ALL FREEZE LONG BEFORE WE REACHED THE GROUND.
FACE IT, SHORTCAKE, THE BALL'S IN MAGNETO'S COURT. LET HIM MAKE THE NEXT MOVE.
"WHY?" CYCLOPS ASKS, AFTER WOLVERINE RELUCTANTLY SHEATHES HIS CLAWS. "WHY US, MAGNETO? WHY NOW?"
"I TOLD YOU, CYCLOPS UNFINISHED BUSINESS. AFTER LEAVING MUIR ISLE, I EVENTUALLY MADE MY WAY TO XAVIER'S MANSION...
"...ONLY TO FIND IT DESERTED. IT WAS OBVIOUS THAT SOMETHING HAD HAPPENED. THE QUESTION WAS...WHAT?
"AND WHO WAS RESPONSIBLE?
"THE BEAST'S SUDDEN ARRIVAL INTERRUPTED ME BEFORE I COULD BEGIN TO TRACK YOU DOWN.
"HIS DEMEANOR SUGGESTED THAT HE NEEDED TO FIND YOU URGENTLY, SO I DECIDED TO LET HIM DO MY WORK FOR ME.
"WHEN HE POINTED HIS AVENGERS QUINJET SOUTH AND WEST TOWARD TEXAS, I FOLLOWED ALONG.

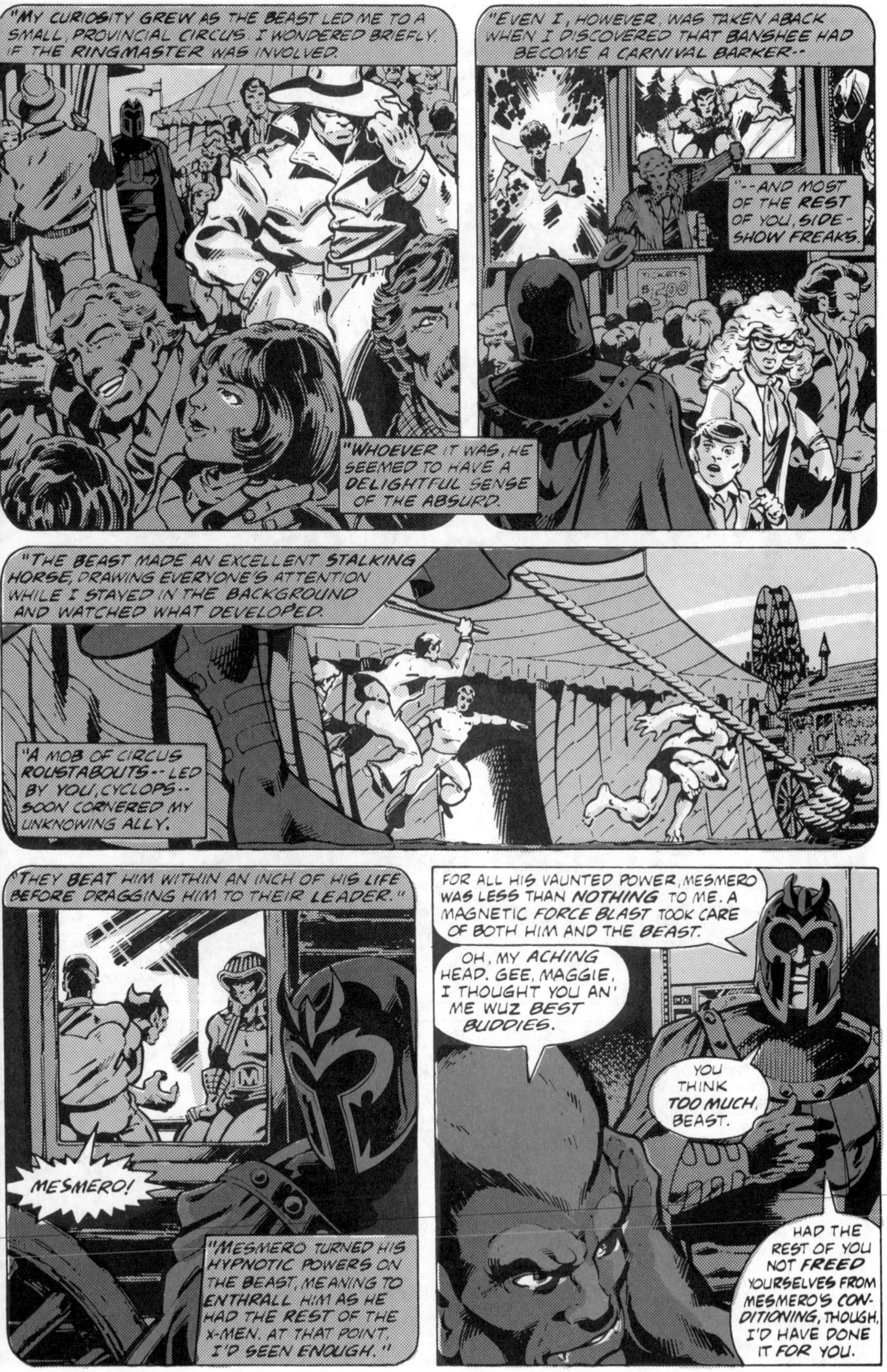
"MY CURIOSITY GREW AS THE BEAST LED ME TO A SMALL, PROVINCIAL CIRCUS. I WONDERED BRIEFLY IF THE RINGMASTER WAS INVOLVED.
"WHOEVER IT WAS, HE SEEMED TO HAVE A DELIGHTFUL SENSE OF THE ABSURD.
"EVEN I, HOWEVER, WAS TAKEN ABACK WHEN I DISCOVERED THAT BANSHEE HAD BECOME A CARNIVAL BARKER--
"--AND MOST OF THE REST OF YOU, SIDE-SHOW FREAKS.
"THE BEAST MADE AN EXCELLENT STALKING HORSE, DRAWING EVERYONE'S ATTENTION WHILE I STAYED IN THE BACKGROUND AND WATCHED WHAT DEVELOPED.
"A MOB OF CIRCUS ROUSTABOUTS--LED BY YOU, CYCLOPS--SOON CORNERED MY UNKNOWING ALLY.
"THEY BEAT HIM WITHIN AN INCH OF HIS LIFE BEFORE DRAGGING HIM TO THEIR LEADER."
MESMERO!
"MESMERO TURNED HIS HYPNOTIC POWERS ON THE BEAST, MEANING TO ENTHRALL HIM AS HE HAD THE REST OF THE X-MEN. AT THAT POINT, I'D SEEN ENOUGH."
FOR ALL HIS VAUNTED POWER, MESMERO WAS LESS THAN NOTHING TO ME. A MAGNETIC FORCE BLAST TOOK CARE OF BOTH HIM AND THE BEAST.
OH, MY ACHING HEAD. GEE, MAGGIE, I THOUGHT YOU AN' ME WUZ BEST BUDDIES.
YOU THINK TOO MUCH, BEAST.
HAD THE REST OF YOU NOT FREED YOURSELVES FROM MESMERO'S CONDITIONING, THOUGH, I'D HAVE DONE IT FOR YOU.

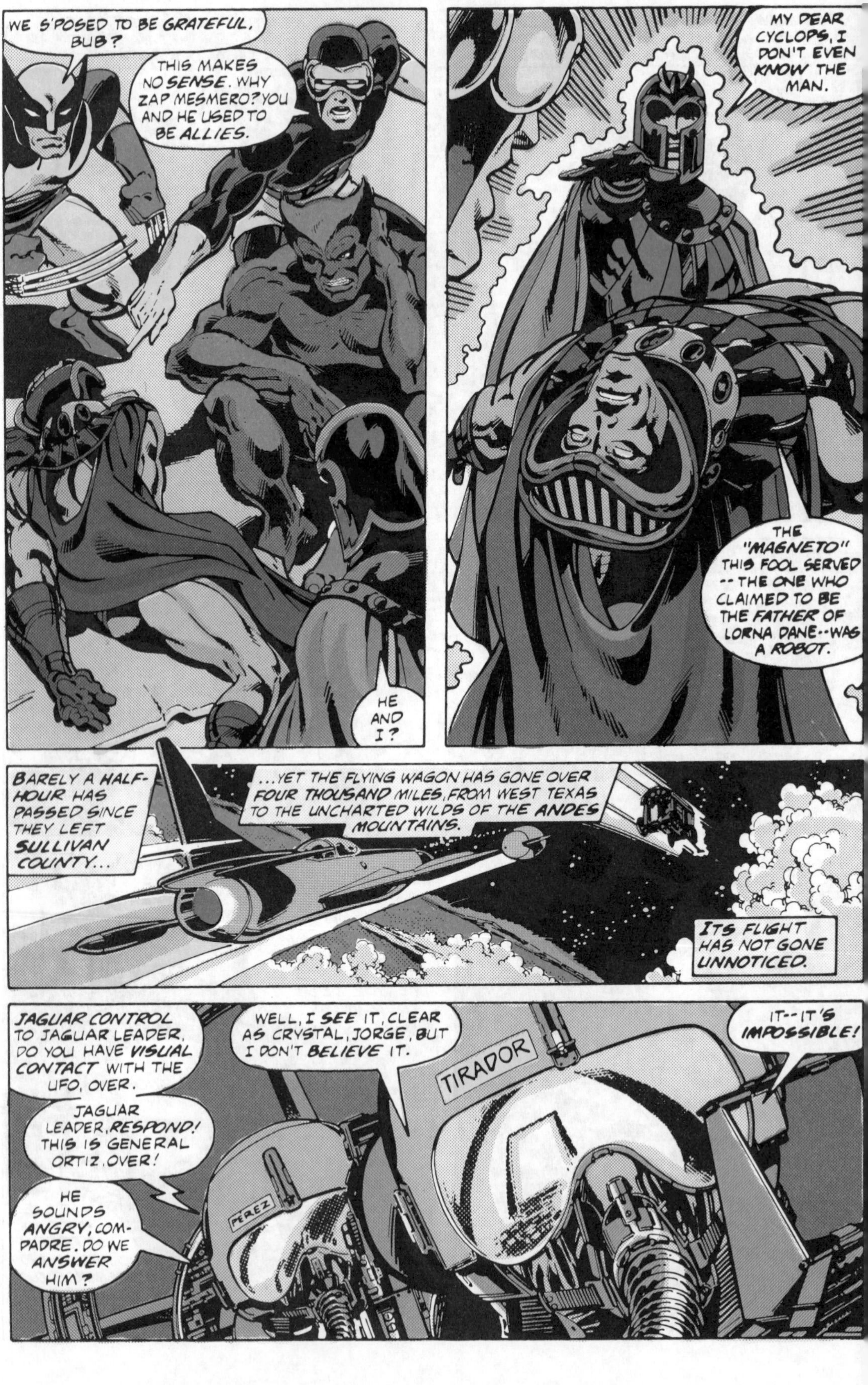

WE S'POSED TO BE GRATEFUL, BUB?
THIS MAKES NO SENSE. WHY ZAP MESMERO? YOU AND HE USED TO BE ALLIES.
HE AND I?
MY DEAR CYCLOPS, I DON'T EVEN KNOW THE MAN.
THE "MAGNETO" THIS FOOL SERVED -- THE ONE WHO CLAIMED TO BE THE FATHER OF LORNA DANE--WAS A ROBOT.
BARELY A HALF-HOUR HAS PASSED SINCE THEY LEFT SULLIVAN COUNTY...
...YET THE FLYING WAGON HAS GONE OVER FOUR THOUSAND MILES, FROM WEST TEXAS TO THE UNCHARTED WILDS OF THE ANDES MOUNTAINS.
ITS FLIGHT HAS NOT GONE UNNOTICED.
JAGUAR CONTROL TO JAGUAR LEADER. DO YOU HAVE VISUAL CONTACT WITH THE UFO, OVER.
JAGUAR LEADER, RESPOND! THIS IS GENERAL ORTIZ, OVER!
HE SOUNDS ANGRY, COMPADRE. DO WE ANSWER HIM?
WELL, I SEE IT, CLEAR AS CRYSTAL, JORGE, BUT I DON'T BELIEVE IT.
IT--IT'S IMPOSSIBLE!
TIRADOR
PEREZ

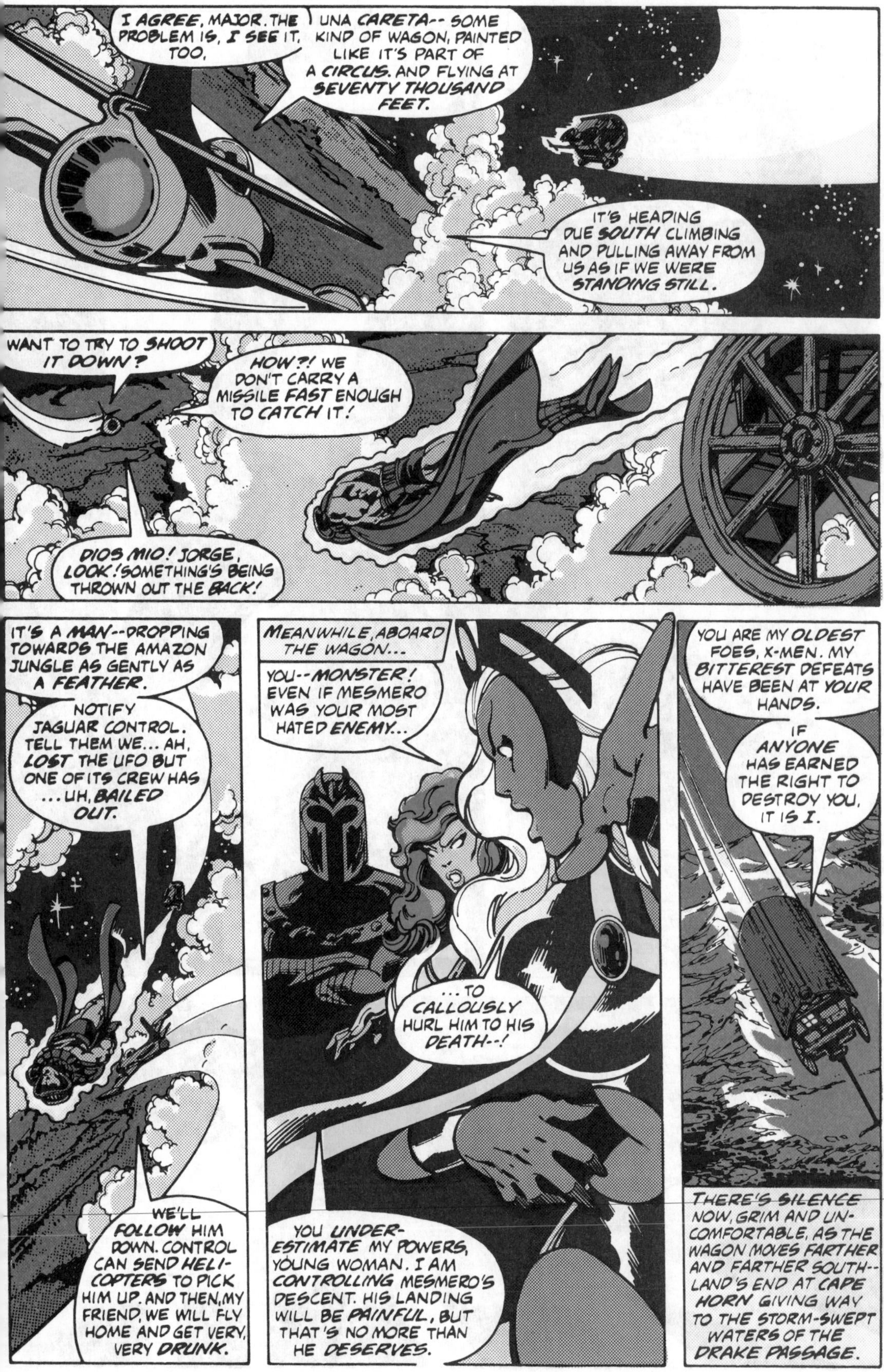
I AGREE, MAJOR. THE PROBLEM IS, I SEE IT, TOO.
UNA CARETA-- SOME KIND OF WAGON, PAINTED LIKE IT'S PART OF A CIRCUS. AND FLYING AT SEVENTY THOUSAND FEET.
IT'S HEADING DUE SOUTH CLIMBING AND PULLING AWAY FROM US AS IF WE WERE STANDING STILL.
WANT TO TRY TO SHOOT IT DOWN?
HOW?! WE DON'T CARRY A MISSILE FAST ENOUGH TO CATCH IT!
DIOS MIO! JORGE, LOOK! SOMETHING'S BEING THROWN OUT THE BACK!
IT'S A MAN--DROPPING TOWARDS THE AMAZON JUNGLE AS GENTLY AS A FEATHER.
NOTIFY JAGUAR CONTROL. TELL THEM WE... AH, LOST THE UFO BUT ONE OF ITS CREW HAS ...UH, BAILED OUT.
WE'LL FOLLOW HIM DOWN. CONTROL CAN SEND HELI-COPTERS TO PICK HIM UP. AND THEN, MY FRIEND, WE WILL FLY HOME AND GET VERY, VERY DRUNK.
MEANWHILE, ABOARD THE WAGON...
YOU--MONSTER! EVEN IF MESMERO WAS YOUR MOST HATED ENEMY...
...TO CALLOUSLY HURL HIM TO HIS DEATH--!
YOU UNDER-ESTIMATE MY POWERS, YOUNG WOMAN. I AM CONTROLLING MESMERO'S DESCENT. HIS LANDING WILL BE PAINFUL, BUT THAT'S NO MORE THAN HE DESERVES.
YOU ARE MY OLDEST FOES, X-MEN. MY BITTEREST DEFEATS HAVE BEEN AT YOUR HANDS.
IF ANYONE HAS EARNED THE RIGHT TO DESTROY YOU, IT IS I.
THERE'S SILENCE NOW, GRIM AND UN-COMFORTABLE, AS THE WAGON MOVES FARTHER AND FARTHER SOUTH-- LAND'S END AT CAPE HORN GIVING WAY TO THE STORM-SWEPT WATERS OF THE DRAKE PASSAGE.

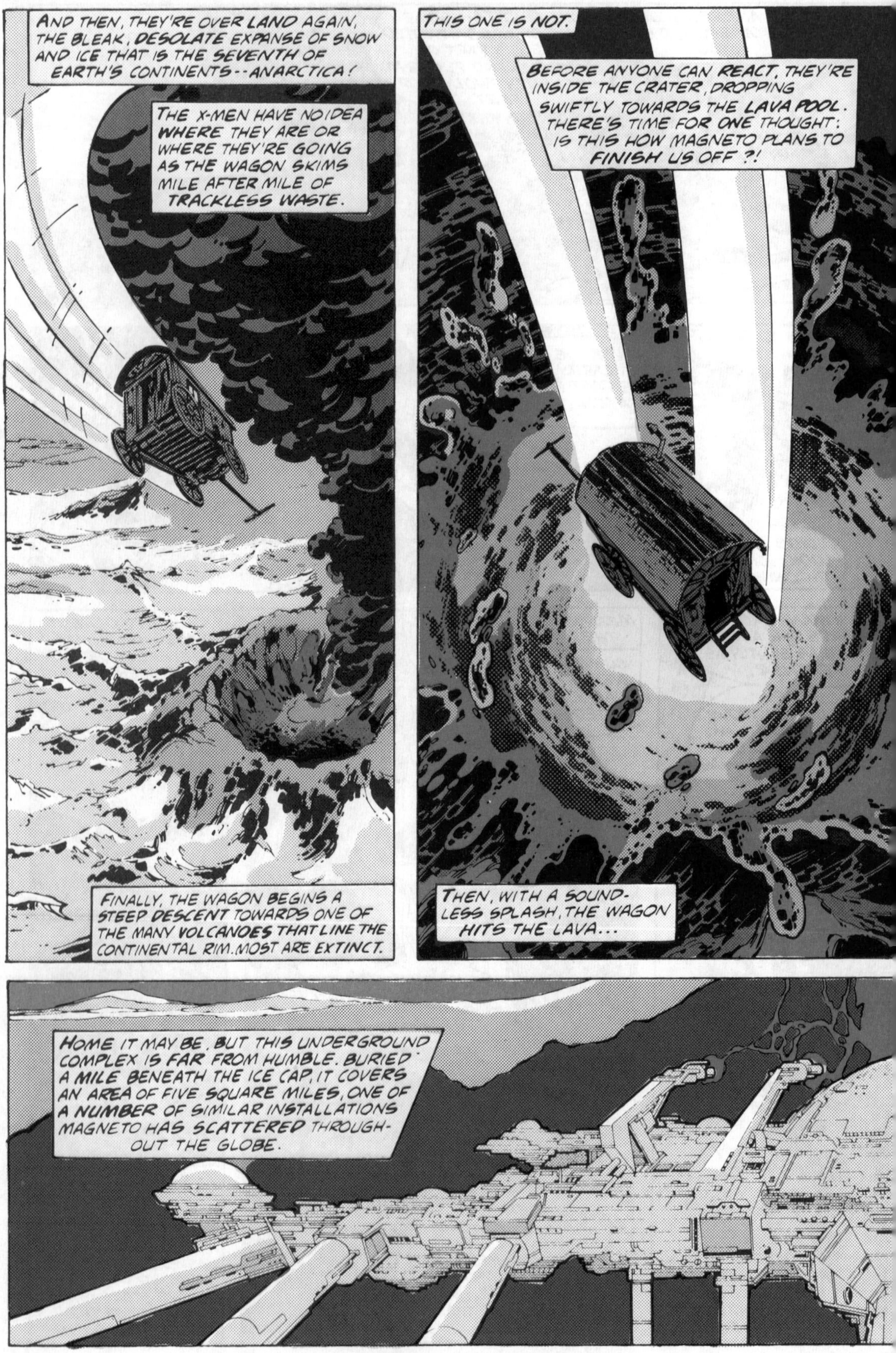
AND THEN, THEY'RE OVER LAND AGAIN, THE BLEAK, DESOLATE EXPANSE OF SNOW AND ICE THAT IS THE SEVENTH OF EARTH'S CONTINENTS--ANARCTICA!
THE X-MEN HAVE NO IDEA WHERE THEY ARE OR WHERE THEY'RE GOING AS THE WAGON SKIMS MILE AFTER MILE OF TRACKLESS WASTE.
FINALLY, THE WAGON BEGINS A STEEP DESCENT TOWARDS ONE OF THE MANY VOLCANOES THAT LINE THE CONTINENTAL RIM. MOST ARE EXTINCT.
THIS ONE IS NOT.
BEFORE ANYONE CAN REACT, THEY'RE INSIDE THE CRATER, DROPPING SWIFTLY TOWARDS THE LAVA POOL. THERE'S TIME FOR ONE THOUGHT: IS THIS HOW MAGNETO PLANS TO FINISH US OFF?!
THEN, WITH A SOUND-LESS SPLASH, THE WAGON HITS THE LAVA...
HOME IT MAY BE, BUT THIS UNDERGROUND COMPLEX IS FAR FROM HUMBLE. BURIED A MILE BENEATH THE ICE CAP, IT COVERS AN AREA OF FIVE SQUARE MILES, ONE OF A NUMBER OF SIMILAR INSTALLATIONS MAGNETO HAS SCATTERED THROUGH-OUT THE GLOBE.

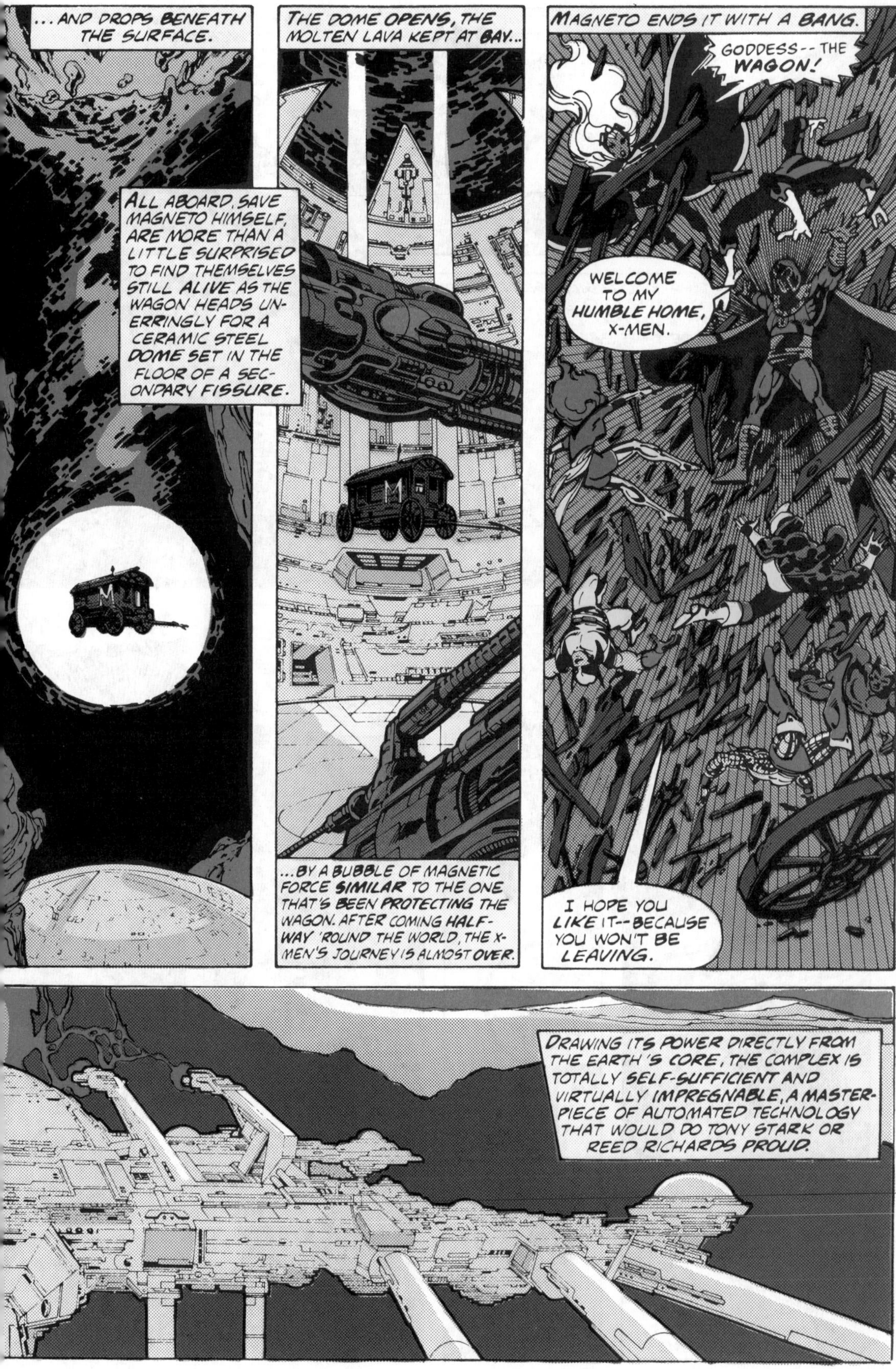
...AND DROPS BENEATH THE SURFACE.
ALL ABOARD, SAVE MAGNETO HIMSELF, ARE MORE THAN A LITTLE SURPRISED TO FIND THEMSELVES STILL ALIVE AS THE WAGON HEADS UNERRINGLY FOR A CERAMIC STEEL DOME SET IN THE FLOOR OF A SECONDARY FISSURE.
THE DOME OPENS, THE MOLTEN LAVA KEPT AT BAY...
...BY A BUBBLE OF MAGNETIC FORCE SIMILAR TO THE ONE THAT'S BEEN PROTECTING THE WAGON. AFTER COMING HALF-WAY 'ROUND THE WORLD, THE X-MEN'S JOURNEY IS ALMOST OVER.
MAGNETO ENDS IT WITH A BANG.
GODDESS--THE WAGON!
WELCOME TO MY HUMBLE HOME, X-MEN.
I HOPE YOU LIKE IT--BECAUSE YOU WON'T BE LEAVING.
DRAWING ITS POWER DIRECTLY FROM THE EARTH'S CORE, THE COMPLEX IS TOTALLY SELF-SUFFICIENT AND VIRTUALLY IMPREGNABLE, A MASTERPIECE OF AUTOMATED TECHNOLOGY THAT WOULD DO TONY STARK OR REED RICHARDS PROUD.

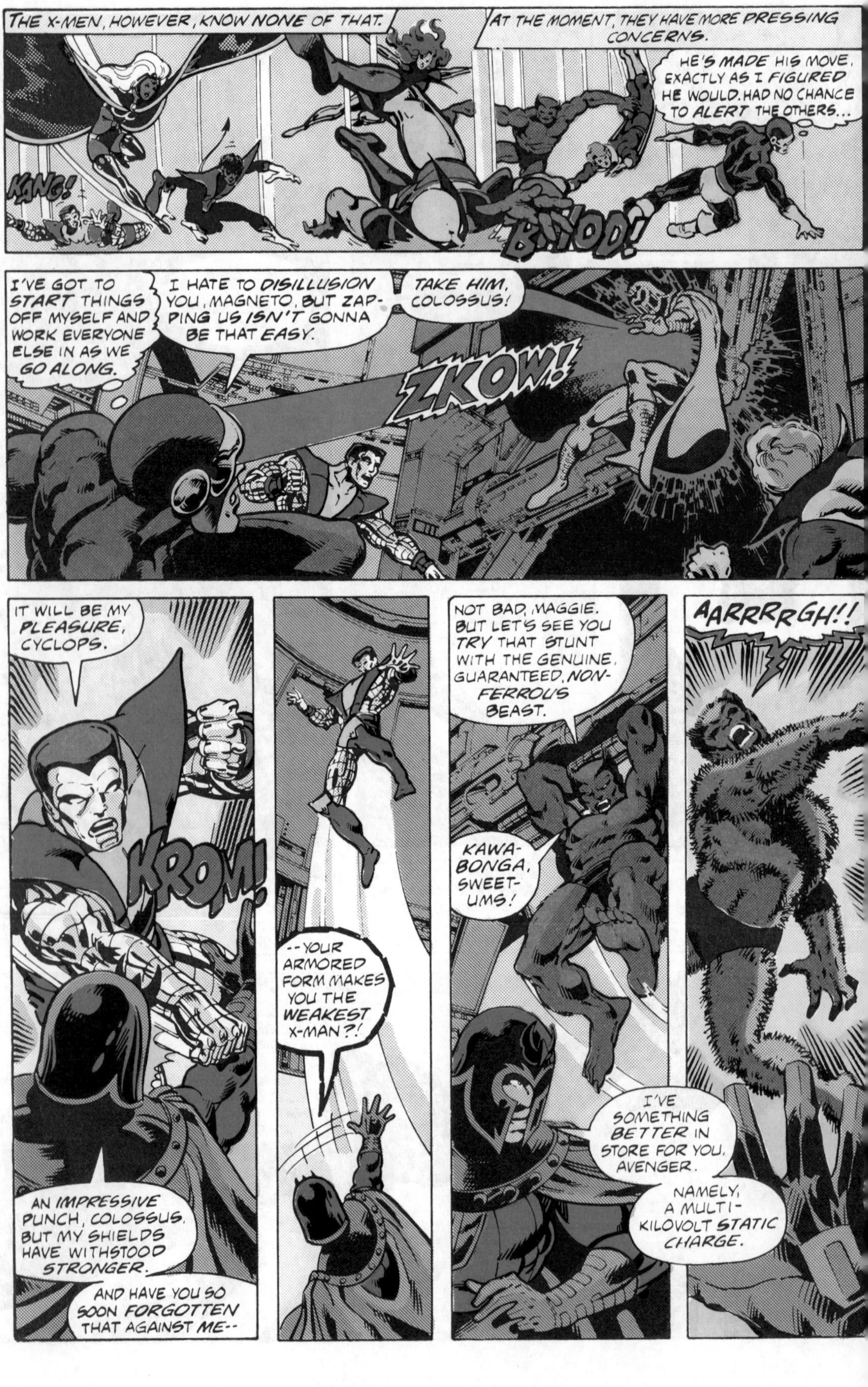
THE X-MEN, HOWEVER, KNOW NONE OF THAT.
AT THE MOMENT, THEY HAVE MORE PRESSING CONCERNS.
HE'S MADE HIS MOVE, EXACTLY AS I FIGURED HE WOULD. HAD NO CHANCE TO ALERT THE OTHERS...
KANG!
BHOOOM!
I'VE GOT TO START THINGS OFF MYSELF AND WORK EVERYONE ELSE IN AS WE GO ALONG.
I HATE TO DISILLUSION YOU, MAGNETO, BUT ZAPPING US ISN'T GONNA BE THAT EASY.
TAKE HIM, COLOSSUS!
ZKOW!
IT WILL BE MY PLEASURE, CYCLOPS.
KROM!
AN IMPRESSIVE PUNCH, COLOSSUS, BUT MY SHIELDS HAVE WITHSTOOD STRONGER.
AND HAVE YOU SO SOON FORGOTTEN THAT AGAINST ME--
--YOUR ARMORED FORM MAKES YOU THE WEAKEST X-MAN?!
NOT BAD, MAGGIE. BUT LET'S SEE YOU TRY THAT STUNT WITH THE GENUINE, GUARANTEED, NON-FERROUS BEAST.
KAWA-BONGA, SWEET-UMS!
I'VE SOMETHING BETTER IN STORE FOR YOU, AVENGER.
NAMELY, A MULTI-KILOVOLT STATIC CHARGE.
AARRRRGH!!

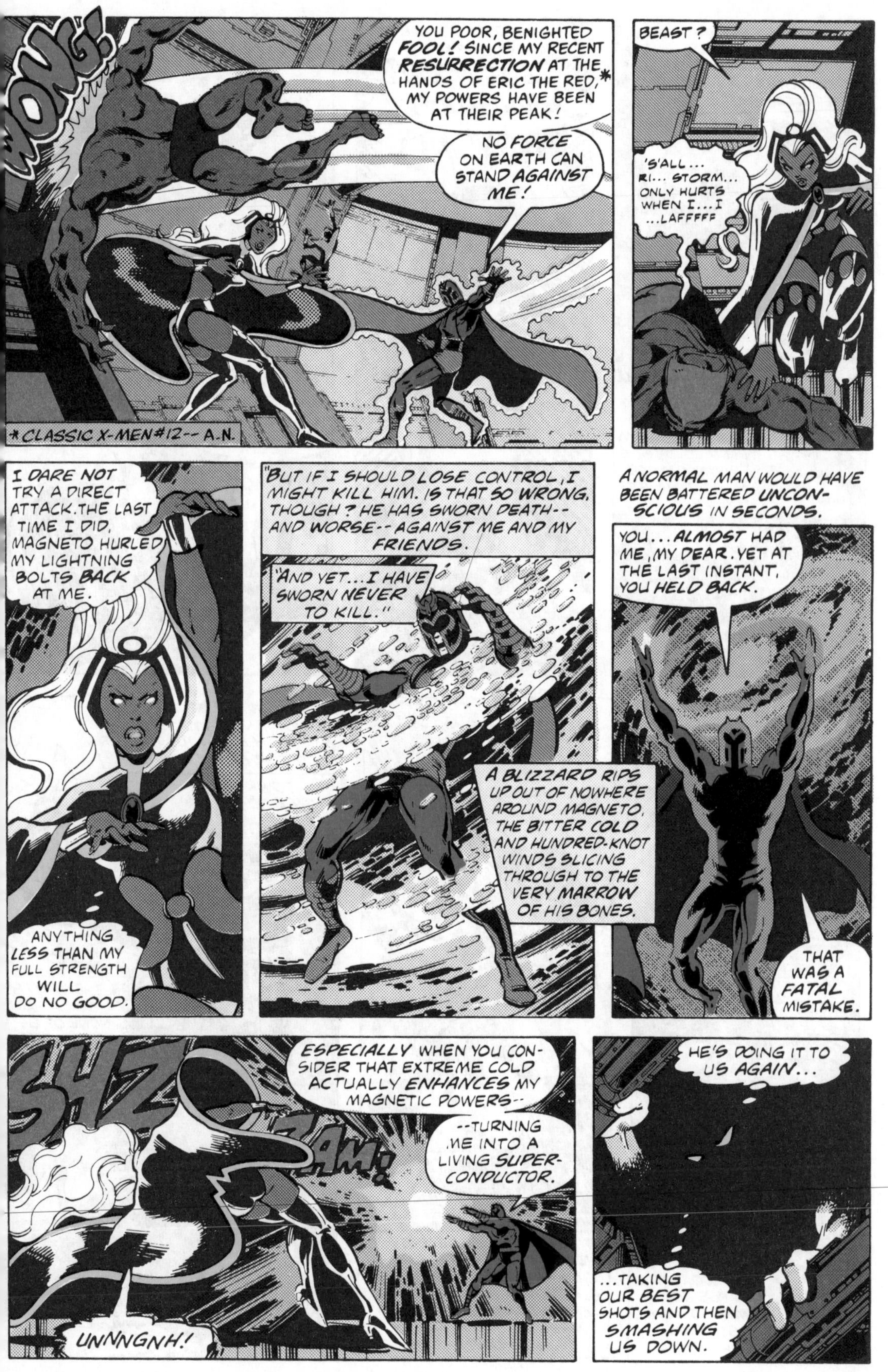
WONG!
YOU POOR, BENIGHTED FOOL! SINCE MY RECENT RESURRECTION AT THE HANDS OF ERIC THE RED,* MY POWERS HAVE BEEN AT THEIR PEAK!
NO FORCE ON EARTH CAN STAND AGAINST ME!
*CLASSIC X-MEN #12-- A.N.
BEAST?
'S'ALL... RI... STORM... ONLY HURTS WHEN I... I ...LAFFFFF
I DARE NOT TRY A DIRECT ATTACK. THE LAST TIME I DID, MAGNETO HURLED MY LIGHTNING BOLTS BACK AT ME.
ANYTHING LESS THAN MY FULL STRENGTH WILL DO NO GOOD.
"BUT IF I SHOULD LOSE CONTROL, I MIGHT KILL HIM. IS THAT SO WRONG, THOUGH? HE HAS SWORN DEATH-- AND WORSE-- AGAINST ME AND MY FRIENDS.
"AND YET... I HAVE SWORN NEVER TO KILL."
A BLIZZARD RIPS UP OUT OF NOWHERE AROUND MAGNETO, THE BITTER COLD AND HUNDRED-KNOT WINDS SLICING THROUGH TO THE VERY MARROW OF HIS BONES.
A NORMAL MAN WOULD HAVE BEEN BATTERED UNCONSCIOUS IN SECONDS.
YOU... ALMOST HAD ME, MY DEAR. YET AT THE LAST INSTANT, YOU HELD BACK.
THAT WAS A FATAL MISTAKE.
SHZ
ZAM!
ESPECIALLY WHEN YOU CONSIDER THAT EXTREME COLD ACTUALLY ENHANCES MY MAGNETIC POWERS--
--TURNING ME INTO A LIVING SUPERCONDUCTOR.
UNNNGNH!
HE'S DOING IT TO US AGAIN...
...TAKING OUR BEST SHOTS AND THEN SMASHING US DOWN.

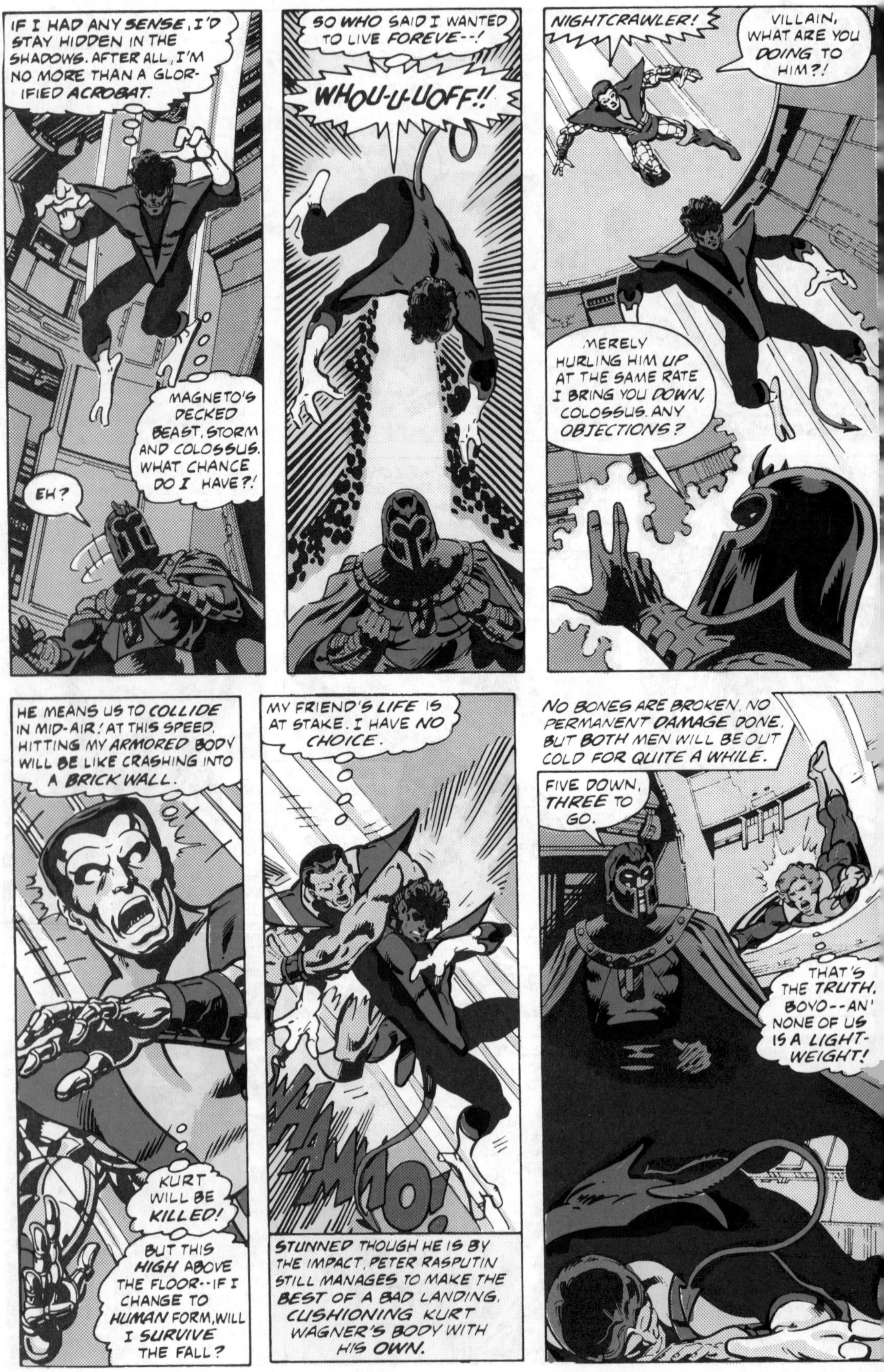

IF I HAD ANY SENSE, I'D STAY HIDDEN IN THE SHADOWS. AFTER ALL, I'M NO MORE THAN A GLORIFIED ACROBAT.
MAGNETO'S DECKED BEAST, STORM AND COLOSSUS. WHAT CHANCE DO I HAVE?!
EH?
SO WHO SAID I WANTED TO LIVE FOREVE--!
WHOU-U-UOFF!!
NIGHTCRAWLER!
VILLAIN, WHAT ARE YOU DOING TO HIM?!
MERELY HURLING HIM UP AT THE SAME RATE I BRING YOU DOWN, COLOSSUS. ANY OBJECTIONS?
HE MEANS US TO COLLIDE IN MID-AIR! AT THIS SPEED, HITTING MY ARMORED BODY WILL BE LIKE CRASHING INTO A BRICK WALL.
KURT WILL BE KILLED!
BUT THIS HIGH ABOVE THE FLOOR--IF I CHANGE TO HUMAN FORM, WILL I SURVIVE THE FALL?
MY FRIEND'S LIFE IS AT STAKE. I HAVE NO CHOICE.
WHAM!
STUNNED THOUGH HE IS BY THE IMPACT, PETER RASPUTIN STILL MANAGES TO MAKE THE BEST OF A BAD LANDING, CUSHIONING KURT WAGNER'S BODY WITH HIS OWN.
NO BONES ARE BROKEN, NO PERMANENT DAMAGE DONE, BUT BOTH MEN WILL BE OUT COLD FOR QUITE A WHILE.
FIVE DOWN, THREE TO GO.
THAT'S THE TRUTH, BOYO--AN' NONE OF US IS A LIGHTWEIGHT!

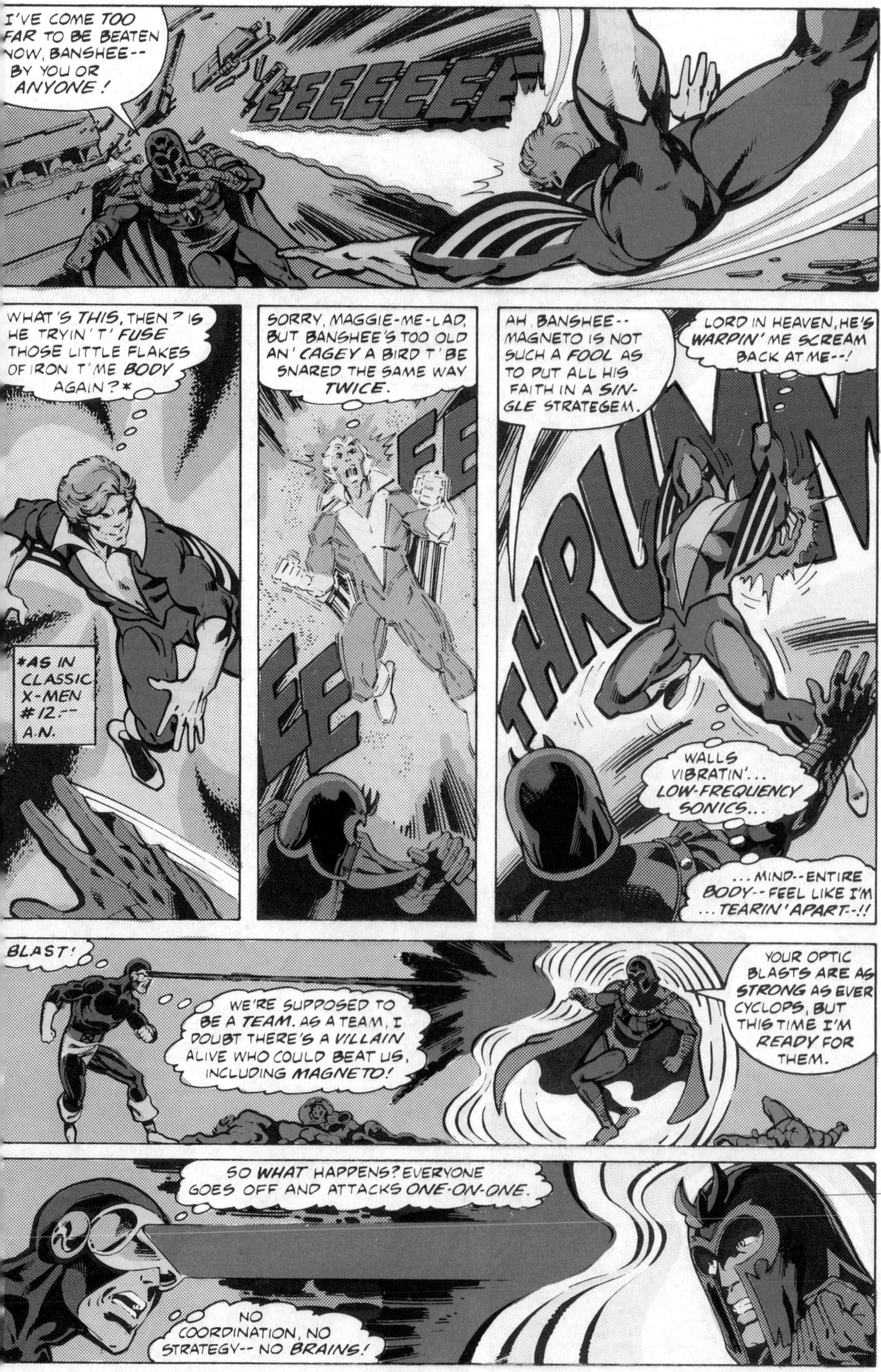
I'VE COME TOO FAR TO BE BEATEN NOW, BANSHEE-- BY YOU OR ANYONE!
EEEEEEE
WHAT'S THIS, THEN? IS HE TRYIN' T' FUSE THOSE LITTLE FLAKES OF IRON T'ME BODY AGAIN?*
*AS IN CLASSIC X-MEN #12.-- A.N.
SORRY, MAGGIE-ME-LAD, BUT BANSHEE'S TOO OLD AN' CAGEY A BIRD T' BE SNARED THE SAME WAY TWICE.
EE
FE
AH, BANSHEE-- MAGNETO IS NOT SUCH A FOOL AS TO PUT ALL HIS FAITH IN A SINGLE STRATEGEM.
LORD IN HEAVEN, HE'S WARPIN' ME SCREAM BACK AT ME--!
THRUMM
WALLS VIBRATIN'... LOW-FREQUENCY SONICS...
...MIND--ENTIRE BODY-- FEEL LIKE I'M ...TEARIN' APART--!!
BLAST!
WE'RE SUPPOSED TO BE A TEAM. AS A TEAM, I DOUBT THERE'S A VILLAIN ALIVE WHO COULD BEAT US, INCLUDING MAGNETO!
YOUR OPTIC BLASTS ARE AS STRONG AS EVER CYCLOPS, BUT THIS TIME I'M READY FOR THEM.
SO WHAT HAPPENS? EVERYONE GOES OFF AND ATTACKS ONE-ON-ONE.
NO COORDINATION, NO STRATEGY-- NO BRAINS!

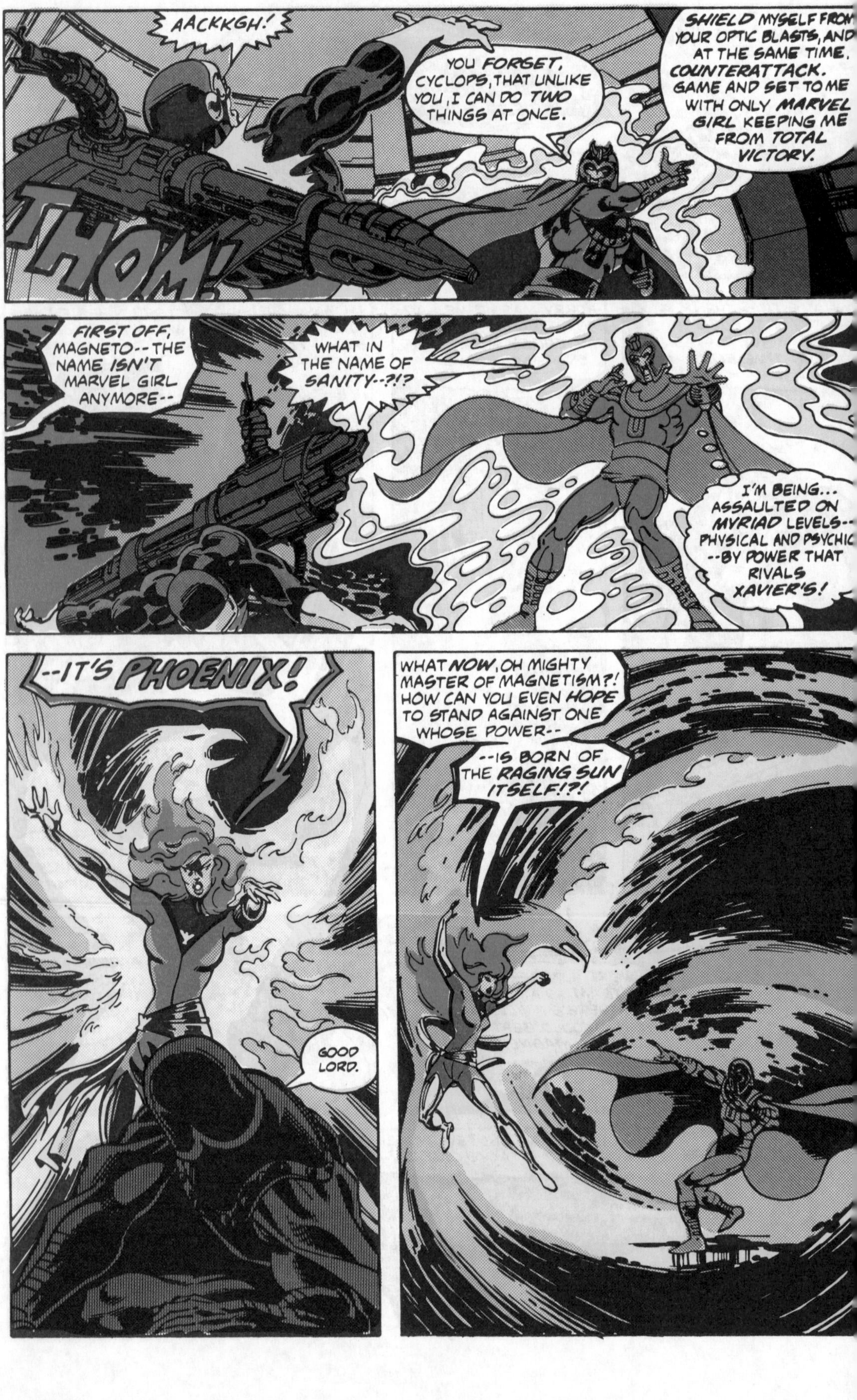
AACKKGH!
YOU FORGET, CYCLOPS, THAT UNLIKE YOU, I CAN DO TWO THINGS AT ONCE.
SHIELD MYSELF FROM YOUR OPTIC BLASTS, AND AT THE SAME TIME, COUNTERATTACK. GAME AND SET TO ME WITH ONLY MARVEL GIRL KEEPING ME FROM TOTAL VICTORY.
THOM!
FIRST OFF, MAGNETO--THE NAME ISN'T MARVEL GIRL ANYMORE--
WHAT IN THE NAME OF SANITY--?!?
I'M BEING... ASSAULTED ON MYRIAD LEVELS--PHYSICAL AND PSYCHIC--BY POWER THAT RIVALS XAVIER'S!
--IT'S PHOENIX!
GOOD LORD.
WHAT NOW, OH MIGHTY MASTER OF MAGNETISM?! HOW CAN YOU EVEN HOPE TO STAND AGAINST ONE WHOSE POWER--
--IS BORN OF THE RAGING SUN ITSELF!?!

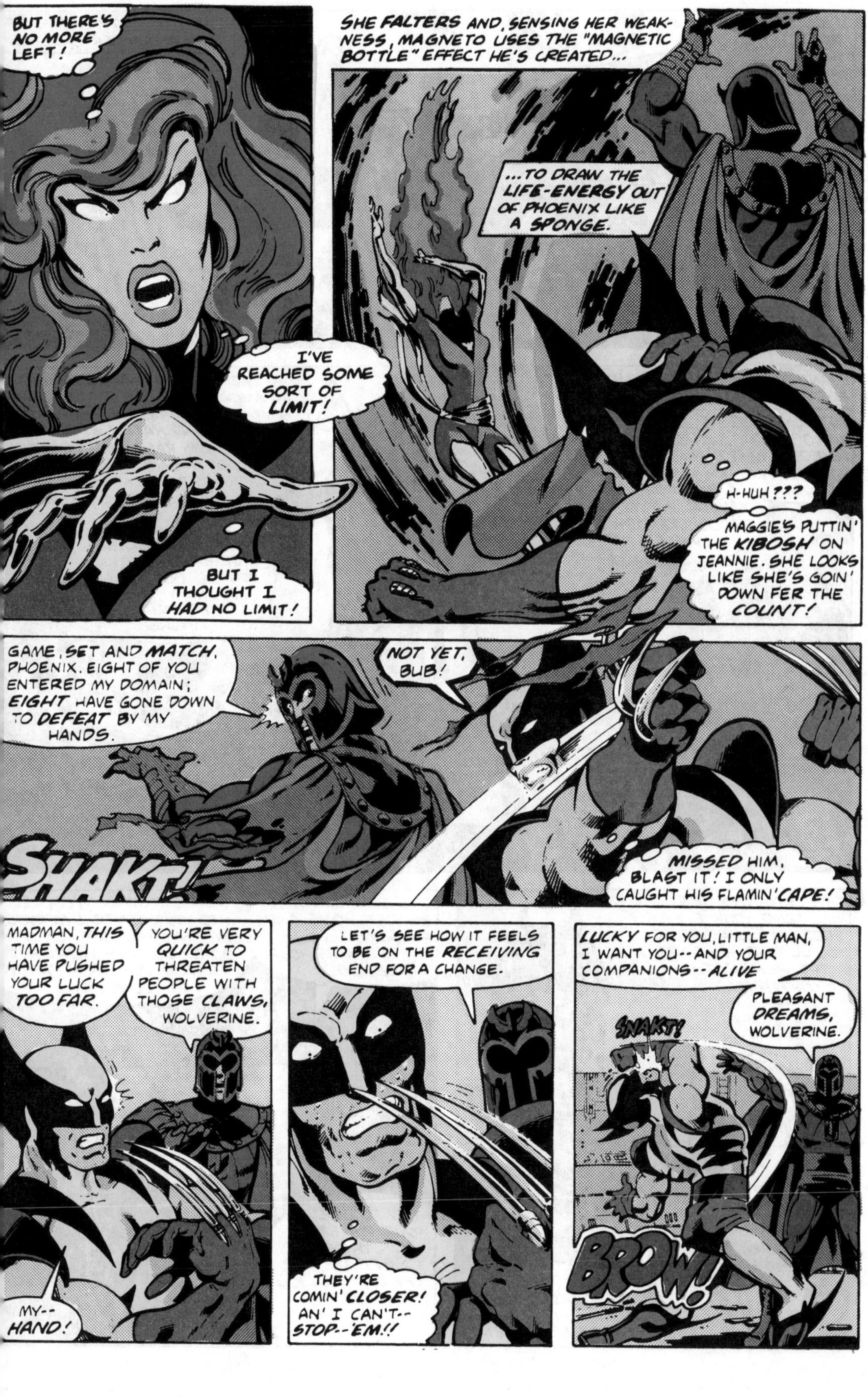

BUT THERE'S NO MORE LEFT!
I'VE REACHED SOME SORT OF LIMIT!
BUT I THOUGHT I HAD NO LIMIT!
SHE FALTERS AND, SENSING HER WEAKNESS, MAGNETO USES THE "MAGNETIC BOTTLE" EFFECT HE'S CREATED...
...TO DRAW THE LIFE-ENERGY OUT OF PHOENIX LIKE A SPONGE.
H-HUH???
MAGGIE'S PUTTIN' THE KIBOSH ON JEANNIE. SHE LOOKS LIKE SHE'S GOIN' DOWN FER THE COUNT!
GAME, SET AND MATCH, PHOENIX. EIGHT OF YOU ENTERED MY DOMAIN; EIGHT HAVE GONE DOWN TO DEFEAT BY MY HANDS.
NOT YET, BUB!
SHAKT!
MISSED HIM, BLAST IT! I ONLY CAUGHT HIS FLAMIN' CAPE!
MADMAN, THIS TIME YOU HAVE PUSHED YOUR LUCK TOO FAR.
YOU'RE VERY QUICK TO THREATEN PEOPLE WITH THOSE CLAWS, WOLVERINE.
MY-- HAND!
LET'S SEE HOW IT FEELS TO BE ON THE RECEIVING END FOR A CHANGE.
THEY'RE COMIN' CLOSER! AN' I CAN'T-- STOP--'EM!!
LUCKY FOR YOU, LITTLE MAN, I WANT YOU--AND YOUR COMPANIONS--ALIVE
PLEASANT DREAMS, WOLVERINE.
SNAKT!
BROW!

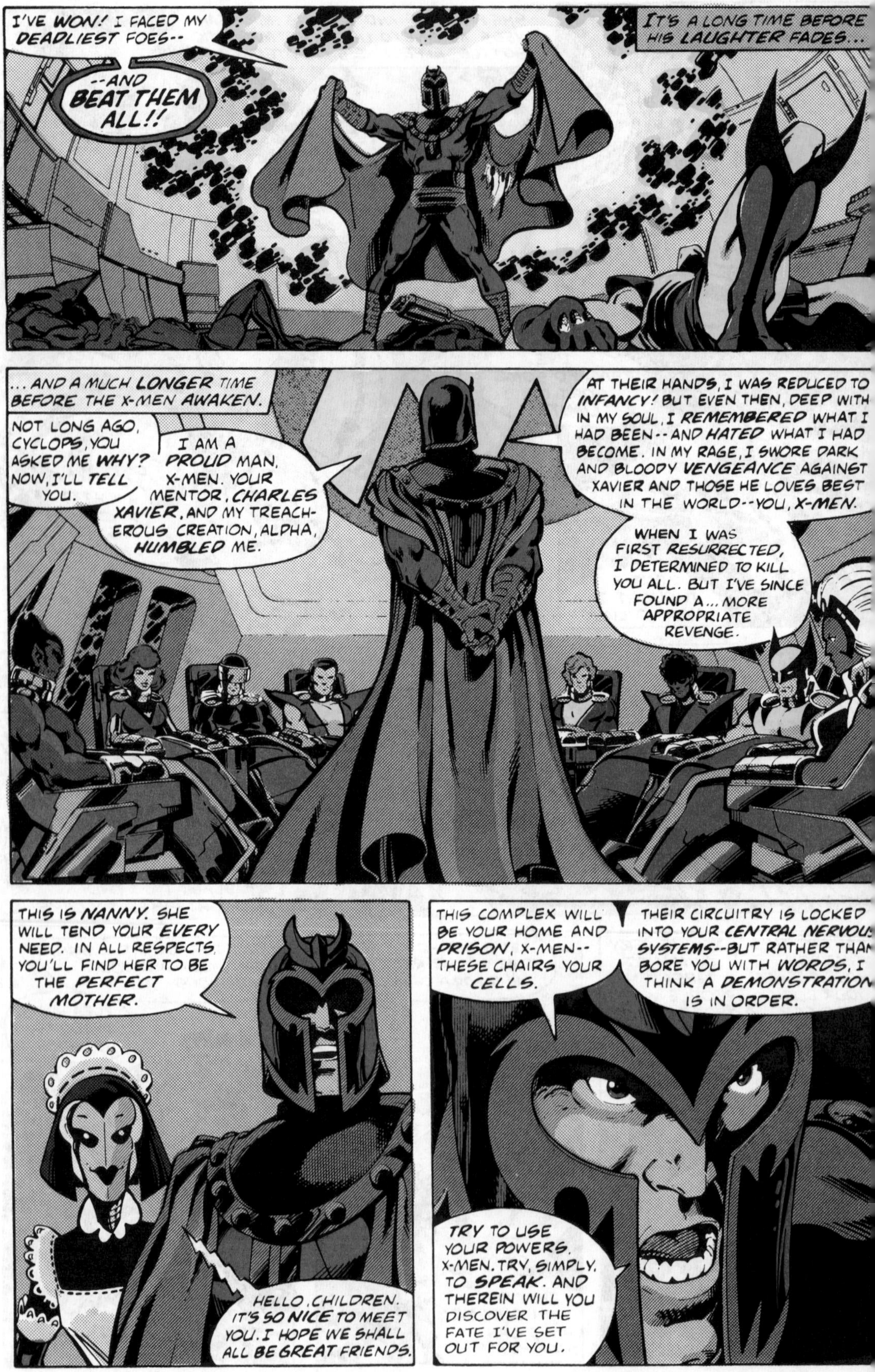
I'VE WON! I FACED MY DEADLIEST FOES--
--AND BEAT THEM ALL!!
IT'S A LONG TIME BEFORE HIS LAUGHTER FADES...
...AND A MUCH LONGER TIME BEFORE THE X-MEN AWAKEN.
NOT LONG AGO, CYCLOPS, YOU ASKED ME WHY? NOW, I'LL TELL YOU.
I AM A PROUD MAN, X-MEN. YOUR MENTOR, CHARLES XAVIER, AND MY TREACHEROUS CREATION, ALPHA, HUMBLED ME.
AT THEIR HANDS, I WAS REDUCED TO INFANCY! BUT EVEN THEN, DEEP WITHIN MY SOUL, I REMEMBERED WHAT I HAD BEEN--AND HATED WHAT I HAD BECOME. IN MY RAGE, I SWORE DARK AND BLOODY VENGEANCE AGAINST XAVIER AND THOSE HE LOVES BEST IN THE WORLD--YOU, X-MEN.
WHEN I WAS FIRST RESURRECTED, I DETERMINED TO KILL YOU ALL. BUT I'VE SINCE FOUND A... MORE APPROPRIATE REVENGE.
THIS IS NANNY. SHE WILL TEND YOUR EVERY NEED. IN ALL RESPECTS, YOU'LL FIND HER TO BE THE PERFECT MOTHER.
HELLO, CHILDREN. IT'S SO NICE TO MEET YOU. I HOPE WE SHALL ALL BE GREAT FRIENDS.
THIS COMPLEX WILL BE YOUR HOME AND PRISON, X-MEN-- THESE CHAIRS YOUR CELLS.
THEIR CIRCUITRY IS LOCKED INTO YOUR CENTRAL NERVOUS SYSTEMS--BUT RATHER THAN BORE YOU WITH WORDS, I THINK A DEMONSTRATION IS IN ORDER.
TRY TO USE YOUR POWERS, X-MEN. TRY, SIMPLY, TO SPEAK. AND THEREIN WILL YOU DISCOVER THE FATE I'VE SET OUT FOR YOU.

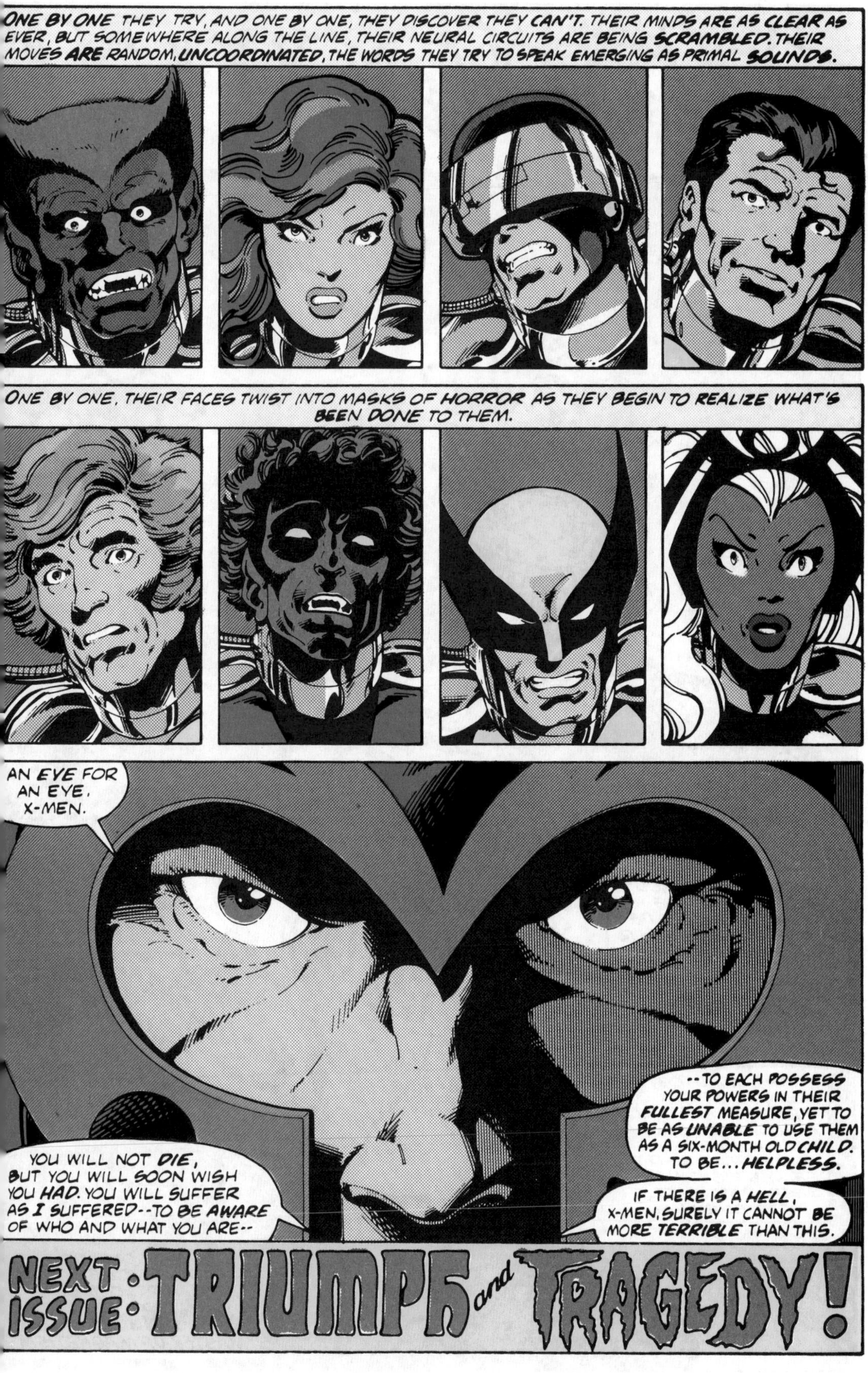
ONE BY ONE THEY TRY, AND ONE BY ONE, THEY DISCOVER THEY CAN'T. THEIR MINDS ARE AS CLEAR AS EVER, BUT SOMEWHERE ALONG THE LINE, THEIR NEURAL CIRCUITS ARE BEING SCRAMBLED. THEIR MOVES ARE RANDOM, UNCOORDINATED, THE WORDS THEY TRY TO SPEAK EMERGING AS PRIMAL SOUNDS.
ONE BY ONE, THEIR FACES TWIST INTO MASKS OF HORROR AS THEY BEGIN TO REALIZE WHAT'S BEEN DONE TO THEM.
AN EYE FOR AN EYE, X-MEN.
YOU WILL NOT DIE, BUT YOU WILL SOON WISH YOU HAD. YOU WILL SUFFER AS I SUFFERED--TO BE AWARE OF WHO AND WHAT YOU ARE--
--TO EACH POSSESS YOUR POWERS IN THEIR FULLEST MEASURE, YET TO BE AS UNABLE TO USE THEM AS A SIX-MONTH OLD CHILD. TO BE... HELPLESS.
IF THERE IS A HELL, X-MEN, SURELY IT CANNOT BE MORE TERRIBLE THAN THIS.
NEXT ISSUE: TRIUMPH and TRAGEDY!

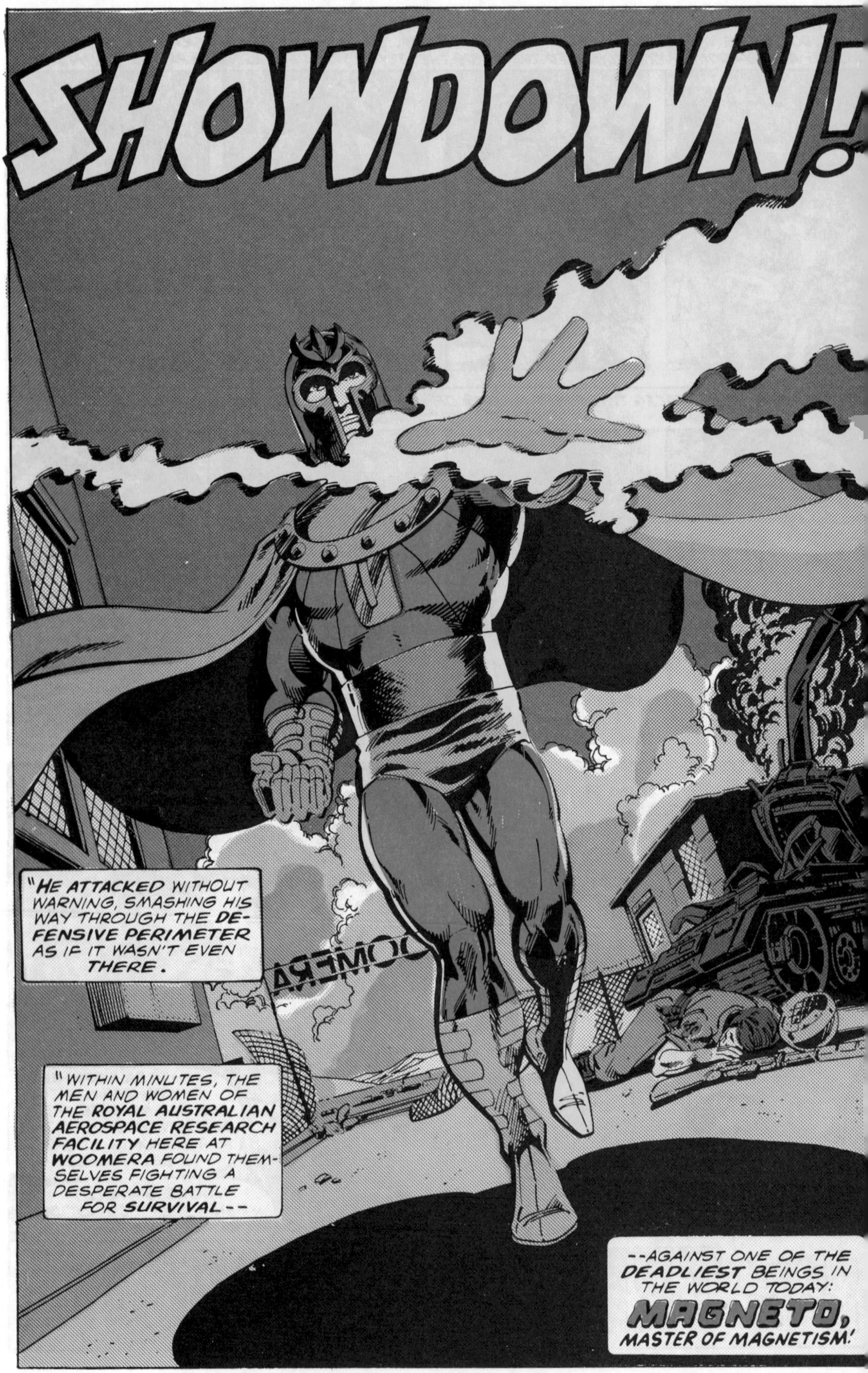
SHOWDOWN!
"HE ATTACKED WITHOUT WARNING, SMASHING HIS WAY THROUGH THE DEFENSIVE PERIMETER AS IF IT WASN'T EVEN THERE.
"WITHIN MINUTES, THE MEN AND WOMEN OF THE ROYAL AUSTRALIAN AEROSPACE RESEARCH FACILITY HERE AT WOOMERA FOUND THEMSELVES FIGHTING A DESPERATE BATTLE FOR SURVIVAL--
--AGAINST ONE OF THE DEADLIEST BEINGS IN THE WORLD TODAY: MAGNETO, MASTER OF MAGNETISM!'

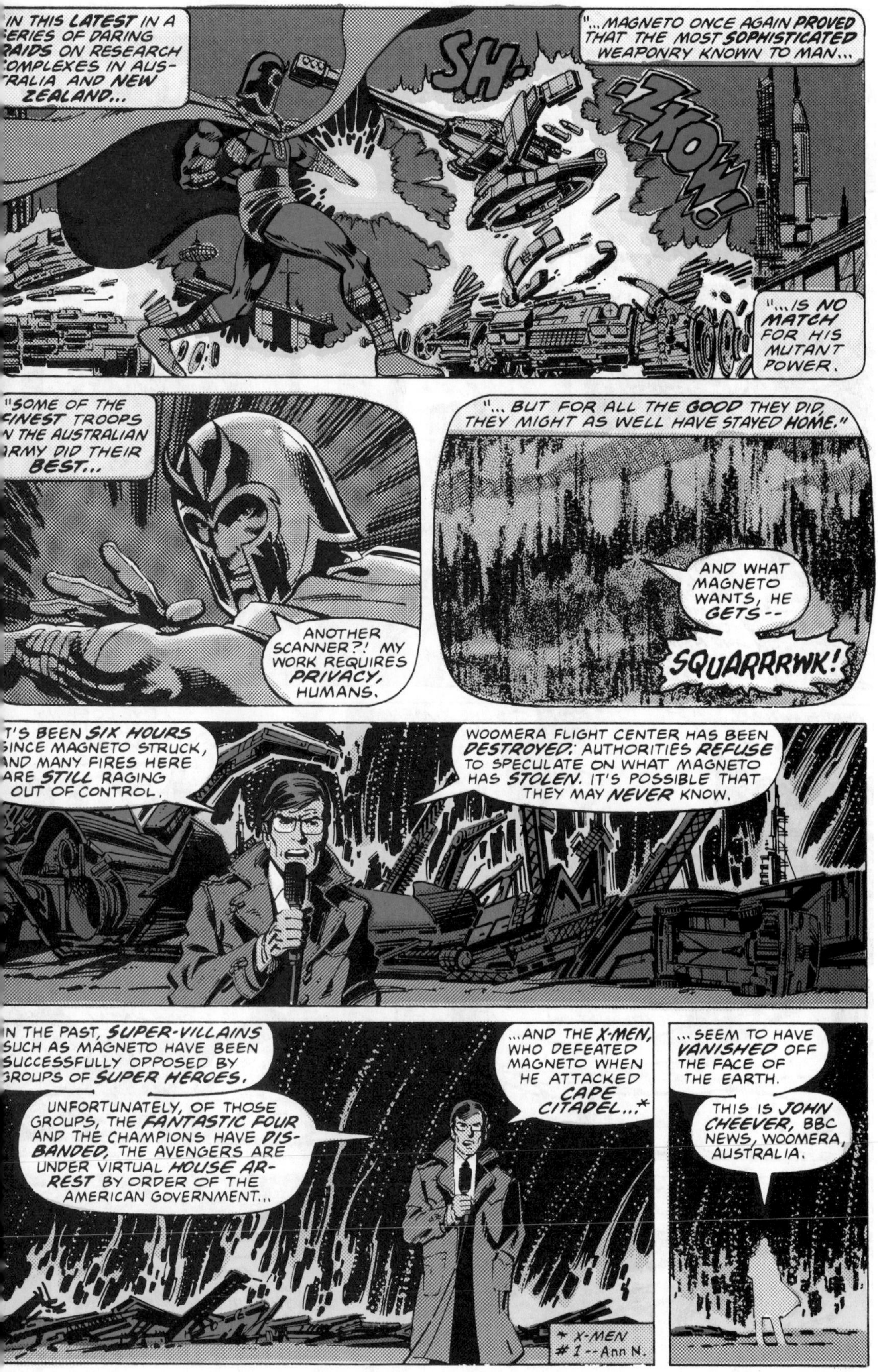
IN THIS LATEST IN A ERIES OF DARING RAIDS ON RESEARCH OMPLEXES IN AUS-RALIA AND NEW ZEALAND...
"...MAGNETO ONCE AGAIN PROVED THAT THE MOST SOPHISTICATED WEAPONRY KNOWN TO MAN...
SH-
-ZKOW!
"...IS NO MATCH FOR HIS MUTANT POWER.
"SOME OF THE FINEST TROOPS N THE AUSTRALIAN RMY DID THEIR BEST...
ANOTHER SCANNER?! MY WORK REQUIRES PRIVACY, HUMANS.
"...BUT FOR ALL THE GOOD THEY DID, THEY MIGHT AS WELL HAVE STAYED HOME."
AND WHAT MAGNETO WANTS, HE GETS--
SQUARRRWK!
T'S BEEN SIX HOURS INCE MAGNETO STRUCK, AND MANY FIRES HERE ARE STILL RAGING OUT OF CONTROL.
WOOMERA FLIGHT CENTER HAS BEEN DESTROYED: AUTHORITIES REFUSE TO SPECULATE ON WHAT MAGNETO HAS STOLEN. IT'S POSSIBLE THAT THEY MAY NEVER KNOW.
N THE PAST, SUPER-VILLAINS SUCH AS MAGNETO HAVE BEEN SUCCESSFULLY OPPOSED BY GROUPS OF SUPER HEROES.
UNFORTUNATELY, OF THOSE GROUPS, THE FANTASTIC FOUR AND THE CHAMPIONS HAVE DISBANDED, THE AVENGERS ARE UNDER VIRTUAL HOUSE ARREST BY ORDER OF THE AMERICAN GOVERNMENT...
...AND THE X-MEN, WHO DEFEATED MAGNETO WHEN HE ATTACKED CAPE CITADEL...*
* X-MEN #1 --Ann N.
...SEEM TO HAVE VANISHED OFF THE FACE OF THE EARTH.
THIS IS JOHN CHEEVER, BBC NEWS, WOOMERA, AUSTRALIA.

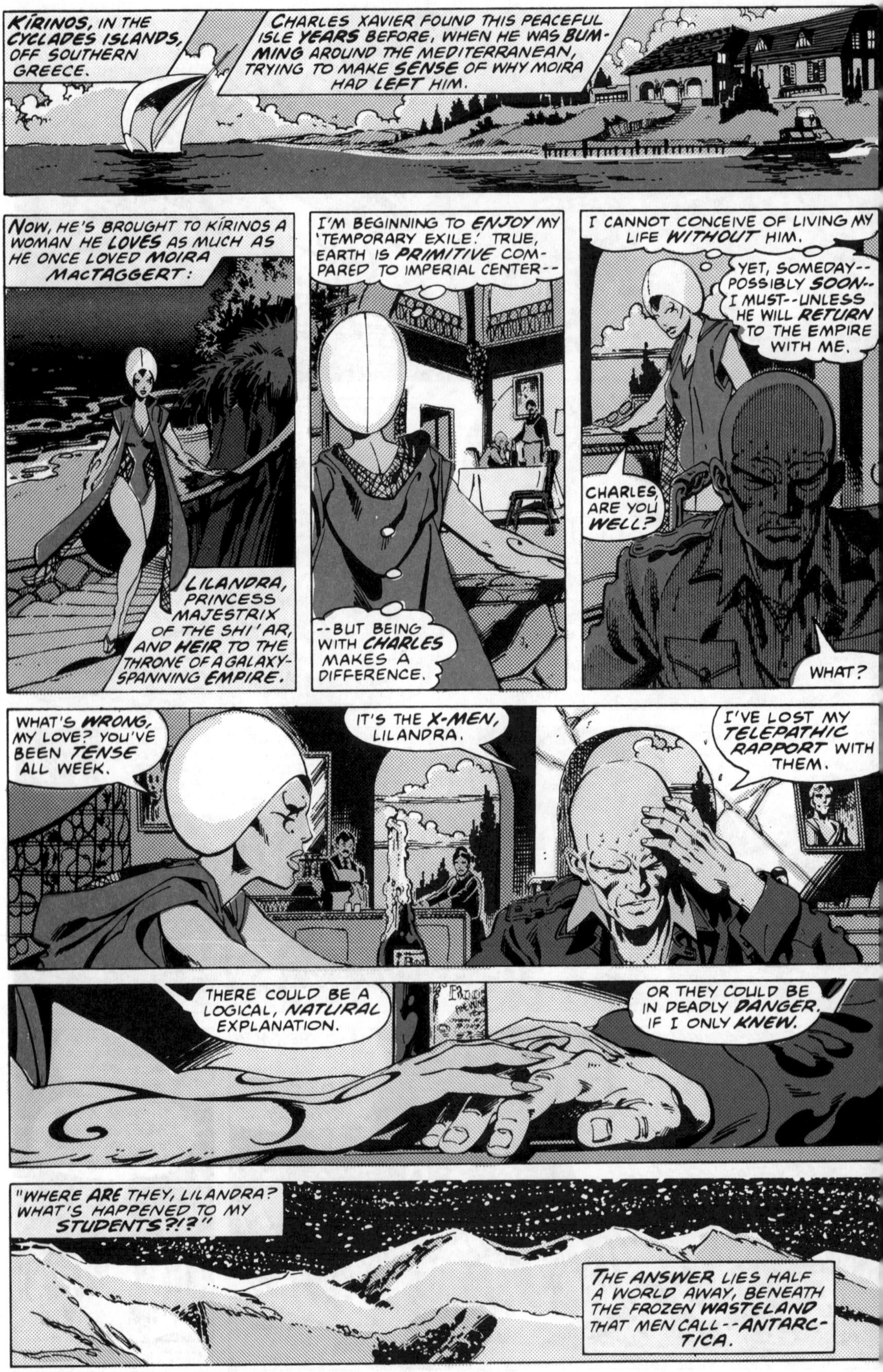
KIRINOS, IN THE CYCLADES ISLANDS, OFF SOUTHERN GREECE.
CHARLES XAVIER FOUND THIS PEACEFUL ISLE YEARS BEFORE, WHEN HE WAS BUMMING AROUND THE MEDITERRANEAN, TRYING TO MAKE SENSE OF WHY MOIRA HAD LEFT HIM.
NOW, HE'S BROUGHT TO KIRINOS A WOMAN HE LOVES AS MUCH AS HE ONCE LOVED MOIRA MacTAGGERT:
LILANDRA, PRINCESS MAJESTRIX OF THE SHI'AR, AND HEIR TO THE THRONE OF A GALAXY-SPANNING EMPIRE.
I'M BEGINNING TO ENJOY MY 'TEMPORARY EXILE.' TRUE, EARTH IS PRIMITIVE COMPARED TO IMPERIAL CENTER--
--BUT BEING WITH CHARLES MAKES A DIFFERENCE.
I CANNOT CONCEIVE OF LIVING MY LIFE WITHOUT HIM.
YET, SOMEDAY--POSSIBLY SOON--I MUST--UNLESS HE WILL RETURN TO THE EMPIRE WITH ME.
CHARLES, ARE YOU WELL?
WHAT?
WHAT'S WRONG, MY LOVE? YOU'VE BEEN TENSE ALL WEEK.
IT'S THE X-MEN, LILANDRA.
I'VE LOST MY TELEPATHIC RAPPORT WITH THEM.
THERE COULD BE A LOGICAL, NATURAL EXPLANATION.
OR THEY COULD BE IN DEADLY DANGER. IF I ONLY KNEW.
"WHERE ARE THEY, LILANDRA? WHAT'S HAPPENED TO MY STUDENTS?!?"
THE ANSWER LIES HALF A WORLD AWAY, BENEATH THE FROZEN WASTELAND THAT MEN CALL--ANTARCTICA.

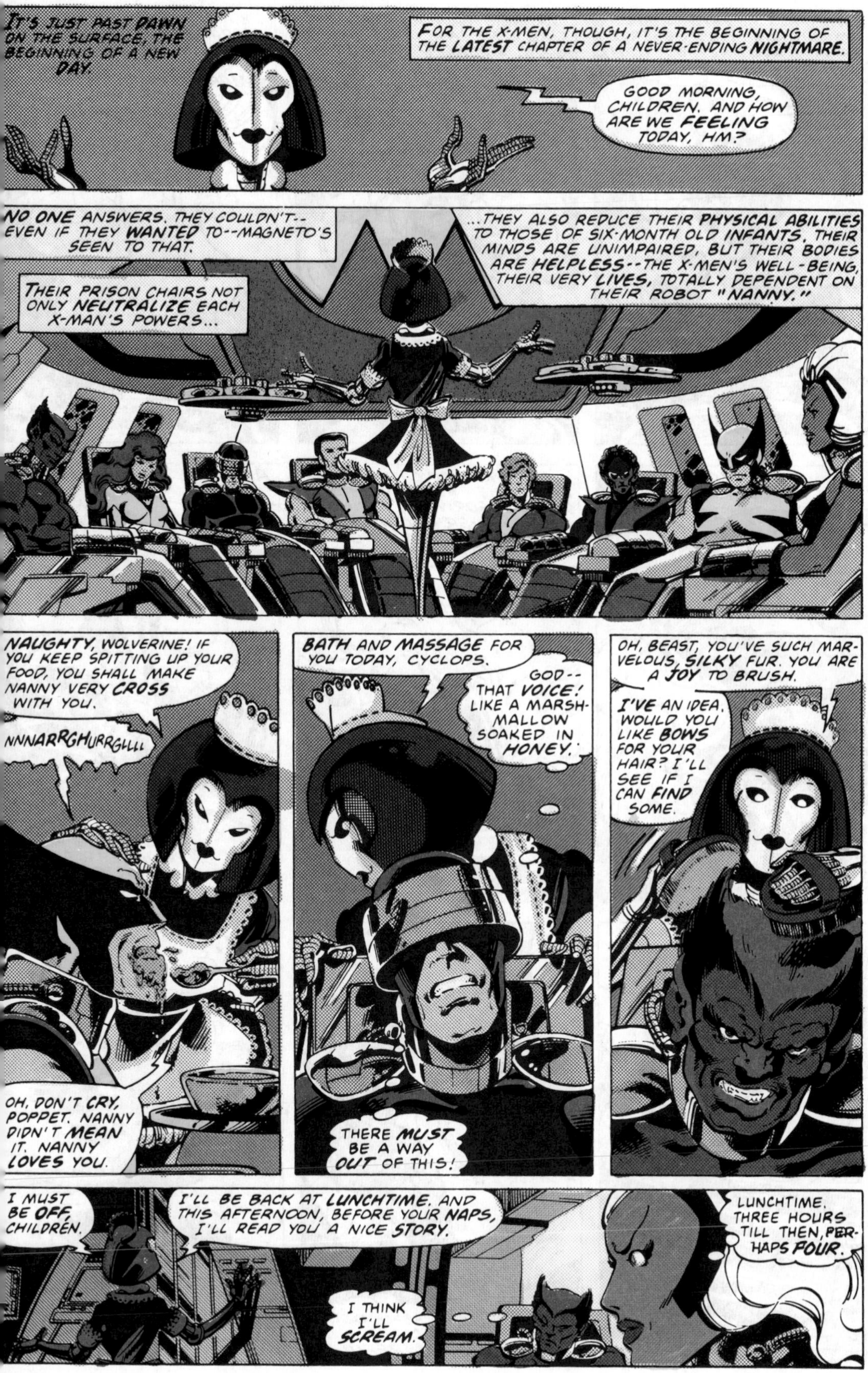
IT'S JUST PAST DAWN ON THE SURFACE, THE BEGINNING OF A NEW DAY.
FOR THE X-MEN, THOUGH, IT'S THE BEGINNING OF THE LATEST CHAPTER OF A NEVER-ENDING NIGHTMARE.
GOOD MORNING, CHILDREN. AND HOW ARE WE FEELING TODAY, HM?
NO ONE ANSWERS. THEY COULDN'T-- EVEN IF THEY WANTED TO--MAGNETO'S SEEN TO THAT.
THEIR PRISON CHAIRS NOT ONLY NEUTRALIZE EACH X-MAN'S POWERS...
...THEY ALSO REDUCE THEIR PHYSICAL ABILITIES TO THOSE OF SIX-MONTH OLD INFANTS. THEIR MINDS ARE UNIMPAIRED, BUT THEIR BODIES ARE HELPLESS--THE X-MEN'S WELL-BEING, THEIR VERY LIVES, TOTALLY DEPENDENT ON THEIR ROBOT "NANNY."
NAUGHTY, WOLVERINE! IF YOU KEEP SPITTING UP YOUR FOOD, YOU SHALL MAKE NANNY VERY CROSS WITH YOU.
NNNARRGHURRGLLLL
OH, DON'T CRY, POPPET. NANNY DIDN'T MEAN IT. NANNY LOVES YOU.
BATH AND MASSAGE FOR YOU TODAY, CYCLOPS.
GOD-- THAT VOICE! LIKE A MARSH-MALLOW SOAKED IN HONEY.
THERE MUST BE A WAY OUT OF THIS!
OH, BEAST, YOU'VE SUCH MAR-VELOUS, SILKY FUR. YOU ARE A JOY TO BRUSH.
I'VE AN IDEA. WOULD YOU LIKE BOWS FOR YOUR HAIR? I'LL SEE IF I CAN FIND SOME.
I MUST BE OFF, CHILDREN.
I'LL BE BACK AT LUNCHTIME. AND THIS AFTERNOON, BEFORE YOUR NAPS, I'LL READ YOU A NICE STORY.
LUNCHTIME. THREE HOURS TILL THEN, PER-HAPS FOUR.
I THINK I'LL SCREAM.

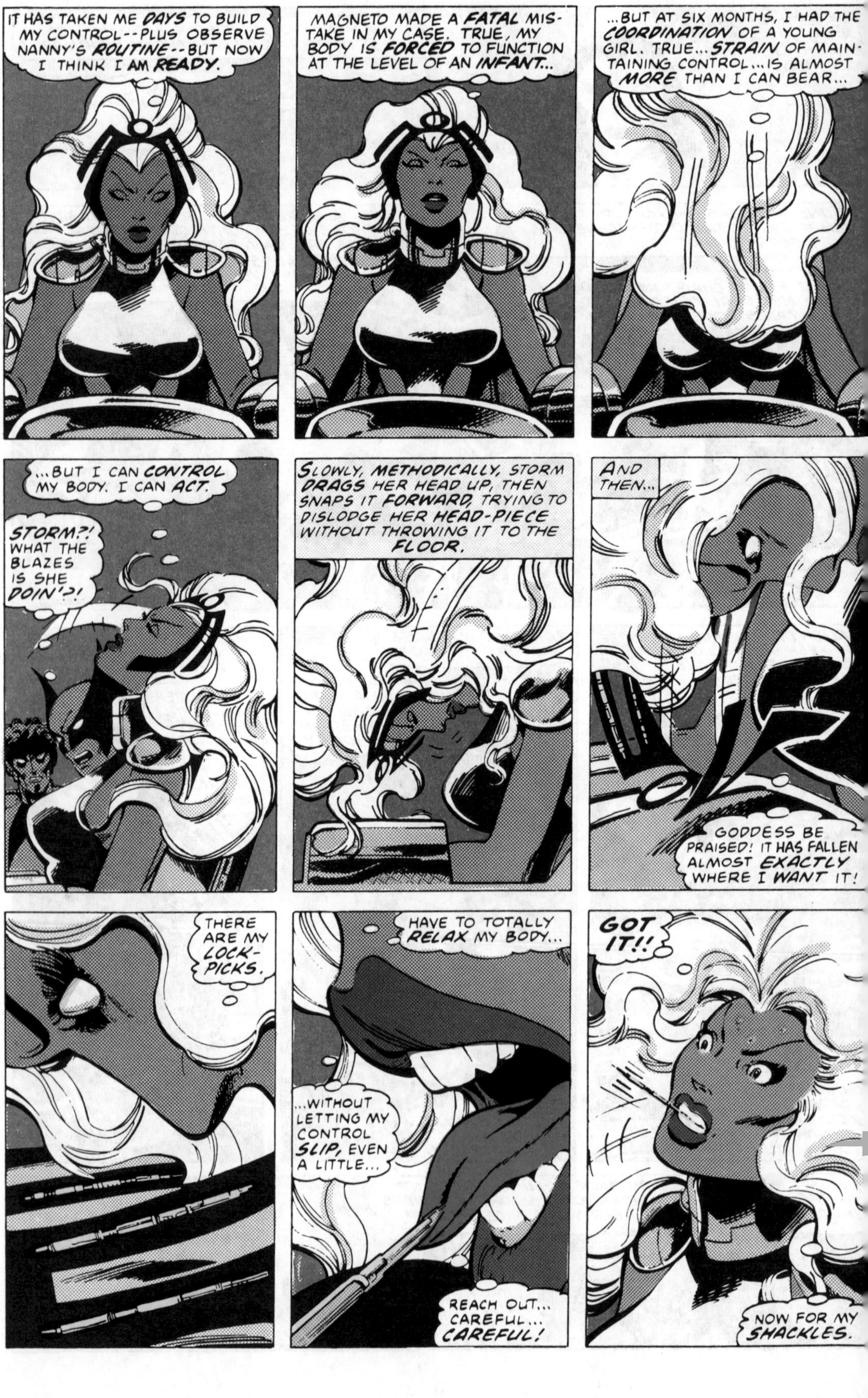
IT HAS TAKEN ME DAYS TO BUILD MY CONTROL--PLUS OBSERVE NANNY'S ROUTINE--BUT NOW I THINK I AM READY.
MAGNETO MADE A FATAL MISTAKE IN MY CASE. TRUE, MY BODY IS FORCED TO FUNCTION AT THE LEVEL OF AN INFANT...
...BUT AT SIX MONTHS, I HAD THE COORDINATION OF A YOUNG GIRL. TRUE... STRAIN OF MAINTAINING CONTROL... IS ALMOST MORE THAN I CAN BEAR...
...BUT I CAN CONTROL MY BODY. I CAN ACT.
STORM?! WHAT THE BLAZES IS SHE DOIN'?!
SLOWLY, METHODICALLY, STORM DRAGS HER HEAD UP, THEN SNAPS IT FORWARD, TRYING TO DISLODGE HER HEAD-PIECE WITHOUT THROWING IT TO THE FLOOR.
AND THEN...
GODDESS BE PRAISED! IT HAS FALLEN ALMOST EXACTLY WHERE I WANT IT!
THERE ARE MY LOCK-PICKS.
HAVE TO TOTALLY RELAX MY BODY...
...WITHOUT LETTING MY CONTROL SLIP, EVEN A LITTLE...
REACH OUT... CAREFUL... CAREFUL!
GOT IT!!
NOW FOR MY SHACKLES.

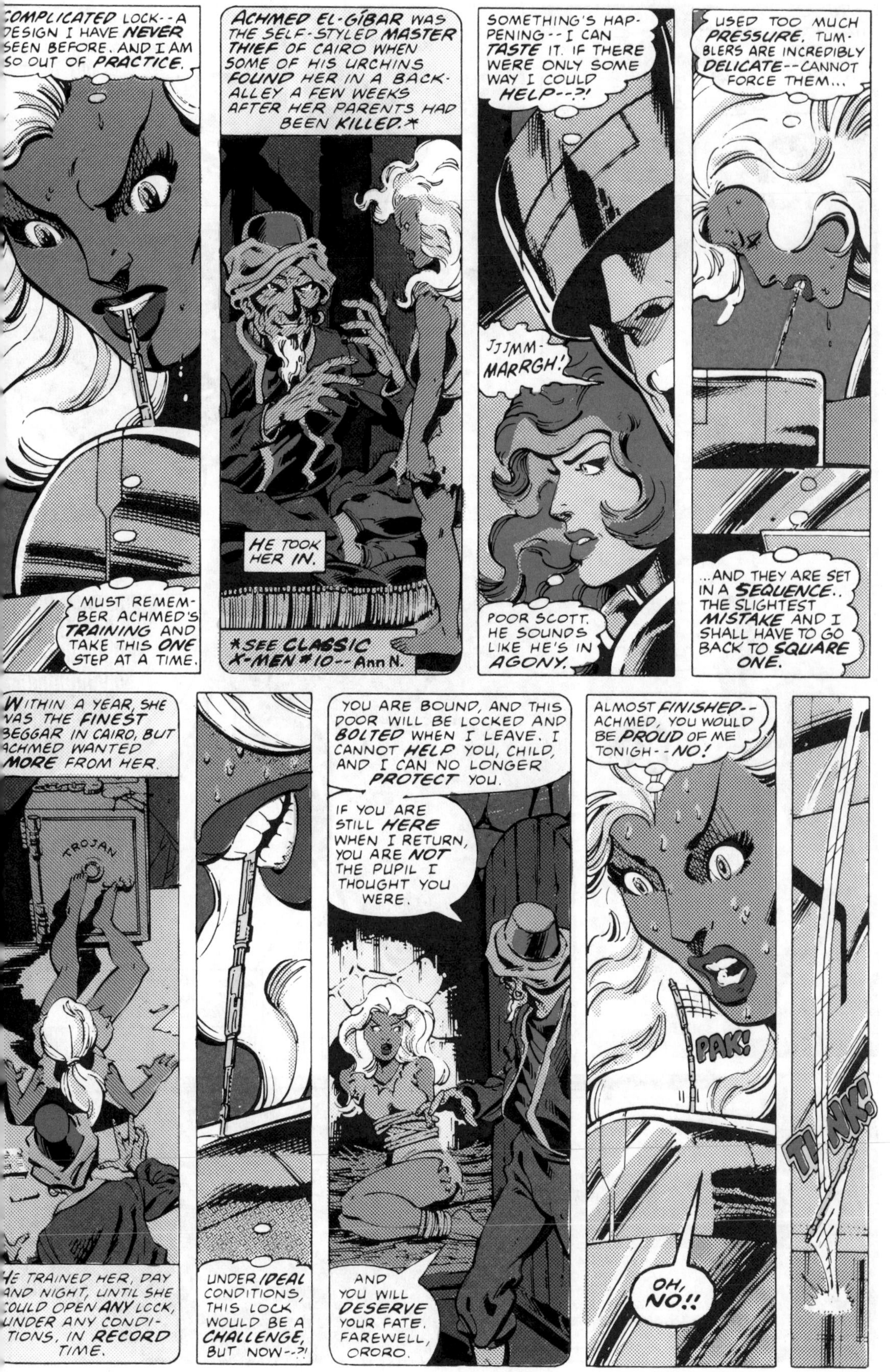

COMPLICATED LOCK--A DESIGN I HAVE NEVER SEEN BEFORE. AND I AM SO OUT OF PRACTICE.
MUST REMEMBER ACHMED'S TRAINING AND TAKE THIS ONE STEP AT A TIME.
ACHMED EL-GIBAR WAS THE SELF-STYLED MASTER THIEF OF CAIRO WHEN SOME OF HIS URCHINS FOUND HER IN A BACK-ALLEY A FEW WEEKS AFTER HER PARENTS HAD BEEN KILLED.*
HE TOOK HER IN.
*SEE CLASSIC X-MEN #10--Ann N.
SOMETHING'S HAPPENING--I CAN TASTE IT. IF THERE WERE ONLY SOME WAY I COULD HELP--?!
JJJMM-MARRGH!
POOR SCOTT. HE SOUNDS LIKE HE'S IN AGONY.
USED TOO MUCH PRESSURE. TUMBLERS ARE INCREDIBLY DELICATE--CANNOT FORCE THEM...
...AND THEY ARE SET IN A SEQUENCE.. THE SLIGHTEST MISTAKE AND I SHALL HAVE TO GO BACK TO SQUARE ONE.
WITHIN A YEAR, SHE WAS THE FINEST BEGGAR IN CAIRO, BUT ACHMED WANTED MORE FROM HER.
TROJAN
HE TRAINED HER, DAY AND NIGHT, UNTIL SHE COULD OPEN ANY LOCK, UNDER ANY CONDITIONS, IN RECORD TIME.
UNDER IDEAL CONDITIONS, THIS LOCK WOULD BE A CHALLENGE, BUT NOW--?!
YOU ARE BOUND, AND THIS DOOR WILL BE LOCKED AND BOLTED WHEN I LEAVE. I CANNOT HELP YOU, CHILD, AND I CAN NO LONGER PROTECT YOU.
IF YOU ARE STILL HERE WHEN I RETURN, YOU ARE NOT THE PUPIL I THOUGHT YOU WERE.
AND YOU WILL DESERVE YOUR FATE. FAREWELL, ORORO.
ALMOST FINISHED--ACHMED, YOU WOULD BE PROUD OF ME TONIGH--NO!
PAK!
OH, NO!!
TINK!

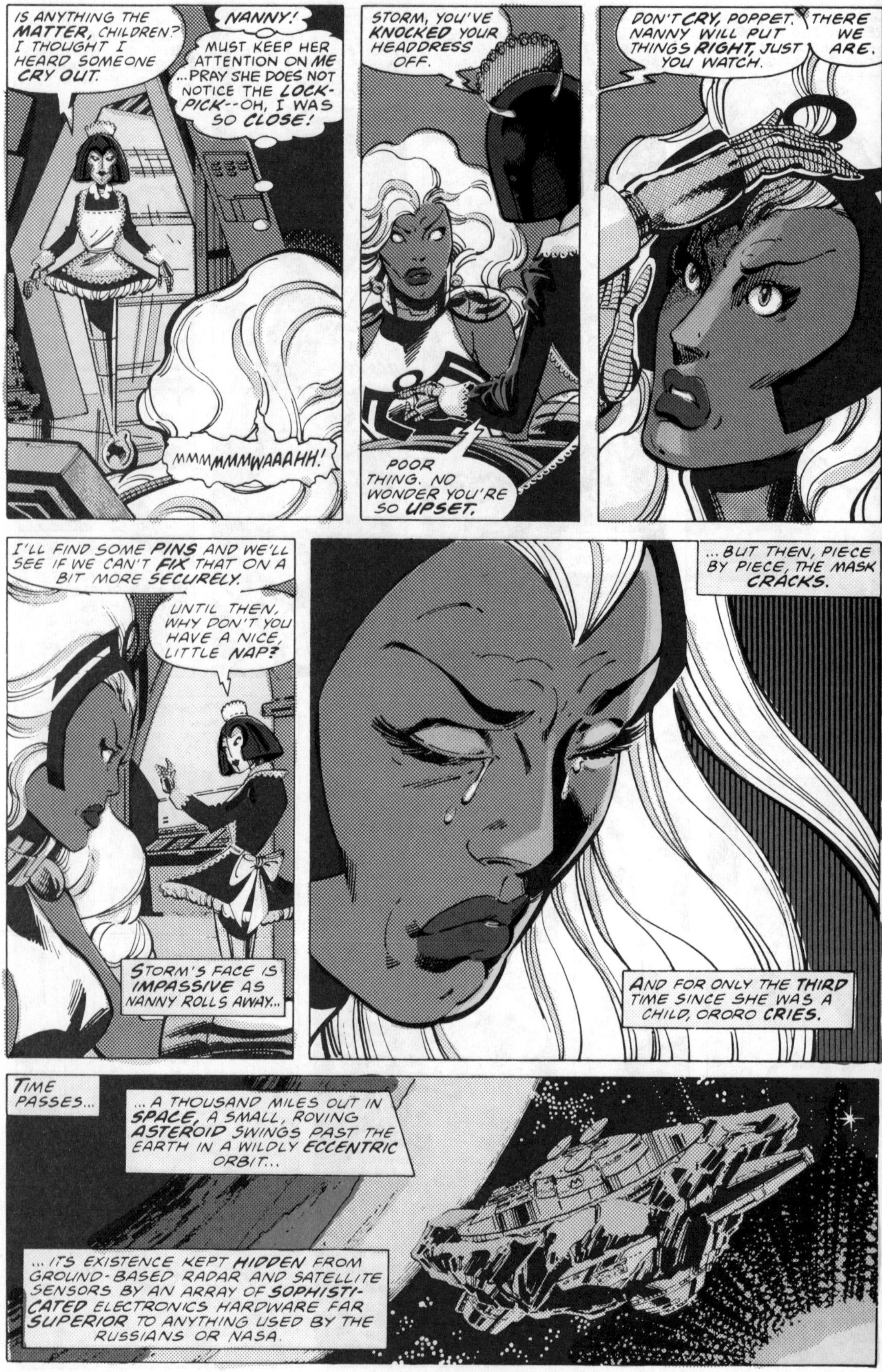
IS ANYTHING THE MATTER, CHILDREN? I THOUGHT I HEARD SOMEONE CRY OUT.
NANNY!
MUST KEEP HER ATTENTION ON ME ...PRAY SHE DOES NOT NOTICE THE LOCK-PICK--OH, I WAS SO CLOSE!
MMMMMMWAAAHH!
STORM, YOU'VE KNOCKED YOUR HEADDRESS OFF.
POOR THING. NO WONDER YOU'RE SO UPSET.
DON'T CRY, POPPET. NANNY WILL PUT THINGS RIGHT, JUST YOU WATCH.
THERE WE ARE.
I'LL FIND SOME PINS AND WE'LL SEE IF WE CAN'T FIX THAT ON A BIT MORE SECURELY.
UNTIL THEN, WHY DON'T YOU HAVE A NICE, LITTLE NAP?
STORM'S FACE IS IMPASSIVE AS NANNY ROLLS AWAY...
...BUT THEN, PIECE BY PIECE, THE MASK CRACKS.
AND FOR ONLY THE THIRD TIME SINCE SHE WAS A CHILD, ORORO CRIES.
TIME PASSES...
...A THOUSAND MILES OUT IN SPACE, A SMALL, ROVING ASTEROID SWINGS PAST THE EARTH IN A WILDLY ECCENTRIC ORBIT...
...ITS EXISTENCE KEPT HIDDEN FROM GROUND-BASED RADAR AND SATELLITE SENSORS BY AN ARRAY OF SOPHISTICATED ELECTRONICS HARDWARE FAR SUPERIOR TO ANYTHING USED BY THE RUSSIANS OR NASA.

AND YOU WILL NEVER KNOW THEIR FATE -- UNLESS I WILL IT.

PING!

SINCE MY RESURRECTION, I HAVE BEEN SUBTLY ALTERING THE MAGNETIC FIELD OF THE EARTH -- GENERATING AN IMPENETRABLE WALL OF PSYCHIC STATIC TO INHIBIT ANY AND ALL LONG-RANGE TELEPATHIC BROADCASTS. YOUR PSI-LINK WITH YOUR PROTÉGÉS, OLD FRIEND, HAS BEEN FOREVER SHATTERED.

STILL, FOR ALL OF THAT, THEY ARE NOBLE COURAGEOUS FOES -- YOU TAUGHT THEM WELL -- I FIND MYSELF WISHING THINGS HAD TURNED OUT DIFFERENTLY, AND THAT WE HAD BEEN ALLIES. HMMM--?!

SOME SORT OF MINOR SYSTEMS MALFUNCTION AT MY ANTARCTIC COMPLEX. ODD -- WHY HASN'T NANNY REPAIRED IT?

IT COULD BE NOTHING, BUT IT'S BEST TO TAKE NO CHANCES. THAT BASE IS STILL VITAL TO ME...

...AND MUCH OF THE DATA IN ITS COMPUTER MEMORY BANK IS IRREPLACEABLE.

IN THE PAST, MY POWERS WERE SO DILUTED BY MY DEFEATS...

...THAT I NO LONGER HAD THE STRENGTH EVEN TO RETURN TO MY ASTEROID BASE, LET ALONE REBUILD IT. *

* AFTER ITS DESTRUCTION IN X-MEN #5--Ann N

THANKS TO ERIC THE RED, THAT HAS CHANGED. I AM STRONG BEYOND BELIEF, MY POWER UNTAINTED BY TIME OR WASTED BATTLES.

ONCE I'VE FINISHED WORK ON MY ASTEROID, I'LL HAVE AN IMPREGNABLE FORTRESS FROM WHICH I WILL TEACH ALL MANKIND THAT MAGNETO IS TRULY MASTER OF THE WORLD!

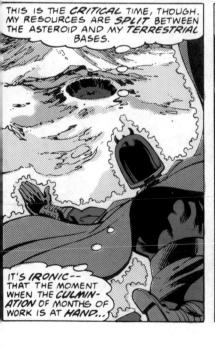

THIS IS THE CRITICAL TIME, THOUGH. MY RESOURCES ARE SPLIT BETWEEN THE ASTEROID AND MY TERRESTRIAL BASES.

IT'S IRONIC -- THAT THE MOMENT WHEN THE CULMINATION OF MONTHS OF WORK IS AT HAND...

...SHOULD ALSO BE WHEN I AM MOST VULNERABLE TO ATTACK.

THIS SUDDEN MALFUNCTION -- COULD IT HAVE BEEN CAUSED BY THE X-MEN?!

IMPOSSIBLE! THERE ARE A SCORE OF ALARM SYSTEMS IN THE COMPLEX -- ALL SET TO GO OFF IF THOSE CURSED MUTANTS BROKE FREE.

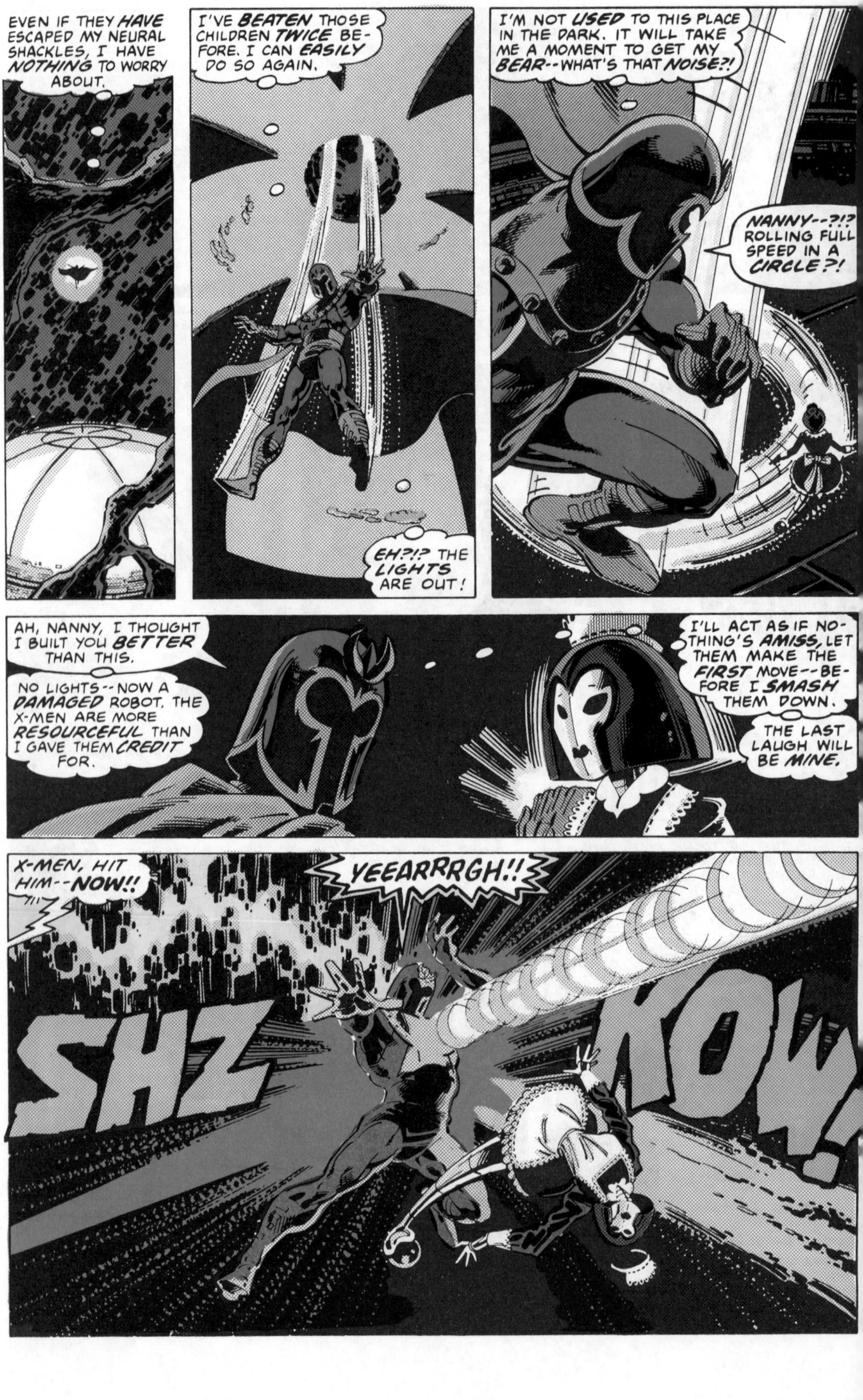
EVEN IF THEY HAVE ESCAPED MY NEURAL SHACKLES, I HAVE NOTHING TO WORRY ABOUT.
I'VE BEATEN THOSE CHILDREN TWICE BEFORE. I CAN EASILY DO SO AGAIN.
EH?!? THE LIGHTS ARE OUT!
I'M NOT USED TO THIS PLACE IN THE DARK. IT WILL TAKE ME A MOMENT TO GET MY BEAR--WHAT'S THAT NOISE?!
NANNY--?!? ROLLING FULL SPEED IN A CIRCLE?!
AH, NANNY, I THOUGHT I BUILT YOU BETTER THAN THIS.
NO LIGHTS--NOW A DAMAGED ROBOT. THE X-MEN ARE MORE RESOURCEFUL THAN I GAVE THEM CREDIT FOR.
I'LL ACT AS IF NOTHING'S AMISS, LET THEM MAKE THE FIRST MOVE--BEFORE I SMASH THEM DOWN.
THE LAST LAUGH WILL BE MINE.
X-MEN, HIT HIM--NOW!!
YEEARRRGH!!
SHZ
KOW!

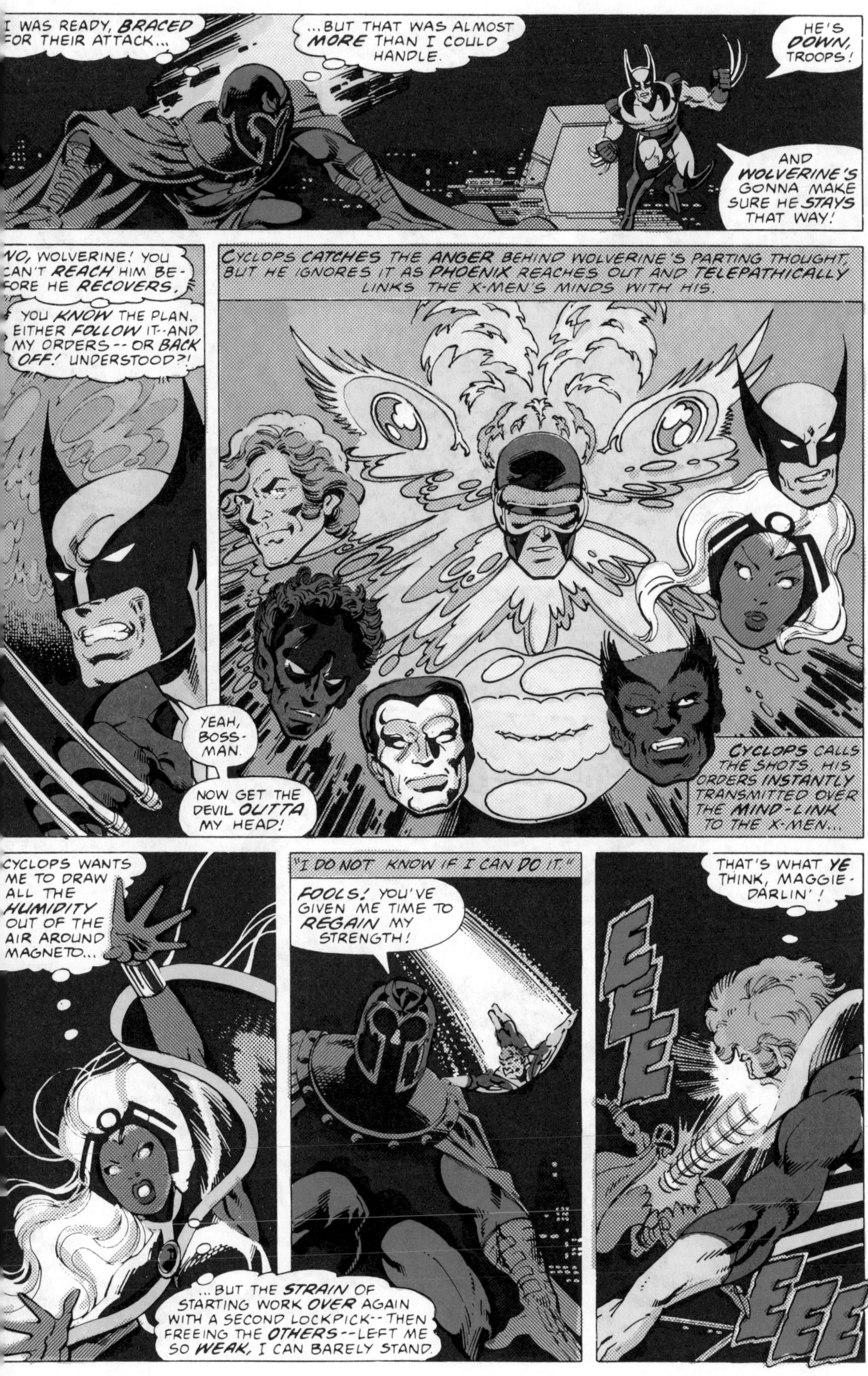

I WAS READY, BRACED FOR THEIR ATTACK...
...BUT THAT WAS ALMOST MORE THAN I COULD HANDLE.
HE'S DOWN, TROOPS!
AND WOLVERINE'S GONNA MAKE SURE HE STAYS THAT WAY!
NO, WOLVERINE! YOU CAN'T REACH HIM BEFORE HE RECOVERS.
YOU KNOW THE PLAN. EITHER FOLLOW IT--AND MY ORDERS--OR BACK OFF! UNDERSTOOD?!
YEAH, BOSS-MAN.
NOW GET THE DEVIL OUTTA MY HEAD!
CYCLOPS CATCHES THE ANGER BEHIND WOLVERINE'S PARTING THOUGHT, BUT HE IGNORES IT AS PHOENIX REACHES OUT AND TELEPATHICALLY LINKS THE X-MEN'S MINDS WITH HIS.
CYCLOPS CALLS THE SHOTS, HIS ORDERS INSTANTLY TRANSMITTED OVER THE MIND-LINK TO THE X-MEN...
CYCLOPS WANTS ME TO DRAW ALL THE HUMIDITY OUT OF THE AIR AROUND MAGNETO...
"I DO NOT KNOW IF I CAN DO IT."
FOOLS! YOU'VE GIVEN ME TIME TO REGAIN MY STRENGTH!
...BUT THE STRAIN OF STARTING WORK OVER AGAIN WITH A SECOND LOCKPICK--THEN FREEING THE OTHERS--LEFT ME SO WEAK, I CAN BARELY STAND.
THAT'S WHAT YE THINK, MAGGIE-DARLIN'!
EEE
EEE

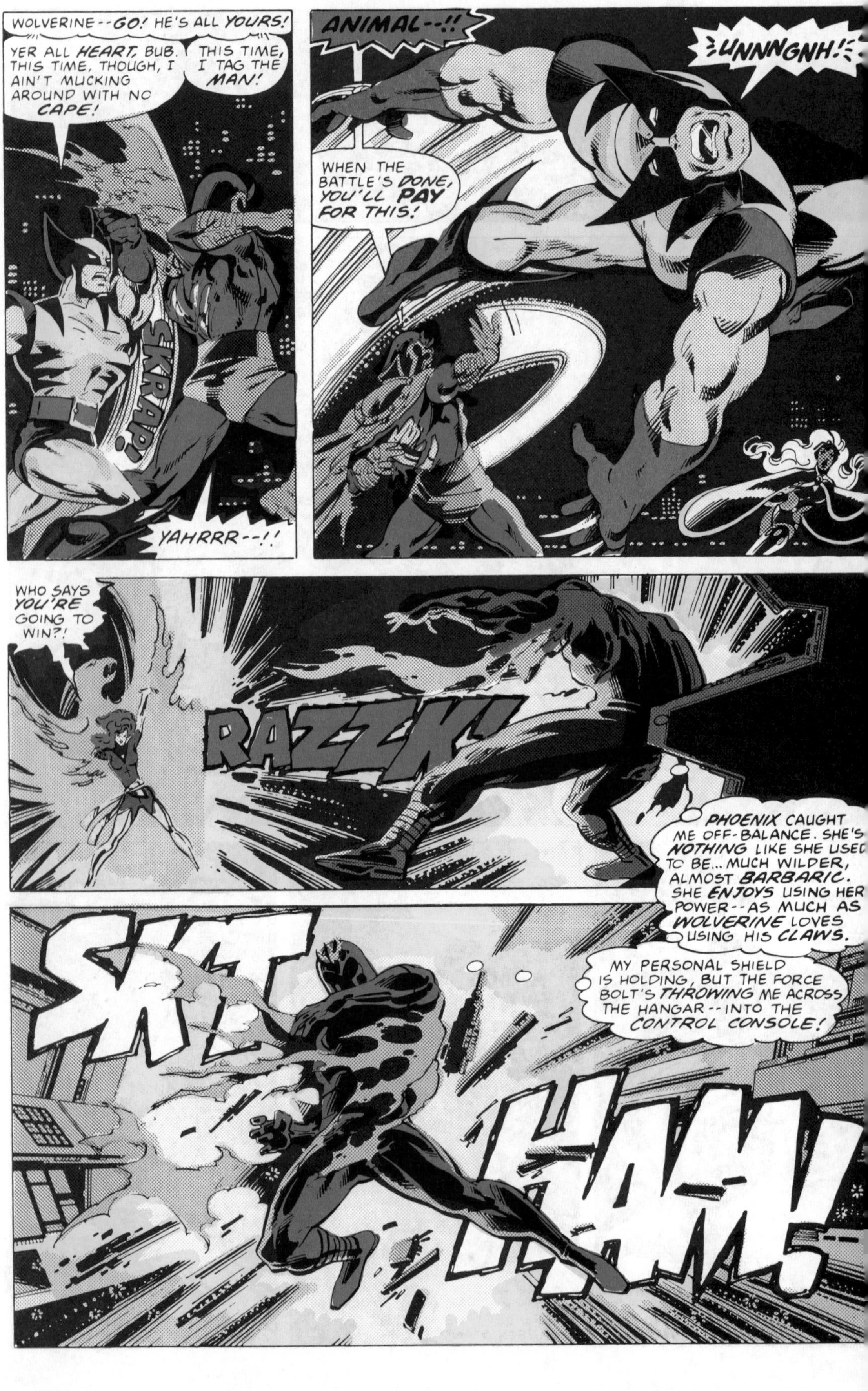
WOLVERINE--GO! HE'S ALL YOURS!
YER ALL HEART, BUB. THIS TIME, THOUGH, I AIN'T MUCKING AROUND WITH NO CAPE!
THIS TIME, I TAG THE MAN!
SKRAP!
YAHRRR--!!
ANIMAL--!!
UNNNGNH!
WHEN THE BATTLE'S DONE, YOU'LL PAY FOR THIS!
WHO SAYS YOU'RE GOING TO WIN?!
RAZZK!
PHOENIX CAUGHT ME OFF-BALANCE. SHE'S NOTHING LIKE SHE USED TO BE... MUCH WILDER, ALMOST BARBARIC. SHE ENJOYS USING HER POWER--AS MUCH AS WOLVERINE LOVES USING HIS CLAWS.
MY PERSONAL SHIELD IS HOLDING, BUT THE FORCE BOLT'S THROWING ME ACROSS THE HANGAR--INTO THE CONTROL CONSOLE!

THEY'RE USING *HIT-AND-RUN* STRATEGY...GIVING ME NO OPPORTUNITY TO *STRIKE BACK.*

LORD, IT'S *HOT* ALL OF A SUDDEN.

I'M *SWEATING* LIKE A PIG. IS THIS PART OF THEIR *PLAN?!*

YOU'VE FACED THE *OTHER* X-MEN, VILLAIN. NOW IT IS *MY TURN.*

COLOSSUS!

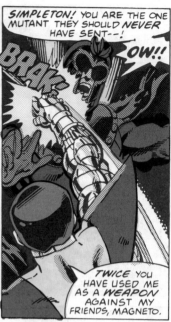

SIMPLETON! YOU ARE THE ONE MUTANT THEY SHOULD *NEVER* HAVE SENT--!

BRAK

OW!!

TWICE YOU HAVE USED ME AS A *WEAPON* AGAINST MY FRIENDS, MAGNETO.

IT WILL *NOT* HAPPEN AGAIN!

I MUST NOT ALLOW HIM EVEN A *MOMENT'S* PEACE, OR HIS MAGNETIC POWERS WILL GIVE HIM *ABSOLUTE* CONTROL OVER MY *ARMORED* FORM.

I MUST KEEP *HAMMERING* AT HIM UNTIL HE *DROPS.*

PETER--COLOSSUS--OF ALL THE *STUPID* STUNTS! I TOLD YOU TO STAY ON THE SIDELINES IN *HUMAN* FORM--WHY THE BLAZES DIDN'T YOU *LISTEN?!*

AT LEAST HE'S HOLD- ING HIS *OWN* SO FAR--THAT'S *SOMETHING.*

HANK, NIGHT- CRAWLER-- GIVE COLOSSUS A *HAND!*

WE'RE WAY *AHEAD* OF YOU, CYKE.

THERE MUST BE A BETTER WAY!

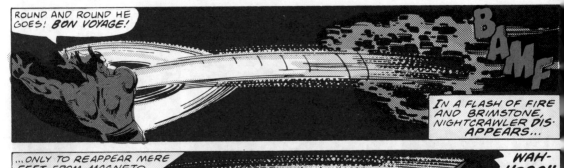

ROUND AND ROUND HE GOES! *BON VOYAGE!*

BAMF

IN A FLASH OF FIRE AND BRIMSTONE, NIGHTCRAWLER DISAPPEARS...

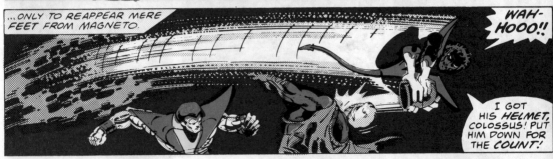

...ONLY TO REAPPEAR MERE FEET FROM MAGNETO.

WAH-HOOO!!

I GOT HIS *HELMET,* COLOSSUS! PUT HIM DOWN FOR THE *COUNT!*

COMRADE, IT WILL BE *MY PLEASURE!*

UNGLAUBLICH! THAT PUNCH WOULD HAVE TORN A NORMAL MAN'S *HEAD* OFF--YET MAGNETO'S STILL ON HIS *FEET.*

CYCLOPS HAD THE *RIGHT* IDEA--WE KEEP MAGNETO *OCCUPIED* WITH HIT-AND-RUN ATTACKS WHILE STORM SUBTLY *DEHYDRATES--* EH?!?

MEIN GOTT.

CYCLOPS-- *ALL OF YOU!* THE ROOF DOME--IT'S *OPENING!*

KROM!

THAT IS *MOLTEN ROCK.* WHAT'S IT DOING HE--?!

VILLAIN, WHAT HAVE YOU *DONE?!*

IF WE'RE *DOOMED,* X-MAN, THE BLAME IS *YOURS!*

PHOENIX'S BLAST *DESTROYED* THE MAIN CONTROL CONSOLE. SYSTEMS ALL OVER THE COMPLEX ARE RUNNING *WILD*--AND YOU CAN'T DO A THING TO *STOP THEM!*

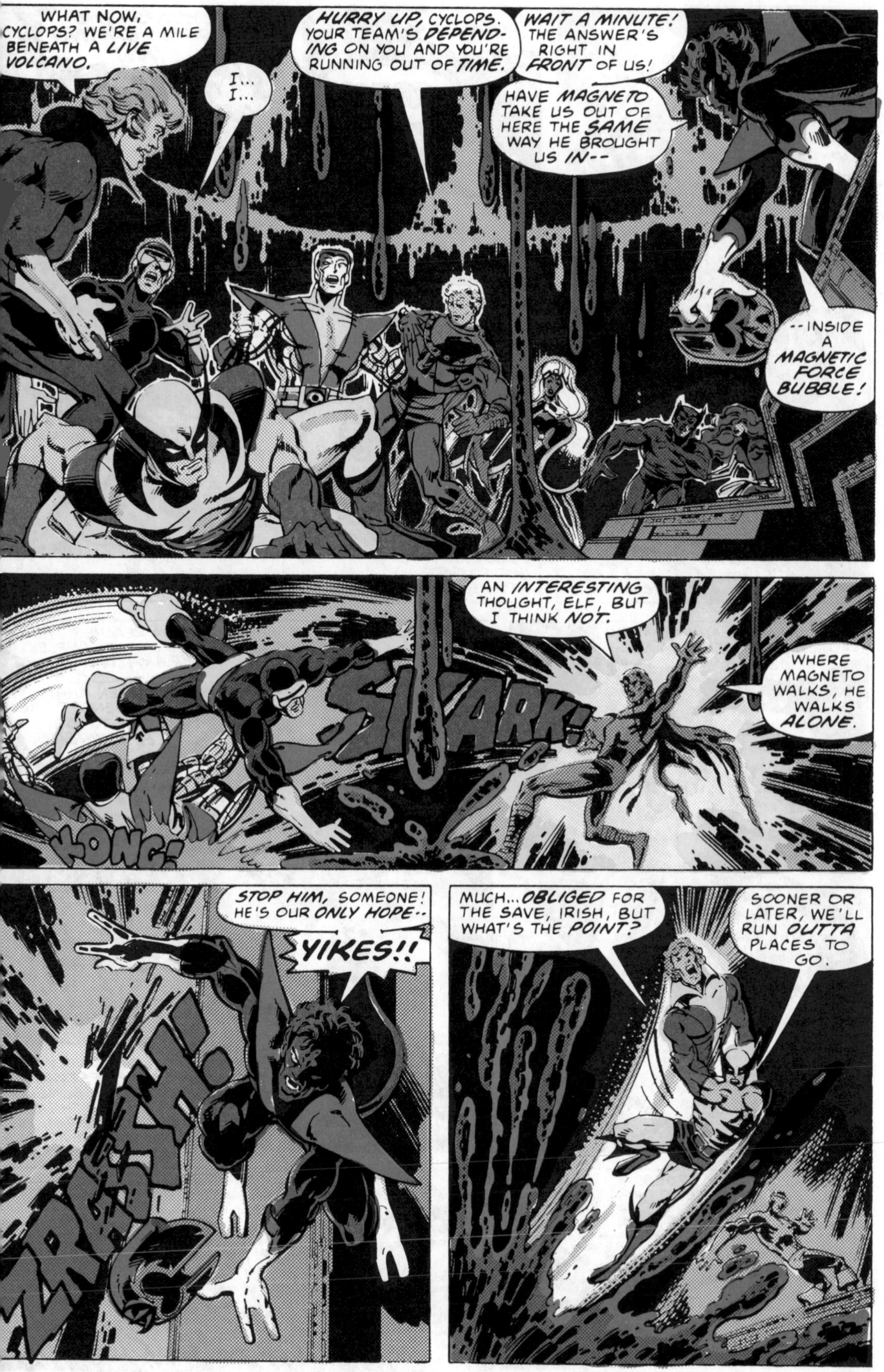

WHAT NOW, CYCLOPS? WE'RE A MILE BENEATH A LIVE VOLCANO.
I... I...
HURRY UP, CYCLOPS. YOUR TEAM'S DEPENDING ON YOU AND YOU'RE RUNNING OUT OF TIME.
WAIT A MINUTE! THE ANSWER'S RIGHT IN FRONT OF US!
HAVE MAGNETO TAKE US OUT OF HERE THE SAME WAY HE BROUGHT US IN--
--INSIDE A MAGNETIC FORCE BUBBLE!
AN INTERESTING THOUGHT, ELF, BUT I THINK NOT.
WHERE MAGNETO WALKS, HE WALKS ALONE.
KONG!
STOP HIM, SOMEONE! HE'S OUR ONLY HOPE--
YIKES!!
MUCH...OBLIGED FOR THE SAVE, IRISH, BUT WHAT'S THE POINT?
SOONER OR LATER, WE'LL RUN OUTTA PLACES TO GO.

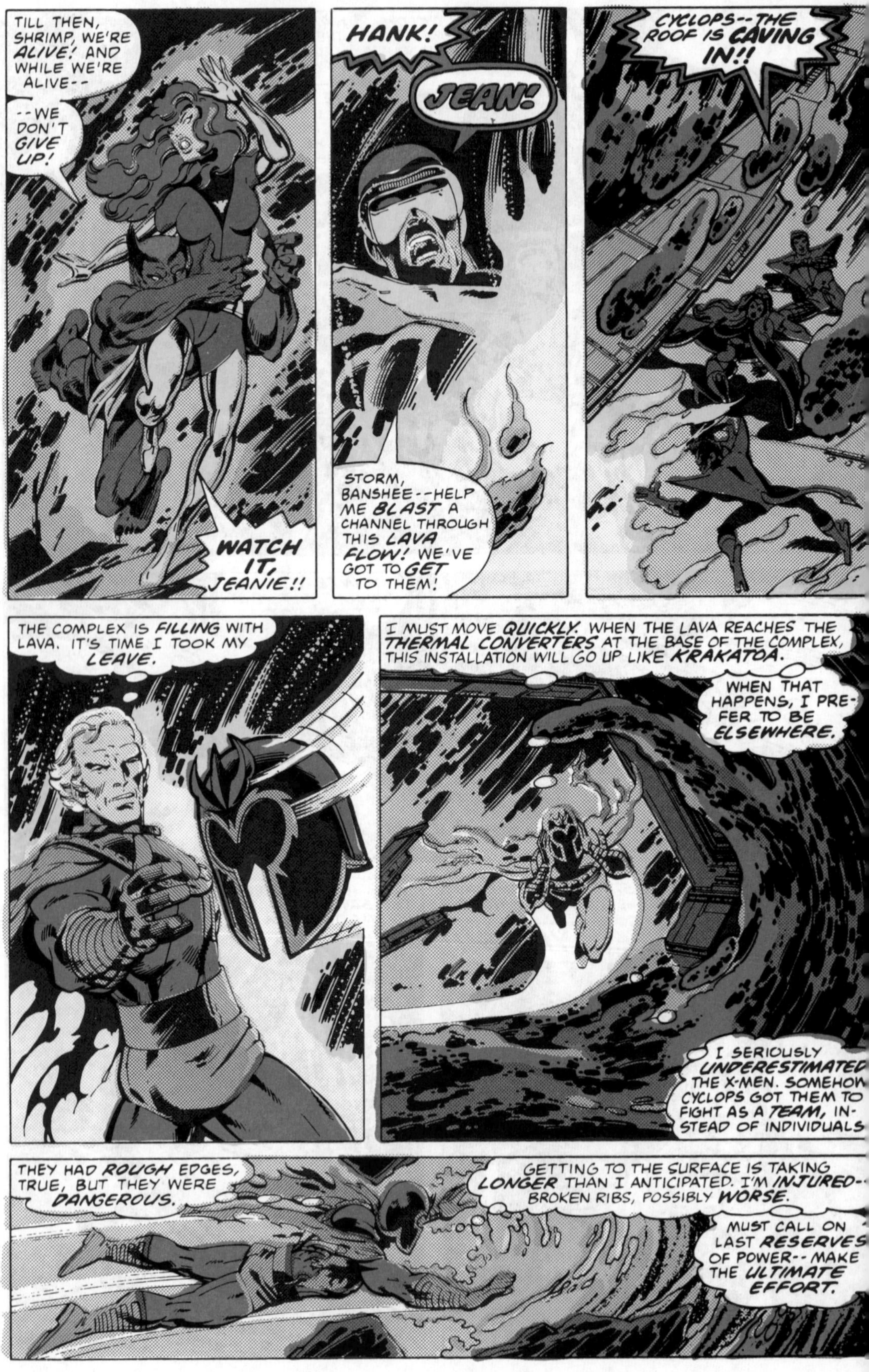
TILL THEN, SHRIMP, WE'RE ALIVE! AND WHILE WE'RE ALIVE--
--WE DON'T GIVE UP!
WATCH IT, JEANIE!!
HANK!
JEAN!
STORM, BANSHEE--HELP ME BLAST A CHANNEL THROUGH THIS LAVA FLOW! WE'VE GOT TO GET TO THEM!
CYCLOPS--THE ROOF IS CAVING IN!!
THE COMPLEX IS FILLING WITH LAVA. IT'S TIME I TOOK MY LEAVE.
I MUST MOVE QUICKLY. WHEN THE LAVA REACHES THE THERMAL CONVERTERS AT THE BASE OF THE COMPLEX, THIS INSTALLATION WILL GO UP LIKE KRAKATOA.
WHEN THAT HAPPENS, I PREFER TO BE ELSEWHERE.
I SERIOUSLY UNDERESTIMATED THE X-MEN. SOMEHOW CYCLOPS GOT THEM TO FIGHT AS A TEAM, INSTEAD OF INDIVIDUALS.
THEY HAD ROUGH EDGES, TRUE, BUT THEY WERE DANGEROUS.
GETTING TO THE SURFACE IS TAKING LONGER THAN I ANTICIPATED. I'M INJURED--BROKEN RIBS, POSSIBLY WORSE.
MUST CALL ON LAST RESERVES OF POWER--MAKE THE ULTIMATE EFFORT.

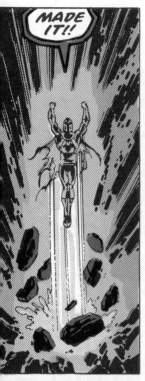

MADE IT!!

THERE'S SADNESS IN HIS EYES AS THE VOLCANO EXPLODES BEHIND HIM. THE WORK AND MEMORIES OF A *LIFE-TIME* HAD BEEN STORED THERE.

NOW THEY'RE GONE.

IT... IS OVER.

EVEN IN *DEATH*, X-MEN, YOU SEEK TO *THWART* MY PLANS. I AM ALIVE, BUT THANKS TO *COLOSSUS*--

--IT WILL BE *MONTHS* BEFORE I'M *WELL* ENOUGH TO RESUME MY WORK. MONTHS DURING WHICH MY PLANS WILL LIE *DORMANT*, GATHERING *DUST*.

BUT *I* AM *ALIVE*, X-MEN.

AND MY ONE *CONSOLATION* IS THAT WHEN, AT LAST, I BRING MY PLANS TO *FRUITION*--AND MANKIND TO ITS COLLECTIVE *KNEES*--

--YOU WILL *NOT* BE THERE TO *INTERFERE!*

FOR A TIME, THE ICE CAP IS *SILENT*--SAVE FOR THE VOLCANO'S BASSO RUMBLINGS AND THE *SKIRLING* HOWL OF THE WIND--AND THEN...

SKRAKOW!

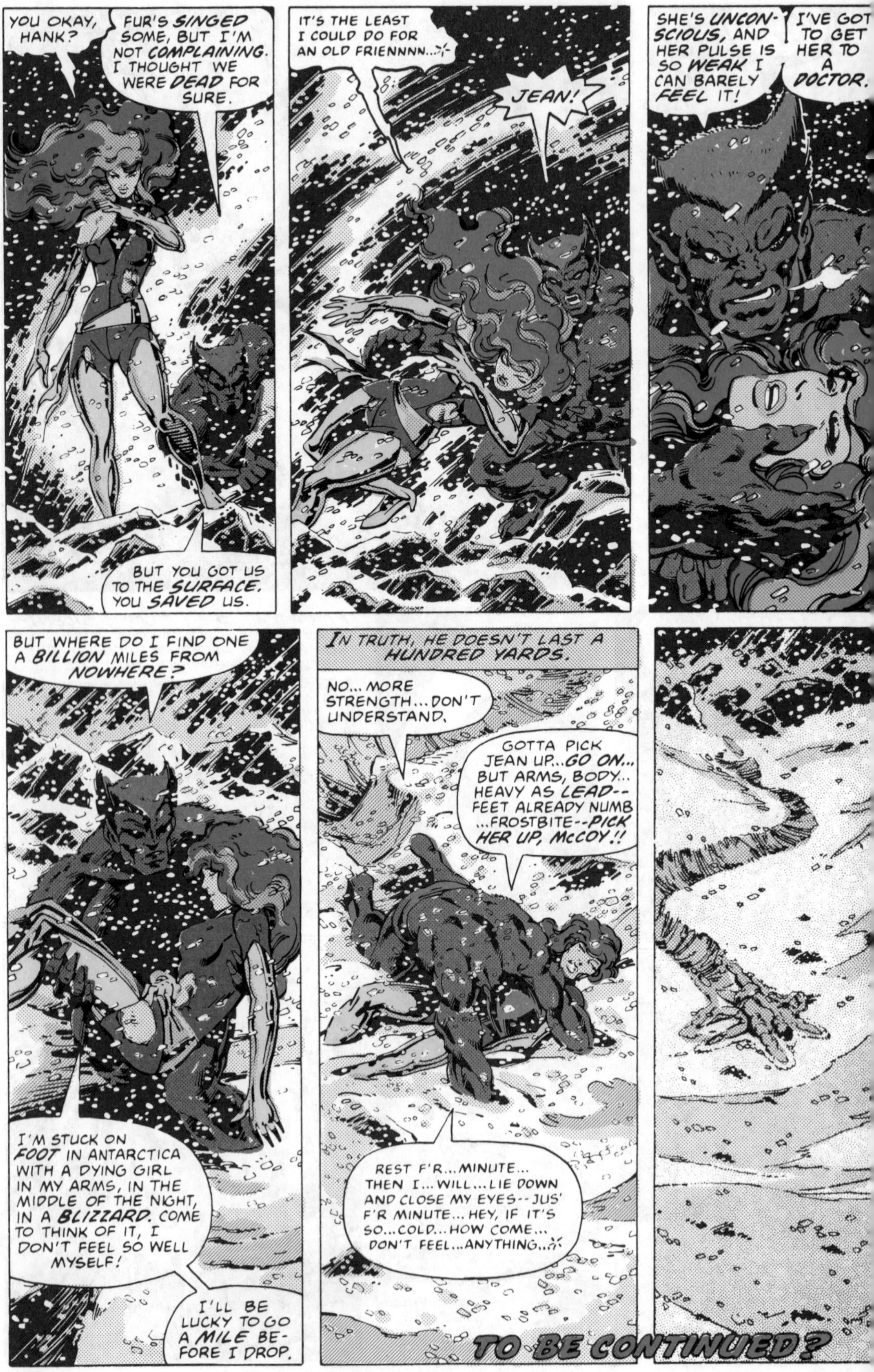
YOU OKAY, HANK?
FUR'S SINGED SOME, BUT I'M NOT COMPLAINING. I THOUGHT WE WERE DEAD FOR SURE.
BUT YOU GOT US TO THE SURFACE. YOU SAVED US.
IT'S THE LEAST I COULD DO FOR AN OLD FRIENNNN...
JEAN!
SHE'S UNCONSCIOUS, AND HER PULSE IS SO WEAK I CAN BARELY FEEL IT!
I'VE GOT TO GET HER TO A DOCTOR.
BUT WHERE DO I FIND ONE A BILLION MILES FROM NOWHERE?
I'M STUCK ON FOOT IN ANTARCTICA WITH A DYING GIRL IN MY ARMS, IN THE MIDDLE OF THE NIGHT, IN A BLIZZARD. COME TO THINK OF IT, I DON'T FEEL SO WELL MYSELF!
I'LL BE LUCKY TO GO A MILE BEFORE I DROP.
IN TRUTH, HE DOESN'T LAST A HUNDRED YARDS.
NO... MORE STRENGTH... DON'T UNDERSTAND.
GOTTA PICK JEAN UP...GO ON... BUT ARMS, BODY... HEAVY AS LEAD-- FEET ALREADY NUMB ...FROSTBITE--PICK HER UP, McCOY!!
REST F'R... MINUTE... THEN I... WILL... LIE DOWN AND CLOSE MY EYES-- JUS' F'R MINUTE... HEY, IF IT'S SO...COLD... HOW COME... DON'T FEEL...ANYTHING...
TO BE CONTINUED?

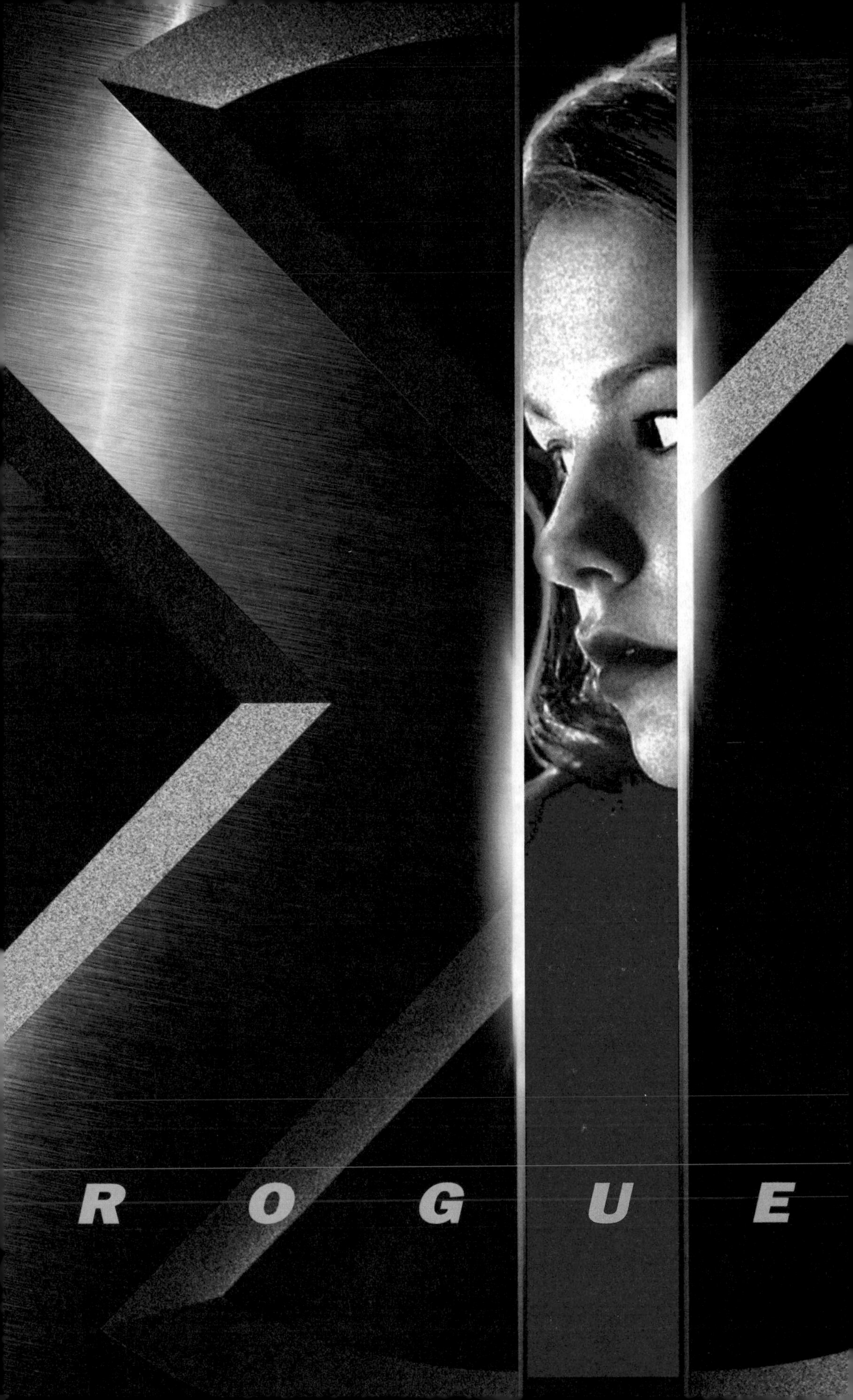
R O G U E

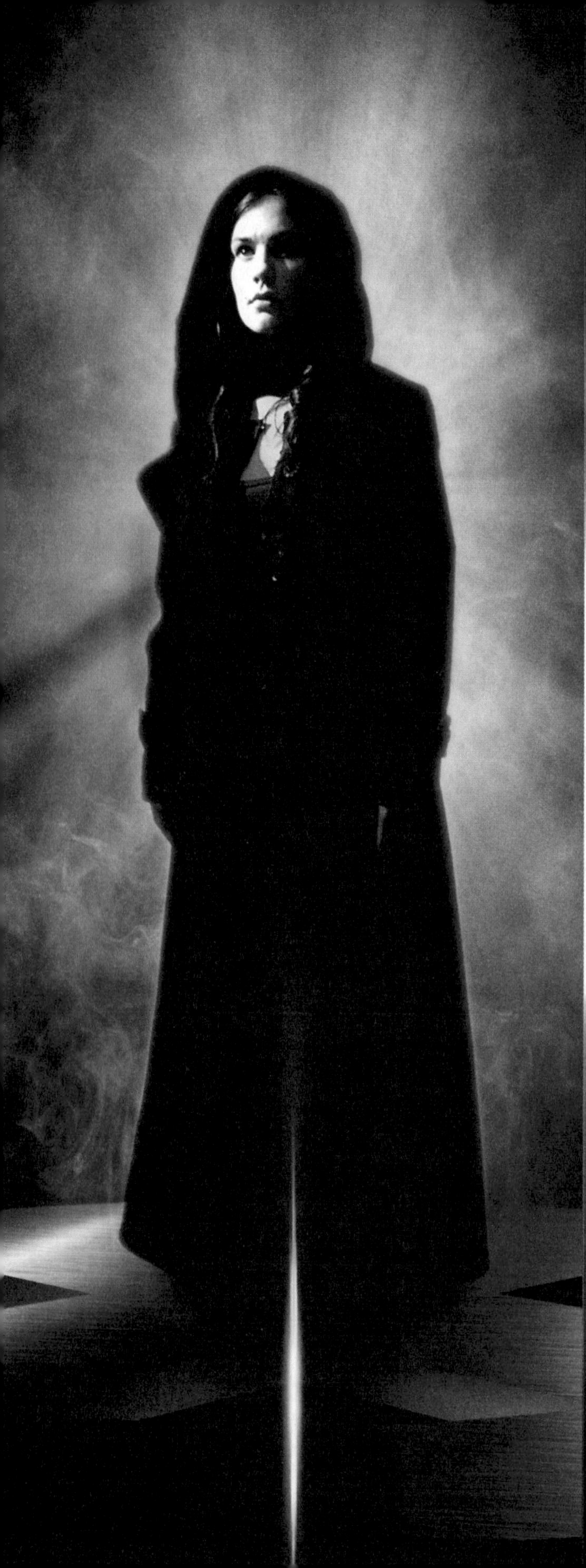

ROGUE

MADE

HER FIRST

APPEARANCE

IN

UNCANNY

X-MEN

#171.

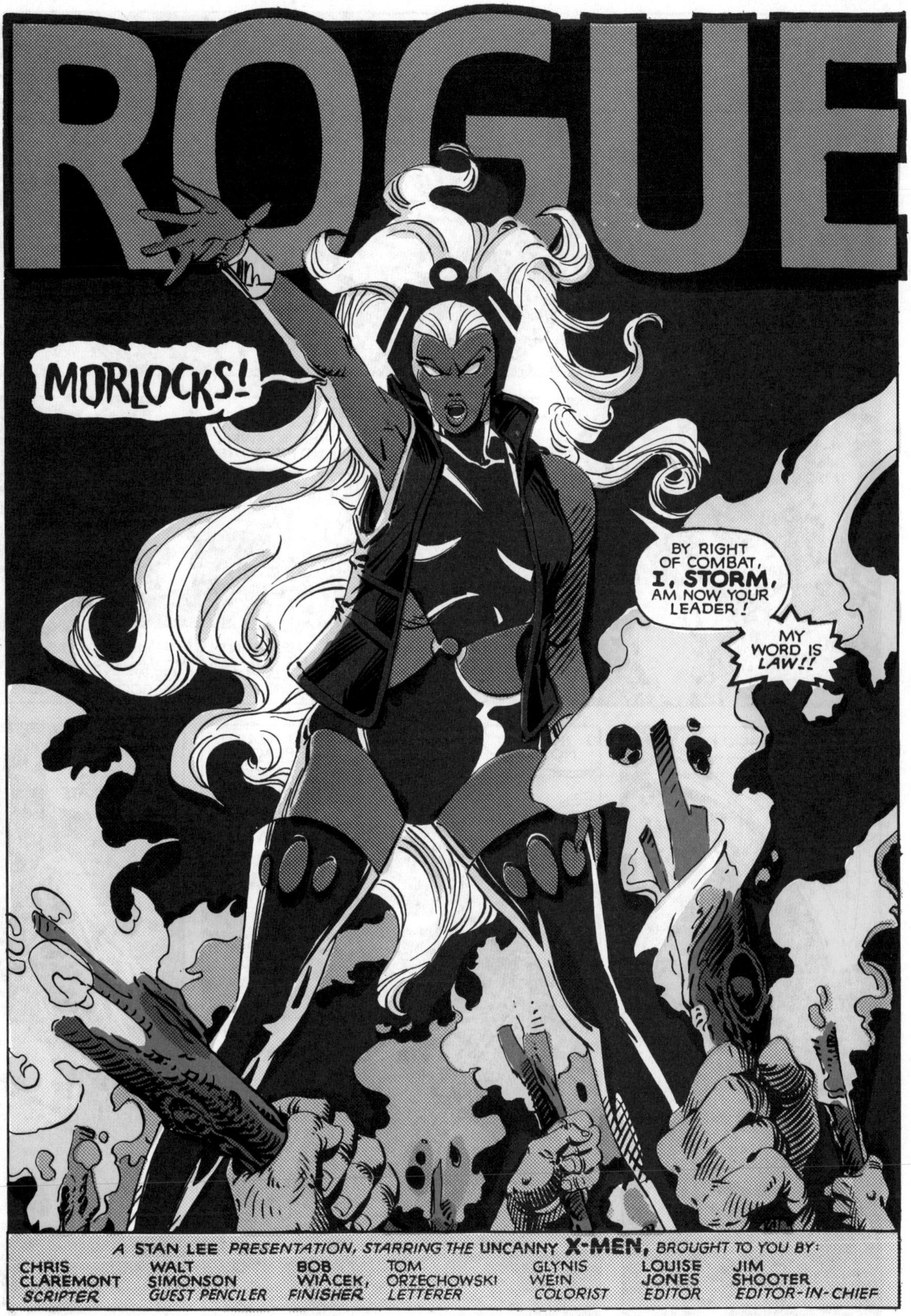
ROGUE
MORLOCKS!
BY RIGHT OF COMBAT, I, STORM, AM NOW YOUR LEADER!
MY WORD IS LAW!!

A STAN LEE *PRESENTATION, STARRING THE* UNCANNY **X-MEN,** *BROUGHT TO YOU BY:*

CHRIS CLAREMONT *SCRIPTER* · WALT SIMONSON *GUEST PENCILER* · BOB WIACEK, *FINISHER* · TOM ORZECHOWSKI *LETTERER* · GLYNIS WEIN *COLORIST* · LOUISE JONES *EDITOR* · JIM SHOOTER *EDITOR-IN-CHIEF*

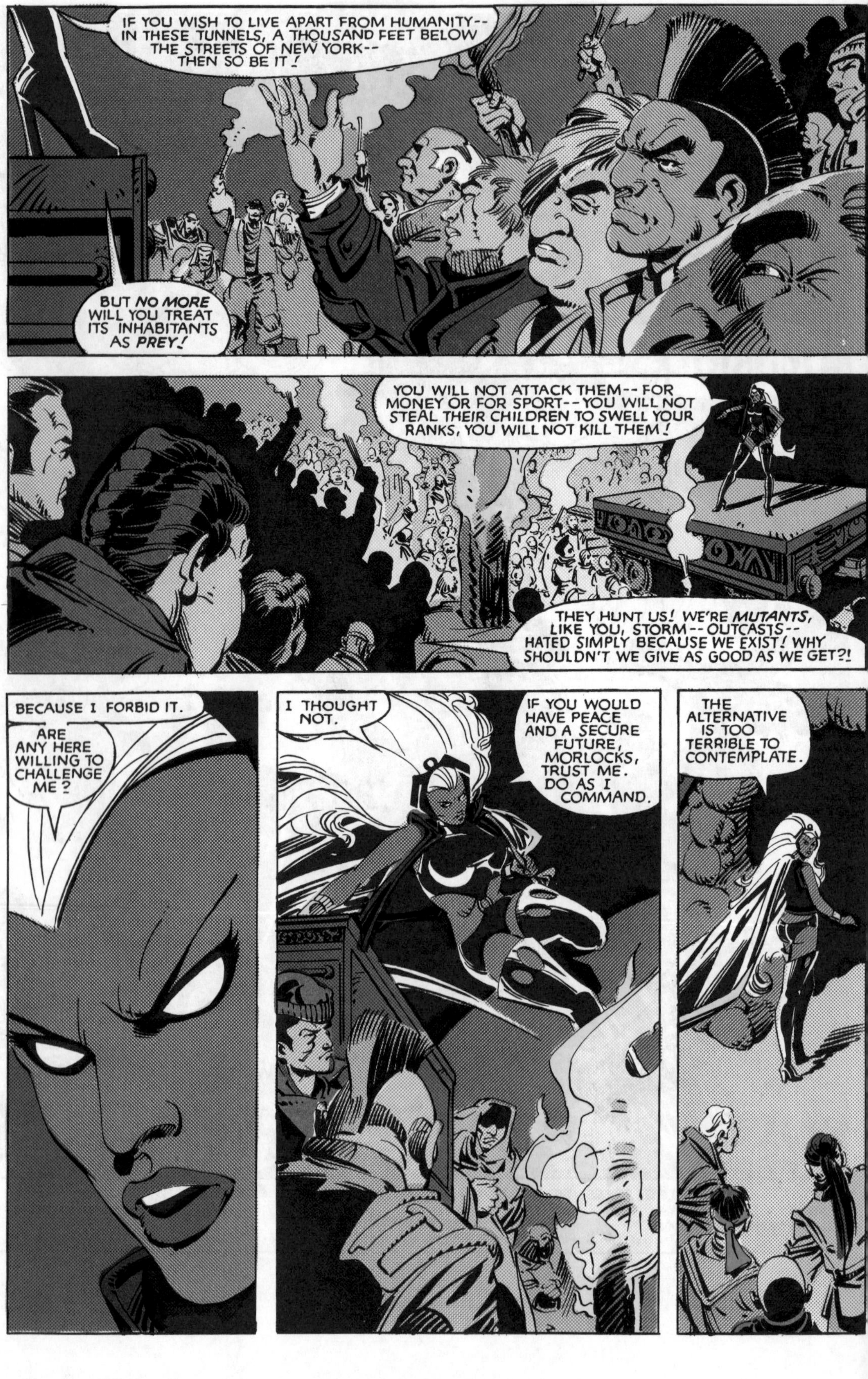
IF YOU WISH TO LIVE APART FROM HUMANITY-- IN THESE TUNNELS, A THOUSAND FEET BELOW THE STREETS OF NEW YORK-- THEN SO BE IT!
BUT NO MORE WILL YOU TREAT ITS INHABITANTS AS PREY!
YOU WILL NOT ATTACK THEM-- FOR MONEY OR FOR SPORT--YOU WILL NOT STEAL THEIR CHILDREN TO SWELL YOUR RANKS, YOU WILL NOT KILL THEM!
THEY HUNT US! WE'RE MUTANTS, LIKE YOU, STORM--OUTCASTS-- HATED SIMPLY BECAUSE WE EXIST! WHY SHOULDN'T WE GIVE AS GOOD AS WE GET?!
BECAUSE I FORBID IT.
ARE ANY HERE WILLING TO CHALLENGE ME?
I THOUGHT NOT.
IF YOU WOULD HAVE PEACE AND A SECURE FUTURE, MORLOCKS, TRUST ME. DO AS I COMMAND.
THE ALTERNATIVE IS TOO TERRIBLE TO CONTEMPLATE.

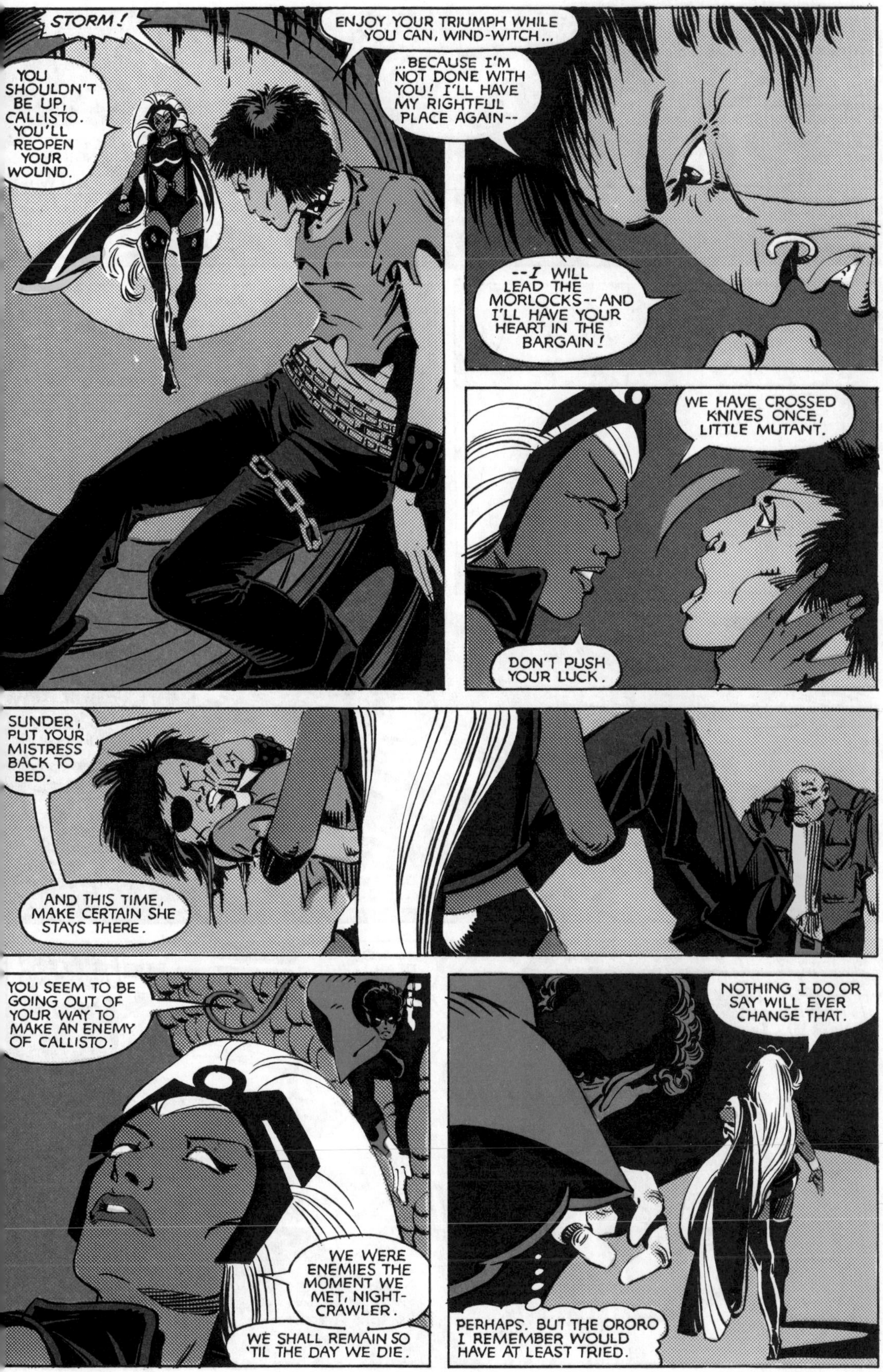
STORM!
YOU SHOULDN'T BE UP, CALLISTO. YOU'LL REOPEN YOUR WOUND.
ENJOY YOUR TRIUMPH WHILE YOU CAN, WIND-WITCH...
...BECAUSE I'M NOT DONE WITH YOU! I'LL HAVE MY RIGHTFUL PLACE AGAIN--
--I WILL LEAD THE MORLOCKS--AND I'LL HAVE YOUR HEART IN THE BARGAIN!
WE HAVE CROSSED KNIVES ONCE, LITTLE MUTANT.
DON'T PUSH YOUR LUCK.
SUNDER, PUT YOUR MISTRESS BACK TO BED.
AND THIS TIME, MAKE CERTAIN SHE STAYS THERE.
YOU SEEM TO BE GOING OUT OF YOUR WAY TO MAKE AN ENEMY OF CALLISTO.
WE WERE ENEMIES THE MOMENT WE MET, NIGHT-CRAWLER.
WE SHALL REMAIN SO 'TIL THE DAY WE DIE.
NOTHING I DO OR SAY WILL EVER CHANGE THAT.
PERHAPS. BUT THE ORORO I REMEMBER WOULD HAVE AT LEAST TRIED.

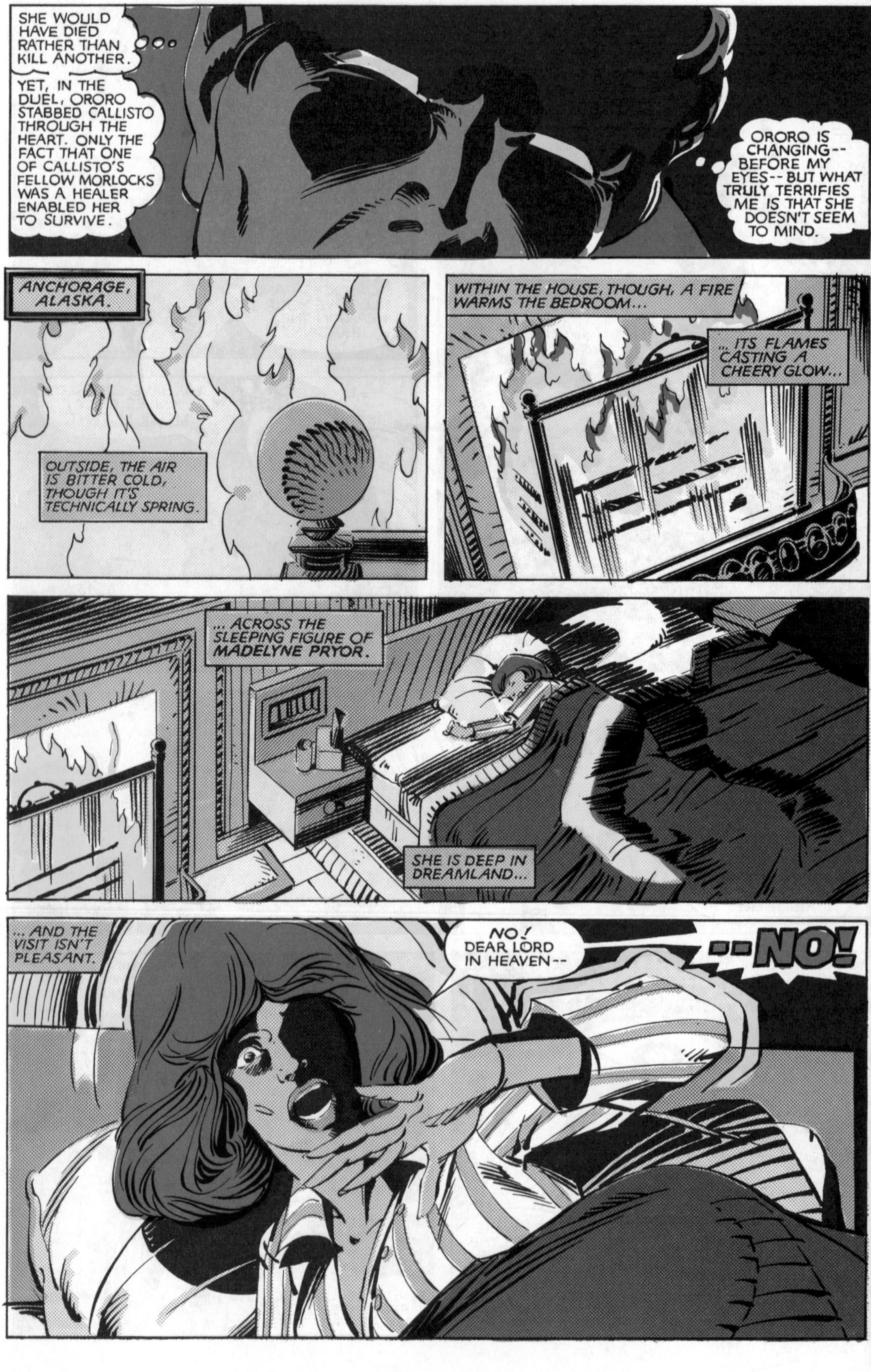
SHE WOULD HAVE DIED RATHER THAN KILL ANOTHER.
YET, IN THE DUEL, ORORO STABBED CALLISTO THROUGH THE HEART. ONLY THE FACT THAT ONE OF CALLISTO'S FELLOW MORLOCKS WAS A HEALER ENABLED HER TO SURVIVE.
ORORO IS CHANGING-- BEFORE MY EYES-- BUT WHAT TRULY TERRIFIES ME IS THAT SHE DOESN'T SEEM TO MIND.
ANCHORAGE, ALASKA.
OUTSIDE, THE AIR IS BITTER COLD, THOUGH IT'S TECHNICALLY SPRING.
WITHIN THE HOUSE, THOUGH, A FIRE WARMS THE BEDROOM...
...ITS FLAMES CASTING A CHEERY GLOW...
...ACROSS THE SLEEPING FIGURE OF MADELYNE PRYOR.
SHE IS DEEP IN DREAMLAND...
... AND THE VISIT ISN'T PLEASANT.
NO! DEAR LORD IN HEAVEN--
--NO!

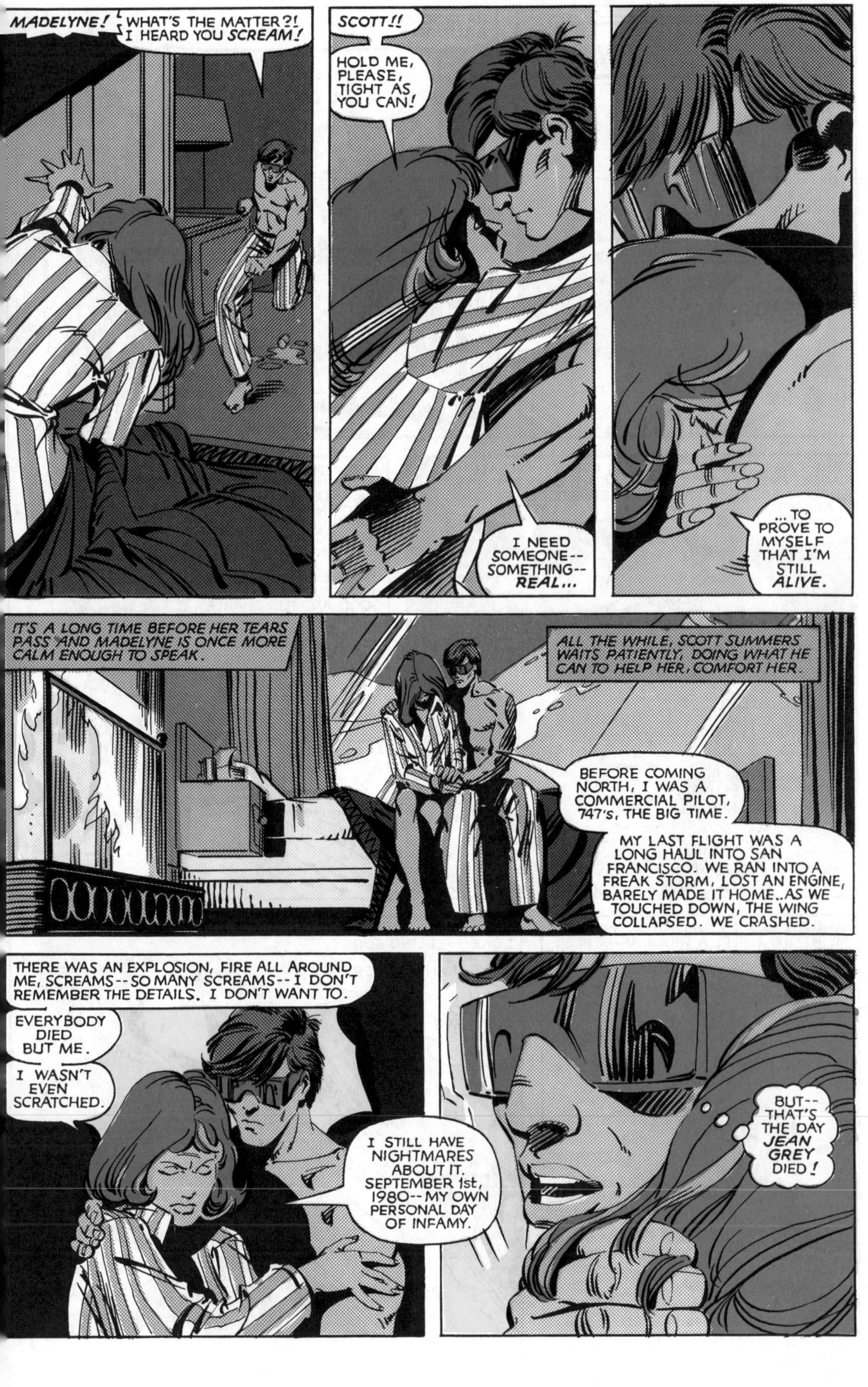

MADELYNE!
WHAT'S THE MATTER?! I HEARD YOU SCREAM!
SCOTT!!
HOLD ME, PLEASE, TIGHT AS YOU CAN!
I NEED SOMEONE-- SOMETHING-- REAL...
...TO PROVE TO MYSELF THAT I'M STILL ALIVE.
IT'S A LONG TIME BEFORE HER TEARS PASS AND MADELYNE IS ONCE MORE CALM ENOUGH TO SPEAK.
ALL THE WHILE, SCOTT SUMMERS WAITS PATIENTLY, DOING WHAT HE CAN TO HELP HER, COMFORT HER.
BEFORE COMING NORTH, I WAS A COMMERCIAL PILOT, 747's, THE BIG TIME.
MY LAST FLIGHT WAS A LONG HAUL INTO SAN FRANCISCO. WE RAN INTO A FREAK STORM, LOST AN ENGINE, BARELY MADE IT HOME..AS WE TOUCHED DOWN, THE WING COLLAPSED. WE CRASHED.
THERE WAS AN EXPLOSION, FIRE ALL AROUND ME, SCREAMS--SO MANY SCREAMS--I DON'T REMEMBER THE DETAILS. I DON'T WANT TO.
EVERYBODY DIED BUT ME.
I WASN'T EVEN SCRATCHED.
I STILL HAVE NIGHTMARES ABOUT IT. SEPTEMBER 1st, 1980--MY OWN PERSONAL DAY OF INFAMY.
BUT-- THAT'S THE DAY JEAN GREY DIED!

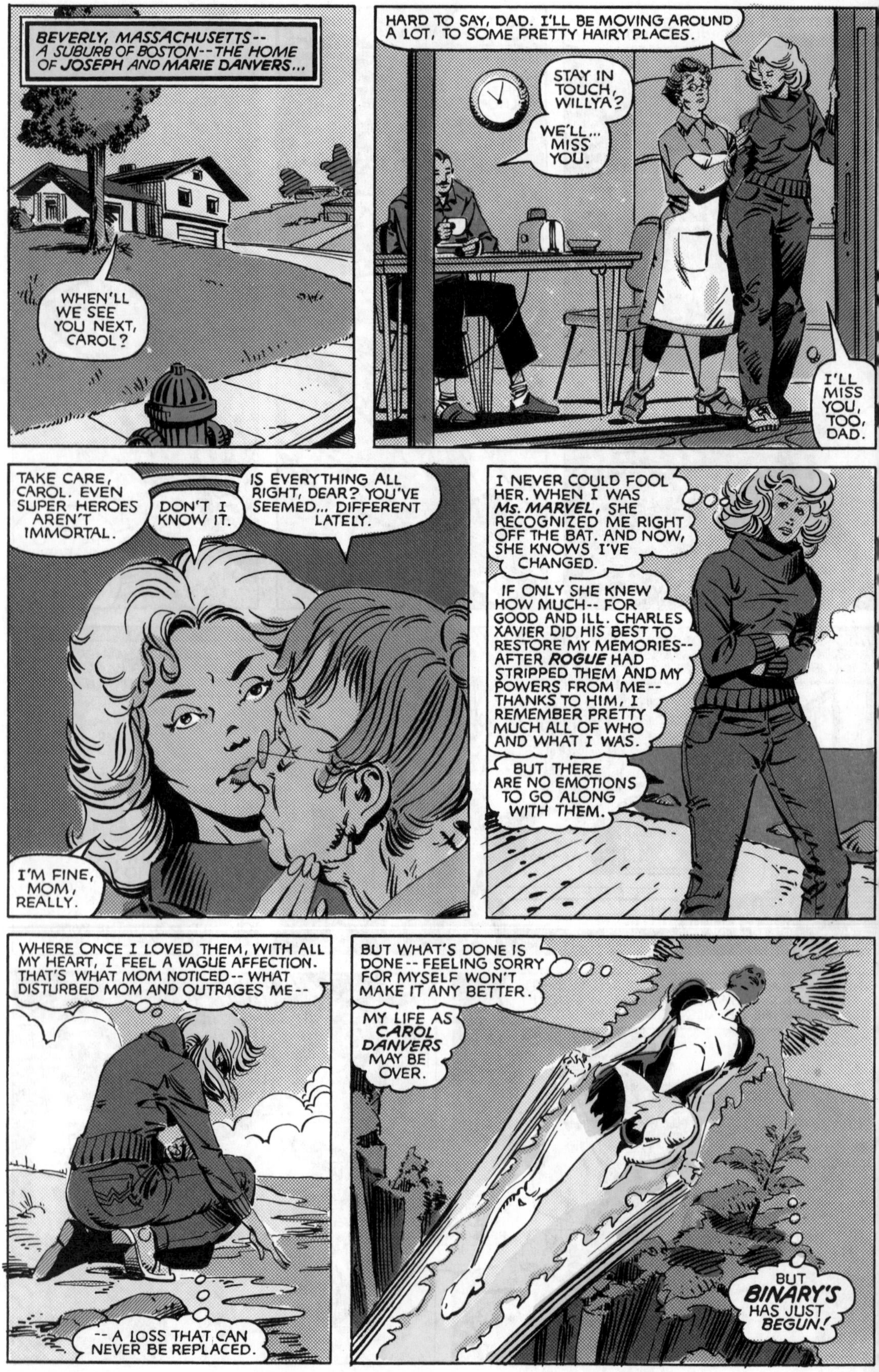
BEVERLY, MASSACHUSETTS-- A SUBURB OF BOSTON--THE HOME OF JOSEPH AND MARIE DANVERS...
WHEN'LL WE SEE YOU NEXT, CAROL?
HARD TO SAY, DAD. I'LL BE MOVING AROUND A LOT, TO SOME PRETTY HAIRY PLACES.
STAY IN TOUCH, WILLYA?
WE'LL... MISS YOU.
I'LL MISS YOU, TOO, DAD.
TAKE CARE, CAROL. EVEN SUPER HEROES AREN'T IMMORTAL.
DON'T I KNOW IT.
IS EVERYTHING ALL RIGHT, DEAR? YOU'VE SEEMED... DIFFERENT LATELY.
I'M FINE, MOM, REALLY.
I NEVER COULD FOOL HER. WHEN I WAS Ms. MARVEL, SHE RECOGNIZED ME RIGHT OFF THE BAT. AND NOW, SHE KNOWS I'VE CHANGED.
IF ONLY SHE KNEW HOW MUCH-- FOR GOOD AND ILL. CHARLES XAVIER DID HIS BEST TO RESTORE MY MEMORIES-- AFTER ROGUE HAD STRIPPED THEM AND MY POWERS FROM ME-- THANKS TO HIM, I REMEMBER PRETTY MUCH ALL OF WHO AND WHAT I WAS.
BUT THERE ARE NO EMOTIONS TO GO ALONG WITH THEM.
WHERE ONCE I LOVED THEM, WITH ALL MY HEART, I FEEL A VAGUE AFFECTION. THAT'S WHAT MOM NOTICED-- WHAT DISTURBED MOM AND OUTRAGES ME--
-- A LOSS THAT CAN NEVER BE REPLACED.
BUT WHAT'S DONE IS DONE-- FEELING SORRY FOR MYSELF WON'T MAKE IT ANY BETTER.
MY LIFE AS CAROL DANVERS MAY BE OVER.
BUT BINARY'S HAS JUST BEGUN!

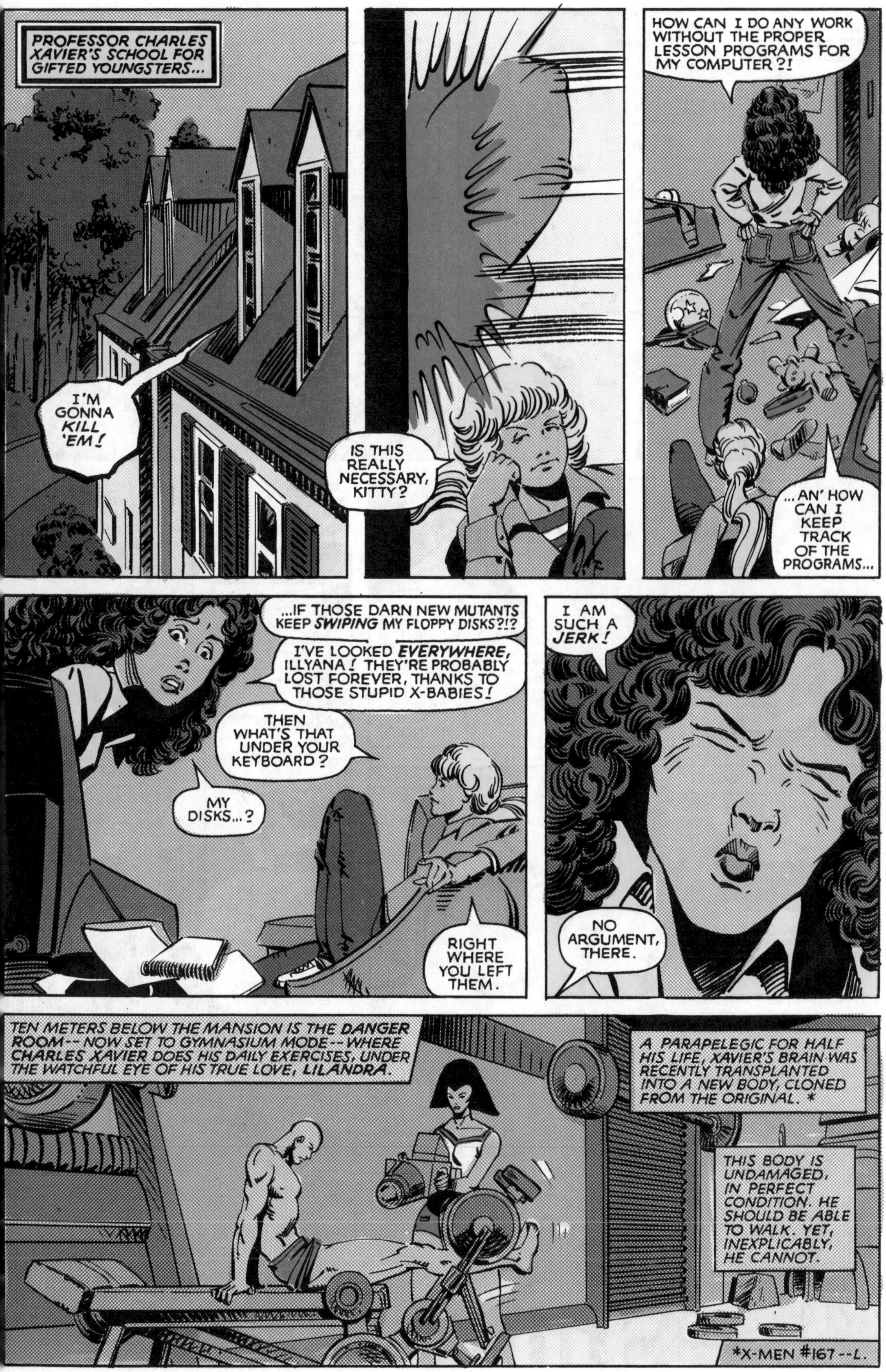
PROFESSOR CHARLES XAVIER'S SCHOOL FOR GIFTED YOUNGSTERS...
I'M GONNA KILL 'EM!
IS THIS REALLY NECESSARY, KITTY?
HOW CAN I DO ANY WORK WITHOUT THE PROPER LESSON PROGRAMS FOR MY COMPUTER?!
...AN' HOW CAN I KEEP TRACK OF THE PROGRAMS...
...IF THOSE DARN NEW MUTANTS KEEP SWIPING MY FLOPPY DISKS?!?
I'VE LOOKED EVERYWHERE, ILLYANA! THEY'RE PROBABLY LOST FOREVER, THANKS TO THOSE STUPID X-BABIES!
THEN WHAT'S THAT UNDER YOUR KEYBOARD?
MY DISKS...?
RIGHT WHERE YOU LEFT THEM.
I AM SUCH A JERK!
NO ARGUMENT, THERE.
TEN METERS BELOW THE MANSION IS THE DANGER ROOM-- NOW SET TO GYMNASIUM MODE--WHERE CHARLES XAVIER DOES HIS DAILY EXERCISES, UNDER THE WATCHFUL EYE OF HIS TRUE LOVE, LILANDRA.
A PARAPELEGIC FOR HALF HIS LIFE, XAVIER'S BRAIN WAS RECENTLY TRANSPLANTED INTO A NEW BODY, CLONED FROM THE ORIGINAL. *
THIS BODY IS UNDAMAGED, IN PERFECT CONDITION. HE SHOULD BE ABLE TO WALK. YET, INEXPLICABLY, HE CANNOT.
*X-MEN #167 --L.

NO MORE, LIL, I BEG YOU!

PROBLEMS?

WHEN I USE MY LEGS, THE PSYCHO-SOMATIC PAIN I FEEL INHIBITS MY PSIONIC POWERS, ESPECIALLY MY ABILITY TO SCREEN OUT OTHER PEOPLE'S THOUGHTS.

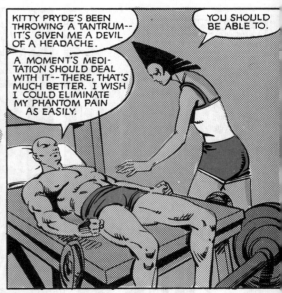

KITTY PRYDE'S BEEN THROWING A TANTRUM-- IT'S GIVEN ME A DEVIL OF A HEADACHE.

YOU SHOULD BE ABLE TO.

A MOMENT'S MEDI-TATION SHOULD DEAL WITH IT--THERE, THAT'S MUCH BETTER. I WISH I COULD ELIMINATE MY PHANTOM PAIN AS EASILY.

YOU ARE, AFTER ALL, THE STRONGEST MUTANT MIND ON EARTH... AMONG OTHER THINGS.

UPSTAIRS, IN THE KITCHEN, ANOTHER OF XAVIER'S STUDENTS, *PIOTR NIKOLIEVITCH RASPUTIN*, PONDERS THE COMPLEX MYSTERIE AND INHERENT CONTRADICTIONS...

... OF A COOKBOOK.

WHAT DO YOU SUGGEST?

WE COULD PLAY DOCTOR.

LILANDRA!

SERIOUSLY, CHARLES, I WOULD LIKE TO GIVE YOU A THOROUGH EXAMI-NATION. PERHAPS YOUR CONDITION ISN'T PSYCHIC IN NATURE, BUT *PHYSICAL*.

EGGS, BACON, CREAM, BUTTER, SPICES-- SLICE, BEAT, MIX, BAKE-- AND IN HALF AN HOUR: *QUICHE LORRAINE*. IT LOOKS SIMPLE ENOUGH.

COLOSSUS, WE HAVE A VISITOR.

AT ONCE, PROFESSOR.

I FELT THE PROFESSOR'S FATIGUE THROUGH HIS THOUGHT PROJECTION. I HOPE HE IS NOT PUSHING HIMSELF TOO HARD.

HE ADDRESSED ME AS *COLOSSUS*. THAT INDICATES AN ELEMENT OF DANGER.

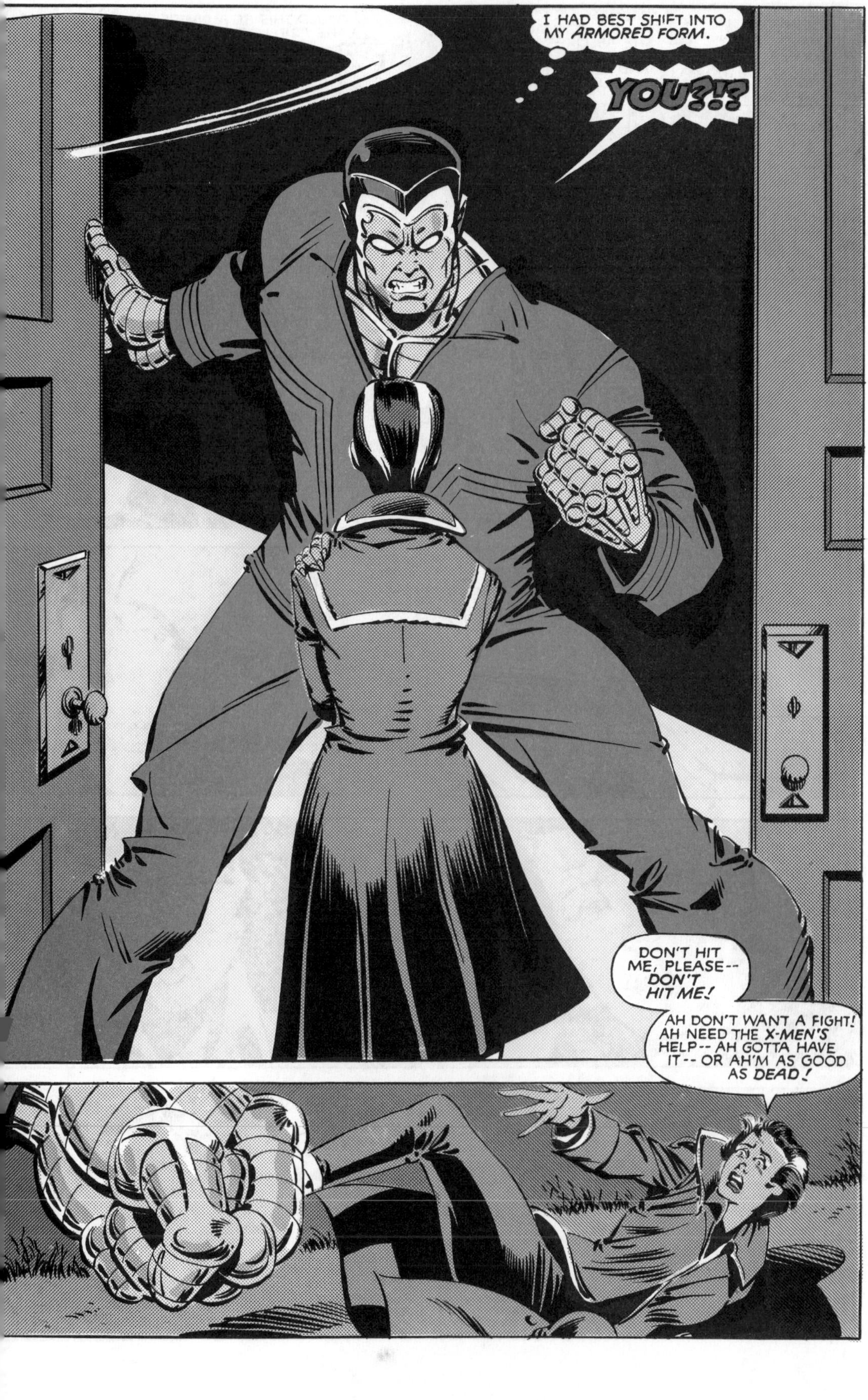
I HAD BEST SHIFT INTO MY ARMORED FORM.
YOU?!?
DON'T HIT ME, PLEASE-- DON'T HIT ME!
AH DON'T WANT A FIGHT! AH NEED THE X-MEN'S HELP-- AH GOTTA HAVE IT-- OR AH'M AS GOOD AS DEAD!

LATER... HER NAME IS *ROGUE*, A MEMBER OF THE *BROTHER-HOOD OF EVIL MUTANTS*.

THROUGH DIRECT PHYSICAL CONTACT, SHE ABSORBS THE ABILITIES AND MEMORIES OF OTHERS.

COULD THIS BE A DIVERSION-- THE PRELUDE TO AN ATTACK?

I'VE PSI-SCANNED THE ESTATE, NIGHT-CRAWLER. SHE IS QUITE ALONE.

WHY ARE YOU HERE, CHILD? WHAT DO YOU WANT?

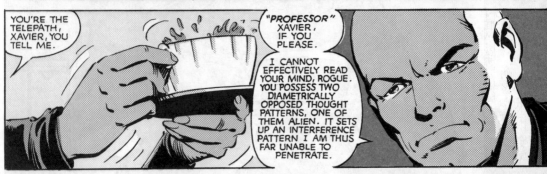

YOU'RE THE TELEPATH, XAVIER, YOU TELL ME.

"*PROFESSOR*" XAVIER, IF YOU PLEASE.

I CANNOT EFFECTIVELY READ YOUR MIND, ROGUE. YOU POSSESS TWO DIAMETRICALLY OPPOSED THOUGHT PATTERNS, ONE OF THEM ALIEN. IT SETS UP AN INTERFERENCE PATTERN I AM THUS FAR UNABLE TO PENETRATE.

THAT'S THE PERSONA AH ABSORBED FROM *CAROL DANVERS* WHEN AH ABSORBED HER POWERS, LAST YEAR.

AH DIDN'T INTEND THE TRANSFER TO BE PERMANENT. IT WAS AN ACCIDENT!

IT'S DRIVING ME CRAZY, PROFESSOR. YOU'VE GOTTA HELP ME!

YOU'VE GOT SOME NERVE, ROGUE, ASKIN' THAT AFTER ALL YOU'VE DONE!

HUSH, KITTY!
GO ON, ROGUE

MAH POWERS ARE OUT OF CONTROL. THE SLIGHTEST TOUCH TRIGGERS THE TRANSFER. IT'S GETTIN' SO AH DON'T KNOW ANYMORE WHICH THOUGHTS-- OR MEM'RIES, OR FEELIN'S-- ARE MINE!

AH LOOK INTO A MIRROR, AN' SEE A *STRANGER'S* FACE!

IF YOU ASK ME, A MOST APT PUNISHMENT FOR YOUR CRIMES.

AH TRIED T'MAKE MYSTIQUE UNDERSTAND, BUT SHE WOULDN'T LISTEN. SHE WAS CERTAIN WE COULD WORK THINGS OUT ON OUR OWN.

AH LOVE HER, PROFESSOR-- SHE'S BEEN LIKE MY MOM TO ME-- BUT AH KNEW SHE WAS WRONG. AH TURNED TO THE X-MEN-- EVEN THOUGH WE'RE ENEMIES--

--BECAUSE YOU'RE MAH ONLY HOPE.

GIMME A BREAK!

KITTY!

I DIDN'T SAY ANY-THING!

YOUR THOUGHTS WERE PLAIN ENOUGH.

THAT'S NOT FAIR!

ARE YOU BEING FAIR TO ROGUE?

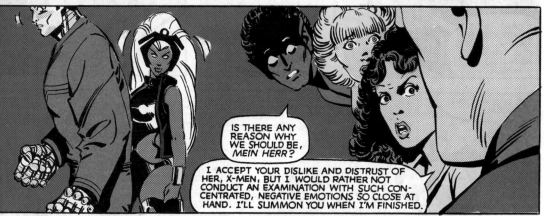

IS THERE ANY REASON WHY WE SHOULD BE, MEIN HERR?

I ACCEPT YOUR DISLIKE AND DISTRUST OF HER, X-MEN, BUT I WOULD RATHER NOT CONDUCT AN EXAMINATION WITH SUCH CON-CENTRATED, NEGATIVE EMOTIONS SO CLOSE AT HAND. I'LL SUMMON YOU WHEN I'M FINISHED.

ARE YOU SURE THIS IS WISE, PROFESSOR? SHE IS DANGEROUS.

LILANDRA AND I CAN TAKE CARE OF OUR-SELVES, STORM. AND AS FOR ROGUE...

... I BELIEVE WE HAVE NOTHING TO FEAR FROM HER.

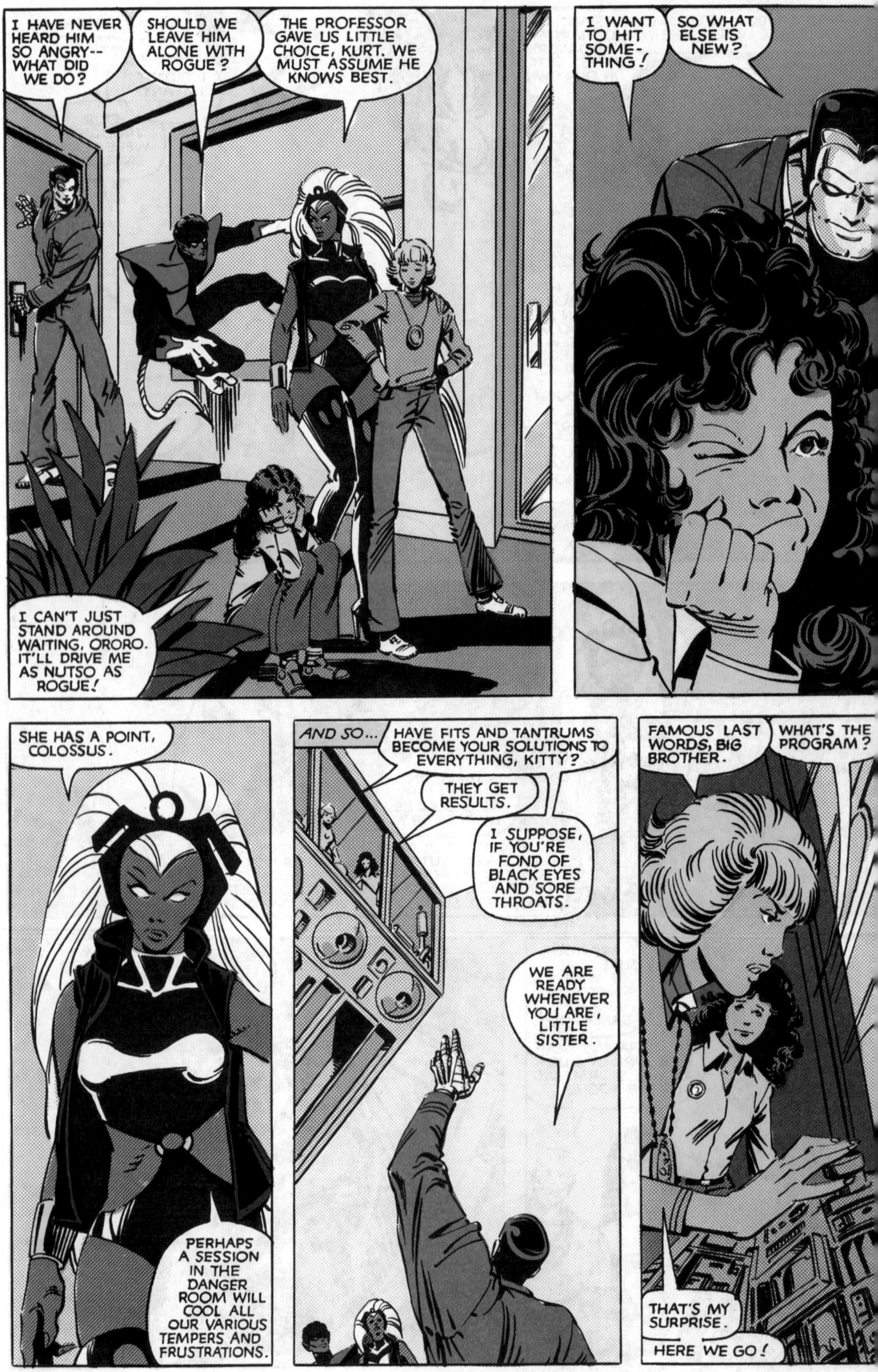
I HAVE NEVER HEARD HIM SO ANGRY-- WHAT DID WE DO?
SHOULD WE LEAVE HIM ALONE WITH ROGUE?
THE PROFESSOR GAVE US LITTLE CHOICE, KURT. WE MUST ASSUME HE KNOWS BEST.
I CAN'T JUST STAND AROUND WAITING, ORORO. IT'LL DRIVE ME AS NUTSO AS ROGUE!
I WANT TO HIT SOME-THING!
SO WHAT ELSE IS NEW?
SHE HAS A POINT, COLOSSUS.
PERHAPS A SESSION IN THE DANGER ROOM WILL COOL ALL OUR VARIOUS TEMPERS AND FRUSTRATIONS.
AND SO...
HAVE FITS AND TANTRUMS BECOME YOUR SOLUTIONS TO EVERYTHING, KITTY?
THEY GET RESULTS.
I SUPPOSE, IF YOU'RE FOND OF BLACK EYES AND SORE THROATS.
WE ARE READY WHENEVER YOU ARE, LITTLE SISTER.
FAMOUS LAST WORDS, BIG BROTHER.
WHAT'S THE PROGRAM?
THAT'S MY SURPRISE.
HERE WE GO!

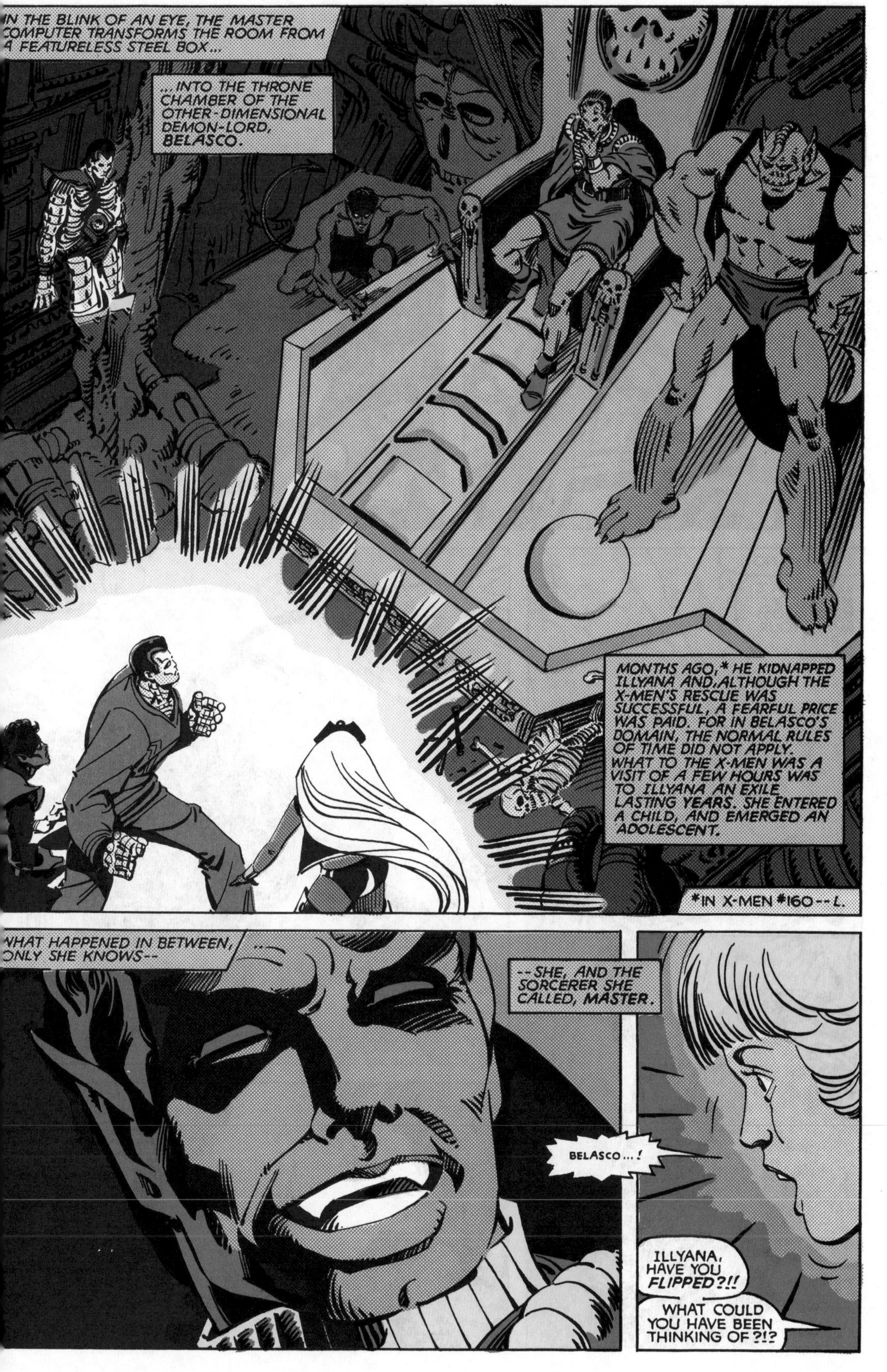
IN THE BLINK OF AN EYE, THE MASTER COMPUTER TRANSFORMS THE ROOM FROM A FEATURELESS STEEL BOX...
...INTO THE THRONE CHAMBER OF THE OTHER-DIMENSIONAL DEMON-LORD, BELASCO.
MONTHS AGO,* HE KIDNAPPED ILLYANA AND, ALTHOUGH THE X-MEN'S RESCUE WAS SUCCESSFUL, A FEARFUL PRICE WAS PAID. FOR IN BELASCO'S DOMAIN, THE NORMAL RULES OF TIME DID NOT APPLY. WHAT TO THE X-MEN WAS A VISIT OF A FEW HOURS WAS TO ILLYANA AN EXILE LASTING YEARS. SHE ENTERED A CHILD, AND EMERGED AN ADOLESCENT.
*IN X-MEN #160 -- L.
WHAT HAPPENED IN BETWEEN, ONLY SHE KNOWS--
--SHE, AND THE SORCERER SHE CALLED, MASTER.
BELASCO...!
ILLYANA, HAVE YOU FLIPPED?!!
WHAT COULD YOU HAVE BEEN THINKING OF?!?

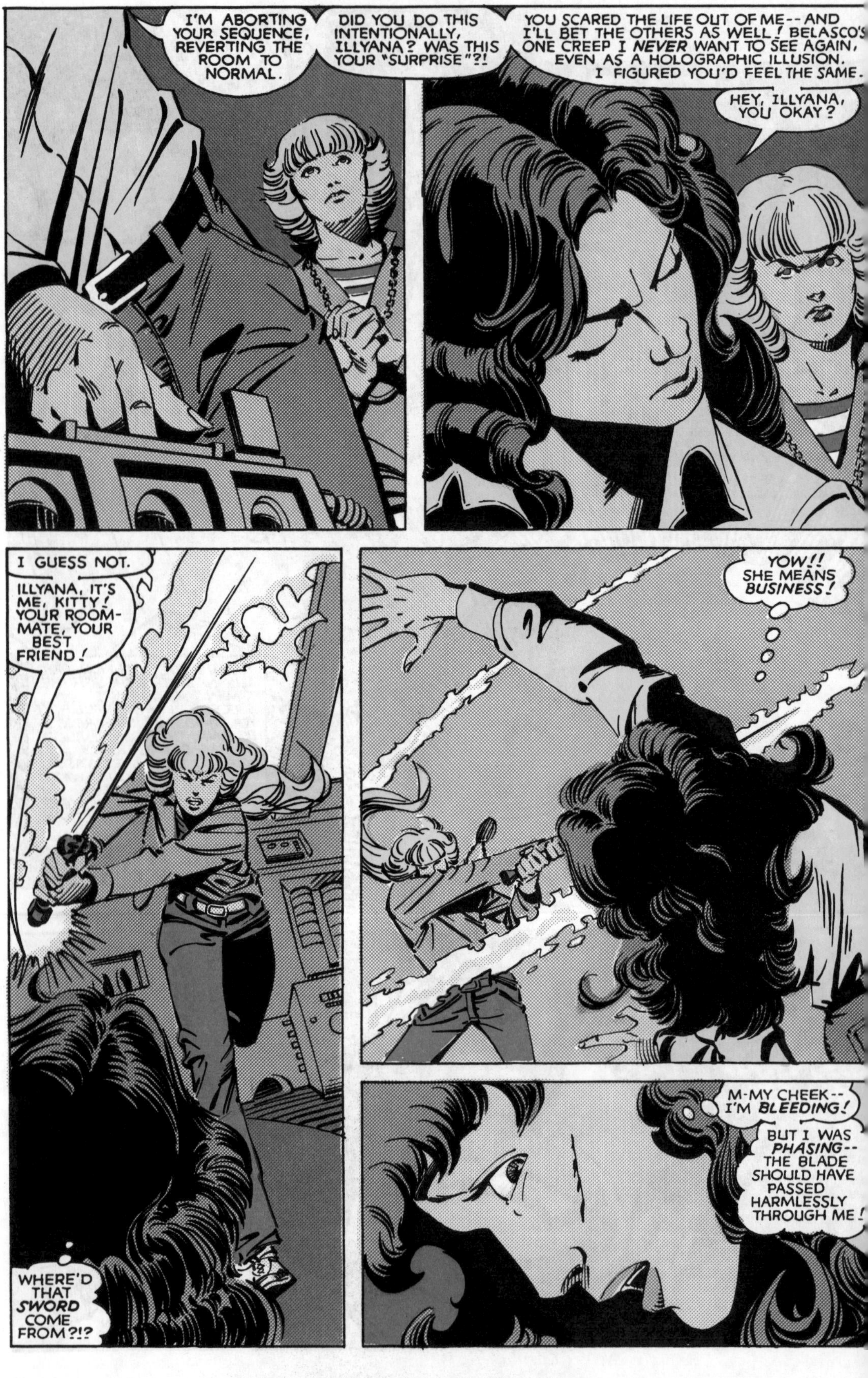
I'M ABORTING YOUR SEQUENCE, REVERTING THE ROOM TO NORMAL.
DID YOU DO THIS INTENTIONALLY, ILLYANA? WAS THIS YOUR "SURPRISE"?!
YOU SCARED THE LIFE OUT OF ME--AND I'LL BET THE OTHERS AS WELL! BELASCO'S ONE CREEP I NEVER WANT TO SEE AGAIN, EVEN AS A HOLOGRAPHIC ILLUSION. I FIGURED YOU'D FEEL THE SAME.
HEY, ILLYANA, YOU OKAY?
I GUESS NOT.
ILLYANA, IT'S ME, KITTY! YOUR ROOM-MATE, YOUR BEST FRIEND!
WHERE'D THAT SWORD COME FROM?!?
YOW!! SHE MEANS BUSINESS!
M-MY CHEEK--I'M BLEEDING!
BUT I WAS PHASING--THE BLADE SHOULD HAVE PASSED HARMLESSLY THROUGH ME!

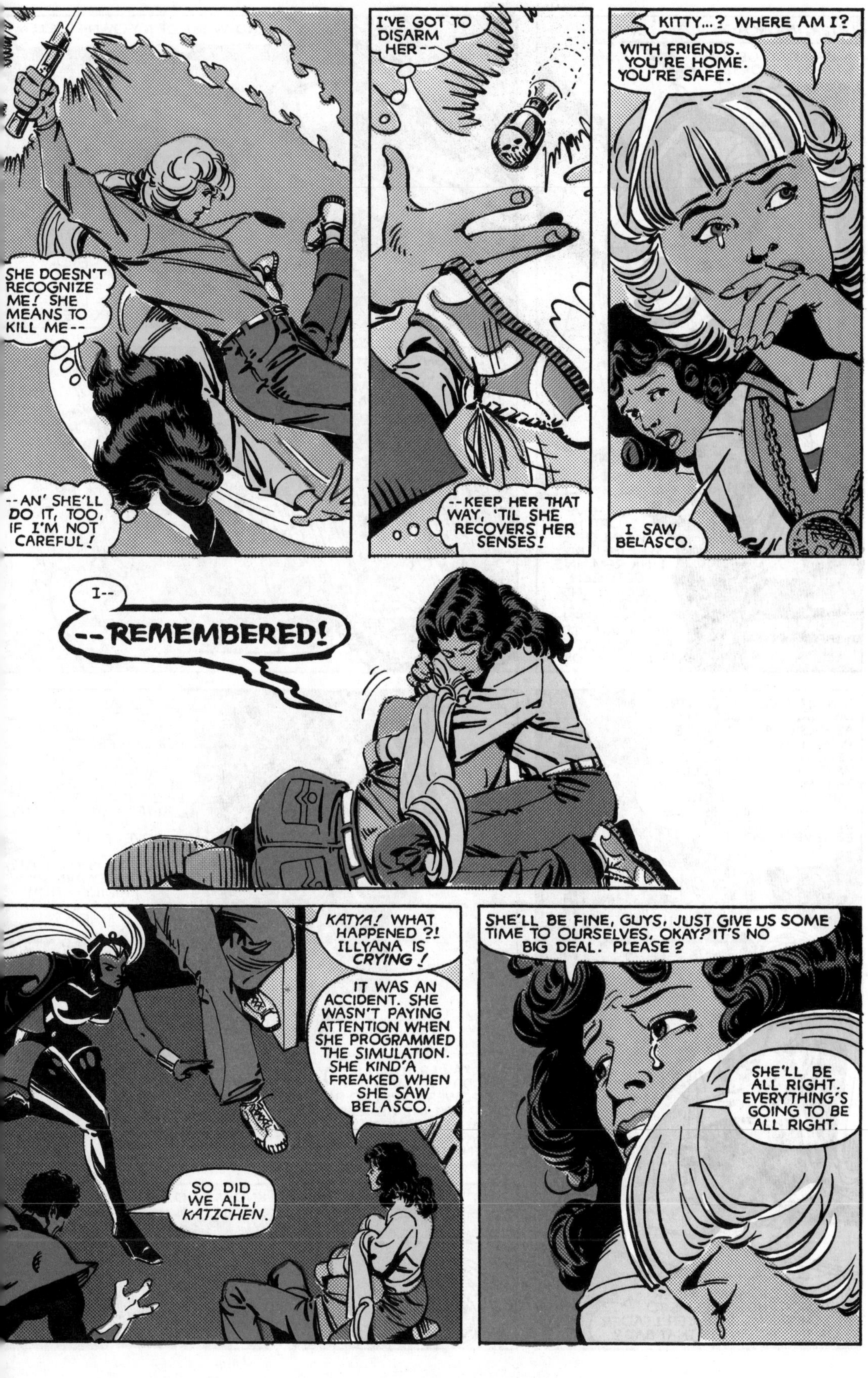
SHE DOESN'T RECOGNIZE ME! SHE MEANS TO KILL ME--
--AN' SHE'LL DO IT, TOO, IF I'M NOT CAREFUL!
I'VE GOT TO DISARM HER--
--KEEP HER THAT WAY, 'TIL SHE RECOVERS HER SENSES!
KITTY...? WHERE AM I?
WITH FRIENDS. YOU'RE HOME. YOU'RE SAFE.
I SAW BELASCO.
I--
--REMEMBERED!
KATYA! WHAT HAPPENED ?! ILLYANA IS CRYING!
IT WAS AN ACCIDENT. SHE WASN'T PAYING ATTENTION WHEN SHE PROGRAMMED THE SIMULATION. SHE KIND'A FREAKED WHEN SHE SAW BELASCO.
SO DID WE ALL, KATZCHEN.
SHE'LL BE FINE, GUYS, JUST GIVE US SOME TIME TO OURSELVES, OKAY? IT'S NO BIG DEAL. PLEASE?
SHE'LL BE ALL RIGHT. EVERYTHING'S GOING TO BE ALL RIGHT.

LATER, IN ORORO'S ATTIC LOFT...

A BAD DAY, GETTING STEADILY WORSE.

WE HAVE OFTEN WONDERED WHETHER ANY LINK REMAINS BETWEEN ILLYANA AND BELASCO, BUT HAVE BEEN RELUCTANT TO PRY. PERHAPS IT IS TIME WE DID.

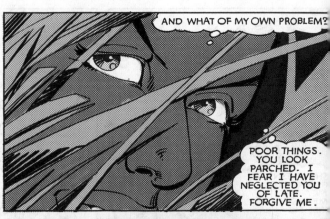

AND WHAT OF MY OWN PROBLEM?

POOR THINGS. YOU LOOK PARCHED. I FEAR I HAVE NEGLECTED YOU OF LATE. FORGIVE ME.

A THOUGHT SUMMONS CLOUDS, CREATES RAIN, SENDS IT SWEEPING ACROSS THE ROOM.

I WISH I COULD CONTROL MY LIFE-- MY DESTINY-- AS EASILY AS I DO THE WEATHER. I CANNOT BELIEVE THE THINGS I HAVE DONE. THE DUEL-- THIS MORNING'S CONFRON- TATION WITH CALLISTO-- THEY ALL FLY IN THE FACE OF ALL I HAVE EVER BELIEVED ABOUT MYSELF.

AND YET, THIS SAME INNER METAMORPHOSIS SEEMS TO BE MAKING ME A BETTER LEADER OF THE X-MEN. IS THAT BAD?

I FEEL AS THOUGH I STAND AT A CROSS- ROADS. TO REMAIN AN X-MAN-- ESPECIALLY AS LEADER-- I MUST SACRIFICE THE BELIEFS THAT GIVE MY LIFE MEANING. YET THE ALTERNATIVE MEANS LEAVING THOSE I LOVE, FOREVER.

THIS IS MY HOME, THEY ARE MY FAMILY-- HOW CAN I DESERT THEM?!

AND XAVIER TOLD ME, THE DAY WE MET, THAT MY POWERS SHOULD BE USED FOR THE BENEFIT OF ALL HUMANITY. WAS I WRONG TO LISTEN? CAN I DENY THAT RESPONSIBILITY?

I DO NOT KNOW, I DO NOT *KNOW*-- eh?!!

THUNDER ?!?

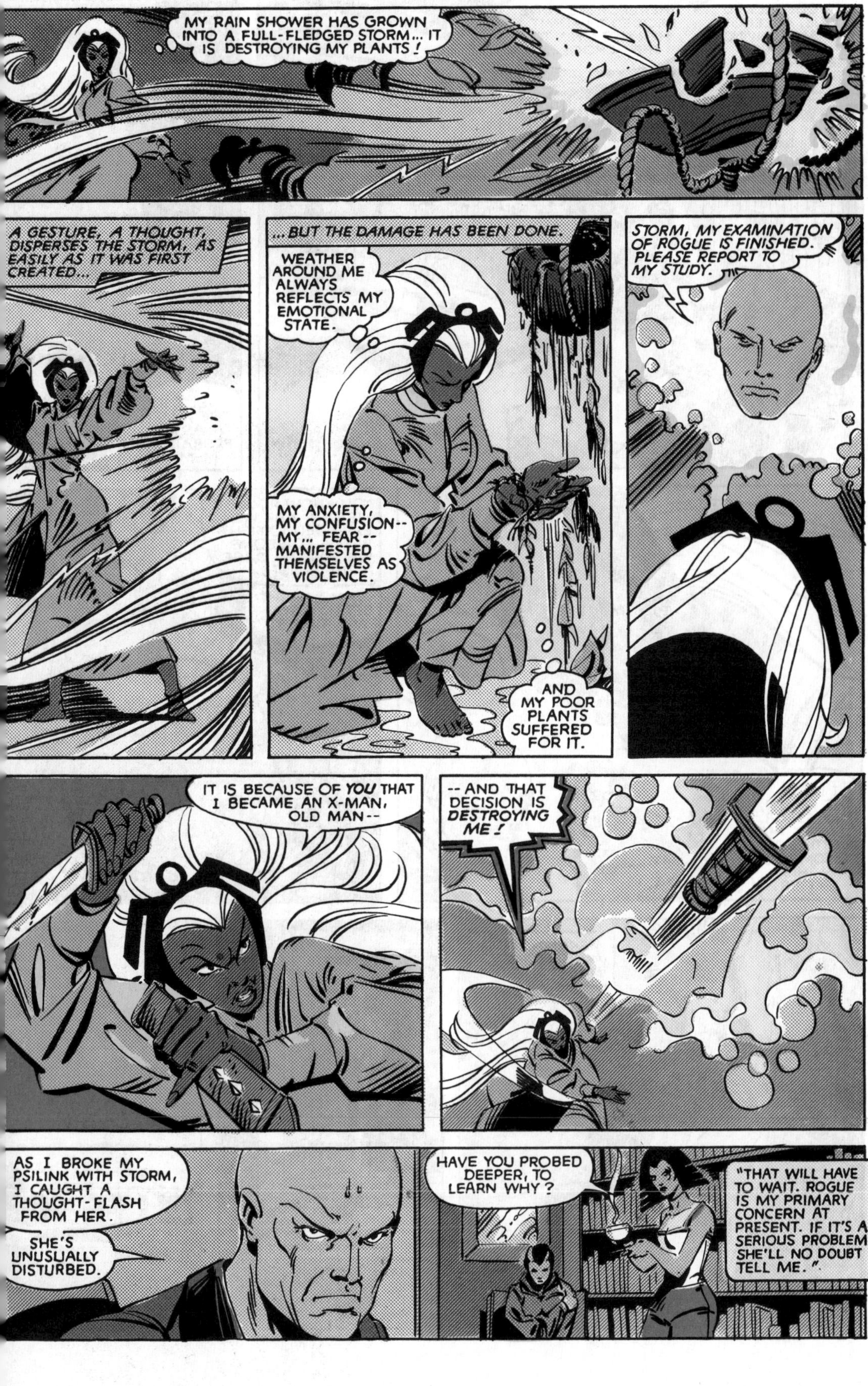
MY RAIN SHOWER HAS GROWN INTO A FULL-FLEDGED STORM... IT IS DESTROYING MY PLANTS!
A GESTURE, A THOUGHT, DISPERSES THE STORM, AS EASILY AS IT WAS FIRST CREATED...
...BUT THE DAMAGE HAS BEEN DONE.
WEATHER AROUND ME ALWAYS REFLECTS MY EMOTIONAL STATE.
MY ANXIETY, MY CONFUSION-- MY... FEAR-- MANIFESTED THEMSELVES AS VIOLENCE.
AND MY POOR PLANTS SUFFERED FOR IT.
STORM, MY EXAMINATION OF ROGUE IS FINISHED. PLEASE REPORT TO MY STUDY.
IT IS BECAUSE OF YOU THAT I BECAME AN X-MAN, OLD MAN--
--AND THAT DECISION IS DESTROYING ME!
AS I BROKE MY PSILINK WITH STORM, I CAUGHT A THOUGHT-FLASH FROM HER.
SHE'S UNUSUALLY DISTURBED.
HAVE YOU PROBED DEEPER, TO LEARN WHY?
"THAT WILL HAVE TO WAIT. ROGUE IS MY PRIMARY CONCERN AT PRESENT. IF IT'S A SERIOUS PROBLEM, SHE'LL NO DOUBT TELL ME."

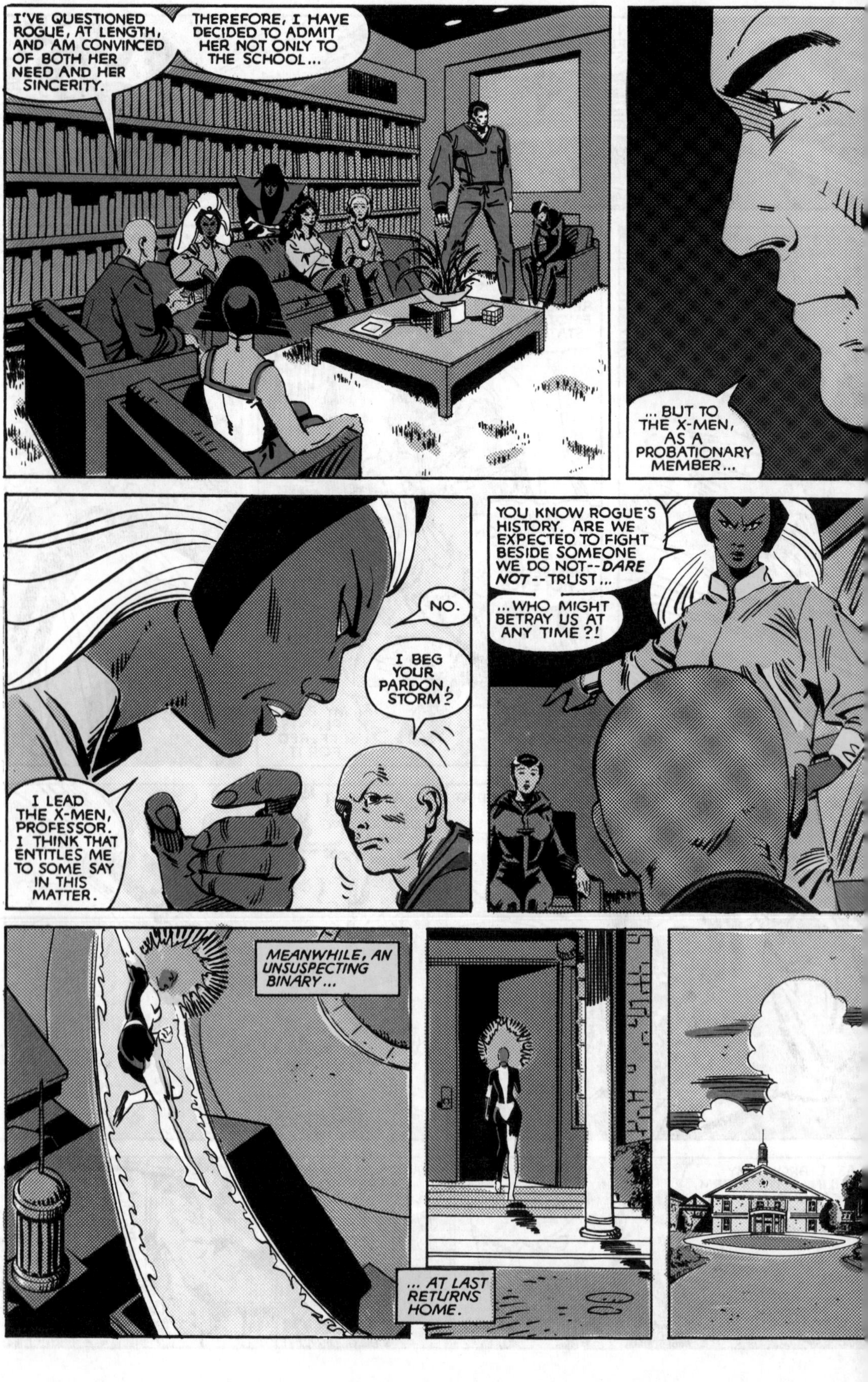
I'VE QUESTIONED ROGUE, AT LENGTH, AND AM CONVINCED OF BOTH HER NEED AND HER SINCERITY.
THEREFORE, I HAVE DECIDED TO ADMIT HER NOT ONLY TO THE SCHOOL...
... BUT TO THE X-MEN, AS A PROBATIONARY MEMBER...
NO.
I BEG YOUR PARDON, STORM?
I LEAD THE X-MEN, PROFESSOR. I THINK THAT ENTITLES ME TO SOME SAY IN THIS MATTER.
YOU KNOW ROGUE'S HISTORY. ARE WE EXPECTED TO FIGHT BESIDE SOMEONE WE DO NOT--DARE NOT--TRUST...
...WHO MIGHT BETRAY US AT ANY TIME?!
MEANWHILE, AN UNSUSPECTING BINARY...
... AT LAST RETURNS HOME.

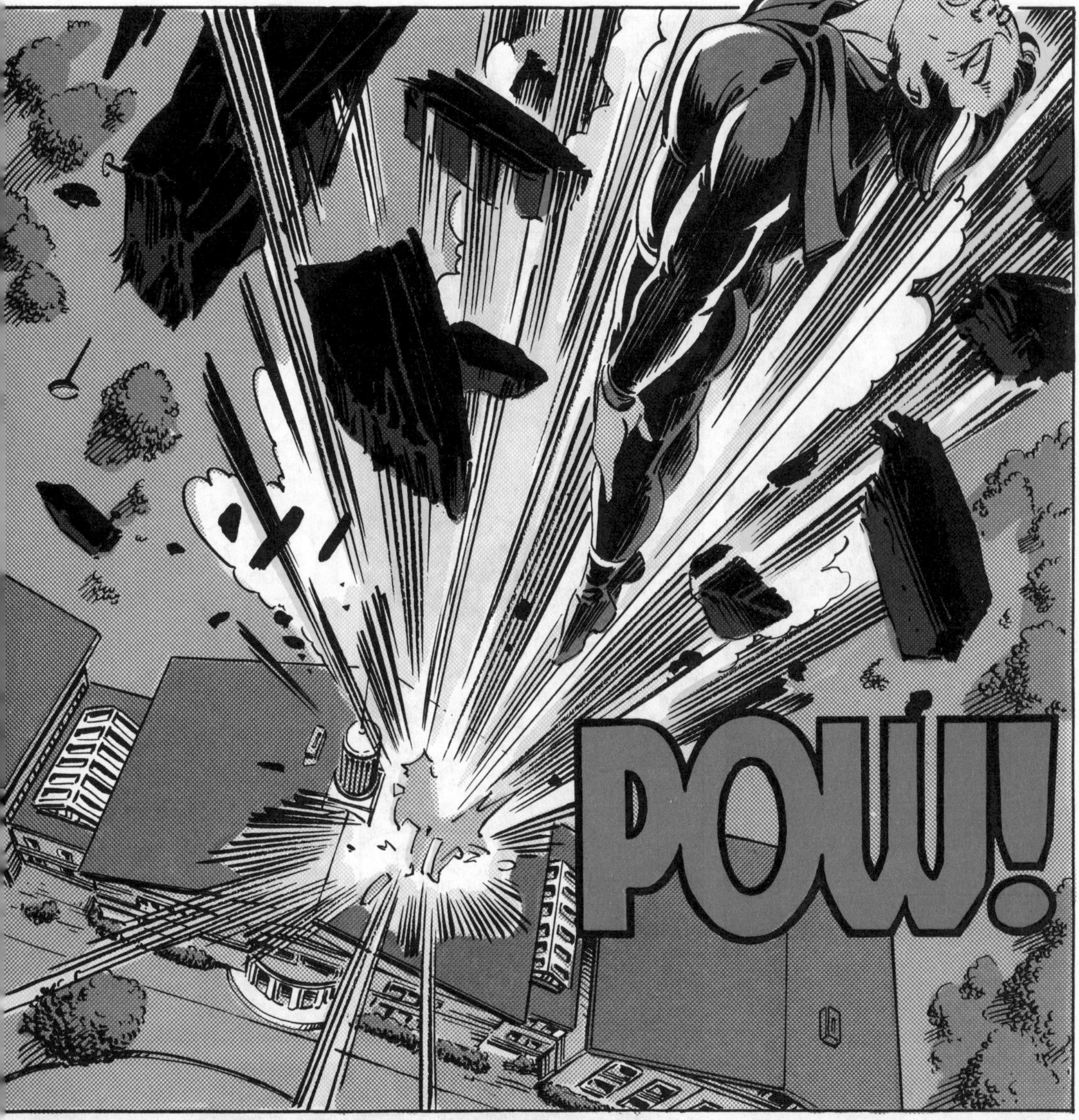
POW!

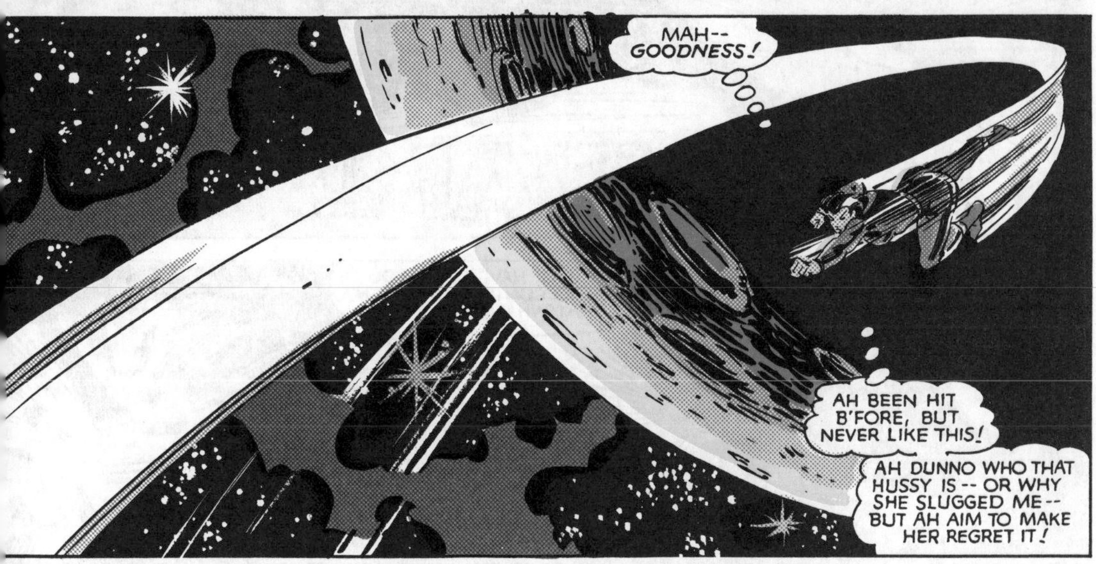
MAH-- GOODNESS!
AH BEEN HIT B'FORE, BUT NEVER LIKE THIS!
AH DUNNO WHO THAT HUSSY IS -- OR WHY SHE SLUGGED ME -- BUT AH AIM TO MAKE HER REGRET IT!

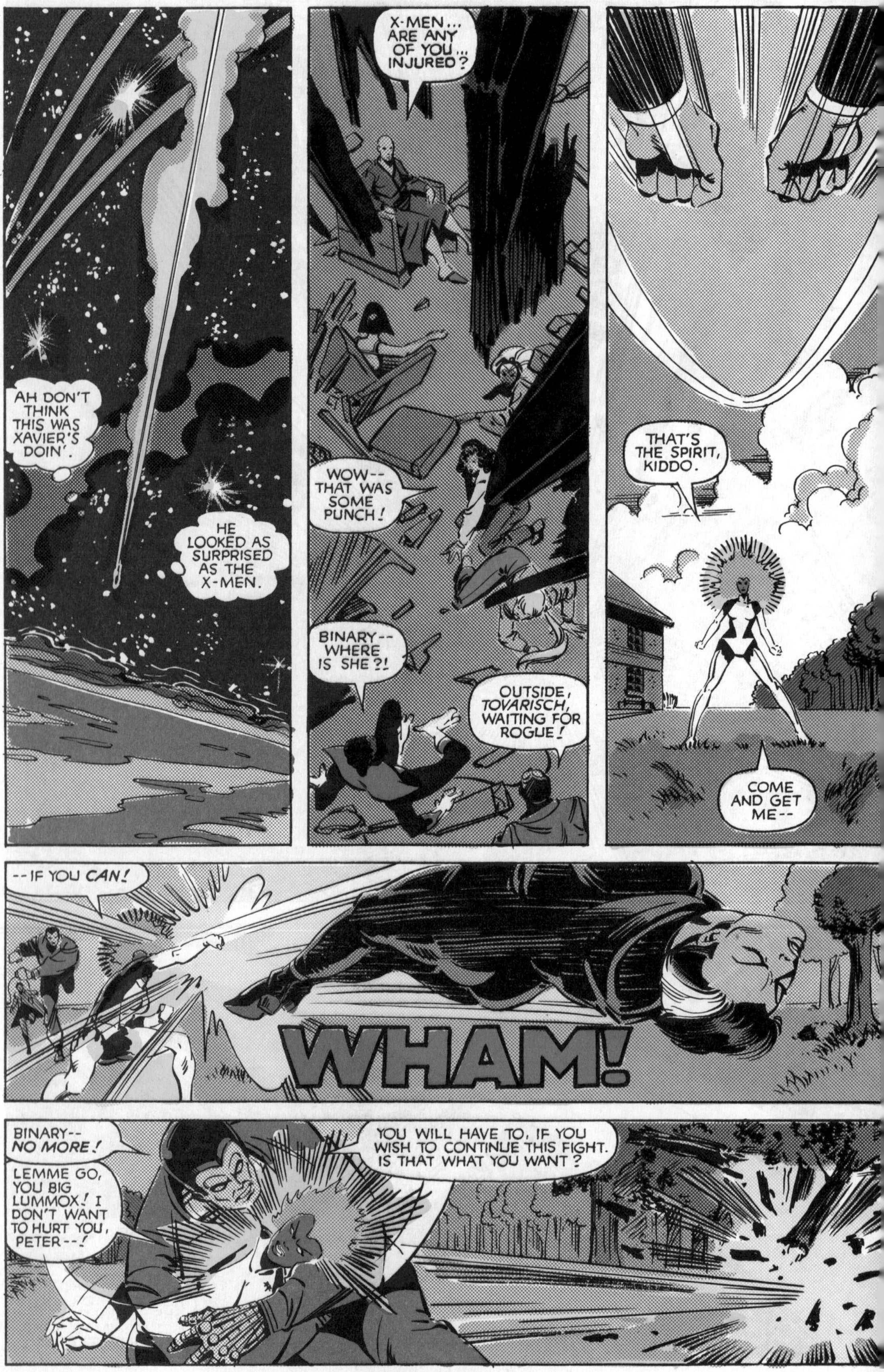
AH DON'T THINK THIS WAS XAVIER'S DOIN'.
HE LOOKED AS SURPRISED AS THE X-MEN.
X-MEN... ARE ANY OF YOU... INJURED?
WOW-- THAT WAS SOME PUNCH!
BINARY-- WHERE IS SHE?!
OUTSIDE, *TOVARISCH*, WAITING FOR ROGUE!
THAT'S THE SPIRIT, KIDDO.
COME AND GET ME--
--IF YOU *CAN!*
WHAM!
BINARY-- ***NO MORE!***
LEMME GO, YOU BIG LUMMOX! I DON'T WANT TO HURT YOU, PETER--!
YOU WILL HAVE TO, IF YOU WISH TO CONTINUE THIS FIGHT. IS THAT WHAT YOU WANT?

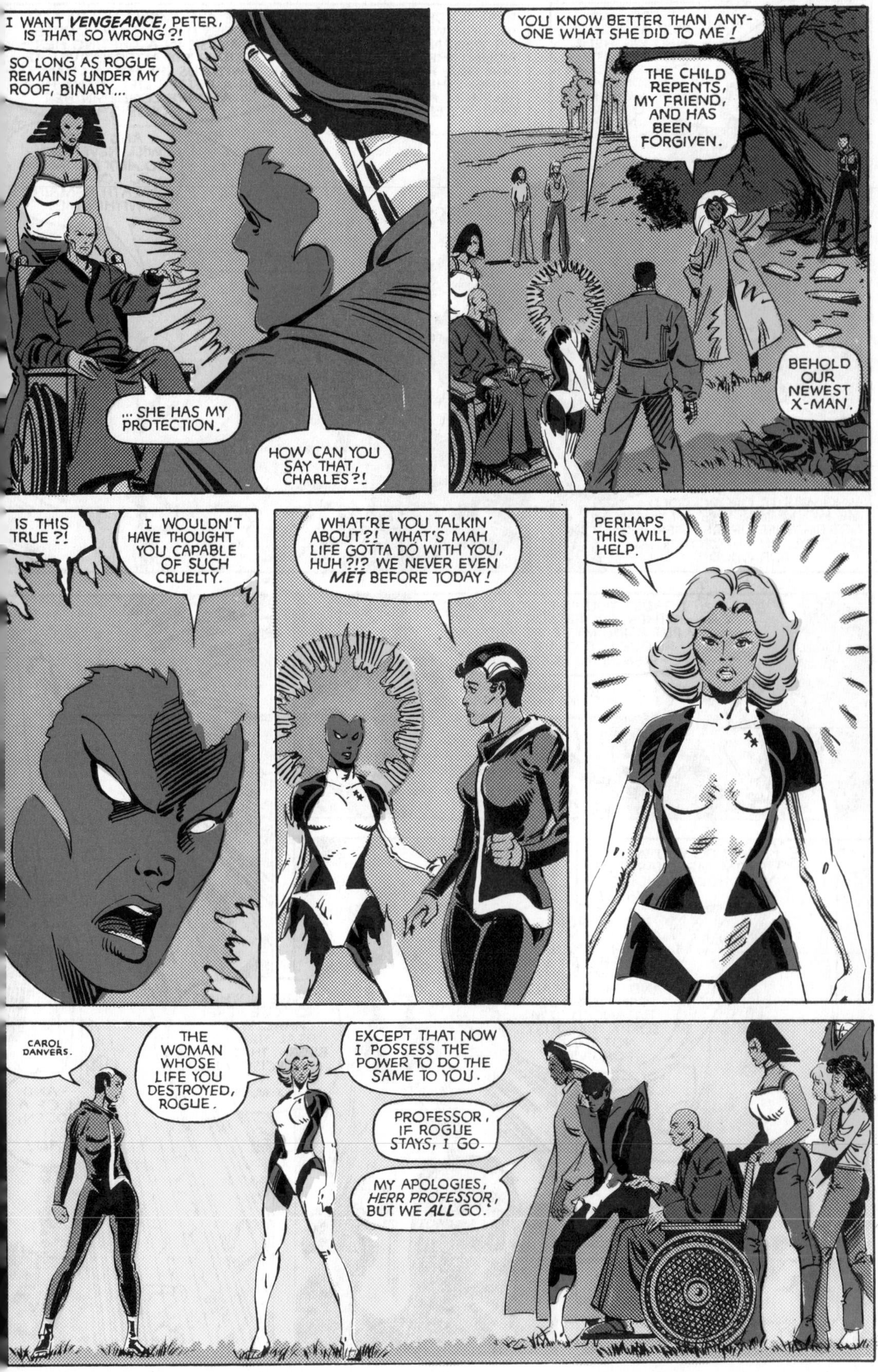
I WANT VENGEANCE, PETER. IS THAT SO WRONG?!
SO LONG AS ROGUE REMAINS UNDER MY ROOF, BINARY...
...SHE HAS MY PROTECTION.
HOW CAN YOU SAY THAT, CHARLES?!
YOU KNOW BETTER THAN ANYONE WHAT SHE DID TO ME!
THE CHILD REPENTS, MY FRIEND, AND HAS BEEN FORGIVEN.
BEHOLD OUR NEWEST X-MAN.
IS THIS TRUE?!
I WOULDN'T HAVE THOUGHT YOU CAPABLE OF SUCH CRUELTY.
WHAT'RE YOU TALKIN' ABOUT?! WHAT'S MAH LIFE GOTTA DO WITH YOU, HUH?!? WE NEVER EVEN MET BEFORE TODAY!
PERHAPS THIS WILL HELP.
CAROL DANVERS.
THE WOMAN WHOSE LIFE YOU DESTROYED, ROGUE.
EXCEPT THAT NOW I POSSESS THE POWER TO DO THE SAME TO YOU.
PROFESSOR, IF ROGUE STAYS, I GO.
MY APOLOGIES, HERR PROFESSOR, BUT WE ALL GO.

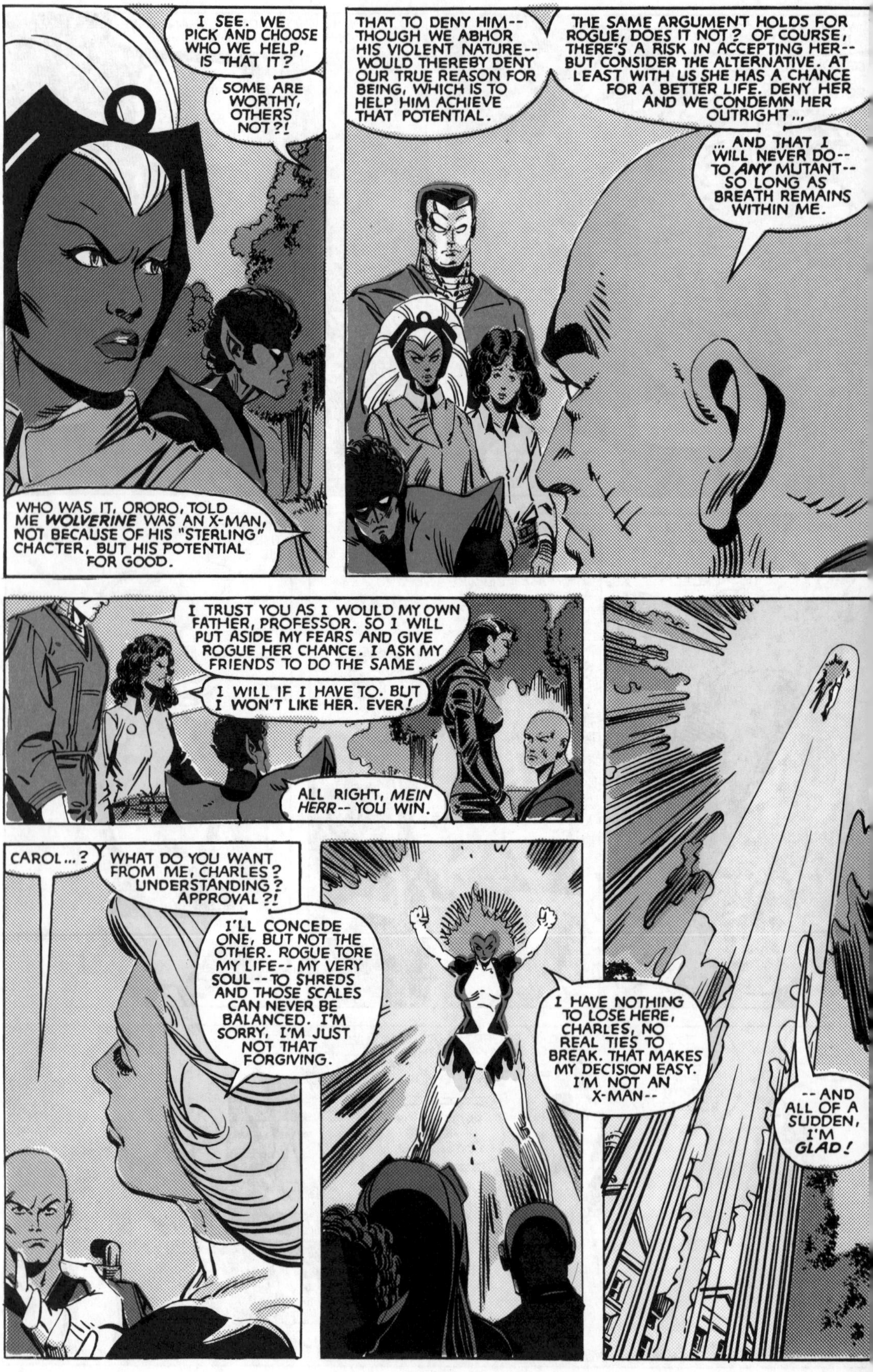
I SEE. WE PICK AND CHOOSE WHO WE HELP, IS THAT IT?
SOME ARE WORTHY, OTHERS NOT?!
WHO WAS IT, ORORO, TOLD ME WOLVERINE WAS AN X-MAN, NOT BECAUSE OF HIS "STERLING" CHACTER, BUT HIS POTENTIAL FOR GOOD.
THAT TO DENY HIM-- THOUGH WE ABHOR HIS VIOLENT NATURE-- WOULD THEREBY DENY OUR TRUE REASON FOR BEING, WHICH IS TO HELP HIM ACHIEVE THAT POTENTIAL.
THE SAME ARGUMENT HOLDS FOR ROGUE, DOES IT NOT? OF COURSE, THERE'S A RISK IN ACCEPTING HER-- BUT CONSIDER THE ALTERNATIVE. AT LEAST WITH US SHE HAS A CHANCE FOR A BETTER LIFE. DENY HER AND WE CONDEMN HER OUTRIGHT...
... AND THAT I WILL NEVER DO-- TO ANY MUTANT-- SO LONG AS BREATH REMAINS WITHIN ME.
I TRUST YOU AS I WOULD MY OWN FATHER, PROFESSOR. SO I WILL PUT ASIDE MY FEARS AND GIVE ROGUE HER CHANCE. I ASK MY FRIENDS TO DO THE SAME.
I WILL IF I HAVE TO. BUT I WON'T LIKE HER. EVER!
ALL RIGHT, MEIN HERR-- YOU WIN.
CAROL...?
WHAT DO YOU WANT FROM ME, CHARLES? UNDERSTANDING? APPROVAL?!
I'LL CONCEDE ONE, BUT NOT THE OTHER. ROGUE TORE MY LIFE-- MY VERY SOUL--TO SHREDS AND THOSE SCALES CAN NEVER BE BALANCED. I'M SORRY, I'M JUST NOT THAT FORGIVING.
I HAVE NOTHING TO LOSE HERE, CHARLES, NO REAL TIES TO BREAK. THAT MAKES MY DECISION EASY. I'M NOT AN X-MAN--
--AND ALL OF A SUDDEN, I'M GLAD!

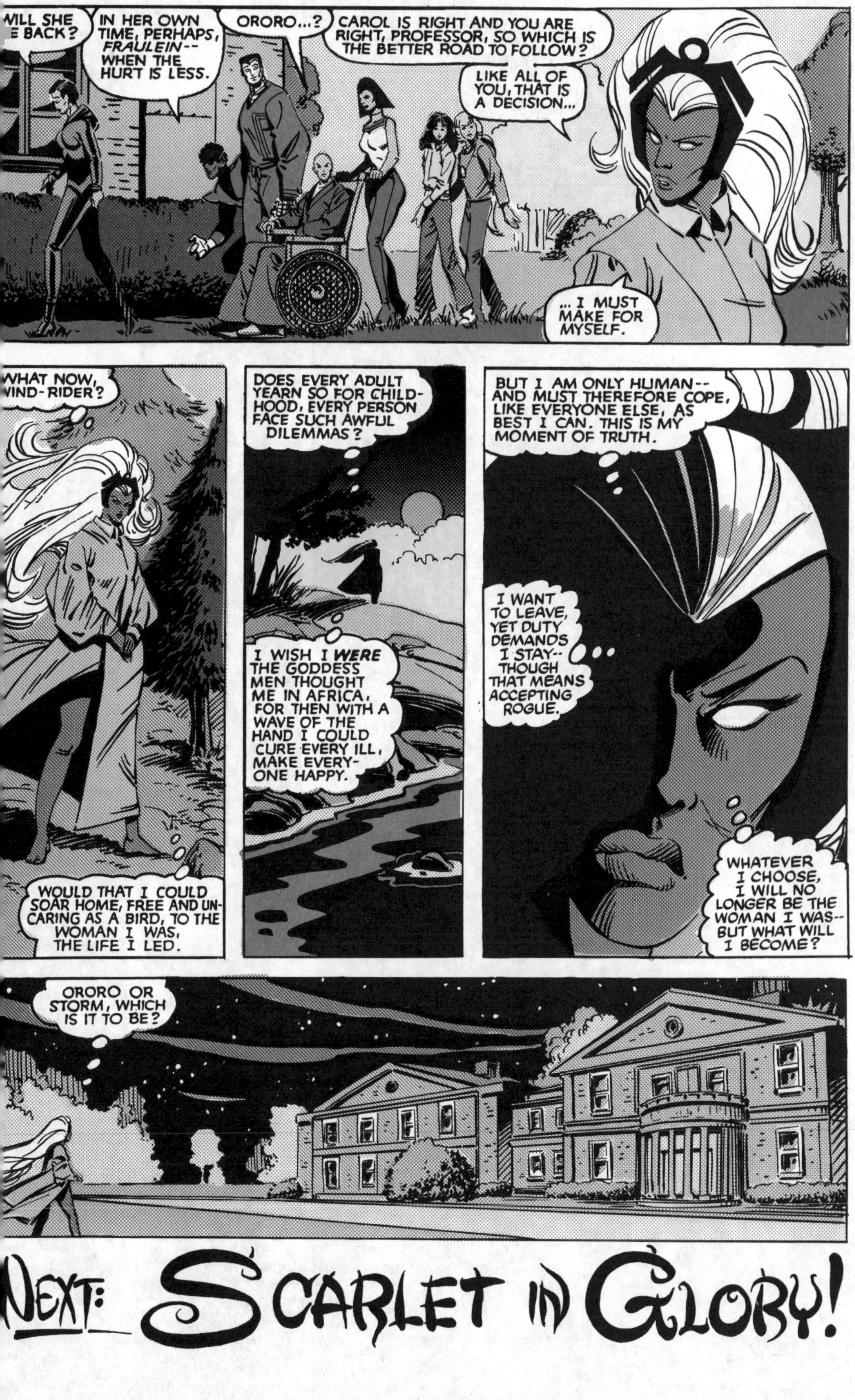
WILL SHE E BACK?
IN HER OWN TIME, PERHAPS, FRAULEIN-- WHEN THE HURT IS LESS.
ORORO...?
CAROL IS RIGHT AND YOU ARE RIGHT, PROFESSOR, SO WHICH IS THE BETTER ROAD TO FOLLOW?
LIKE ALL OF YOU, THAT IS A DECISION...
...I MUST MAKE FOR MYSELF.
WHAT NOW, WIND-RIDER?
WOULD THAT I COULD SOAR HOME, FREE AND UNCARING AS A BIRD, TO THE WOMAN I WAS, THE LIFE I LED.
DOES EVERY ADULT YEARN SO FOR CHILDHOOD, EVERY PERSON FACE SUCH AWFUL DILEMMAS?
I WISH I WERE THE GODDESS MEN THOUGHT ME IN AFRICA, FOR THEN WITH A WAVE OF THE HAND I COULD CURE EVERY ILL, MAKE EVERYONE HAPPY.
BUT I AM ONLY HUMAN-- AND MUST THEREFORE COPE, LIKE EVERYONE ELSE, AS BEST I CAN. THIS IS MY MOMENT OF TRUTH.
I WANT TO LEAVE, YET DUTY DEMANDS I STAY-- THOUGH THAT MEANS ACCEPTING ROGUE.
WHATEVER I CHOOSE, I WILL NO LONGER BE THE WOMAN I WAS-- BUT WHAT WILL I BECOME?
ORORO OR STORM, WHICH IS IT TO BE?
NEXT: SCARLET IN GLORY!

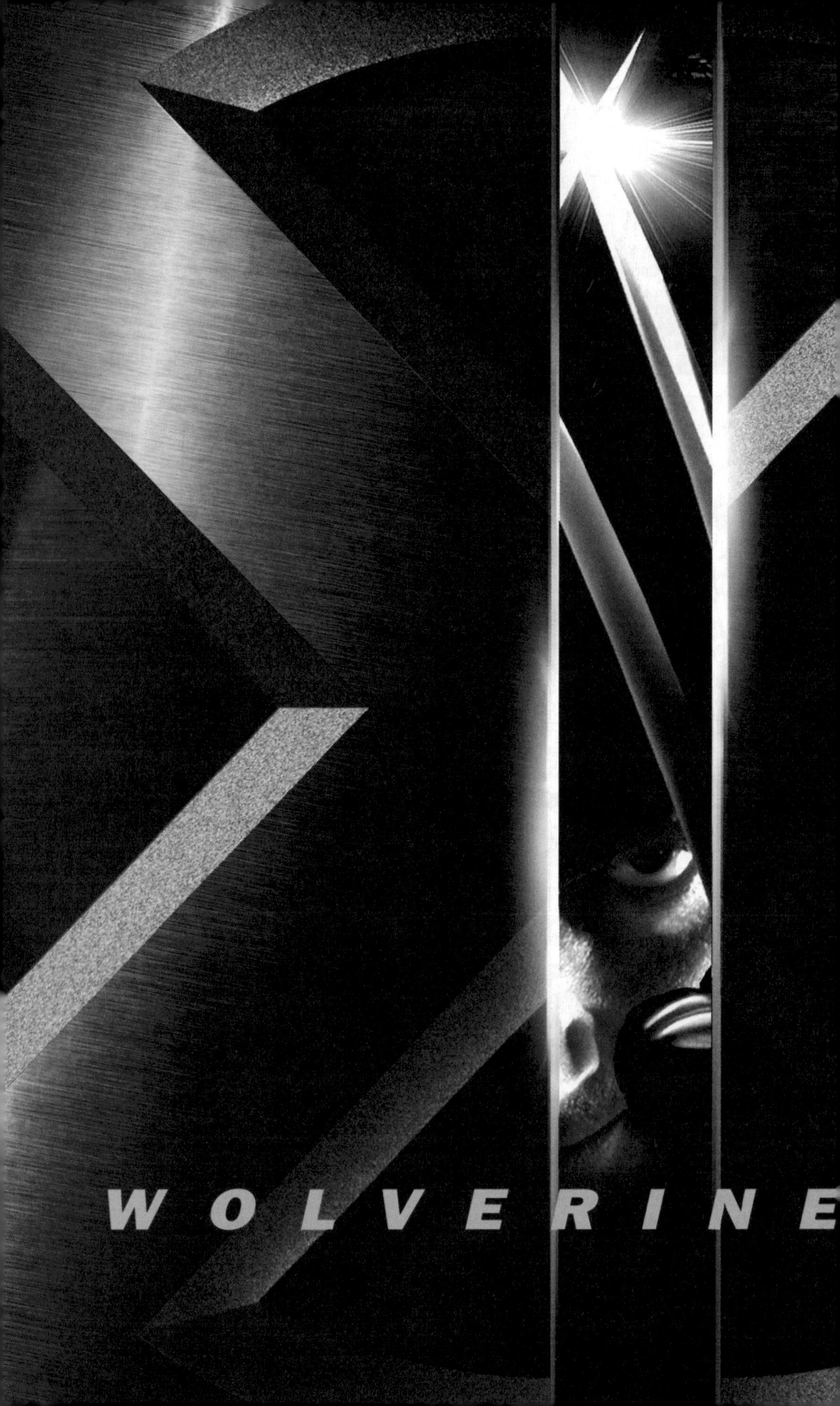
WOLVERINE

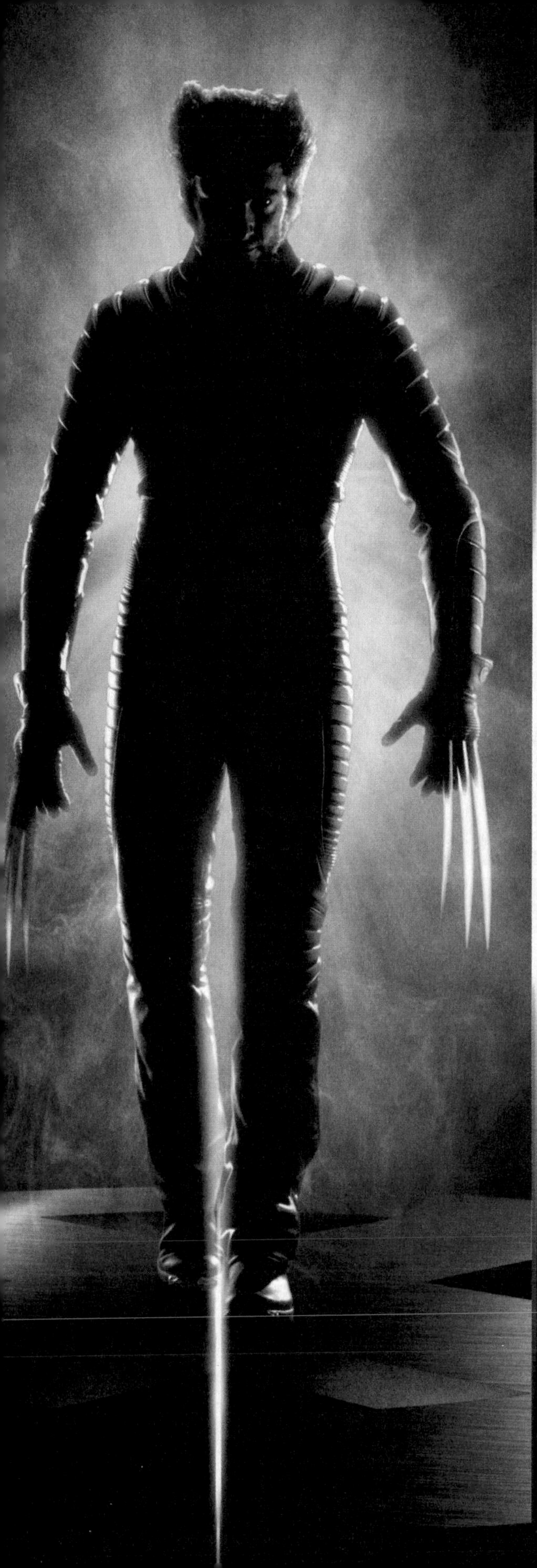

WITNESS

FIRST-HAND

THE

CREATION

OF

WEAPON X!

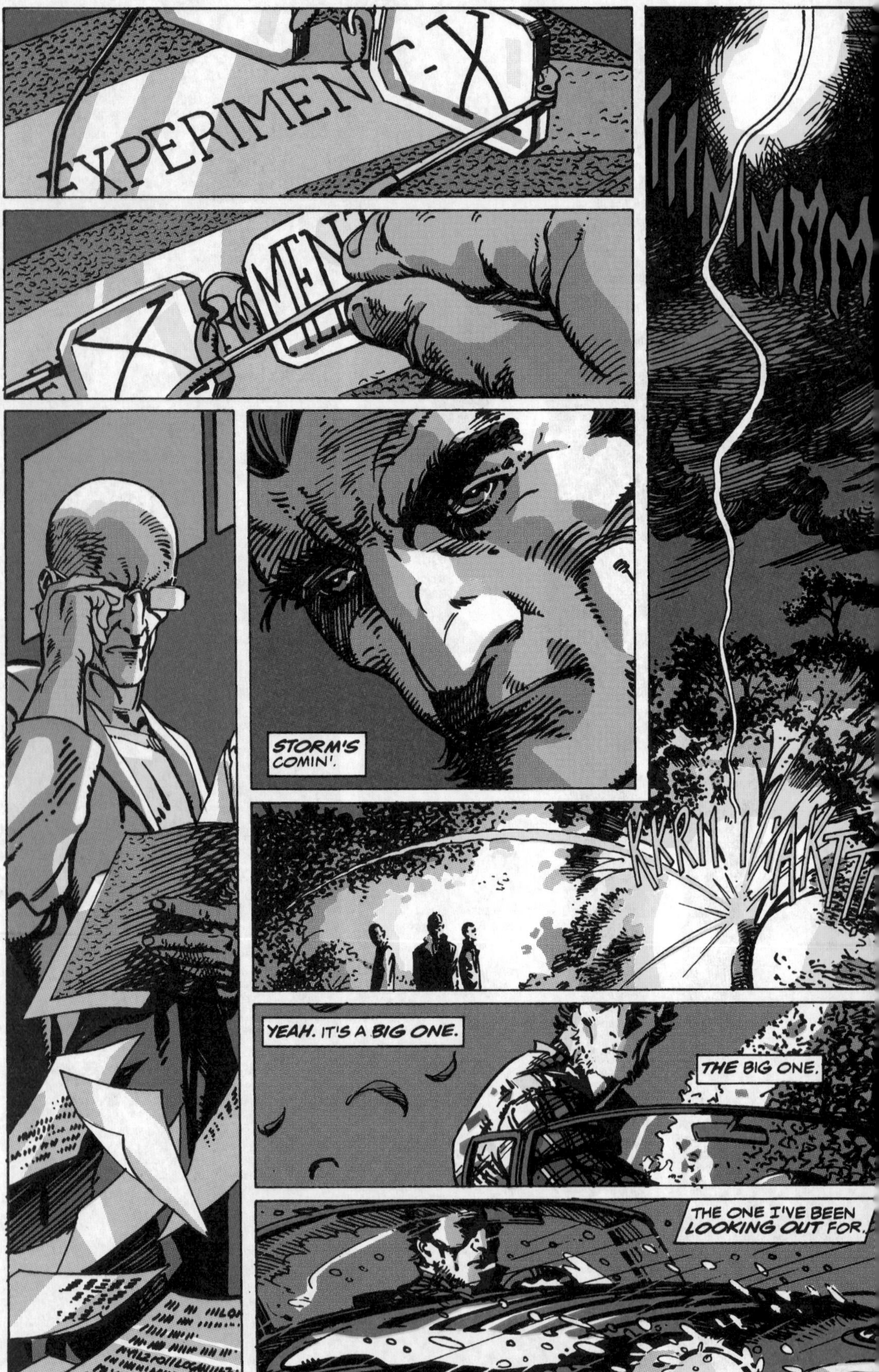
EXPERIMENT-X
THMMMM
STORM'S COMIN'.
KKRM WAKT
YEAH. IT'S A BIG ONE.
THE BIG ONE.
THE ONE I'VE BEEN LOOKING OUT FOR.

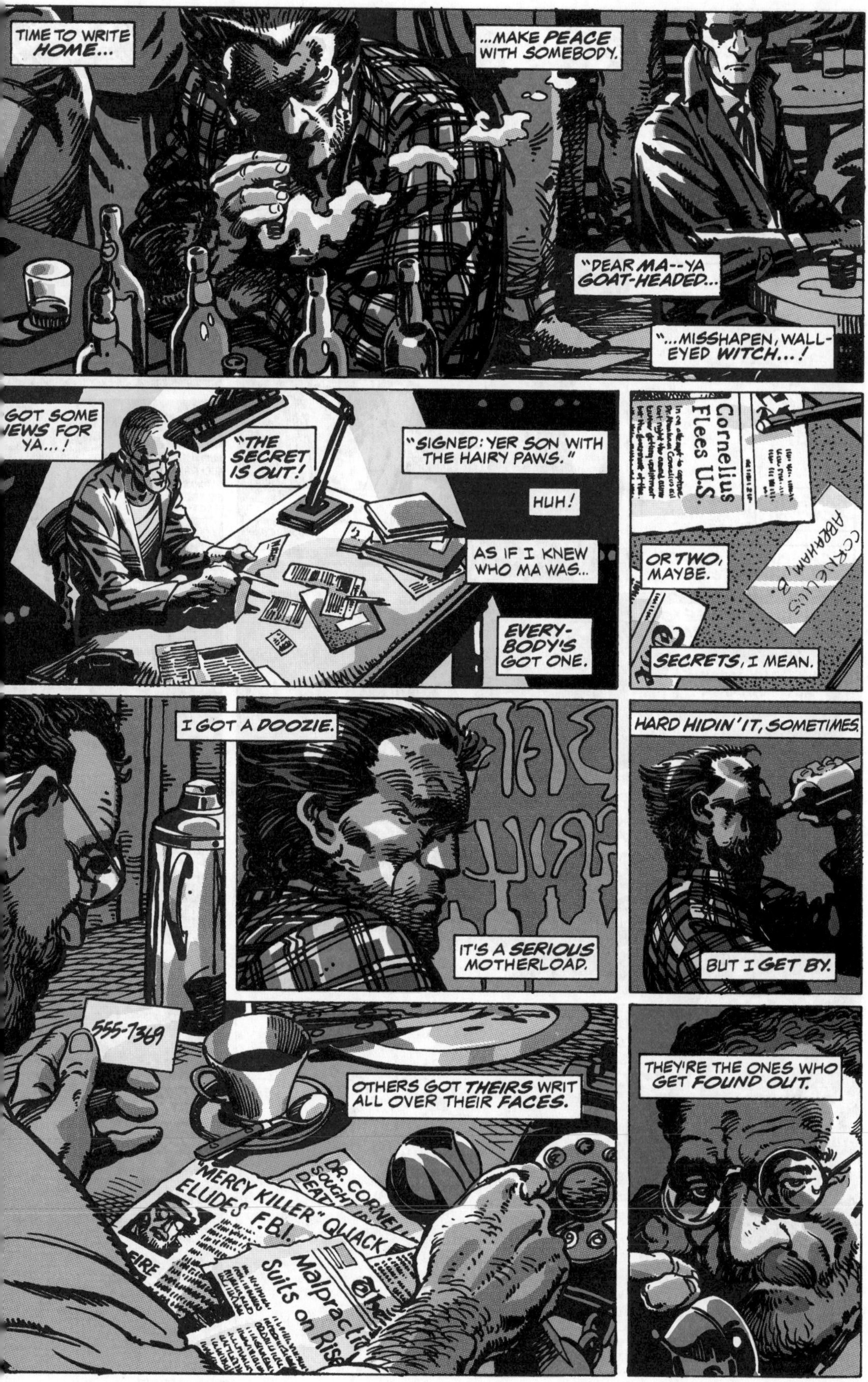

TIME TO WRITE HOME...
...MAKE PEACE WITH SOMEBODY.
"DEAR MA--YA GOAT-HEADED...
"...MISSHAPEN, WALL-EYED WITCH...!
GOT SOME NEWS FOR YA...!
"THE SECRET IS OUT!
"SIGNED: YER SON WITH THE HAIRY PAWS."
HUH!
AS IF I KNEW WHO MA WAS...
EVERY-BODY'S GOT ONE.
Cornelius Flees U.S.
CORNELIUS ABRAHAM, B.
OR TWO, MAYBE.
SECRETS, I MEAN.
I GOT A DOOZIE.
IT'S A SERIOUS MOTHERLOAD.
HARD HIDIN' IT, SOMETIMES.
BUT I GET BY.
555-7369
OTHERS GOT THEIRS WRIT ALL OVER THEIR FACES.
"MERCY KILLER" QUACK ELUDES F.B.I.
THEY'RE THE ONES WHO GET FOUND OUT.

AND END UP DANGLIN' FROM SOMEBODY'S LINE.

BUT YOU ONLY GET *HOOKED* IF YOU TAKE THE *BAIT*, RIGHT?

Hines, Carol MAYBE.

230 Lebeque

Previous Employer Nasa

No Years 12½ months

Have you been exposed to Radiation or Irradiation in the past 12 months? no

Will you submit to a lie detector test? yes

Will you take an Oath of Security? yes

RANGE IS *ROUTINE*.

I CAN PUT *SIX SHOTS* INTO A *QUARTER*...

...AN' GET *CHANGE* FOR THE *GUM-MACHINE*.

WHEN MY *HANDS* AIN'T SHAKIN'.

SO I WING SOME *GEEK* WITH A *RICOCHET*...

LIKE... WHO *GIVES A TOSS*.

DUE TO VIOLENT NATURE OF RETIREE EXTREME CAUTION IS SUGGESTED IN ANY SUBSEQUENT RACTION

REPORT 4 OF 4
FR 1727 1306 Ont.

SUMMAR REPORT OF FIRING E INCIDENT. LOGAN 27 1306 Ont. PRINC. WORKER A1. SUFF D CRITICAL AND .HEAD WOUND D 38 CAL. ENTRY LEFT TEMPLE D

LOGAN. #1727 1306 ONTARI

LOGAN (1727 1306 Ont.) strongly suggest likel ric behaviour and possible self-destructive ten rega ulting from chronic alcohol abuse. morbid preoccupation with current "mutant" sca press and trivia-related sources suggests poss nervous disorder or psychosis. This last is inconclusive, however. A leave of absence is recommended. Alternative measure wo d dismissal from service with standard pay distributed o the 3 year period. due to violent nature of retiree extreme caution is sugge n any subsequent interaction.

SUITS DO, I GUESS.

SOME *ATTITUDE* THEY GOT.

t and advisory ref. 1727 1306 Ont.

CRITICAL WOUNDING (5/11) OF THE RING RANGE STAFF MEMBER. (#602 Ont.) DIATE DISMISSAL IS IMPERATIVE. AND NDING INVESTIGATION.

Report 4 of 4, F.R. #1727 1308 O cc. Beloise, Dore

NG AS PRIORITY. ALL UNITS PLUS CE OPERATIVES ACKNOWLEDGE BY EN REPORTS TO THIS OFFIC

LOGAN 1727 130

SCREW 'EM.

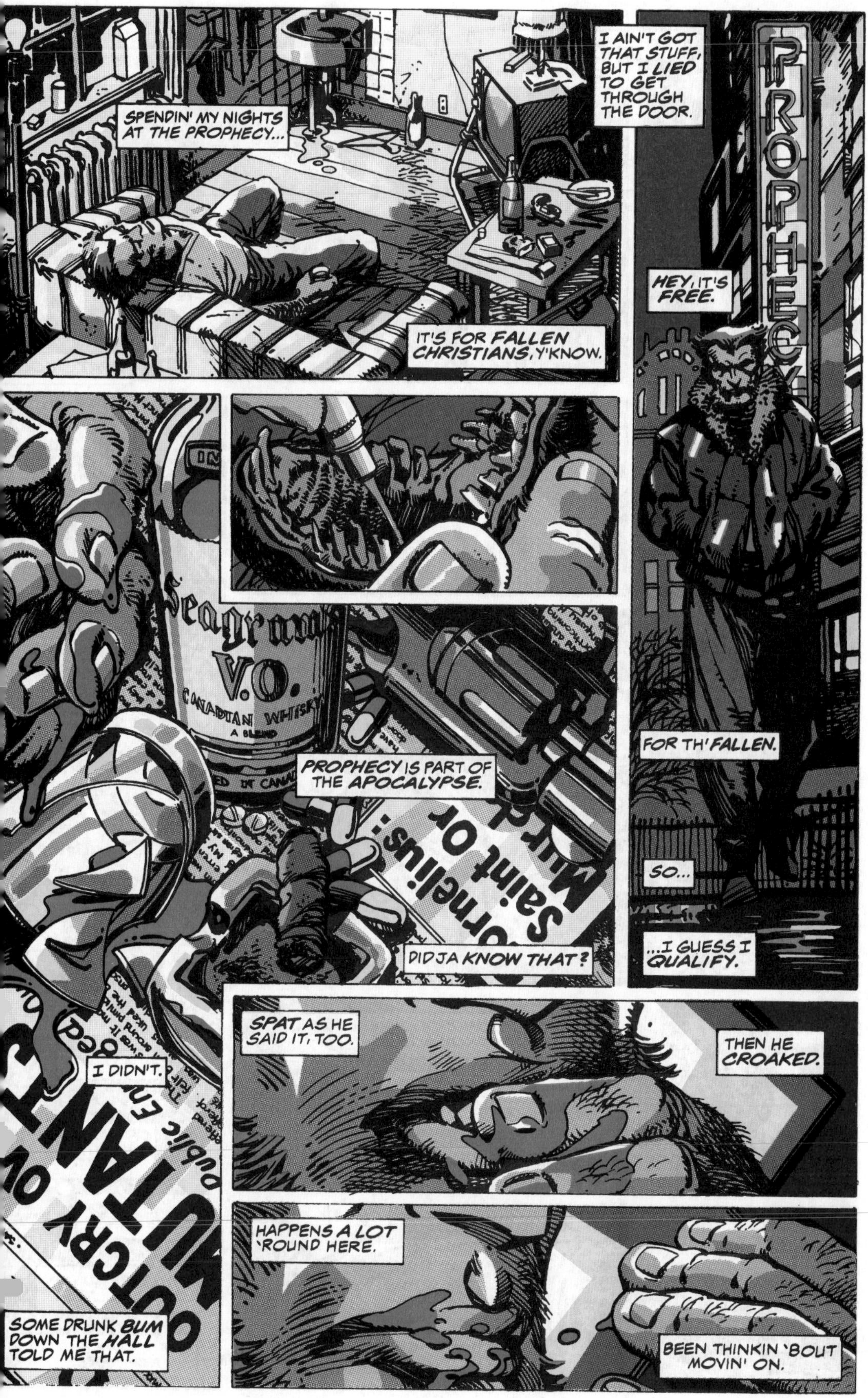
SPENDIN' MY NIGHTS AT THE PROPHECY...
IT'S FOR FALLEN CHRISTIANS, Y'KNOW.
I AIN'T GOT THAT STUFF, BUT I LIED TO GET THROUGH THE DOOR.
PROPHECY
HEY, IT'S FREE.
FOR TH' FALLEN.
SO...
...I GUESS I QUALIFY.
V.O.
CANADIAN WHISKY
A BLEND
PROPHECY IS PART OF THE APOCALYPSE.
DIDJA KNOW THAT?
I DIDN'T.
SOME DRUNK BUM DOWN THE HALL TOLD ME THAT.
SPAT AS HE SAID IT, TOO.
THEN HE CROAKED.
HAPPENS A LOT 'ROUND HERE.
BEEN THINKIN 'BOUT MOVIN' ON.

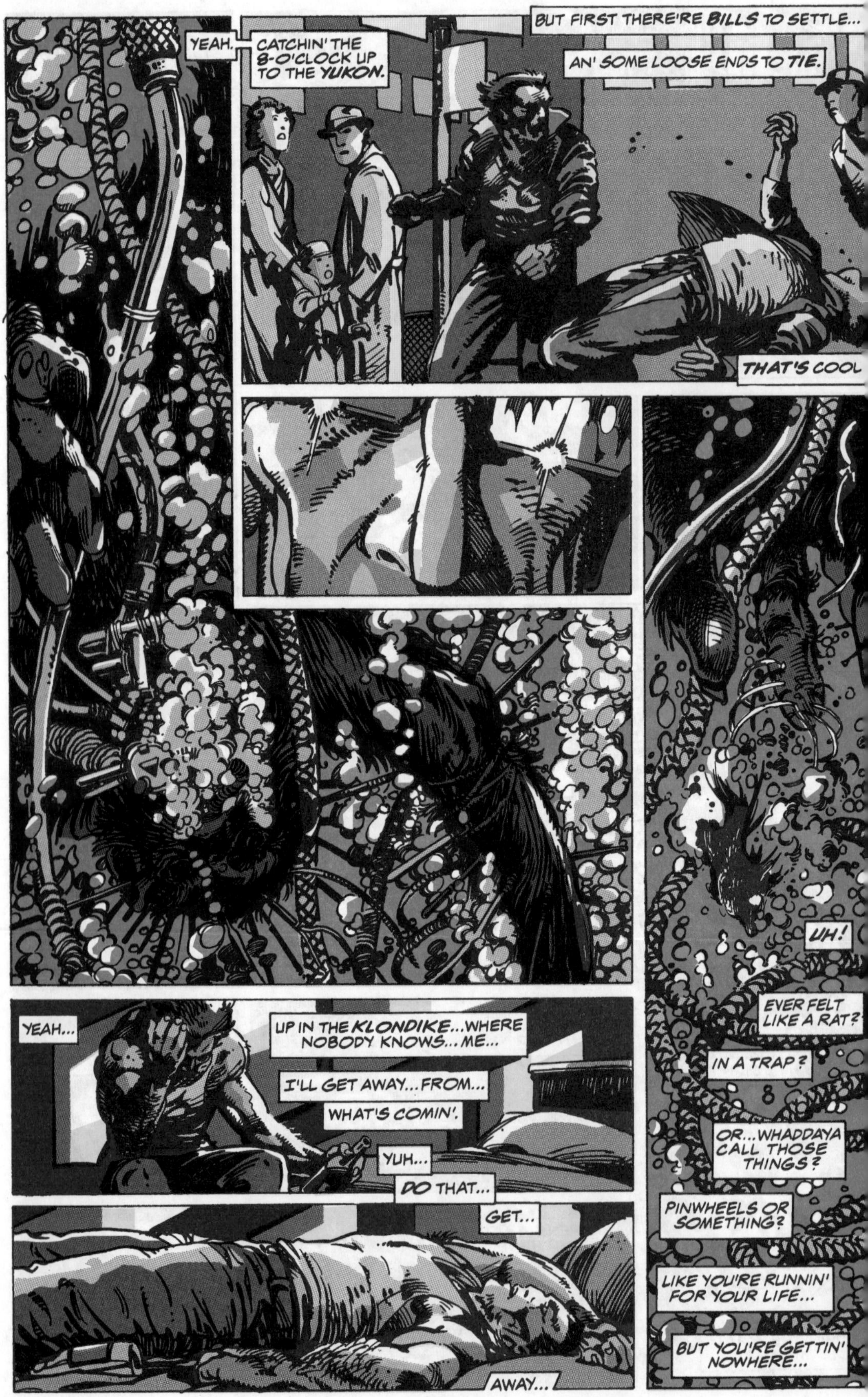
YEAH.
CATCHIN' THE 8-O'CLOCK UP TO THE YUKON.
BUT FIRST THERE'RE BILLS TO SETTLE...
AN' SOME LOOSE ENDS TO TIE.
THAT'S COOL
UH!
EVER FELT LIKE A RAT?
IN A TRAP?
OR...WHADDAYA CALL THOSE THINGS?
PINWHEELS OR SOMETHING?
LIKE YOU'RE RUNNIN' FOR YOUR LIFE...
BUT YOU'RE GETTIN' NOWHERE...
YEAH...
UP IN THE KLONDIKE...WHERE NOBODY KNOWS...ME...
I'LL GET AWAY...FROM...
WHAT'S COMIN'.
YUH...
DO THAT...
GET...
AWAY...

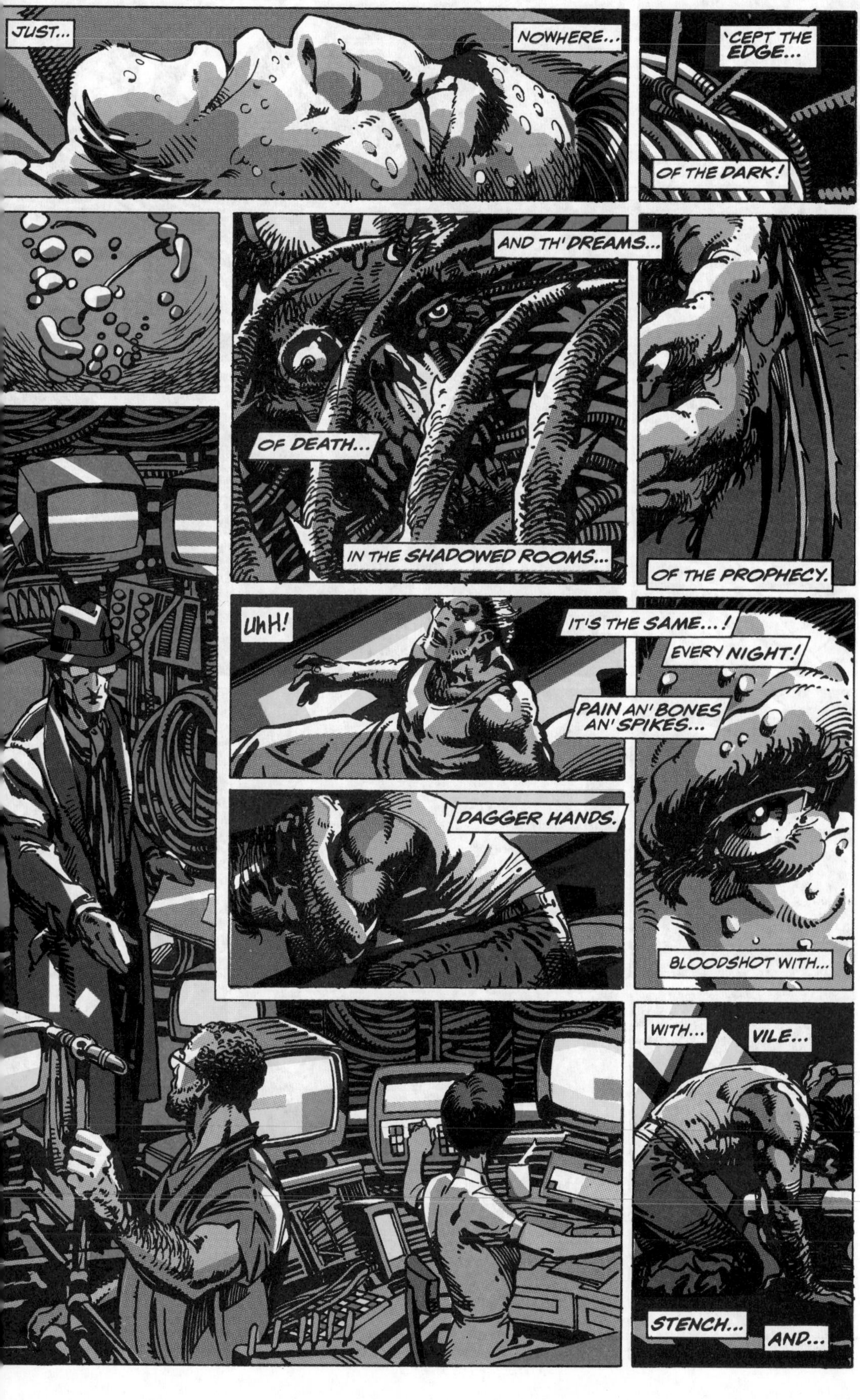
JUST...
NOWHERE...
'CEPT THE EDGE...
OF THE DARK!
AND TH' DREAMS...
OF DEATH...
IN THE SHADOWED ROOMS...
OF THE PROPHECY.
UNH!
IT'S THE SAME...!
EVERY NIGHT!
PAIN AN' BONES AN' SPIKES...
DAGGER HANDS.
BLOODSHOT WITH...
WITH...
VILE...
STENCH...
AND...

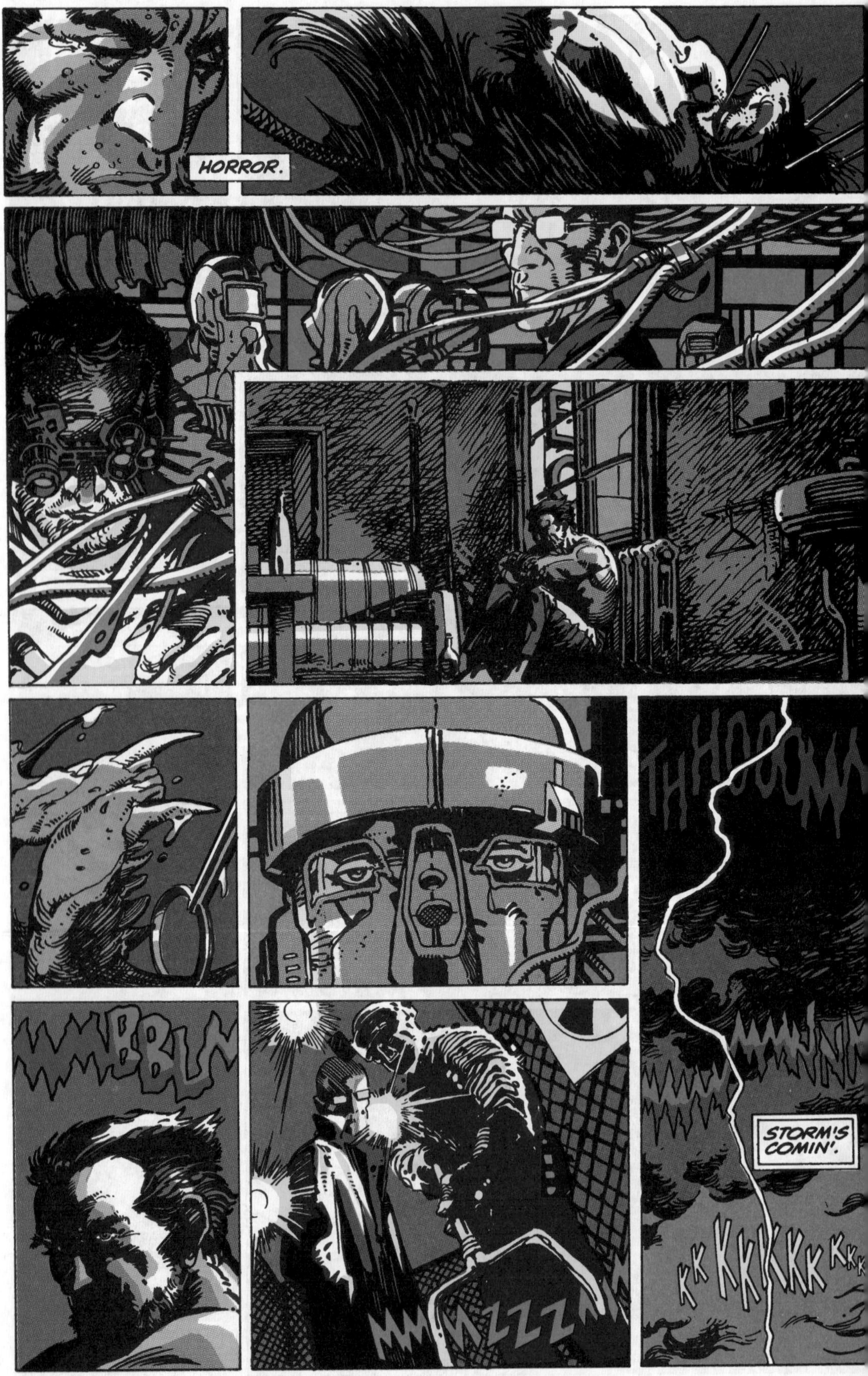
HORROR.
STORM'S COMIN'.

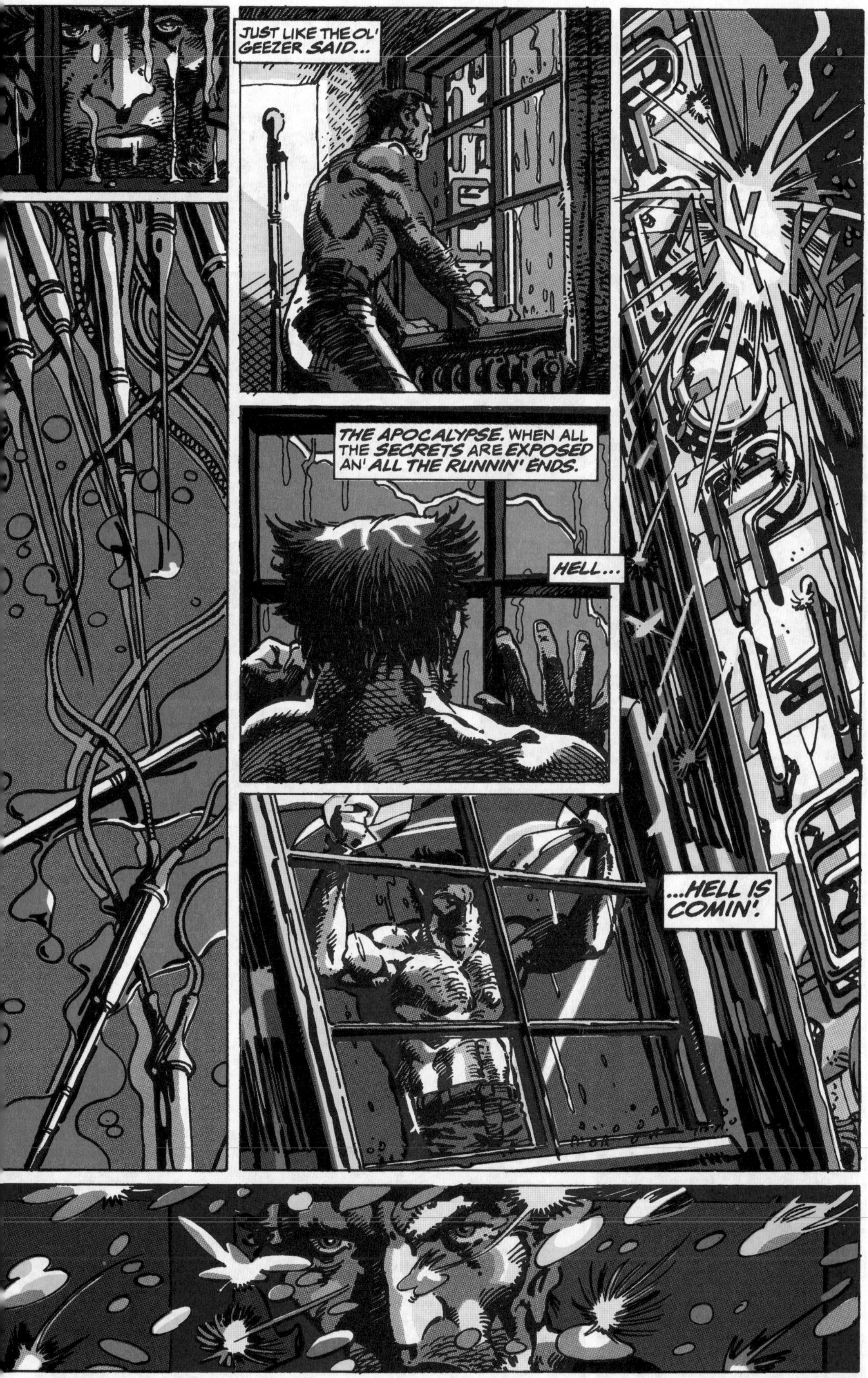
JUST LIKE THE OL' GEEZER SAID...
THE APOCALYPSE. WHEN ALL THE SECRETS ARE EXPOSED AN' ALL THE RUNNIN' ENDS.
HELL...
...HELL IS COMIN'.

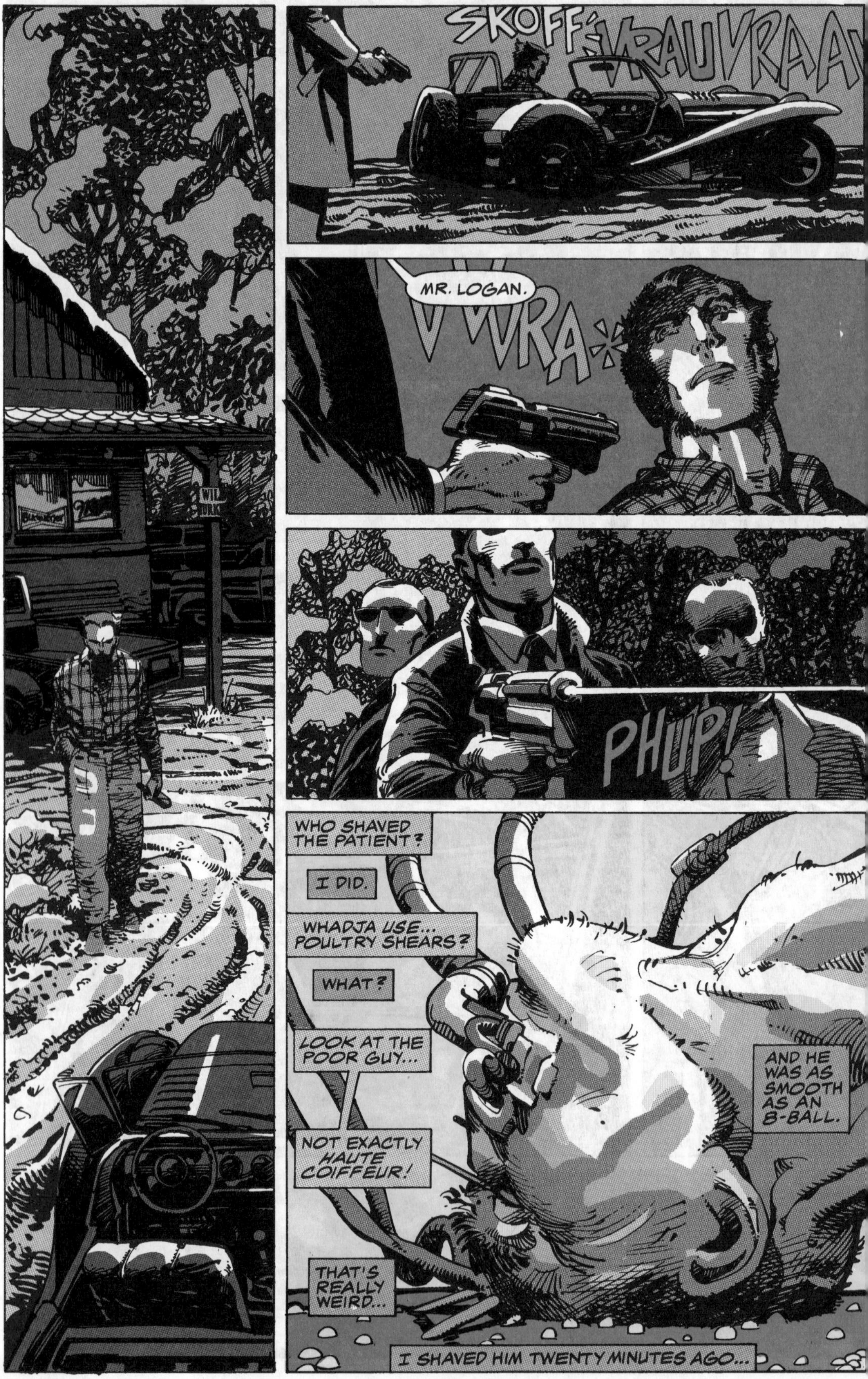
SKOFF
VRAUVRAA
MR. LOGAN.
VWRA
PHUP!
WHO SHAVED THE PATIENT?
I DID.
WHADJA USE... POULTRY SHEARS?
WHAT?
LOOK AT THE POOR GUY...
NOT EXACTLY HAUTE COIFFEUR!
AND HE WAS AS SMOOTH AS AN 8-BALL.
THAT'S REALLY WEIRD...
I SHAVED HIM TWENTY MINUTES AGO...

UHF HELP ME WITH HIM.

YUH HE'S REAL HEAVY FOR JUST...

...A LITTLE GUY...

TOK!

HEADS UP, GENTLEMEN. THE PROFESSOR IS ARRIVING.

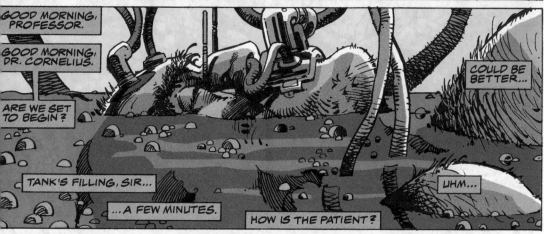

GOOD MORNING, PROFESSOR.

GOOD MORNING, DR. CORNELIUS.

ARE WE SET TO BEGIN?

TANK'S FILLING, SIR...

...A FEW MINUTES.

HOW IS THE PATIENT?

COULD BE BETTER...

UHM...

HE PUT UP SOME RESISTANCE WHEN THE BOYS PICKED HIM UP LAST NIGHT.

AAGH! GET HIM OFFA-MEE!

THEY HAD TO JOSTLE HIM A BIT.

IS HE DAMAGED?

ANY DEEP CUTS?

HE'S O.K.

BUT WE CAN'T AFFORD LEAKAGE.

WE PLUGGED HIM UP TIGHT.

PROFESSOR? DR. CORNELIUS? WE CAN BEGIN NOW.

#!%@! DIDN'T YOU GET HIM WITH THAT STUPID STUN-GUN?!

COURSE I DID!

POINT BLANK!

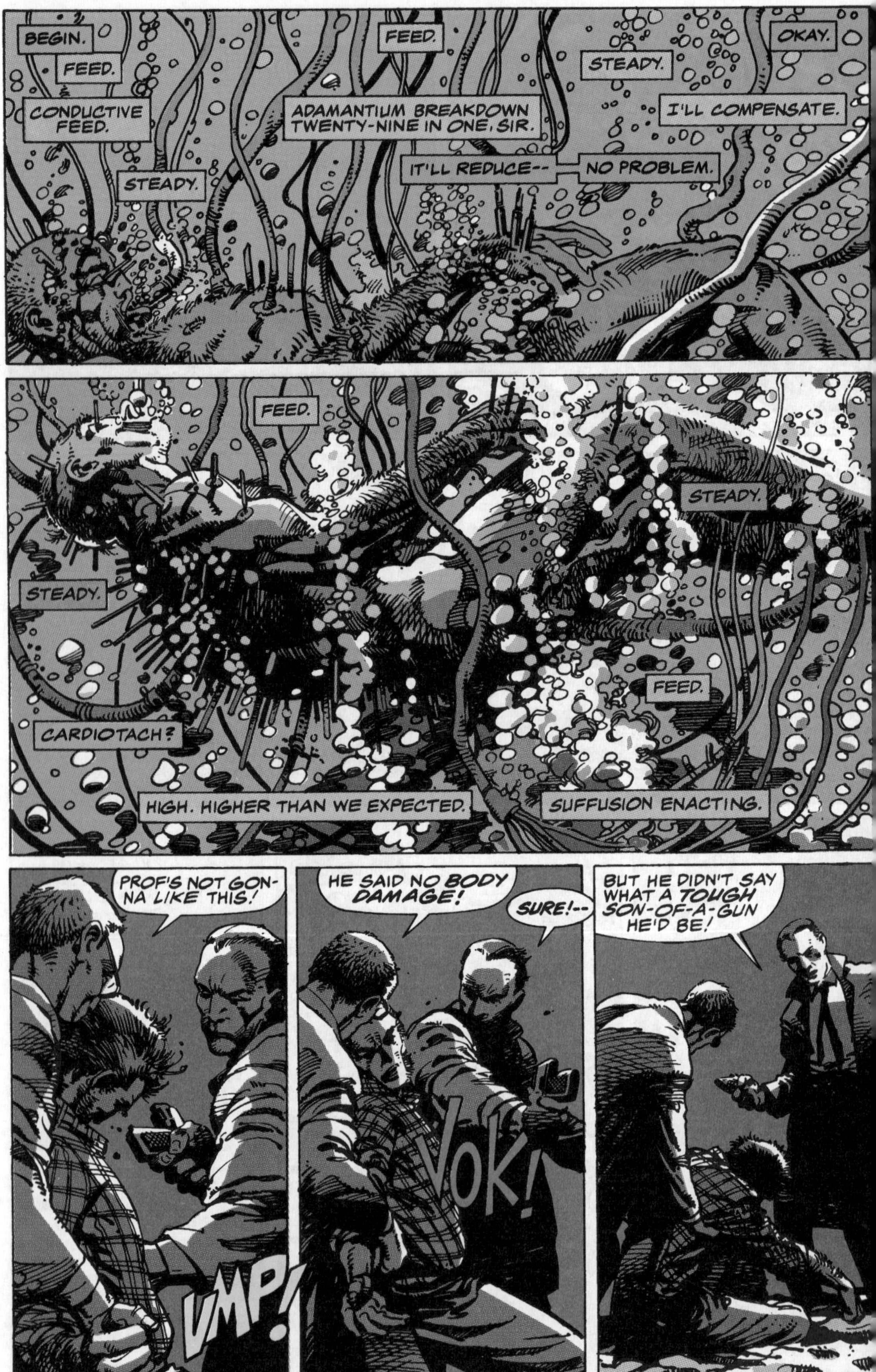
BEGIN.
FEED.
CONDUCTIVE FEED.
STEADY.
ADAMANTIUM BREAKDOWN TWENTY-NINE IN ONE, SIR.
FEED.
IT'LL REDUCE--
NO PROBLEM.
STEADY.
I'LL COMPENSATE.
OKAY.
FEED.
STEADY.
STEADY.
FEED.
CARDIOTACH?
HIGH. HIGHER THAN WE EXPECTED.
SUFFUSION ENACTING.
PROF'S NOT GON-NA LIKE THIS!
UMP!
HE SAID NO BODY DAMAGE!
SURE!--
VOK!
BUT HE DIDN'T SAY WHAT A TOUGH SON-OF-A-GUN HE'D BE!

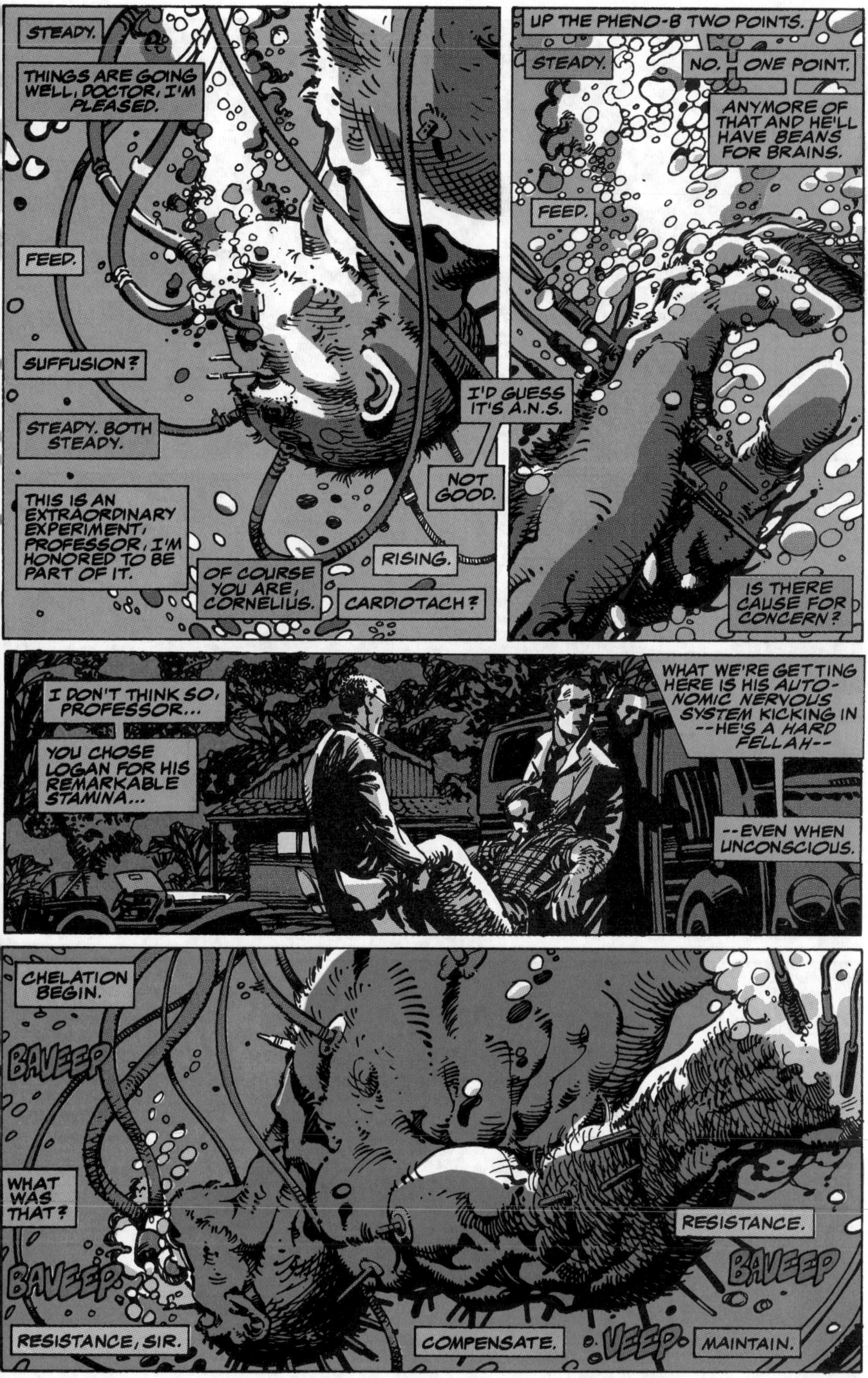
STEADY.
THINGS ARE GOING WELL, DOCTOR. I'M PLEASED.
FEED.
SUFFUSION?
STEADY. BOTH STEADY.
I'D GUESS IT'S A.N.S.
NOT GOOD.
THIS IS AN EXTRAORDINARY EXPERIMENT, PROFESSOR. I'M HONORED TO BE PART OF IT.
OF COURSE YOU ARE, CORNELIUS.
RISING.
CARDIOTACH?
UP THE PHENO-B TWO POINTS.
STEADY.
NO. ONE POINT.
ANYMORE OF THAT AND HE'LL HAVE BEANS FOR BRAINS.
FEED.
IS THERE CAUSE FOR CONCERN?
I DON'T THINK SO, PROFESSOR...
YOU CHOSE LOGAN FOR HIS REMARKABLE STAMINA...
WHAT WE'RE GETTING HERE IS HIS AUTONOMIC NERVOUS SYSTEM KICKING IN --HE'S A HARD FELLAH--
--EVEN WHEN UNCONSCIOUS.
CHELATION BEGIN.
BAVEEP
WHAT WAS THAT?
BAVEEP
RESISTANCE.
BAVEEP
RESISTANCE, SIR.
COMPENSATE.
VEEP
MAINTAIN.

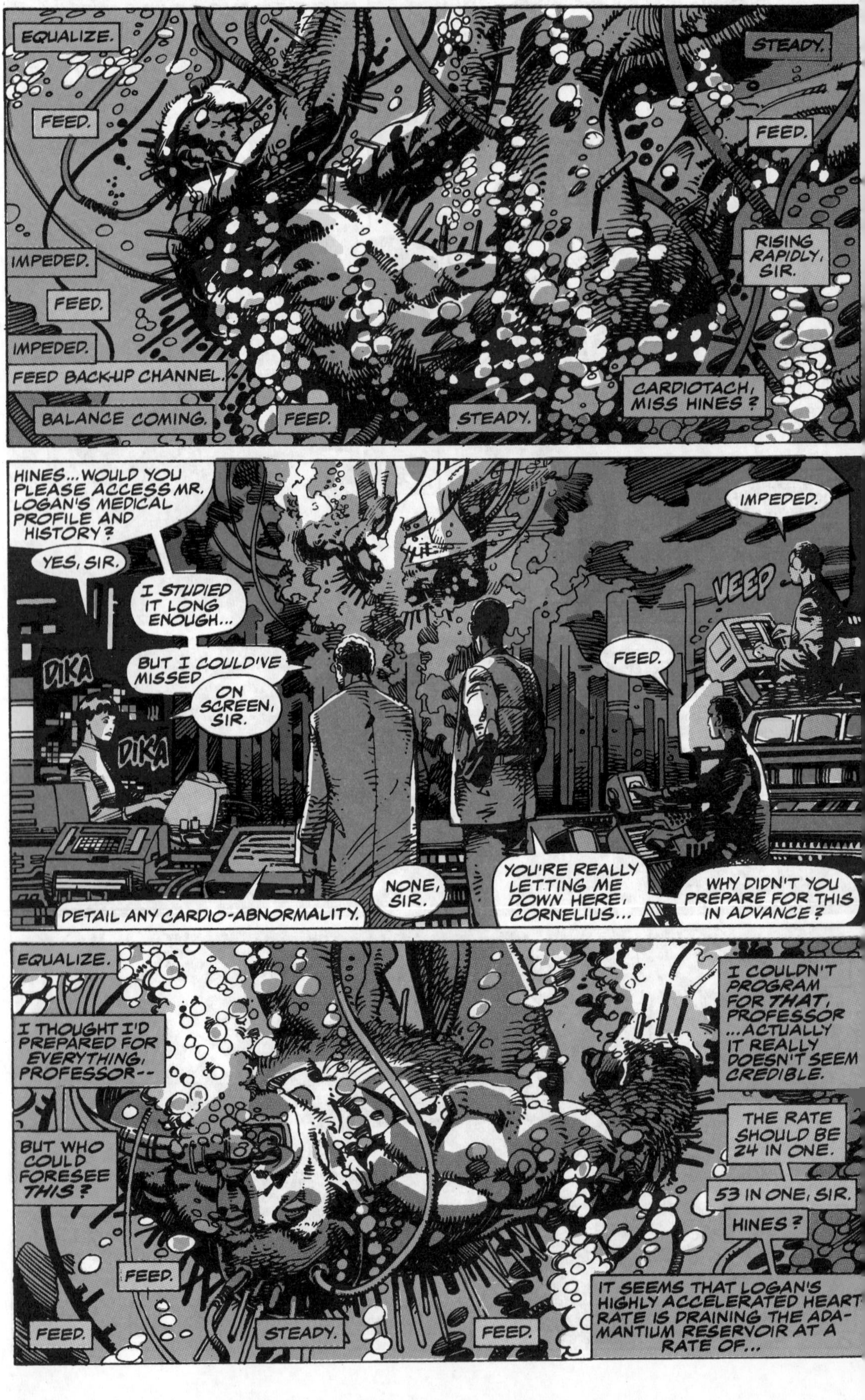
EQUALIZE.
FEED.
STEADY.
FEED.
RISING RAPIDLY, SIR.
IMPEDED.
FEED.
IMPEDED.
FEED BACK-UP CHANNEL.
BALANCE COMING.
FEED.
STEADY.
CARDIOTACH, MISS HINES?
HINES... WOULD YOU PLEASE ACCESS MR. LOGAN'S MEDICAL PROFILE AND HISTORY?
YES, SIR.
I STUDIED IT LONG ENOUGH...
BUT I COULD'VE MISSED
ON SCREEN, SIR.
DIKA
DIKA
IMPEDED.
VEEP
FEED.
DETAIL ANY CARDIO-ABNORMALITY.
NONE, SIR.
YOU'RE REALLY LETTING ME DOWN HERE, CORNELIUS...
WHY DIDN'T YOU PREPARE FOR THIS IN ADVANCE?
EQUALIZE.
I THOUGHT I'D PREPARED FOR EVERYTHING, PROFESSOR--
BUT WHO COULD FORESEE THIS?
I COULDN'T PROGRAM FOR THAT, PROFESSOR ...ACTUALLY IT REALLY DOESN'T SEEM CREDIBLE.
THE RATE SHOULD BE 24 IN ONE.
53 IN ONE, SIR.
HINES?
FEED.
FEED.
STEADY.
FEED.
IT SEEMS THAT LOGAN'S HIGHLY ACCELERATED HEART RATE IS DRAINING THE ADAMANTIUM RESERVOIR AT A RATE OF...

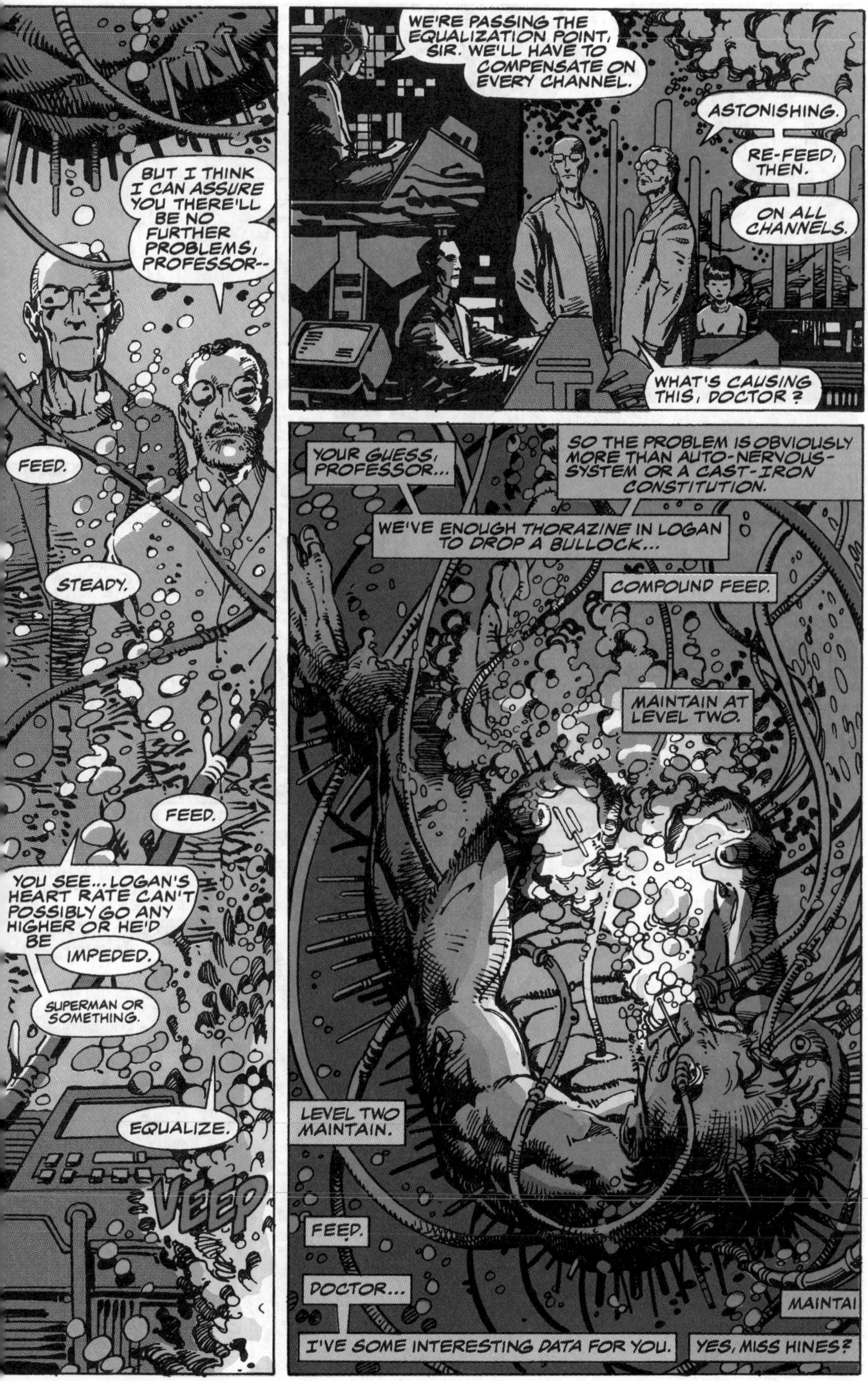
BUT I THINK I CAN ASSURE YOU THERE'LL BE NO FURTHER PROBLEMS, PROFESSOR--
FEED.
STEADY.
FEED.
YOU SEE... LOGAN'S HEART RATE CAN'T POSSIBLY GO ANY HIGHER OR HE'D BE
IMPEDED.
SUPERMAN OR SOMETHING.
EQUALIZE.
VEEP
WE'RE PASSING THE EQUALIZATION POINT, SIR. WE'LL HAVE TO COMPENSATE ON EVERY CHANNEL.
ASTONISHING.
RE-FEED, THEN.
ON ALL CHANNELS.
WHAT'S CAUSING THIS, DOCTOR?
YOUR GUESS, PROFESSOR...
SO THE PROBLEM IS OBVIOUSLY MORE THAN AUTO-NERVOUS-SYSTEM OR A CAST-IRON CONSTITUTION.
WE'VE ENOUGH THORAZINE IN LOGAN TO DROP A BULLOCK...
COMPOUND FEED.
MAINTAIN AT LEVEL TWO.
LEVEL TWO MAINTAIN.
FEED.
DOCTOR...
MAINTAI
I'VE SOME INTERESTING DATA FOR YOU.
YES, MISS HINES?

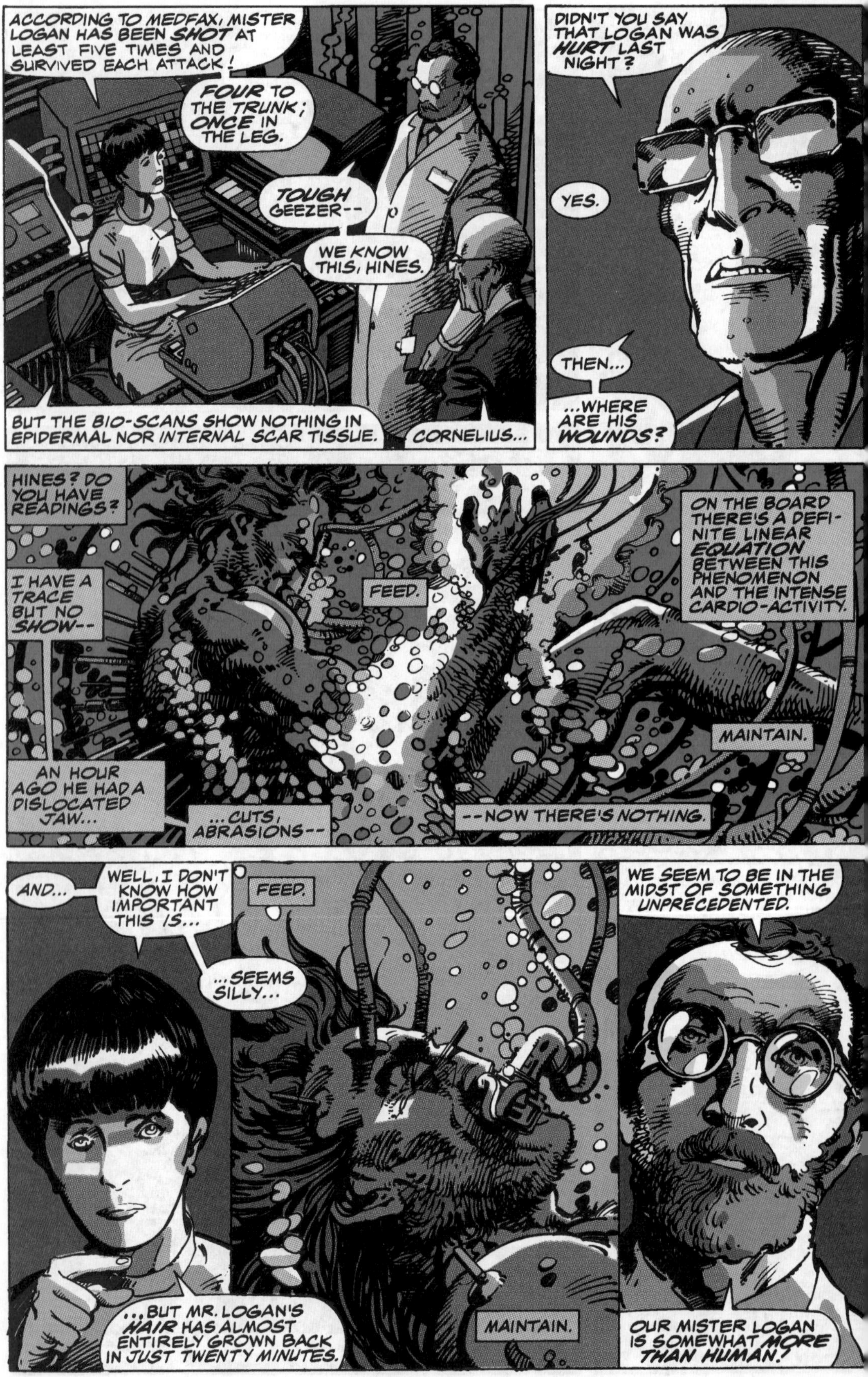

ACCORDING TO MEDFAX, MISTER LOGAN HAS BEEN SHOT AT LEAST FIVE TIMES AND SURVIVED EACH ATTACK!
FOUR TO THE TRUNK; ONCE IN THE LEG.
TOUGH GEEZER--
WE KNOW THIS, HINES.
BUT THE BIO-SCANS SHOW NOTHING IN EPIDERMAL NOR INTERNAL SCAR TISSUE.
CORNELIUS...
DIDN'T YOU SAY THAT LOGAN WAS HURT LAST NIGHT?
YES.
THEN...
...WHERE ARE HIS WOUNDS?
HINES? DO YOU HAVE READINGS?
I HAVE A TRACE BUT NO SHOW--
FEED.
ON THE BOARD THERE'S A DEFINITE LINEAR EQUATION BETWEEN THIS PHENOMENON AND THE INTENSE CARDIO-ACTIVITY.
MAINTAIN.
AN HOUR AGO HE HAD A DISLOCATED JAW...
...CUTS, ABRASIONS--
--NOW THERE'S NOTHING.
AND...
WELL, I DON'T KNOW HOW IMPORTANT THIS IS...
...SEEMS SILLY...
...BUT MR. LOGAN'S HAIR HAS ALMOST ENTIRELY GROWN BACK IN JUST TWENTY MINUTES.
FEED.
MAINTAIN.
WE SEEM TO BE IN THE MIDST OF SOMETHING UNPRECEDENTED.
OUR MISTER LOGAN IS SOMEWHAT MORE THAN HUMAN!

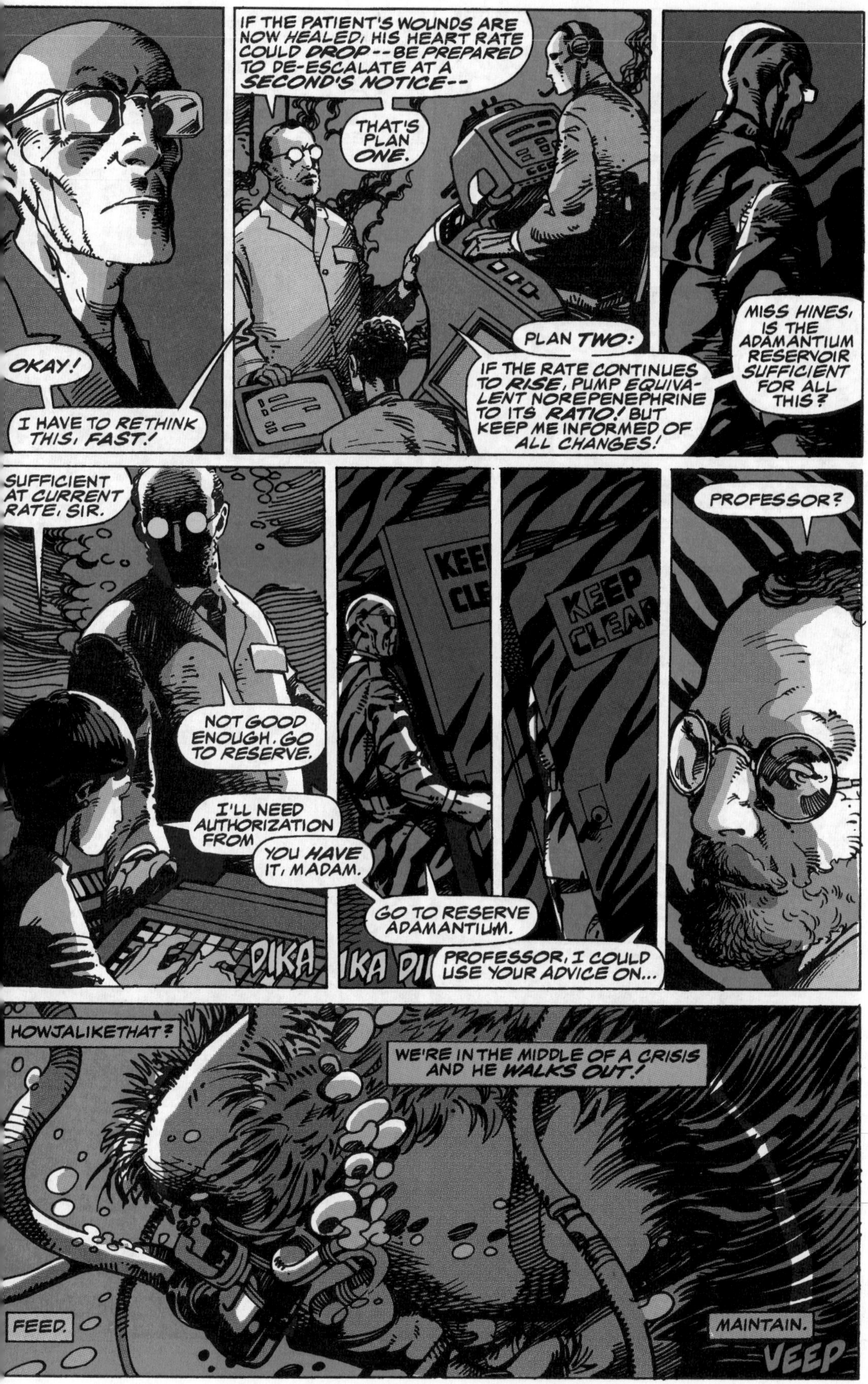
OKAY!
I HAVE TO RETHINK THIS, FAST!
IF THE PATIENT'S WOUNDS ARE NOW HEALED, HIS HEART RATE COULD DROP--BE PREPARED TO DE-ESCALATE AT A SECOND'S NOTICE--
THAT'S PLAN ONE.
PLAN TWO:
IF THE RATE CONTINUES TO RISE, PUMP EQUIVALENT NOREPENEPHRINE TO ITS RATIO! BUT KEEP ME INFORMED OF ALL CHANGES!
MISS HINES, IS THE ADAMANTIUM RESERVOIR SUFFICIENT FOR ALL THIS?
SUFFICIENT AT CURRENT RATE, SIR.
NOT GOOD ENOUGH. GO TO RESERVE.
I'LL NEED AUTHORIZATION FROM
YOU HAVE IT, MADAM.
GO TO RESERVE ADAMANTIUM.
DIKA
KEEP CLEAR
IKA DI
KEEP CLEAR
PROFESSOR, I COULD USE YOUR ADVICE ON...
PROFESSOR?
HOWJALIKETHAT?
WE'RE IN THE MIDDLE OF A CRISIS AND HE WALKS OUT!
FEED.
MAINTAIN.
VEEP

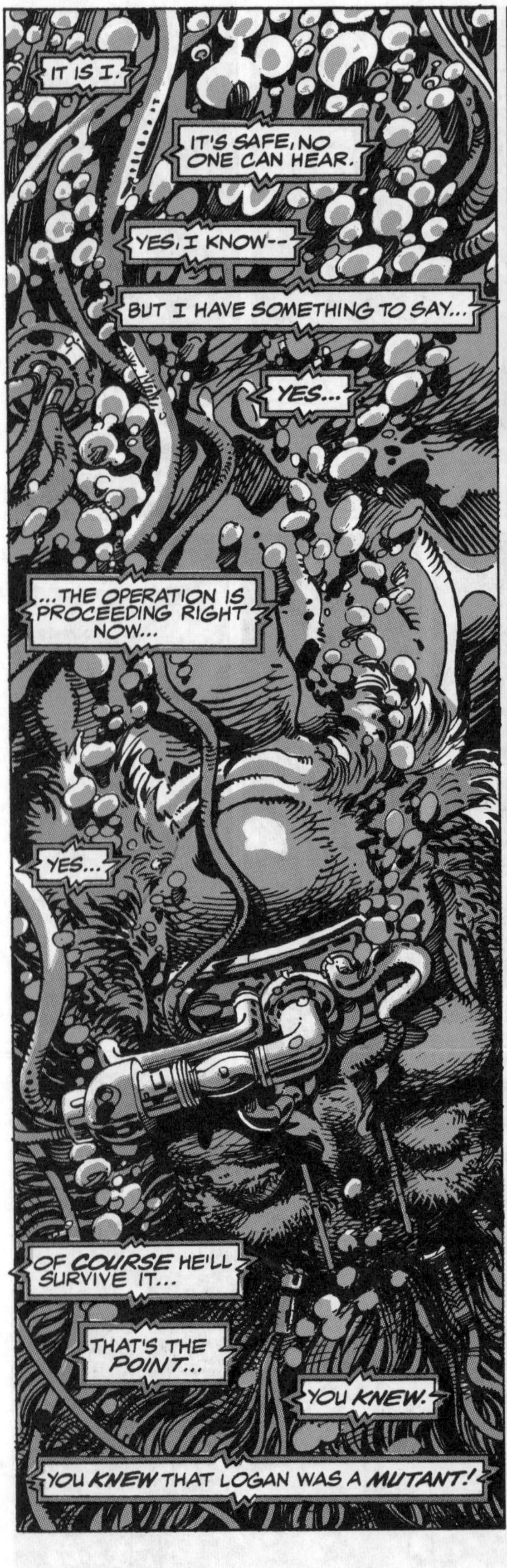
IT IS I.
IT'S SAFE, NO ONE CAN HEAR.
YES, I KNOW--
BUT I HAVE SOMETHING TO SAY...
YES...
...THE OPERATION IS PROCEEDING RIGHT NOW...
YES...
OF COURSE HE'LL SURVIVE IT...
THAT'S THE POINT...
YOU KNEW.
YOU KNEW THAT LOGAN WAS A MUTANT!

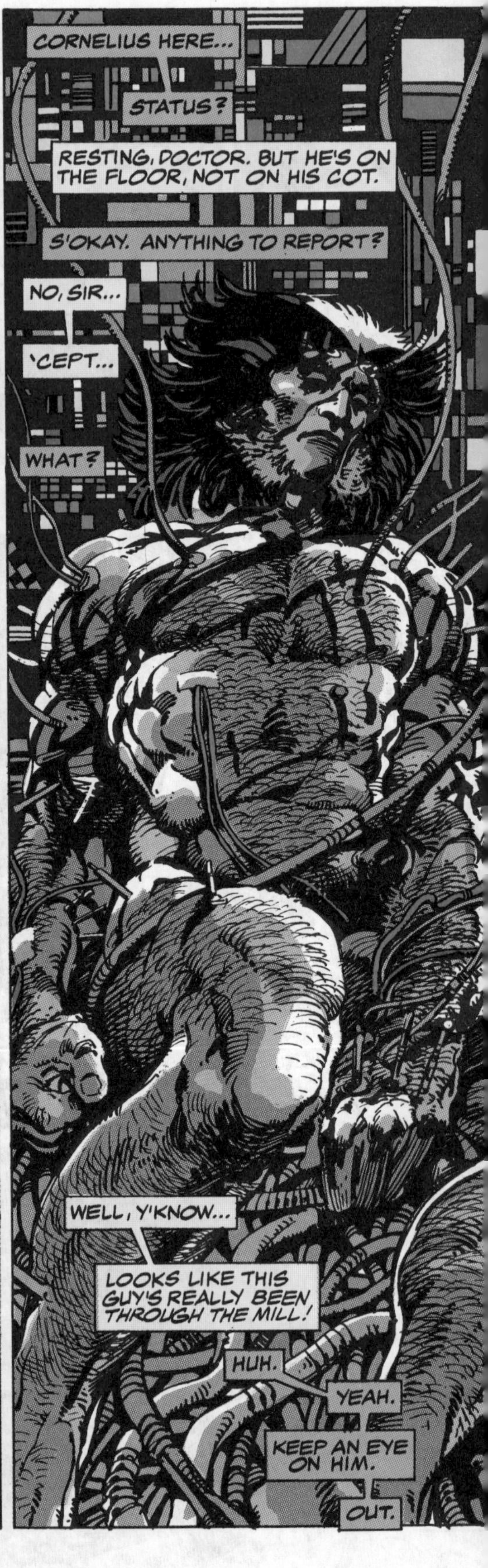
CORNELIUS HERE...
STATUS?
RESTING, DOCTOR. BUT HE'S ON THE FLOOR, NOT ON HIS COT.
S'OKAY. ANYTHING TO REPORT?
NO, SIR...
'CEPT...
WHAT?
WELL, Y'KNOW...
LOOKS LIKE THIS GUY'S REALLY BEEN THROUGH THE MILL!
HUH.
YEAH.
KEEP AN EYE ON HIM.
OUT.

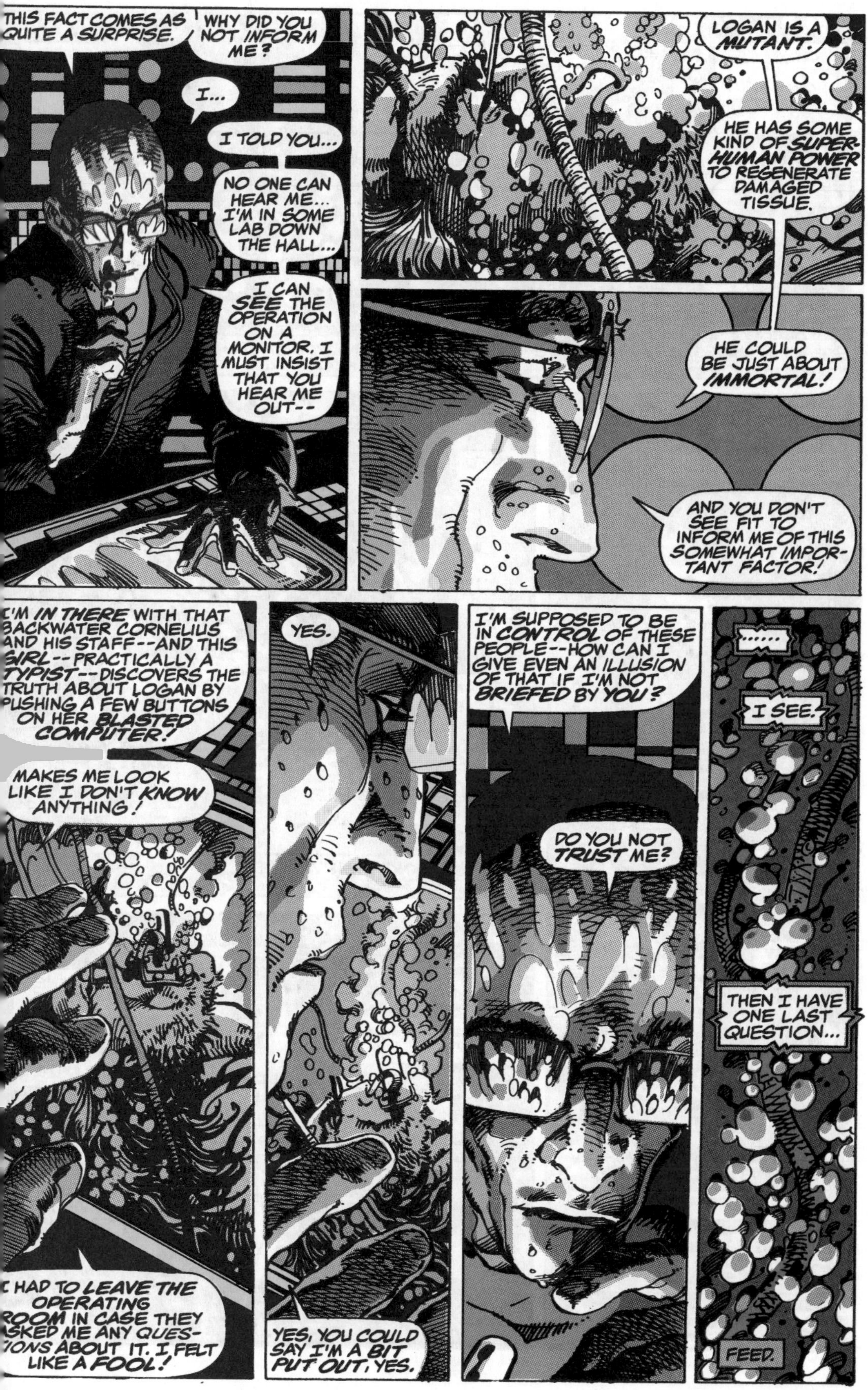
THIS FACT COMES AS QUITE A SURPRISE.
WHY DID YOU NOT INFORM ME?
I...
I TOLD YOU...
NO ONE CAN HEAR ME... I'M IN SOME LAB DOWN THE HALL...
I CAN SEE THE OPERATION ON A MONITOR. I MUST INSIST THAT YOU HEAR ME OUT--
LOGAN IS A MUTANT.
HE HAS SOME KIND OF SUPER-HUMAN POWER TO REGENERATE DAMAGED TISSUE.
HE COULD BE JUST ABOUT IMMORTAL!
AND YOU DON'T SEE FIT TO INFORM ME OF THIS SOMEWHAT IMPORTANT FACTOR!
I'M IN THERE WITH THAT BACKWATER CORNELIUS AND HIS STAFF--AND THIS GIRL--PRACTICALLY A TYPIST--DISCOVERS THE TRUTH ABOUT LOGAN BY PUSHING A FEW BUTTONS ON HER BLASTED COMPUTER!
MAKES ME LOOK LIKE I DON'T KNOW ANYTHING!
I HAD TO LEAVE THE OPERATING ROOM IN CASE THEY ASKED ME ANY QUESTIONS ABOUT IT. I FELT LIKE A FOOL!
YES.
YES, YOU COULD SAY I'M A BIT PUT OUT, YES.
I'M SUPPOSED TO BE IN CONTROL OF THESE PEOPLE--HOW CAN I GIVE EVEN AN ILLUSION OF THAT IF I'M NOT BRIEFED BY YOU?
DO YOU NOT TRUST ME?
......
I SEE.
THEN I HAVE ONE LAST QUESTION...
FEED.

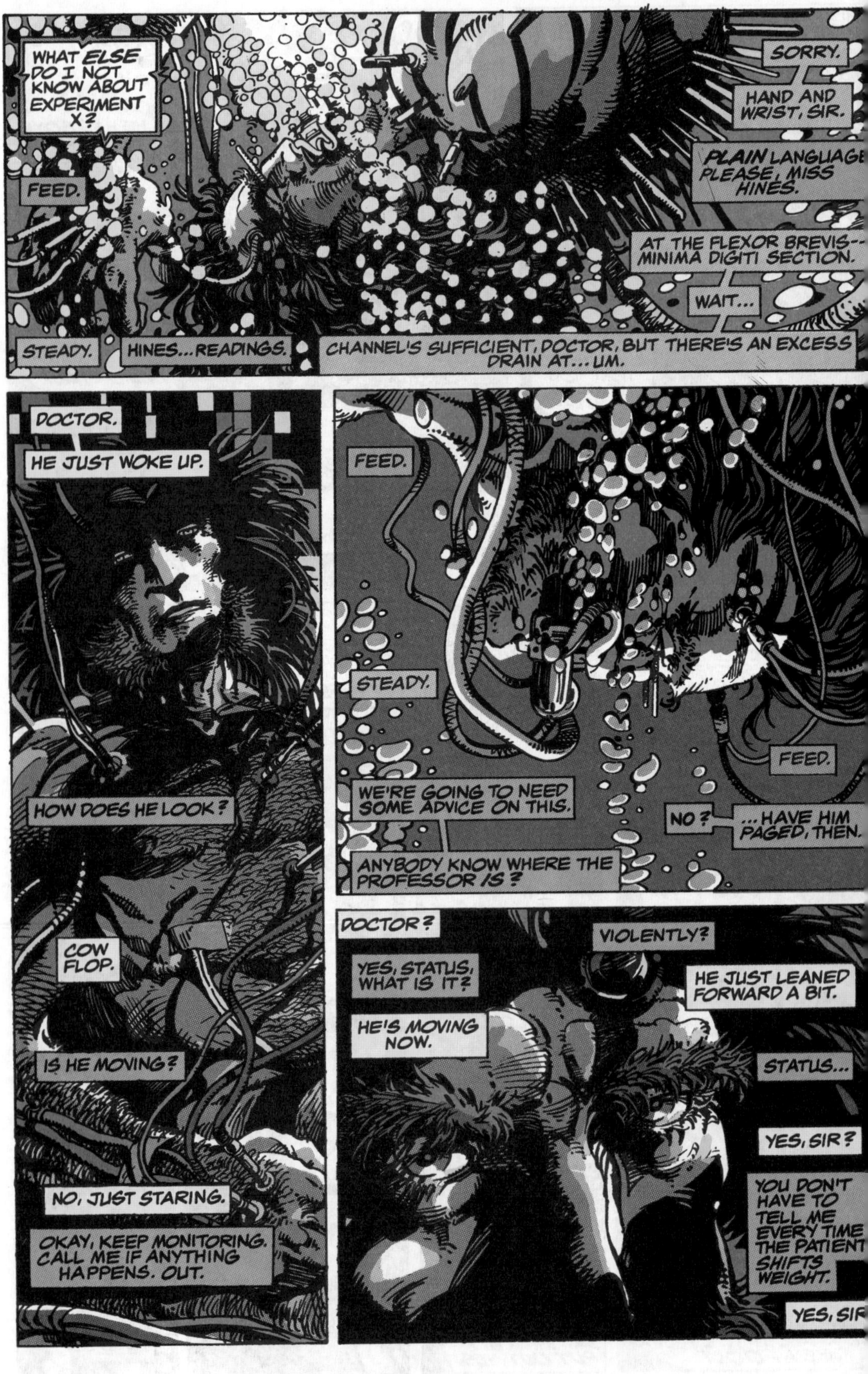
WHAT ELSE DO I NOT KNOW ABOUT EXPERIMENT X?
FEED.
SORRY.
HAND AND WRIST, SIR.
PLAIN LANGUAGE PLEASE, MISS HINES.
AT THE FLEXOR BREVIS-- MINIMA DIGITI SECTION.
WAIT...
STEADY.
HINES... READINGS.
CHANNEL'S SUFFICIENT, DOCTOR, BUT THERE'S AN EXCESS DRAIN AT... UM.
DOCTOR.
HE JUST WOKE UP.
HOW DOES HE LOOK?
COW FLOP.
IS HE MOVING?
NO, JUST STARING.
OKAY, KEEP MONITORING. CALL ME IF ANYTHING HAPPENS. OUT.
FEED.
STEADY.
FEED.
WE'RE GOING TO NEED SOME ADVICE ON THIS.
NO?
...HAVE HIM PAGED, THEN.
ANYBODY KNOW WHERE THE PROFESSOR IS?
DOCTOR?
VIOLENTLY?
YES, STATUS, WHAT IS IT?
HE JUST LEANED FORWARD A BIT.
HE'S MOVING NOW.
STATUS...
YES, SIR?
YOU DON'T HAVE TO TELL ME EVERY TIME THE PATIENT SHIFTS WEIGHT.
YES, SIR

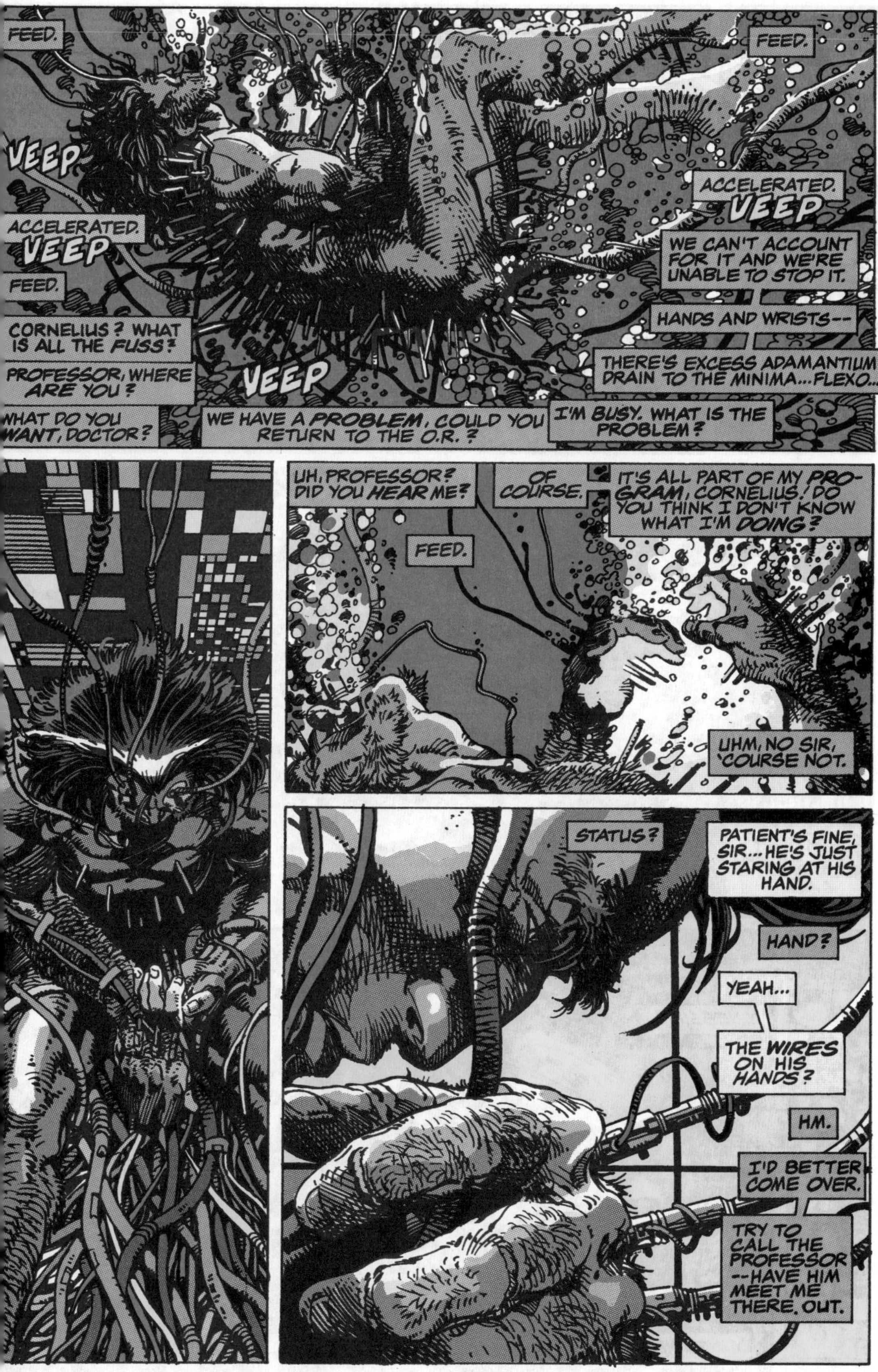
FEED.
FEED.
VEEP
ACCELERATED.
VEEP
FEED.
ACCELERATED.
VEEP
WE CAN'T ACCOUNT FOR IT AND WE'RE UNABLE TO STOP IT.
HANDS AND WRISTS--
CORNELIUS? WHAT IS ALL THE FUSS?
THERE'S EXCESS ADAMANTIUM DRAIN TO THE MINIMA...FLEXO...
PROFESSOR, WHERE ARE YOU?
VEEP
WHAT DO YOU WANT, DOCTOR?
WE HAVE A PROBLEM, COULD YOU RETURN TO THE O.R.?
I'M BUSY. WHAT IS THE PROBLEM?
UH, PROFESSOR? DID YOU HEAR ME?
OF COURSE.
IT'S ALL PART OF MY PROGRAM, CORNELIUS! DO YOU THINK I DON'T KNOW WHAT I'M DOING?
FEED.
UHM, NO SIR, 'COURSE NOT.
STATUS?
PATIENT'S FINE, SIR... HE'S JUST STARING AT HIS HAND.
HAND?
YEAH...
THE WIRES ON HIS HANDS?
HM.
I'D BETTER COME OVER.
TRY TO CALL THE PROFESSOR --HAVE HIM MEET ME THERE. OUT.

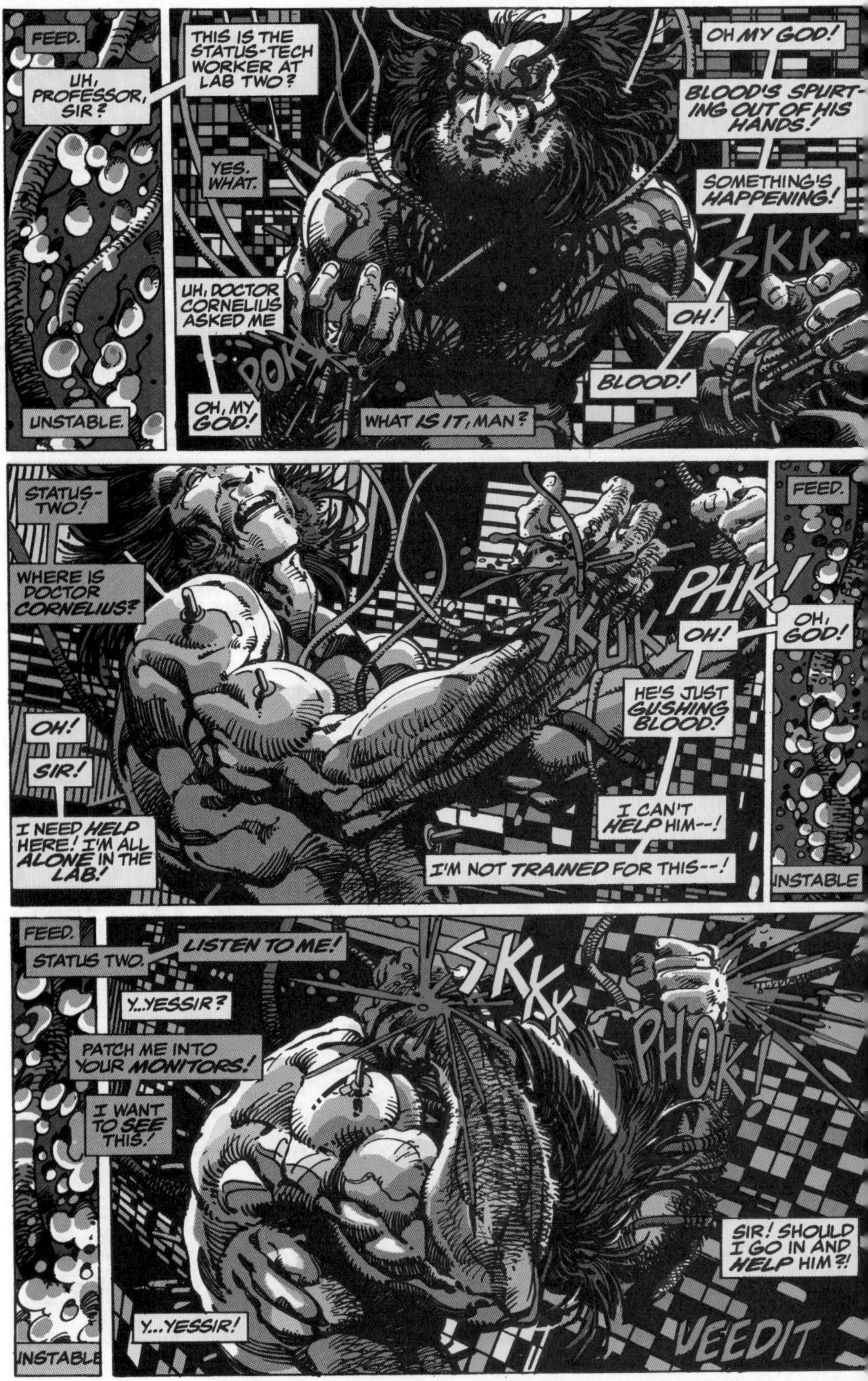

FEED.
UH, PROFESSOR, SIR?
THIS IS THE STATUS-TECH WORKER AT LAB TWO?
YES. WHAT.
UH, DOCTOR CORNELIUS ASKED ME
POK
OH, MY GOD!
UNSTABLE.
WHAT IS IT, MAN?
OH MY GOD!
BLOOD'S SPURTING OUT OF HIS HANDS!
SOMETHING'S HAPPENING!
SKK
OH!
BLOOD!
STATUS-TWO!
WHERE IS DOCTOR CORNELIUS?
OH!
SIR!
I NEED HELP HERE! I'M ALL ALONE IN THE LAB!
SKUK
PHK!
OH!
HE'S JUST GUSHING BLOOD!
I CAN'T HELP HIM--!
I'M NOT TRAINED FOR THIS--!
FEED.
OH, GOD!
UNSTABLE
FEED.
STATUS TWO.
LISTEN TO ME!
Y...YESSIR?
PATCH ME INTO YOUR MONITORS!
I WANT TO SEE THIS!
SKKK
PHOK!
SIR! SHOULD I GO IN AND HELP HIM?!
Y...YESSIR!
UEEDIT
UNSTABLE

UHH!
NO!...

NOT YET, STATUS!

BUT HE MUST BE IN TERRIBLE PAIN, SIR!

YES! I THINK YOU'RE RIGHT!

LOOK AT THAT!

UHHMM...

YOU SAID YOU'RE ALL ALONE IN LAB TWO, DID YOU, STATUS?

YES SIR, AND I'M NOT TRAINED --OH--

--GOD!! HE'S GOT... LIKE... SPIKES COMING OUT OF HIM!

SHCLUK!

RIGHT OUT OF HIS HANDS!!

WHAT SHALL I DO?!

STAY CALM, STATUS...

DO YOU HAVE ACCESS TO THE PATIENT'S BOOTH?

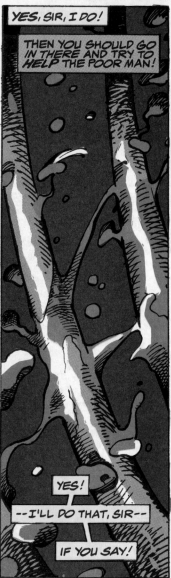

YES, SIR, I DO!

THEN YOU SHOULD GO IN THERE AND TRY TO HELP THE POOR MAN!

YES! --I'LL DO THAT, SIR-- IF YOU SAY!

BE SURE TO CLOSE THE SECURITY DOOR AFTER YOU ENTER, STATUS...

JUST TO BE SAFE.

GOOD LAD.

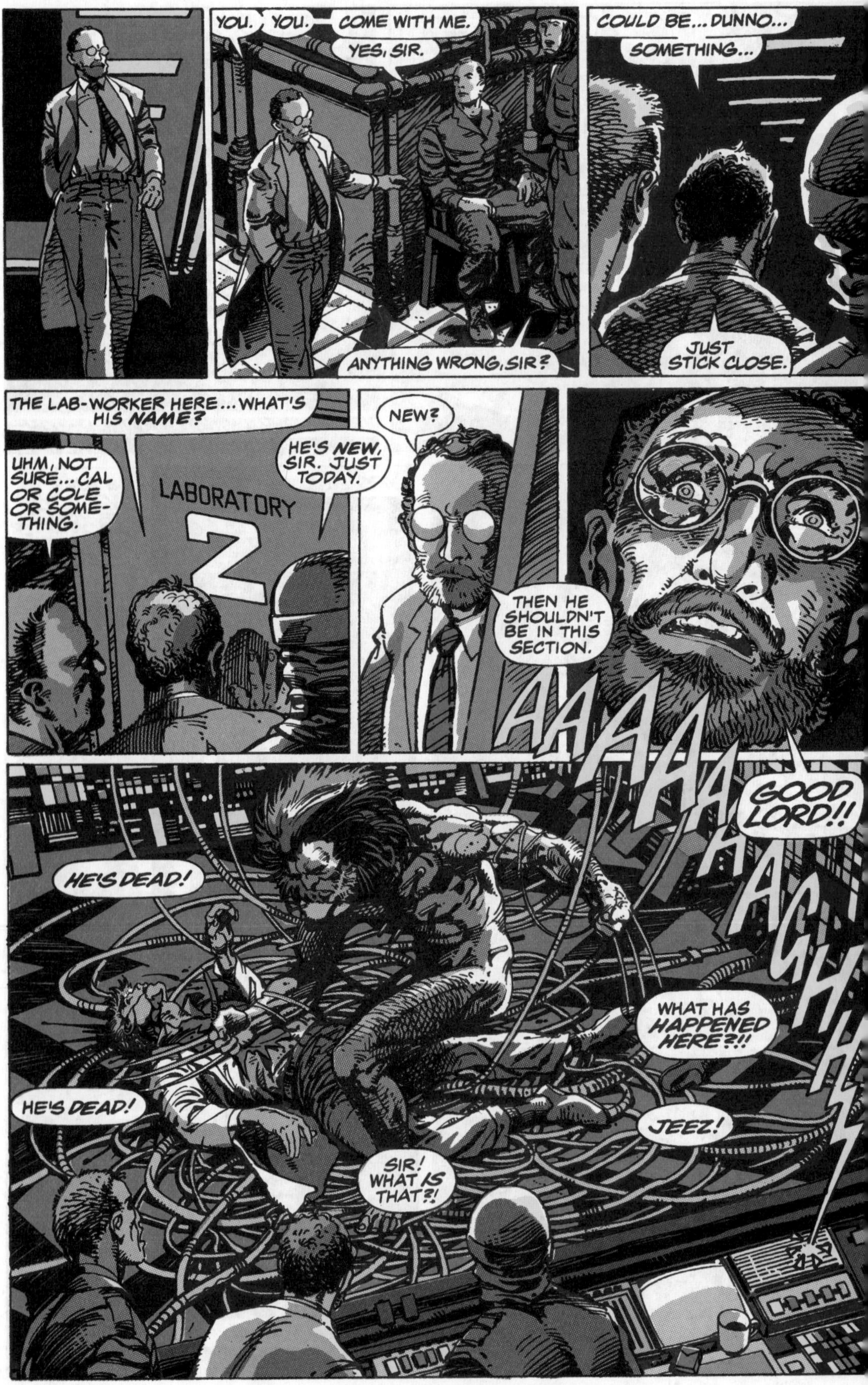
YOU. YOU. COME WITH ME.
YES, SIR.
ANYTHING WRONG, SIR?
COULD BE... DUNNO... SOMETHING...
JUST STICK CLOSE.
THE LAB-WORKER HERE... WHAT'S HIS NAME?
UHM, NOT SURE... CAL OR COLE OR SOME-THING.
LABORATORY 2
HE'S NEW, SIR. JUST TODAY.
NEW?
THEN HE SHOULDN'T BE IN THIS SECTION.
AAAAAAAAGHHH
GOOD LORD!!
HE'S DEAD!
WHAT HAS HAPPENED HERE?!!
HE'S DEAD!
JEEZ!
SIR! WHAT IS THAT?!

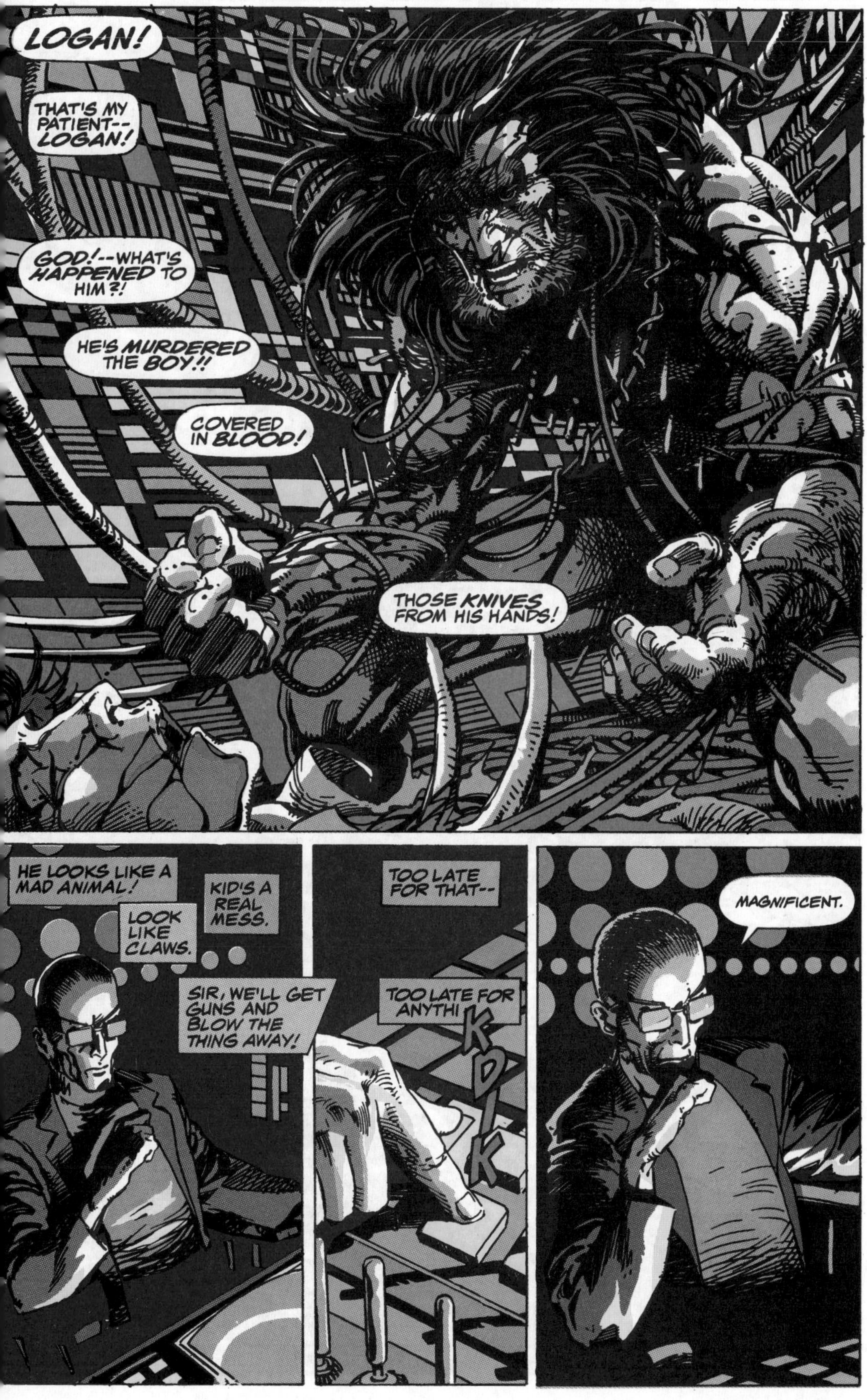
LOGAN!
THAT'S MY PATIENT-- LOGAN!
GOD!--WHAT'S HAPPENED TO HIM?!
HE'S MURDERED THE BOY!!
COVERED IN BLOOD!
THOSE KNIVES FROM HIS HANDS!
HE LOOKS LIKE A MAD ANIMAL!
LOOK LIKE CLAWS.
KID'S A REAL MESS.
SIR, WE'LL GET GUNS AND BLOW THE THING AWAY!
TOO LATE FOR THAT--
TOO LATE FOR ANYTHI
KDIK
MAGNIFICENT.

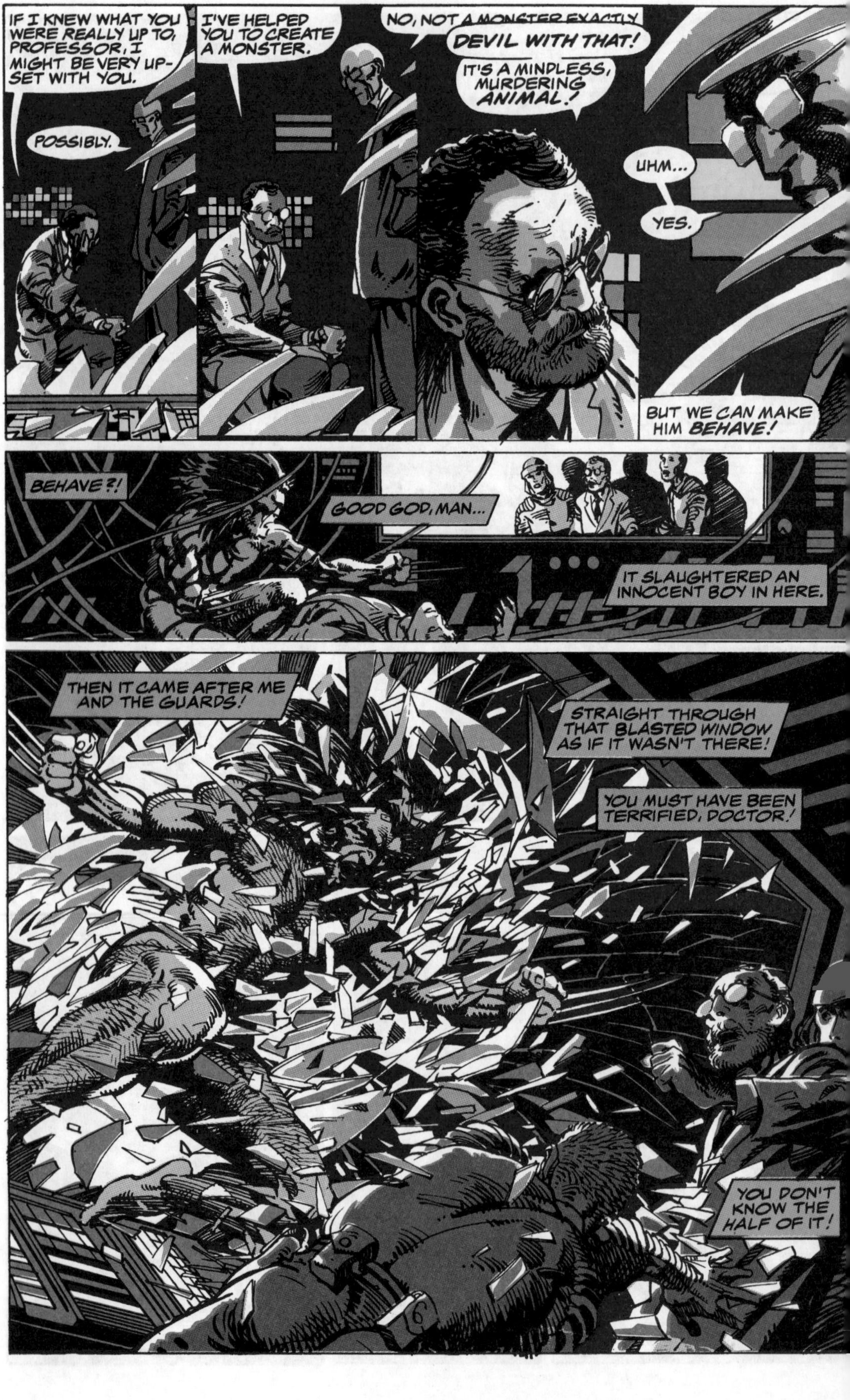
IF I KNEW WHAT YOU WERE REALLY UP TO, PROFESSOR, I MIGHT BE VERY UPSET WITH YOU.
POSSIBLY.
I'VE HELPED YOU TO CREATE A MONSTER.
NO, NOT A MONSTER EXACTLY
DEVIL WITH THAT!
IT'S A MINDLESS, MURDERING ANIMAL!
UHM...
YES.
BUT WE CAN MAKE HIM BEHAVE!
BEHAVE?!
GOOD GOD, MAN...
IT SLAUGHTERED AN INNOCENT BOY IN HERE.
THEN IT CAME AFTER ME AND THE GUARDS!
STRAIGHT THROUGH THAT BLASTED WINDOW AS IF IT WASN'T THERE!
YOU MUST HAVE BEEN TERRIFIED, DOCTOR!
YOU DON'T KNOW THE HALF OF IT!

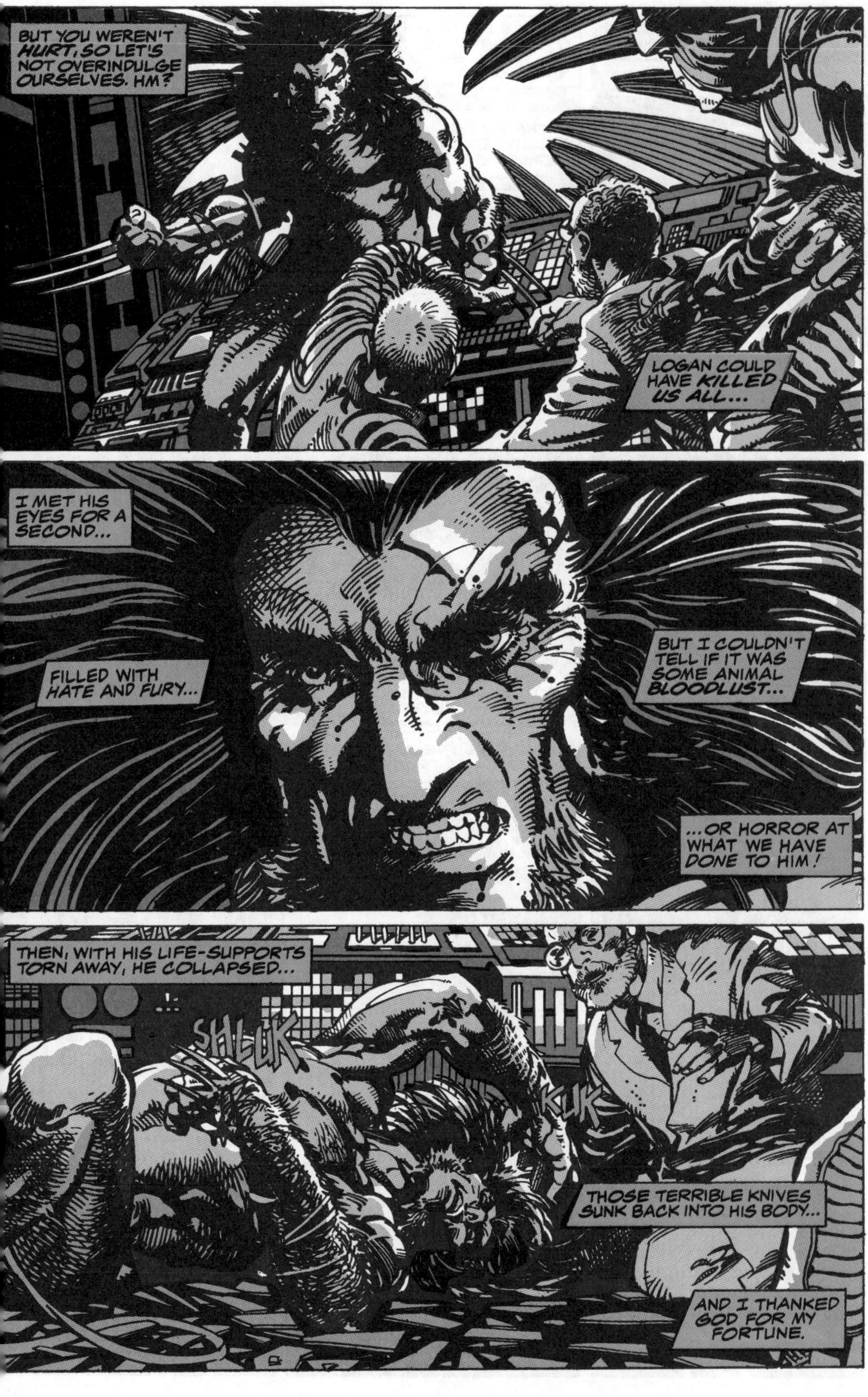

BUT YOU WEREN'T HURT, SO LET'S NOT OVERINDULGE OURSELVES. HM?
LOGAN COULD HAVE KILLED US ALL...
I MET HIS EYES FOR A SECOND...
FILLED WITH HATE AND FURY...
BUT I COULDN'T TELL IF IT WAS SOME ANIMAL BLOODLUST...
...OR HORROR AT WHAT WE HAVE DONE TO HIM!
THEN, WITH HIS LIFE-SUPPORTS TORN AWAY, HE COLLAPSED...
SHLUK
KLUK
THOSE TERRIBLE KNIVES SUNK BACK INTO HIS BODY...
AND I THANKED GOD FOR MY FORTUNE.

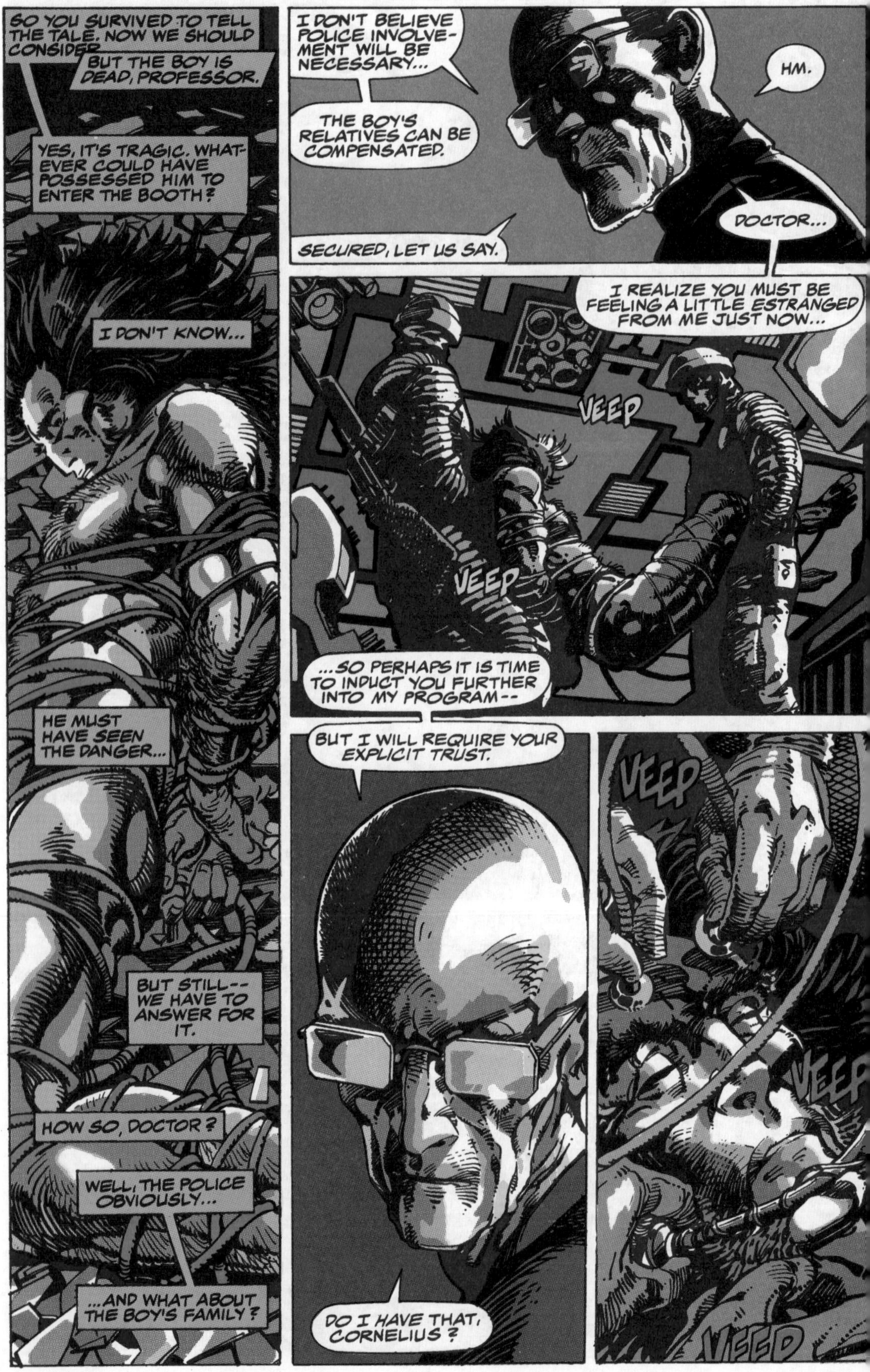

SO YOU SURVIVED TO TELL THE TALE. NOW WE SHOULD CONSIDER
BUT THE BOY IS DEAD, PROFESSOR.
YES, IT'S TRAGIC. WHATEVER COULD HAVE POSSESSED HIM TO ENTER THE BOOTH?
I DON'T KNOW...
HE MUST HAVE SEEN THE DANGER...
BUT STILL-- WE HAVE TO ANSWER FOR IT.
HOW SO, DOCTOR?
WELL, THE POLICE OBVIOUSLY...
...AND WHAT ABOUT THE BOY'S FAMILY?
I DON'T BELIEVE POLICE INVOLVEMENT WILL BE NECESSARY...
THE BOY'S RELATIVES CAN BE COMPENSATED.
SECURED, LET US SAY.
HM.
DOCTOR...
I REALIZE YOU MUST BE FEELING A LITTLE ESTRANGED FROM ME JUST NOW...
VEEP
VEEP
...SO PERHAPS IT IS TIME TO INDUCT YOU FURTHER INTO MY PROGRAM--
BUT I WILL REQUIRE YOUR EXPLICIT TRUST.
DO I HAVE THAT, CORNELIUS?
VEEP
VEEP
VEEP

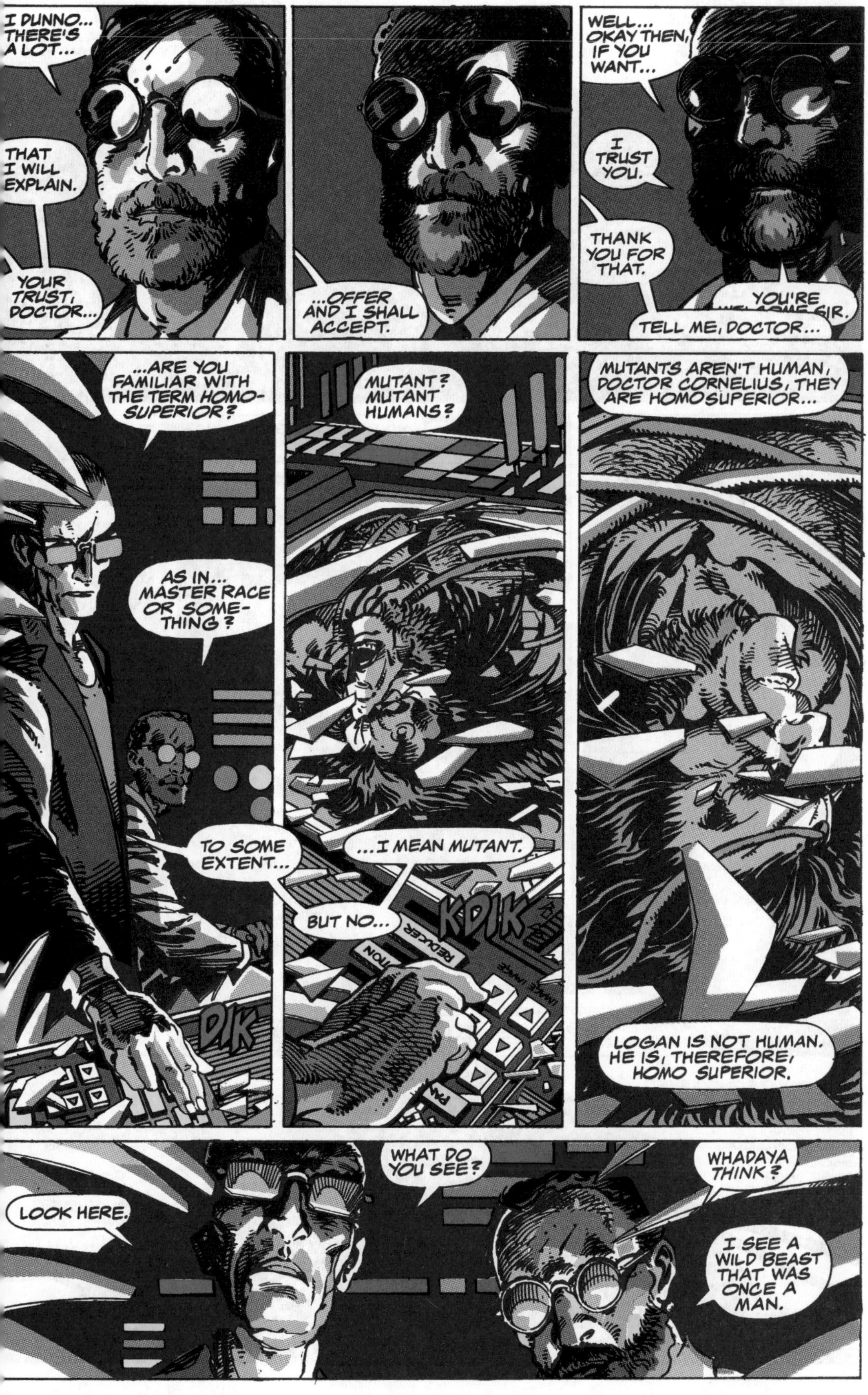
I DUNNO... THERE'S A LOT...
THAT I WILL EXPLAIN.
YOUR TRUST, DOCTOR...
...OFFER AND I SHALL ACCEPT.
WELL... OKAY THEN, IF YOU WANT...
I TRUST YOU.
THANK YOU FOR THAT.
YOU'RE
TELL ME, DOCTOR...
...ARE YOU FAMILIAR WITH THE TERM HOMO-SUPERIOR?
AS IN... MASTER RACE OR SOME-THING?
TO SOME EXTENT...
DIK
MUTANT? MUTANT HUMANS?
...I MEAN MUTANT.
BUT NO...
KDIK
MUTANTS AREN'T HUMAN, DOCTOR CORNELIUS, THEY ARE HOMO SUPERIOR...
LOGAN IS NOT HUMAN. HE IS, THEREFORE, HOMO SUPERIOR.
LOOK HERE.
WHAT DO YOU SEE?
WHADAYA THINK?
I SEE A WILD BEAST THAT WAS ONCE A MAN.

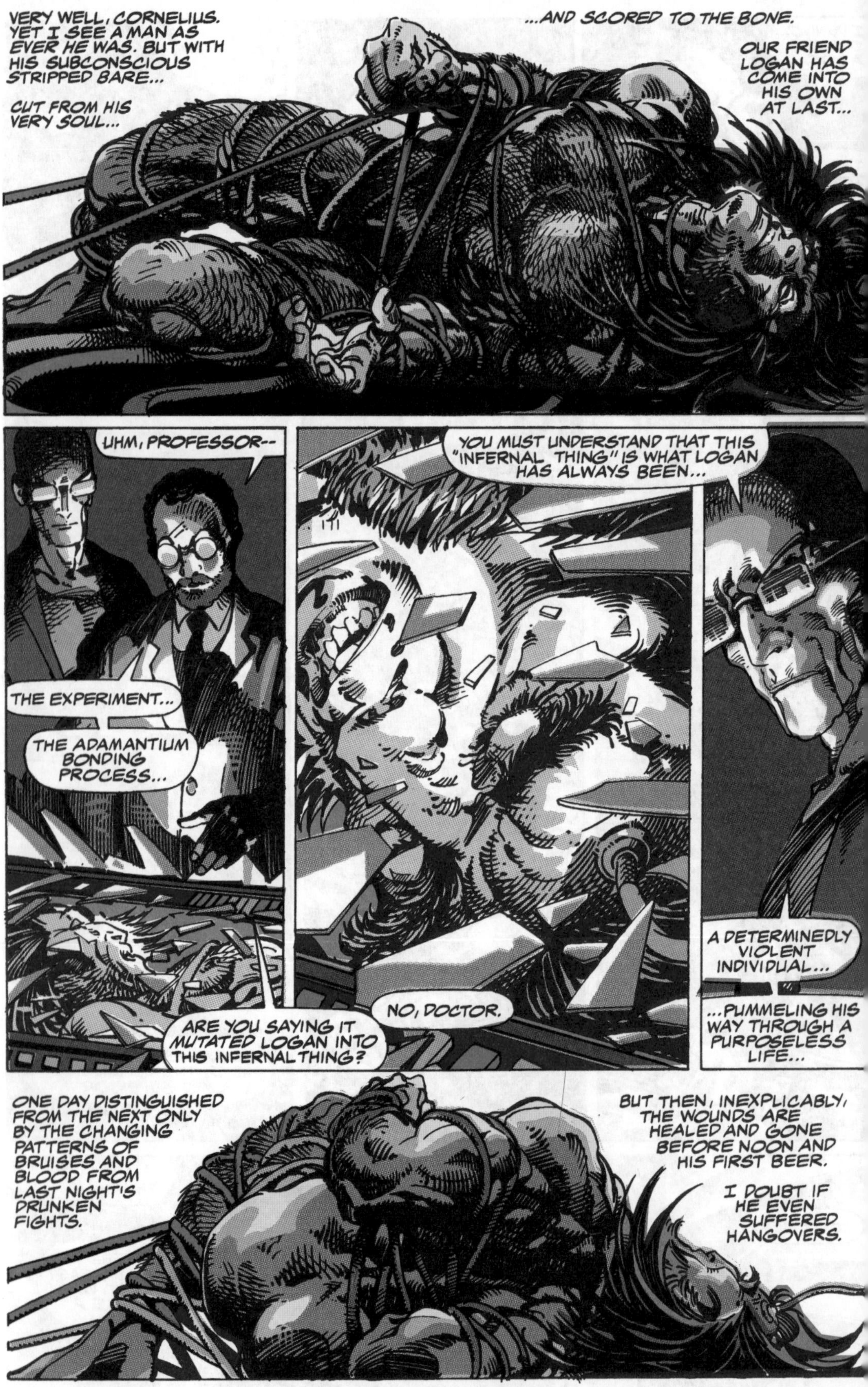
VERY WELL, CORNELIUS. YET I SEE A MAN AS EVER HE WAS. BUT WITH HIS SUBCONSCIOUS STRIPPED BARE...
CUT FROM HIS VERY SOUL...
...AND SCORED TO THE BONE.
OUR FRIEND LOGAN HAS COME INTO HIS OWN AT LAST...
UHM, PROFESSOR--
THE EXPERIMENT...
THE ADAMANTIUM BONDING PROCESS...
ARE YOU SAYING IT MUTATED LOGAN INTO THIS INFERNAL THING?
NO, DOCTOR.
YOU MUST UNDERSTAND THAT THIS "INFERNAL THING" IS WHAT LOGAN HAS ALWAYS BEEN...
A DETERMINEDLY VIOLENT INDIVIDUAL...
...PUMMELING HIS WAY THROUGH A PURPOSELESS LIFE...
ONE DAY DISTINGUISHED FROM THE NEXT ONLY BY THE CHANGING PATTERNS OF BRUISES AND BLOOD FROM LAST NIGHT'S DRUNKEN FIGHTS.
BUT THEN, INEXPLICABLY, THE WOUNDS ARE HEALED AND GONE BEFORE NOON AND HIS FIRST BEER.
I DOUBT IF HE EVEN SUFFERED HANGOVERS.

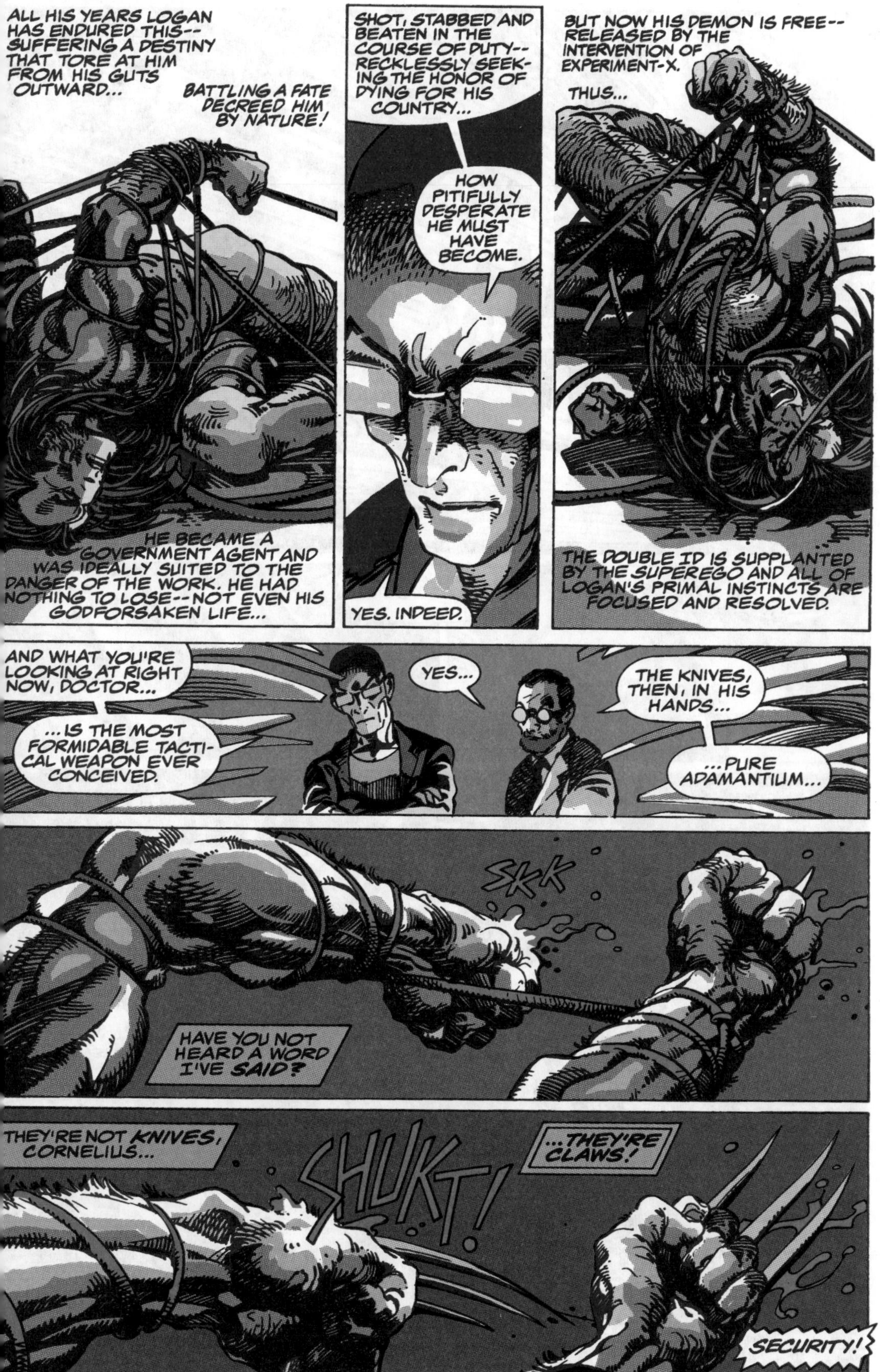
ALL HIS YEARS LOGAN HAS ENDURED THIS-- SUFFERING A DESTINY THAT TORE AT HIM FROM HIS GUTS OUTWARD...
BATTLING A FATE DECREED HIM BY NATURE!
HE BECAME A GOVERNMENT AGENT AND WAS IDEALLY SUITED TO THE DANGER OF THE WORK. HE HAD NOTHING TO LOSE--NOT EVEN HIS GODFORSAKEN LIFE...
SHOT, STABBED AND BEATEN IN THE COURSE OF DUTY-- RECKLESSLY SEEKING THE HONOR OF DYING FOR HIS COUNTRY...
HOW PITIFULLY DESPERATE HE MUST HAVE BECOME.
YES. INDEED.
BUT NOW HIS DEMON IS FREE-- RELEASED BY THE INTERVENTION OF EXPERIMENT-X.
THUS...
THE DOUBLE ID IS SUPPLANTED BY THE SUPEREGO AND ALL OF LOGAN'S PRIMAL INSTINCTS ARE FOCUSED AND RESOLVED.
AND WHAT YOU'RE LOOKING AT RIGHT NOW, DOCTOR...
...IS THE MOST FORMIDABLE TACTICAL WEAPON EVER CONCEIVED.
YES...
THE KNIVES, THEN, IN HIS HANDS...
...PURE ADAMANTIUM...
SKK
HAVE YOU NOT HEARD A WORD I'VE SAID?
THEY'RE NOT KNIVES, CORNELIUS...
SHUKT!
...THEY'RE CLAWS!
SECURITY!

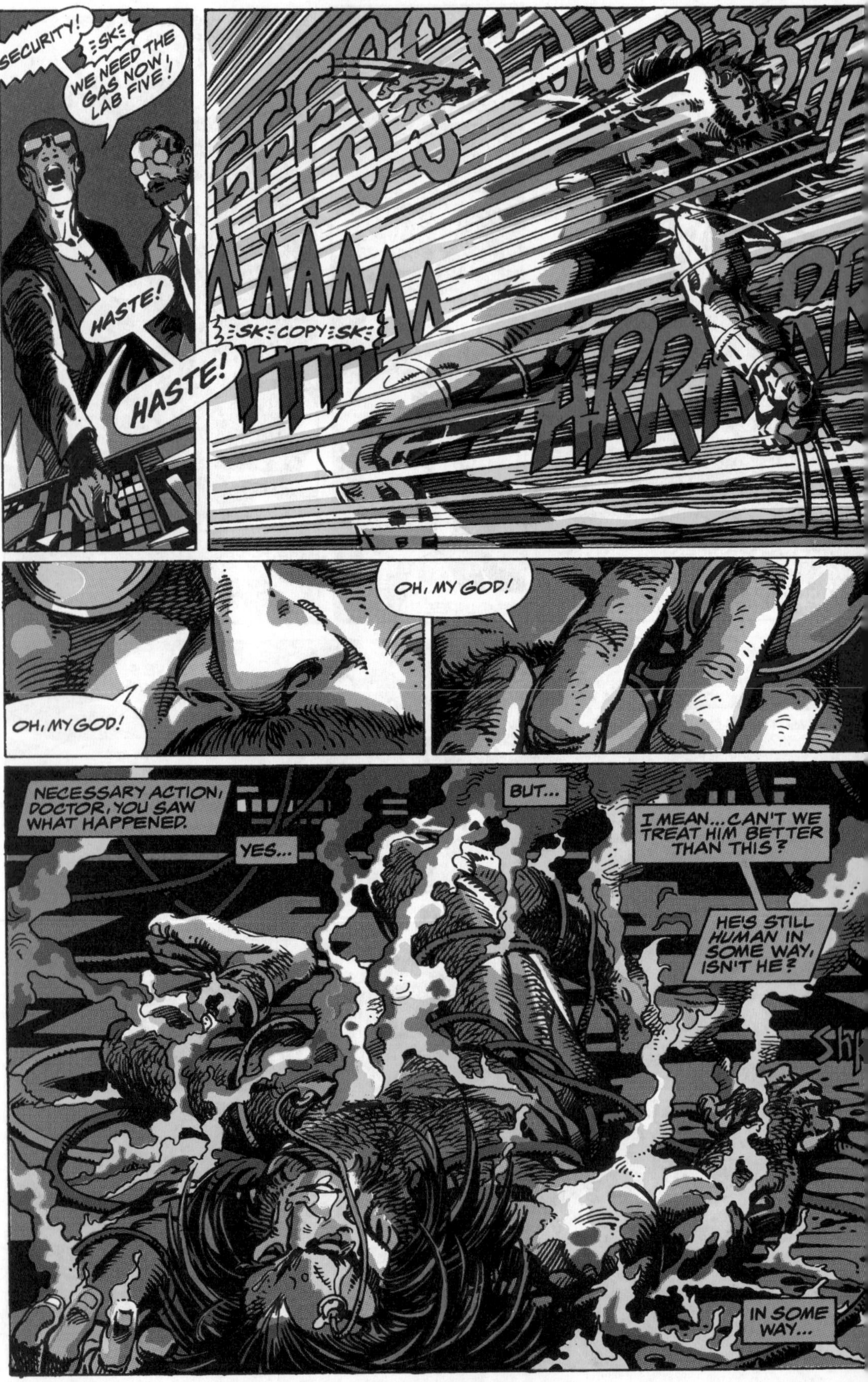
SECURITY!
⁝SK⁝ WE NEED THE GAS NOW, LAB FIVE!
HASTE!
HASTE!
⁝SK⁝COPY⁝SK⁝
OH, MY GOD!
OH, MY GOD!
NECESSARY ACTION, DOCTOR, YOU SAW WHAT HAPPENED.
YES...
BUT...
I MEAN... CAN'T WE TREAT HIM BETTER THAN THIS?
HE'S STILL HUMAN IN SOME WAY, ISN'T HE?
IN SOME WAY...

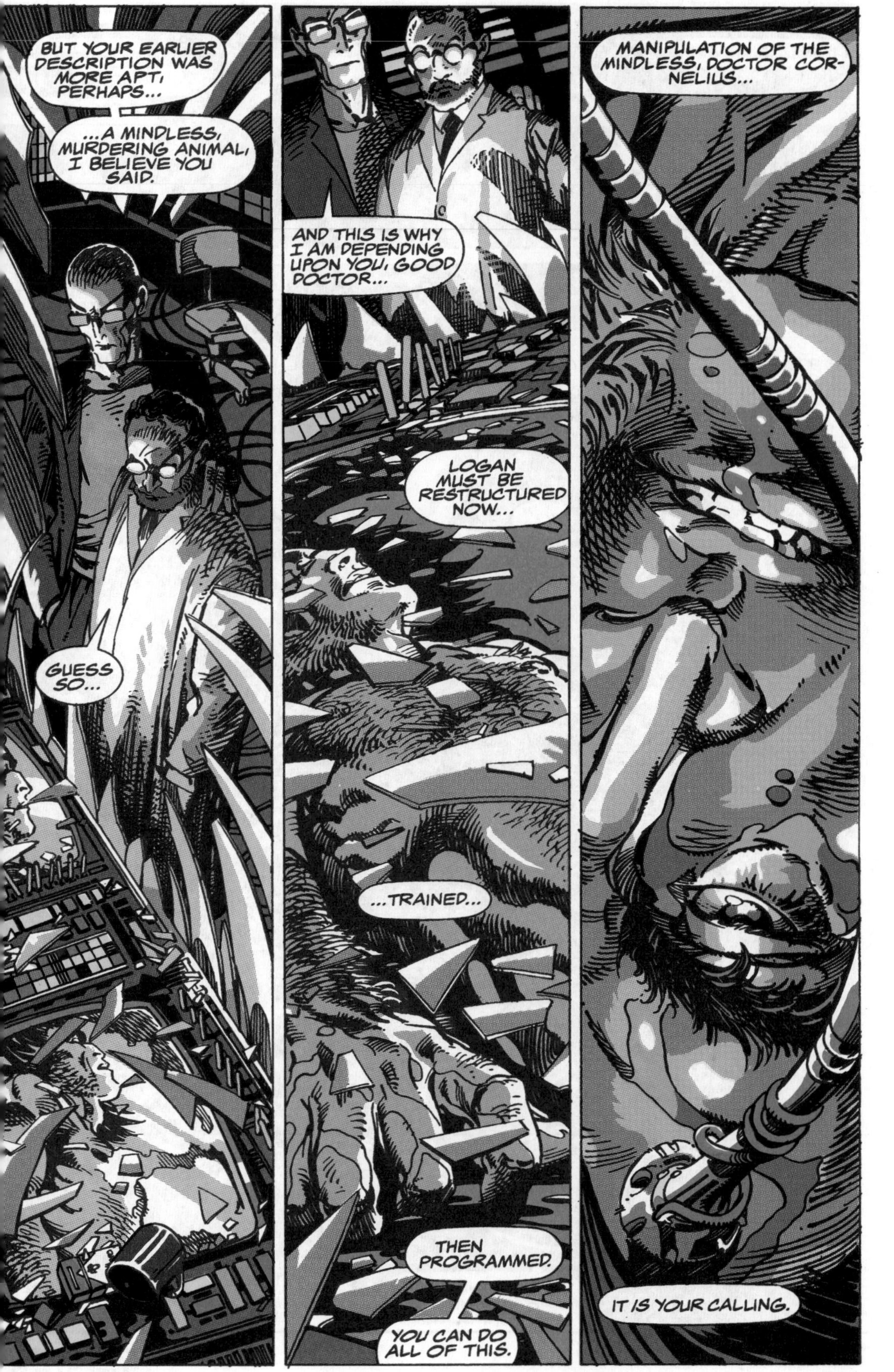
BUT YOUR EARLIER DESCRIPTION WAS MORE APT, PERHAPS...
...A MINDLESS, MURDERING ANIMAL, I BELIEVE YOU SAID.
GUESS SO...
AND THIS IS WHY I AM DEPENDING UPON YOU, GOOD DOCTOR...
LOGAN MUST BE RESTRUCTURED NOW...
...TRAINED...
THEN PROGRAMMED.
YOU CAN DO ALL OF THIS.
MANIPULATION OF THE MINDLESS, DOCTOR CORNELIUS...
IT IS YOUR CALLING.

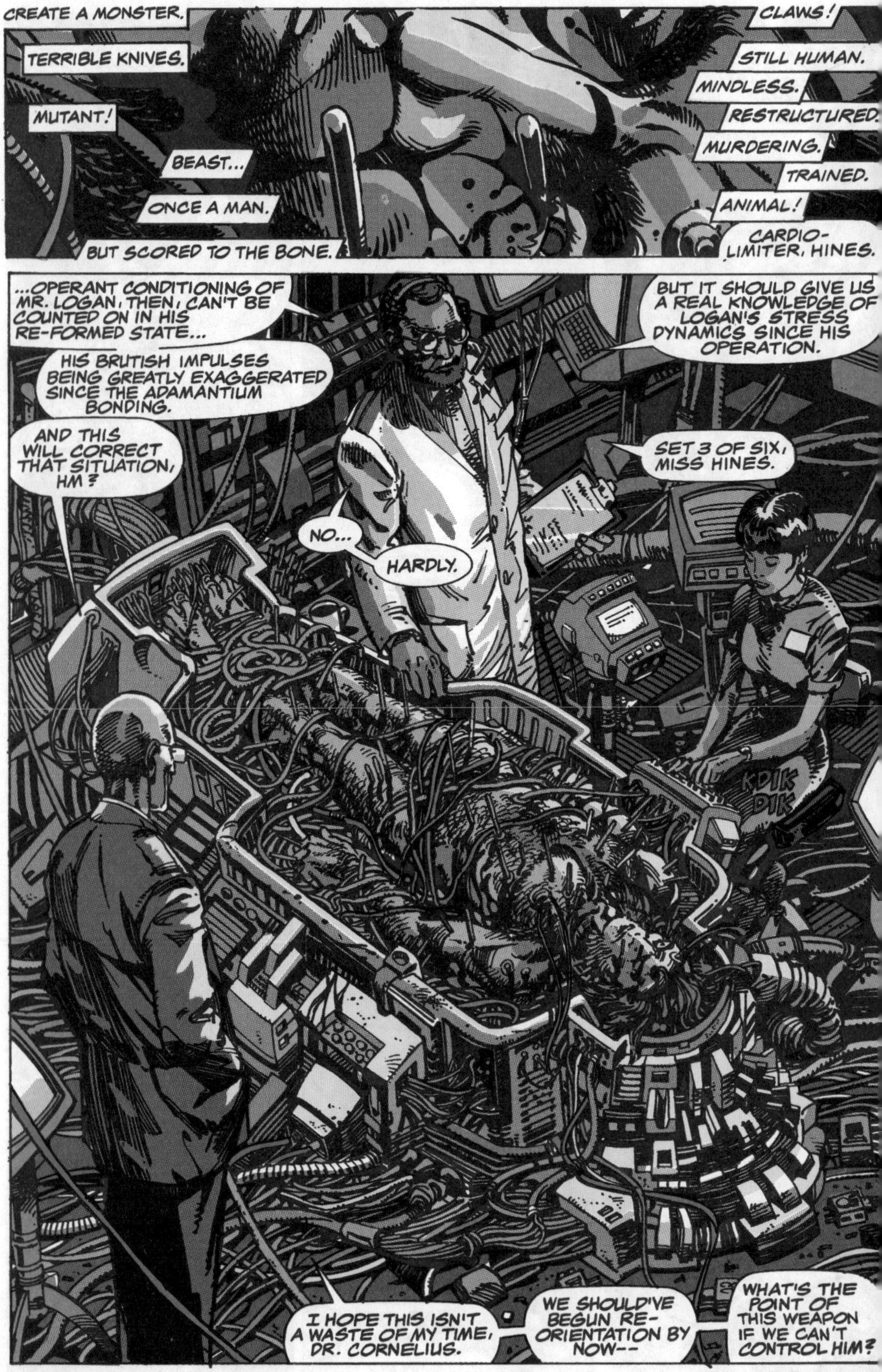

CREATE A MONSTER.
CLAWS!
TERRIBLE KNIVES.
STILL HUMAN.
MINDLESS.
MUTANT!
RESTRUCTURED.
MURDERING.
BEAST...
TRAINED.
ONCE A MAN.
ANIMAL!
BUT SCORED TO THE BONE.
CARDIO-LIMITER, HINES.
...OPERANT CONDITIONING OF MR. LOGAN, THEN, CAN'T BE COUNTED ON IN HIS RE-FORMED STATE...
HIS BRUTISH IMPULSES BEING GREATLY EXAGGERATED SINCE THE ADAMANTIUM BONDING.
AND THIS WILL CORRECT THAT SITUATION, HM?
NO...
HARDLY.
BUT IT SHOULD GIVE US A REAL KNOWLEDGE OF LOGAN'S STRESS DYNAMICS SINCE HIS OPERATION.
SET 3 OF SIX, MISS HINES.
KDIK DIK
I HOPE THIS ISN'T A WASTE OF MY TIME, DR. CORNELIUS.
WE SHOULD'VE BEGUN RE-ORIENTATION BY NOW--
WHAT'S THE POINT OF THIS WEAPON IF WE CAN'T CONTROL HIM?

END